TEXAS
SCIENCE
Fusion

fusion [FYOO • zhuhn] a combination of two
or more things that releases energy

This Write-In Student Edition belongs to

Francisco Esquivel Fuentes Javier

Teacher/Room

Mr. Cajina   Room 107

Consulting Authors

Michael A. DiSpezio
Global Educator
North Falmouth, Massachusetts

Marjorie Frank
Science Writer and Content-Area Reading Specialist
Brooklyn, New York

Michael Heithaus
Executive Director, School of Environment, Arts, and Society
Associate Professor, Department of Biological Sciences
Florida International University
North Miami, Florida

Donna Ogle
Professor of Reading and Language
National-Louis University
Chicago, Illinois

Front Cover: *stingray* ©Jeffrey L. Rotman/Corbis; *moth* ©Millard H. Sharp/Photo Researchers, Inc.; *astronaut* ©NASA; *thermometer* ©StockImages/Alamy; *gear* ©Garry Gay/The Image Bank/Getty Images.

Back Cover: *geyser* ©Frans Lanting/Corbis; *frog* ©DLILLC/Corbis; *flask* ©Gregor Schuster/Getty Images; *rowers* ©Stockbyte/Getty Images.

Copyright © 2015 by Houghton Mifflin Harcourt Publishing Company

All rights reserved. No part of this work may be reproduced or transmitted in any form or by any means, electronic or mechanical, including photocopying or recording, or by any information storage and retrieval system, without the prior written permission of the copyright owner unless such copying is expressly permitted by federal copyright law. Requests for permission to make copies of any part of the work should be addressed to Houghton Mifflin Harcourt Publishing Company, Attn: Contracts, Copyrights, and Licensing, 9400 Southpark Center Loop, Orlando, Florida 32819-8647.

Printed in the U.S.A.

ISBN   978-0-544-02550-9

7 8 9 10   0868   21 20 19 18 17

4500647826   BCDEFG

If you have received these materials as examination copies free of charge, Houghton Mifflin Harcourt Publishing Company retains title to the materials and they may not be resold. Resale of examination copies is strictly prohibited.

Possession of this publication in print format does not entitle users to convert this publication, or any portion of it, into electronic format.

Program Advisors

Paul D. Asimow
Professor of Geology and Geochemistry
California Institute of Technology
Pasadena, California

Bobby Jeanpierre
*Associate Professor of Science
    Education*
University of Central Florida
Orlando, Florida

Gerald H. Krockover
*Professor Emeritus of Earth,
    Atmospheric, and Planetary Science
    Education*
Purdue University
West Lafayette, Indiana

Rose Pringle
*Associate Professor
    School of Teaching and Learning*
College of Education
University of Florida
Gainesville, Florida

Carolyn Staudt
Curriculum Designer for Technology
KidSolve, Inc.
The Concord Consortium
Concord, Massachusetts

Larry Stookey
Science Department
Antigo High School
Antigo, Wisconsin

Carol J. Valenta
*Associate Director of the Museum and
    Senior Vice President*
Saint Louis Science Center
St. Louis, Missouri

Barry A. Van Deman
President and CEO
Museum of Life and Science
Durham, North Carolina

Texas Reviewers

Max Ceballos
District Science Specialist
Edinburg, Texas

Tamara L. Cryar
Cook Elementary
Austin, Texas

Heather Domjan
University of Houston
Houston, Texas

Ashley D. Golden
Washington Elementary
Big Spring, Texas

Linda Churchwell Halliman
Cornelius Elementary School
Houston, Texas

Ellen Lyon
Hays Consolidated ISD
Kyle, Texas

Stephanie McNeil
Bastian Elementary
Houston, Texas

Sue Mendoza
District Science Coach
El Paso ISD
El Paso, Texas

Christine L. Morgan
Emerson Elementary
Midland, Texas

Genaro Ovalle III
Elementary Science Dean
Laredo ISD
Laredo, Texas

Hilda Quintanar
Science Coach
El Paso ISD
El Paso, Texas

Power up with Texas Science Fusion!

Grade 4

Your program fuses . . .

e-Learning & Virtual Labs

Labs & Explorations

Write-In Student Edition

. . . to generate new energy
for today's science learner—**you.**

Write-In Student Edition

Be an active reader and make this book your own!

Describe

...n use all the words you see here to ...
...You can use your senses to find an...
...color, taste, size, shape, odor, or t...

...tive ...ng As you read these two pages, circle words
...hrases t...al a detail about physical properties.

ardness
...hard. The grapes
...cribes how easily
...d or dent.

Co...
...e words we use for ...escribe
...way light bounces ... object.
...at colors do you see ...?

Taste
...ckers are salty. Candy can taste
...t or sour. Can you think of
so...hing that tastes bitter?

Write your ideas, answer questions, make notes, and record activity results right on these pages.

Textur...
feels li...
texture...

These sh...
has a nic...
you if mi...

Learn science concepts and skills by interacting with every page.

e-Learning & Virtual Labs

Digital lessons and virtual labs provide e-learning options for every lesson of *ScienceFusion*.

Do it!

Initial speed (m/s)
1 2 3 4 5 6 7 8 9

Sound is a form of energy made by vibrations.
Click the first bar on the instrument to see how sound travels.

On your own or with a group, explore science concepts in a digital world.

Unit 1   Studying Science

Click to reveal resources.

Digital Lesson

Lesson 1   What Do Scientists Do?

Lesson 2   What Skills Do Scientists Use?

Lesson 3   How Do Scientists Collect and Use Data?

Lesson 4   Why Do Scientists Compare Results?
VIRTUAL LABS

Lesson 5   What Kinds of Models Do Scientists Use?

Lesson 6   How Can You Make a Model?
VIRTUAL LABS

Unit 2   The Engineering Process

Investigate every science concept with multiple virtual labs in every unit.

Continue your science explorations with these online tools:

→ ScienceSaurus   → People in Science

→ NSTA Scilinks   → Media Gallery

→ Video-based Projects   → Vocabulary Cards

→ Science Readers for Texas with complete AUDIO!

Labs & Explorations

Science is all about doing.

Exciting investigations for every lesson.

Ask questions and test your ideas.

Draw conclusions and share what you learn.

How Can You Model a School?

There are many types of models: mental models, two-dimensional, three-dimensional, and computer models. In this activity, you'll model a part of your school in two ways.

With your team, choose the materials you will use. Make any measurements you need, and record them carefully.

Next, choose two types of models to make. Get permission from your teacher to carry out your plans.

ing or modeling program

With a team, choose a part of your school to model. It may be a single room, a floor, or a whole building.

Make the two models, and compare them to those of other teams.

What Is the DESIGN PROCESS?

It has been said that necessity is the mother of invention. But once you find a need, how do you build your invention? That's the design process!

Active Reading As you read these two pages, draw boxes around clue words or phrases that signal a sequence or order.

What is design? **Design** means to conceive something and prepare the plans and drawings for it to be built. Engineers use the design process to develop new technology, but anyone can follow the design process.

From basic to complex, databases have ch...

The design process starts with identifying a need or a problem. Next, you brainstorm and write down ideas on how to plan and build a potential solution. Once you have some options, select a solution to try. Usually, engineers test possible solutions using a prototype.

A prototype is an original or test model on which a real product is based. If the prototype works, then the real product is made. Usually, after testing a prototype, improvements have to be made. The prototype is then tested again. Finally, a finished product is made.

Design Process Steps

- Find a problem
- Plan and build
- Test and improve
- Redesign
- Communicate

Even something seemingly simple takes a lot of thought, planning, testing, and improvement.

66

67

...roved?

Describe two
...e been improved

...tory

...any of your home appliances have ...nd out more about this label. Draw the ...n the timeline. Then, describe what it is ...rators.

S.T.E.M.
Engineering & Technology

Baby, It's Cold Inside
Refrigeration

Have you ever thought about how refrigeration has changed the way we live? We can store foods without having them rot as quickly. Spoiled foods can make people ill.

1800s
People put food on blocks of ice to keep it cold. The ice was cut from lakes or ponds, packed in straw, and stored in warehouses. This ice had to be replaced often.

1900s
By the early 1900s, many homes had iceboxes. Ice was placed in the bottom to cool the air inside the box. It became easier to cool food for longer periods of time until it could be used. These iceboxes were like coolers we use today but larger.

1920s
In the 1920s, electric refrigerators became available for home use. The inside of this refrigerator stayed cold without needing blocks of ice. It used an electric motor and a gas compressor to remove heat from its wooden or metal box.

2010s
Today's refrigerators are larger but use less energy. They have electronic controls that can be adjusted to set different parts of the refrigerator at different temperatures. Some modern refrigerators can alert people when a particular food supply is running low!

Critical Thinking

In addition to slowing food spoilage, what is another advantage of refrigerating food?

383

...that helps you save time. Describe how it helps ...o improve its design.

...sign challenge—complete **Improvise It: Build** ...e Inquiry Flipchart.

By asking questions, testing your ideas, organizing and analyzing data, drawing conclusions, and sharing what you learn...

You are the scientist!

Texas Essential Knowledge and Skills

Dear Students and Family Members,

The *ScienceFusion* Student Edition, Inquiry Flipchart, and Digital Curriculum provide a full year of interactive experiences built around the Texas Essential Knowledge and Skills for Science. As you read, experiment, and interact with print and digital content, you will be learning what you need to know for this school year. The Texas Essential Knowledge and Skills are listed here for you. You will also see them referenced throughout this book. Look for them on the opening pages of each unit and lesson.

Have a great school year!

Sincerely,
The HMH *ScienceFusion* Team

Look in each unit to find the picture.

Check it out: Unit 7
This picture is found on page _____.

TEKS 4.1

Scientific investigation and reasoning.
The student conducts classroom and outdoor investigations, following home and school safety procedures and environmentally appropriate and ethical practices. The student is expected to:

A demonstrate safe practices and the use of safety equipment as described in the Texas Safety Standards during classroom and outdoor investigations; and

B make informed choices in the use and conservation of natural resources and reusing and recycling of materials such as paper, aluminum, glass, cans, and plastic.

© Houghton Mifflin Harcourt Publishing Company   (br) ©Image Source/Getty Images

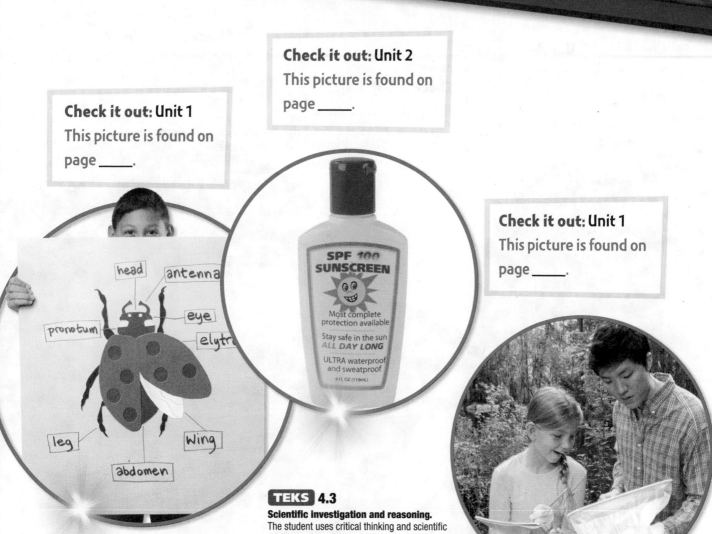

Check it out: Unit 1

This picture is found on page _____.

Check it out: Unit 2

This picture is found on page _____.

Check it out: Unit 1

This picture is found on page _____.

SPF 100 SUNSCREEN

Most complete protection available

Stay safe in the sun
ALL DAY LONG

ULTRA waterproof and sweatproof

4 FL OZ (118mL)

head
antenna
eye
elytra
pronotum
leg
wing
abdomen

TEKS 4.2

Scientific investigation and reasoning.
The student uses scientific inquiry methods during laboratory and outdoor investigations. The student is expected to:

A plan and implement descriptive investigations, including asking well-defined questions, making inferences, and selecting and using appropriate equipment or technology to answer his/her questions;

B collect and record data by observing and measuring, using the metric system, and using descriptive words and numerals such as labeled drawings, writing, and concept maps;

C construct simple tables, charts, bar graphs, and maps using tools and current technology to organize, examine, and evaluate data;

D analyze data and interpret patterns to construct reasonable explanations from data that can be observed and measured;

E perform repeated investigations to increase the reliability of results; and

F communicate valid, oral, and written results supported by data.

TEKS 4.3

Scientific investigation and reasoning.
The student uses critical thinking and scientific problem solving to make informed decisions. The student is expected to:

A in all fields of science, analyze, evaluate, and critique scientific explanations by using empirical evidence, logical reasoning, and experimental and observational testing, including examining all sides of scientific evidence of those scientific explanations, so as to encourage critical thinking by the student;

B draw inferences and evaluate accuracy of services and product claims found in advertisements and labels such as for toys, food, and sunscreen;

C represent the natural world using models such as rivers, stream tables, or fossils and identify their limitations, including accuracy and size; and

D connect grade-level appropriate science concepts with the history of science, science careers, and contributions of scientists.

TEKS 4.4

Science investigation and reasoning.
The student knows how to use a variety of tools, materials, equipment, and models to conduct science inquiry. The student is expected to:

A collect, record, and analyze information using tools, including calculators, microscopes, cameras, computers, hand lenses, metric rulers, Celsius thermometers, mirrors, spring scales, pan balances, triple beam balances, graduated cylinders, beakers, hot plates, meter sticks, compasses, magnets, collecting nets, and notebooks; timing devices, including clocks and stopwatches; and materials to support observation of habitats of organisms such as terrariums and aquariums; and

B use safety equipment as appropriate, including safety goggles and gloves.

© Houghton Mifflin Harcourt Publishing Company   (b) ©Photodisc/Getty Images

Check it out: Unit 3
This picture is found on page _____.

Check it out: Unit 5
This picture is found on page _____.

Check it out: Unit 7
This picture is found on page _____.

TEKS 4.5

Matter and energy. The student knows that matter has measurable physical properties and those properties determine how matter is classified, changed, and used. The student is expected to:

A measure, compare, and contrast physical properties of matter, including size, mass, volume, states (solid, liquid, gas), temperature, magnetism, and the ability to sink or float;

B predict the changes caused by heating and cooling such as ice becoming liquid water and condensation forming on the outside of a glass of ice water; and

C compare and contrast a variety of mixtures and solutions such as rocks in sand, sand in water, or sugar in water.

TEKS 4.6

Force, motion, and energy. The student knows that energy exists in many forms and can be observed in cycles, patterns, and systems. The student is expected to:

A differentiate among forms of energy, including mechanical, sound, electrical, light, and heat/thermal;

B differentiate between conductors and insulators;

C demonstrate that electricity travels in a closed path, creating an electrical circuit, and explore an electromagnetic field; and

D design an experiment to test the effect of force on an object such as a push or a pull, gravity, friction, or magnetism.

TEKS 4.7

Earth and space. The students know that Earth consists of useful resources and its surface is constantly changing. The student is expected to:

A examine properties of soils, including color and texture, capacity to retain water, and ability to support the growth of plants;

B observe and identify slow changes to Earth's surface caused by weathering, erosion, and deposition from water, wind, and ice; and

C identify and classify Earth's renewable resources, including air, plants, water, and animals; and nonrenewable resources, including coal, oil, and natural gas; and the importance of conservation.

© Houghton Mifflin Harcourt Publishing Company   (cl) ©Koichi Hasegawa/Getty Images; (c) ©blickwinkel/Alamy; (cr) ©Digital Vision/Getty Images

Answer Key: page 135, page 250, page 305

© Houghton Mifflin Harcourt Publishing Company   (b) ©Digital Vision/Getty Images;   (c) ©Arco Images GmbH/Alamy; (tr) ©Corbis Super Rf/Alamy Images (c) ©HO/Reuters/Corbis;

Check it out: Unit 8

This picture is found on page _____.

Check it out: Unit 10

This picture is found on page _____.

Check it out: Unit 11

This picture is found on page _____.

TEKS 4.8

Earth and space. The student knows that there are recognizable patterns in the natural world and among the Sun, Earth, and Moon system. The student is expected to:

A measure and record changes in weather and make predictions using weather maps, weather symbols, and a map key;

B describe and illustrate the continuous movement of water above and on the surface of Earth through the water cycle and explain the role of the Sun as a major source of energy in this process; and

C collect and analyze data to identify sequences and predict patterns of change in shadows, tides, seasons, and the observable appearance of the Moon over time.

TEKS 4.9

Organisms and environments. The student knows and understands that living organisms within an ecosystem interact with one another and with their environment. The student is expected to:

A investigate that most producers need sunlight, water, and carbon dioxide to make their own food, while consumers are dependent on other organisms for food; and

B describe the flow of energy through food webs, beginning with the Sun, and predict how changes in the ecosystem affect the food web such as a fire in a forest.

TEKS 4.10

Organisms and environments. The student knows that organisms undergo similar life processes and have structures that help them survive within their environment. The student is expected to:

A explore how adaptations enable organisms to survive in their environment such as comparing birds' beaks and leaves on plants;

B demonstrate that some likenesses between parents and offspring are inherited, passed from generation to generation such as eye color in humans or shapes of leaves in plants. Other likenesses are learned such as table manners or reading a book and seals balancing balls on their noses; and

C explore, illustrate, and compare life cycles in living organisms such as butterflies, beetles, radishes, or lima beans.

Contents

Track Your Progress

Levels of Inquiry Key ■ DIRECTED ■ GUIDED ■ INDEPENDENT

© Houghton Mifflin Harcourt Publishing Company

© Houghton Mifflin Harcourt Publishing Company (b) ©ONOKY - Photononstop/Alamy Images

PHYSICAL SCIENCE

© Houghton Mifflin Harcourt Publishing Company

© Houghton Mifflin Harcourt Publishing Company (b) ©Gaetano Images Inc./Alamy Images

© Houghton Mifflin Harcourt Publishing Company

EARTH SCIENCE

© Houghton Mifflin Harcourt Publishing Company

© Houghton Mifflin Harcourt Publishing Company

© Houghton Mifflin Harcourt Publishing Company (b) ©Digital Vision/Getty Images

© Houghton Mifflin Harcourt Publishing Company · (t) ©MIMOHE/O/Getty Images

Safety in Science

Indoors Doing science is a lot of fun. But, a science lab can be a dangerous place. Falls, cuts, and burns can happen easily. When you are doing a science investigation, you need to be safe. Know the safety rules and listen to your teacher.

Adult scientists have to follow lab safety rules, too.

Pay attention to these safety rules.

1 **Think ahead.** Study the investigation steps so you know what to expect. If you have any questions, ask your teacher. Be sure you understand all caution statements and safety reminders.

2 **Be neat and clean.** Keep your work area clean. If you have long hair, pull it back so it doesn't get in the way. Roll or push up long sleeves to keep them away from your activity.

3 **Oops!** If you spill or break something, or get cut, tell your teacher right away.

4 **Watch your eyes.** Wear safety goggles anytime you are directed to do so. If you get anything in your eyes, tell your teacher right away.

5 **Yuck!** Never eat or drink anything during a science activity.

6 **Don't get shocked.** Be careful if an electric appliance is used. Be sure that electric cords are in a safe place where you can't trip over them. Never use the cord to pull a plug from an outlet.

7 **Keep it clean.** Always clean up when you have finished. Put everything away and wipe your work area. Wash your hands.

8 **Play it safe.** Always know where to find safety equipment, such as fire extinguishers. Know how to use the safety equipment around you.

© Houghton Mifflin Harcourt Publishing Company   (border) ©PhotoObjects.net/Jupiterimages/Getty Images

Outdoors

Lots of science research happens outdoors. It's fun to explore the wild! But, you need to be careful. The weather, the land, and the living things can surprise you.

This scientist has to protect his eyes.

Follow these safety rules when you're doing science outdoors.

1 **Think ahead.** Study the investigation steps so you know what to expect. If you have any questions, ask your teacher. Be sure you understand all caution statements and safety reminders.

2 **Dress right.** Wear appropriate clothes and shoes for the outdoors. Cover up and wear sunscreen and sunglasses for sun safety.

3 **Clean up the area.** Follow your teacher's instructions for when and how to throw away waste.

4 **Oops!** Tell your teacher right away if you break something or get hurt.

5 **Watch your eyes.** Wear safety goggles when directed to do so. If you get anything in your eyes, tell your teacher right away.

6 **Yuck!** Never taste anything outdoors.

7 **Stay with your group.** Work in the area as directed by your teacher. Stay on marked trails.

8 **"Wilderness" doesn't mean go wild.** Never engage in horseplay, games, or pranks.

9 **Always walk.** No running!

10 **Play it safe.** Know where safety equipment can be found and how to use it. Know how to get help.

11 **Clean up.** Wash your hands with soap and water when you come back indoors.

© Houghton Mifflin Harcourt Publishing Company (t) ©Carsten Peter/National Geographic Image Collection/Alamy Images; (border) ©PhotoObjects.net/Jupiterimages/Getty Images

UNIT 1
Studying Science

ughton Mifflin Harcourt Publishing Company (bg) ©Jeff Rotman/Getty Images; (inset) ©Alexis Rosenfeld/Photo Researchers, Inc; (border) ©NDisc/Age Fotostock

Big Idea

Scientists use scientific inquiry methods and critical thinking during investigations to answer questions about the world around us.

TEKS 4.2A, 4.2B, 4.2C, 4.2D, 4.2F, 4.3A, 4.3C, 4.3D, 4.4A

I Wonder Why

Why is the work of a scientist doing field research similar to the work of a scientist doing research in a laboratory? *Turn the page to find out.*

Here's Why All scientists ask questions, answer them with investigations, and communicate their results to other scientists.

In this unit, you will explore the Big Idea, the Essential Questions, and the Investigations on the Inquiry Flipchart.

Levels of Inquiry Key ■ DIRECTED ■ GUIDED ■ INDEPENDENT

Track Your Progress

Big Idea Scientists use scientific inquiry methods and critical thinking during investigations to answer questions about the world around us.

Essential Questions

Now I Get the Big Idea!

Science Notebook

TEKS **4.2A** ...asking well-defined questions... **4.2D** analyze data...to construct reasonable explanations from data that can be...measured **4.2F** communicate valid...written results supported by data **4.4A** collect...information using tools, including...materials to support observation of habitats of organisms such as terrariums and aquariums

Essential Question

What Do Scientists Do?

Engage Your Brain!

Find the answer to the following question in this lesson and record it here.

Biologists make observations about living things. What are some observations you can make about lizards?

_____

_____

_____

_____

_____

Active Reading

Lesson Vocabulary
List the terms. As you learn about each one, make notes in the Interactive Glossary.

_____ _____

_____ _____

_____ _____

Main Ideas
In this lesson, you'll read about how scientists do their work. Active readers look for main ideas before they read to give their reading a purpose. Often, the headings in a lesson state its main ideas. Preview the headings in this lesson to give your reading a purpose.

© Houghton Mifflin Harcourt Publishing Company ©Joe McDonald/Corbis

The Role of Scientists

It's career day for Mr. Green's fourth-grade class! Mr. Green invited a scientist named Dr. Sims to talk to the class. The students are ready, and they have many questions to ask.

Active Reading As you read these two pages, turn the heading into a question in your mind. Then underline the sentence that answers the question.

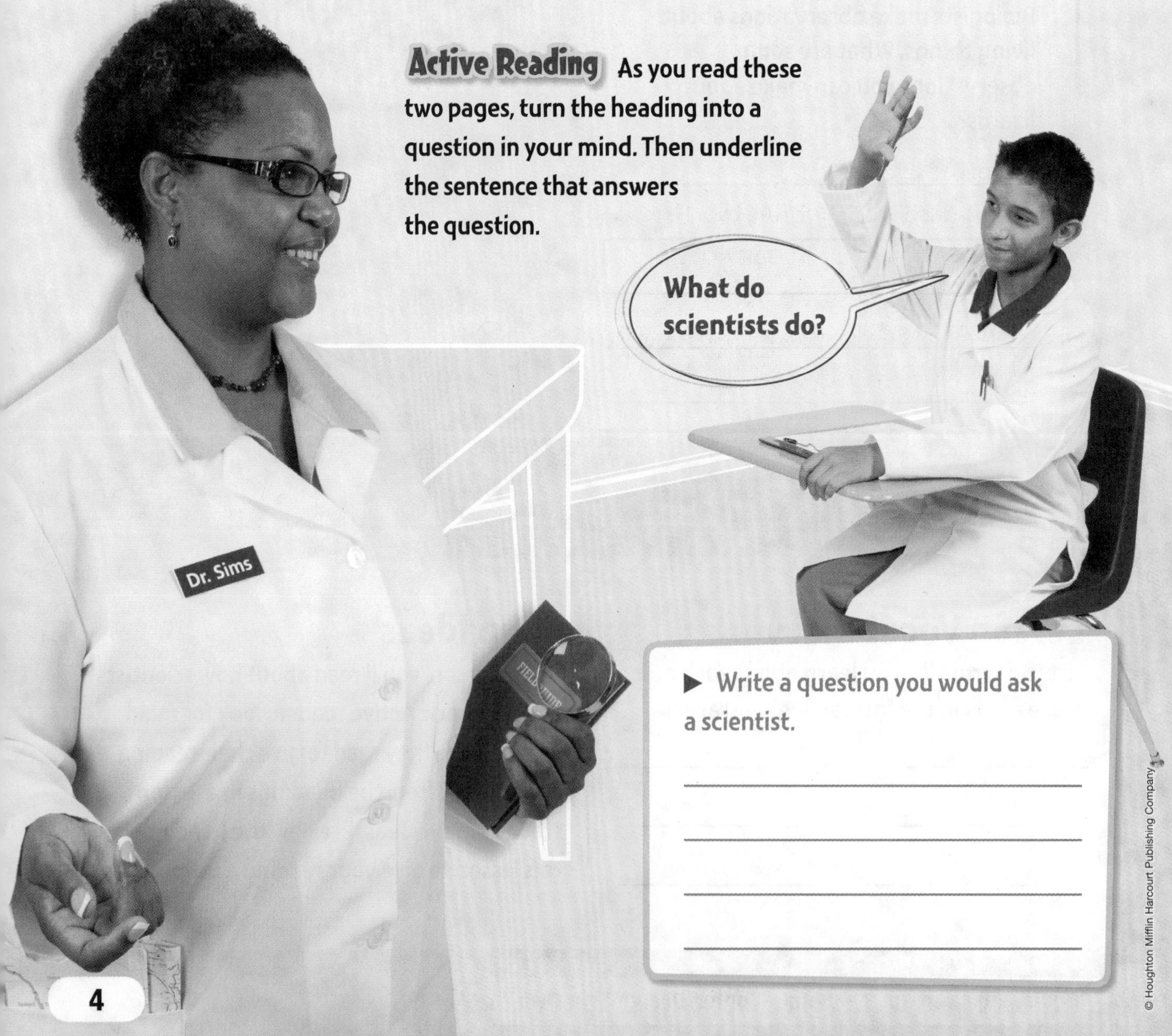

What do scientists do?

▶ Write a question you would ask a scientist.

_____

_____

_____

_____

4

© Houghton Mifflin Harcourt Publishing Company

"Thank you for inviting me to your school! My name is Dr. Sims, and I am a scientist. A **scientist** asks questions about the natural world. There are many kinds of scientists and many questions to ask!

Science is the study of the natural world. Earth scientists study things such as rocks, weather, and the planets. Physical scientists study matter and energy. Life scientists, like me, study living things. I am a wildlife biologist, which means I study animals in the wild.

Scientists work alone and in teams. Sometimes, I travel alone on long hikes to watch animals. At other times, I ask other biologists to go with me. I share ideas with other scientists every day.

Science is hard work but fun, too. I like being outdoors. Discovering something new is exciting. The best part, for me, is helping animals. The best way to explain what a scientist does is to show you."

▶ For each area of science, write one question a scientist might ask.

Earth Science

_____

_____

Life Science

_____

_____

Physical Science

_____

_____

Do you work all by yourself?

Is it fun to be a scientist?

© Houghton Mifflin Harcourt Publishing Company

Making Observations and
Asking Questions

Dr. Sims looks around the classroom. She observes everything for a few moments. Then she asks questions about what she sees.

How does that plant produce offspring?

Does the lizard's skin ever change colors?

Does the goldfish spend more time near the top or at the bottom of the aquarium?

Dr. Sims

▶ Ask your own well-defined question about the classroom in the photo to the right.

_____

_____

_____

© Houghton Mifflin Harcourt Publishing Company

© Houghton Mifflin Harcourt Publishing Company

▶ Name five things you observe in this classroom.

_____

_____

Scientists make observations about the world around them. An **observation** is information collected using the five senses.

Scientists ask well-defined questions about their observations. Notice that Dr. Sims asks questions about the living things in the classroom. That's because she is a wildlife biologist. You might ask different questions if you observed different things.

Dr. Sims asks, "How would you answer my question about the goldfish?" One student suggests recording observations in a Science Notebook. Another student suggests using a stopwatch to collect information about the goldfish.

Dr. Sims says, "I can plan and implement a descriptive investigation." Scientists conduct an **investigation** to answer questions. The steps of planning and implementing an investigation may include asking questions, making inferences, selecting appropriate equipment or technology, collecting and analyzing data, and communicating results supported by data.

7

Experiments

Dr. Sims seems very excited to talk about investigations. She says, "Describing what you see is one kind of investigation. Other investigations include doing an experiment."

Active Reading As you read these two pages, circle the vocabulary term each time it is used.

A Fair Test

An *experiment* is a fair test. It can show that one thing causes another thing to happen. In each test, you change only one factor, or *variable*. To be fair and accurate, you conduct the experiment multiple times.

To test something else, you must start a new experiment. Being creative and working in teams can help scientists conduct experiments.

Carlos is conducting an experiment. He gives the lizard fruit and crickets to see which will be eaten. The food is the only variable that is changed. Each day, the lizard gets two different types of food at the same time and in the same amounts.

© Houghton Mifflin Harcourt Publishing Company

Scientific Methods

Scientific investigations use scientific methods. Scientific methods may include the following activities:

- make observations

- ask a well-defined question

- form a hypothesis

- plan and conduct an experiment

- collect, record, and analyze data

- draw conclusions

- communicate results

Sometimes, these steps are done in this order. At other times, they're not.

A **hypothesis** is an idea or explanation that can be tested with an investigation. Dr. Sims gives the students an example from their classroom. She says, "I hypothesize that this lizard eats more insects than fruit."

▶ Talk with other students in your class. Then write a hypothesis to explain what makes the lizard in the photo change color.

_____

_____

_____

_____

_____

_____

© Houghton Mifflin Harcourt Publishing Company ©Peter Weber/Getty Images

Other Kinds of Investigations

Dr. Sims smiles. She says, "I hope this doesn't confuse anyone, but doing an experiment is not always possible."

Active Reading As you read these two pages, circle the clue words or phrases that signal a detail such as an example or an added fact.

Many science questions cannot be answered by doing an experiment. Here's one question: What kind of lizard have I found? This question can be answered by using an identification guide. Here's another question: What causes the sun to seem to rise and set? This question can be answered by making and using a model of Earth and the sun. Here's another: At what time of year does a state get the most rain? This question can be answered by looking for patterns through many years of rainfall records. Here's another: How did people who lived 100 years ago describe Mars? This question can be answered with research. Research includes reading what others have written and asking experts.

What is the surface of Mars like? This question is hard to answer with an experiment. NASA scientists sent robot spacecraft to Mars. Cameras on these spacecraft take pictures of the planet for scientists to observe.

© Houghton Mifflin Harcourt Publishing Company (inset) ©NASA Jet Propulsion Laboratory; (bkgd) ©Getty Images/PhotoDisc

Use an Identification Guide

Draw lines to match the lizard with its description.

Texas Horned Lizard

- Colors: brownish
- Body: wider and flatter than other lizards
- Tail: straight and shorter than the body
- Spines: several short horns on head, spiny scales on sides of body

Common Chameleon

- Colors: green, yellow, gray, or brown
- Eyes: big and bulge out from side of head
- Body: tall and flat, a ridge of scales along the backbone
- Tail: curls for grasping branches

Common Iguana

- Colors: green, gray, brown, blue, lavender, or black
- Spines: along center of back and tail
- Body: Large flap of skin under the chin

© Houghton Mifflin Harcourt Publishing Company   (l) ©Brownstock Inc./Alamy; (c) ©Tim Davis/Corbis; (r) ©Maria Gritsai/Alamy

Scientists Share Their Results as Evidence

Dr. Sims says, "Tell me something you know. Then tell me *how* do you know."

Active Reading As you read these two pages, draw two lines under the main idea.

When scientists explain how things work, they must give evidence. **Evidence** is data gathered during an investigation. Scientists should examine all sides of scientific evidence as they develop scientific explanations. Evidence might support a hypothesis, or it might not. For example, think about the class with their lizard. The students state this hypothesis: Lizards eat more insects than fruit. They carry out an experiment, putting crickets and fruit in the lizard's tank. After two hours, they observe how much food is left, and repeat the steps each day for a week.

The students report that their lizard ate more crickets than fruit. She says, "What is your evidence?" The students share their recorded results. They report that the lizard ate 13 crickets and no fruit.

Once evidence is gathered, a scientist can analyze the data and interpret patterns. Scientists use data that can be observed and measured to construct reasonable explanations for things that happen in the natural world.

© Houghton Mifflin Harcourt Publishing Company

Science Notebook

A *conclusion* is an explanation based on evidence. Communicate written results by stating conclusions supported by the data below.

Evidence

We used thermometers and found that when the air temperature changed by 5 degrees, a chameleon's skin color changed.

Conclusion

_____

_____

_____

_____

Evidence

We measured the temperature at the same time each morning and each afternoon for one month. Each day, the air temperature was higher in the afternoon than in the morning.

Conclusion

_____

_____

_____

_____

_____

Evidence

Paper Airplane Wingspan (cm)	Time in the Air (sec)
5	7
10	12
15	21
20	28

Conclusion

_____

_____

_____

_____

© Houghton Mifflin Harcourt Publishing Company   (t) ©JH Pete Carmichael/Getty Images; (b) ©Getty Images/PhotoDisc

Fill in the missing words to tell what scientists do.

Summarize

Mr. Brown's fourth-grade class wants a pet in their classroom. Their teacher says they have to think like a (1) _____ to care for animals. The students know that means (2) _____ about the natural world. The class wonders what kinds of animals make good classroom pets. They decide to do an (3) _____ to find out. They go to the library and use books and websites to (4) _____ pets.

The class concludes that guinea pigs are the best pets for their classroom. Mr. Brown asks them what (5) _____ they have to support their conclusion. The students explain that guinea pigs are quiet and gentle. They are also active in the daytime and sleep at night.

Once the guinea pigs are in the classroom, the students watch and listen. They keep a Science Notebook and list all their (6) _____. Then, students ask (7) _____ based on what they observe. One is: What does it mean when the guinea pigs make squeaking sounds? Two students have a (8) _____ : guinea pigs make that noise when they want to be fed.

Mr. Brown suggests that the students record the time when they hear the sound and write down what they are doing at the same time. After a few days, the students see that their guinea pigs make that noise just as the zippered bag that holds the fresh vegetables is opened. So, what do you think the sound means? (9) _____

_____

© Houghton Mifflin Harcourt Publishing Company

Answer Key: 1. scientist, 2. asking questions, 3. investigation, 4. research, 5. evidence, 6. observations, 7. questions, 8. hypothesis, 9. It means they want to eat the vegetables right away.

Name _____

Word Play

1 Use the words in the box to complete the puzzle.

Across

5. An explanation based on evidence

7. Scientists do one of these to answer questions

Down

1. An idea or explanation that can be tested with an investigation

2. To share the results of investigations

3. A person who asks questions about the natural world

4. You ask this

6. A kind of investigation that is a fair test

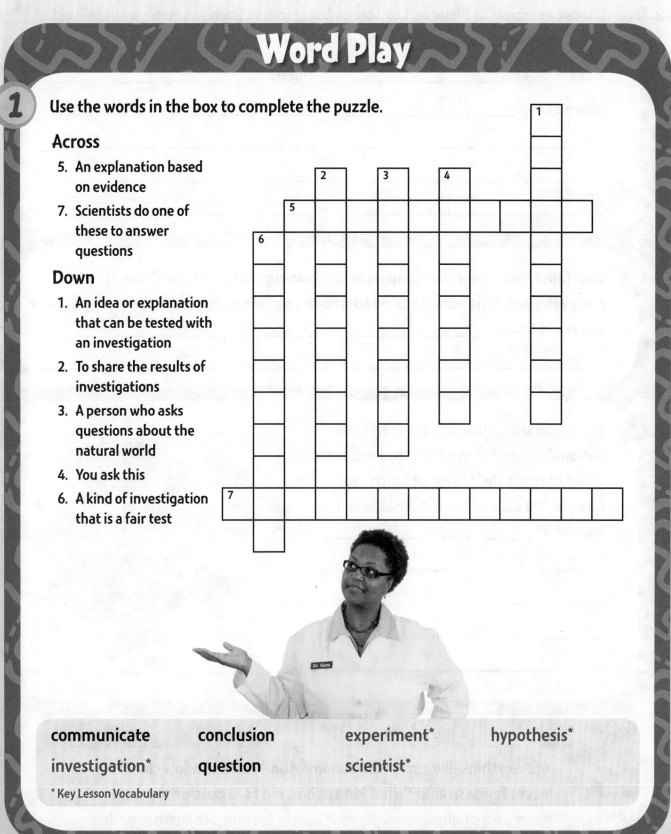

| communicate | conclusion | experiment* | hypothesis* |

| investigation* | question | scientist* |

* Key Lesson Vocabulary

© Houghton Mifflin Harcourt Publishing Company

Apply Concepts

2 Choose an object to observe. List some observations. Then ask some well-defined questions related to your observations.

Name of Object: _____

Observations: _____

_____

_____

_____

Questions: _____

_____

_____

_____

3 Your family uses steel wool soap pads for cleaning pots and pans. Often they get rusty after use. What could you do to stop the pads from rusting? Write a hypothesis you could test. _____

_____

4 The graph shows the data collected from a national online poll in which students were asked to name their favorite lunch food. Analyze the data. What conclusions can you draw? _____

_____

_____

_____

_____

Pita pockets

Grilled cheese

Pizza

Lasagna

Hamburgers

Take It Home! You can think like a scientist at home, too. Which window cleaner leaves fewer streaks? What kind of bird did I see outside my window? Make a list of questions with your family. Investigate them together.

© Houghton Mifflin Harcourt Publishing Company (pita pocket) ©Foodcollection/Getty Images; (grilled cheese) ©Artville/Getty Images; (lasagna) ©Elsing/Getty Images; (burger) ©Artville/Getty Images; (pizza) ©Martin Bennett/Alamy

TEKS **4.2A** ...implement descriptive investigations...making inferences **4.2B** collect...data by observing and measuring **4.2C** construct simple tables...bar graphs...maps...to organize, examine... data **4.3A** ...analyze, evaluate, and critique...explanations by using...evidence, logical reasoning, and experimental and observational testing, including examining all sides...of those...explanations

Essential Question

What Skills Do Scientists Use?

Engage Your Brain!

Find the answer to the following question in the lesson and record it here.

Splash it. Pour it. Freeze it. Make bubbles in it. What skills might a scientist use to test how water behaves?

_____

_____

_____

_____

Active Reading

Lesson Vocabulary

List the terms. As you learn about each one, make notes in the interactive Glossary.

_____

_____

_____

_____

Visual Aids

In this lesson, you'll see large graphics with labels. The labels call attention to important details. Active readers preview a lesson's graphics and decide how the information in them provides details about the main idea.

© Houghton Mifflin Harcourt Publishing Company ©Richard H Johnston/Getty Images

Everyday Science Skills

Do you ask questions about the world around you? If so, you use these science skills all day, every day—just like a scientist!

Active Reading As you read the next four pages, circle the names of nine science skills.

As you read about scientists, think
→ **"Hey, I can do this, too!"**

Infer

Scientists *infer* how things work by thinking about their observations. A biologist may infer that the color patterns of fish enable them to blend in and avoid predators.

Observe

Scientists may *observe* many things, such as changes in color, temperature, and bubbling.

© Houghton Mifflin Harcourt Publishing Company (l) ©Jose Luis Pelaez Inc./Getty Images (r) ©Asia Images Group/Getty Images

Scientists use inquiry skills every day—and so do you. When you observe, you use your five senses to get information. Let's say you smell cheese, bread, and spicy odors. You *infer* "I think we are having pizza for lunch today!" An **inference** is a statement that explains an observation.

When you think about how things are the same and different, you *compare* them. For example, your family wants to adopt a new kitten. You compare different kittens, looking for one that is playful and friendly. When you decide which kitten is the best, you *communicate* that decision to your family. You can communicate by speaking, writing, and by using pictures or models.

Compare

Scientists *compare* objects and things that happen.

▶ Practice the skill of *comparing*. List ways these two fish are similar and different.

| Powder-Blue Tang | Porcupinefish |

Similarities	Differences

Communicate

▶ Scientists *communicate*, or share, their results and inferences with other scientists. What did you communicate today?

_____

_____

_____

© Houghton Mifflin Harcourt Publishing Company (tr) ©blue jean images/Getty Images; (tr) ©Tomas del Amo/PhotoTake/Alamy; (bc) ©Martin Harvey/Alamy; (br) ©lifeonwhite/Alamy

Think Like a Scientist

Scientists use these skills every day in their investigations. Find out what they are and when you might use them.

Predict

Scientists use their observations and existing research to make predictions about what will happen in the future. For example, a meteorologist uses weather patterns to determine whether it will rain over the weekend.

Use Variables

When scientists plan experiments, they think, "What is the one thing I will change?" That one thing is a variable. Let's say you want to find out how cold a freezer has to be to make fruit pops. The variable that you will change is the temperature inside the freezer.

Some science skills are part of doing science investigations, including experiments. They may sound unfamiliar to you. But when you read about these skills, you might realize that you already use them.

© Houghton Mifflin Harcourt Publishing Company

Plan and Conduct Investigations

Scientists plan and conduct investigations that will answer science questions. Say you want to know how salty water must be to make an egg float. First, you think about the steps you'll take to find the answer. Next, you gather the materials you'll use. Then, you test the amount of salt.

▶ You are a marine biologist. You study living things in the ocean. What is one investigation you might plan?

_____

_____

_____

Predict what a marine biologist might look for on a dive.

_____

_____

_____

Hypothesize

Scientists hypothesize when they think of a testable statement that tries to explain an observation. Suppose you notice that water seems to evaporate at different rates from containers with different shapes. What would you hypothesize is a cause?

Draw Conclusions

Scientists draw conclusions when they use evidence to evaluate a hypothesis. If you investigate how the size of a sail affects how quickly a toy boat moves, you might conclude that boats with larger sails move faster because larger sails collect more wind.

© Houghton Mifflin Harcourt Publishing Company

Math and Science Skills

Using rulers and balances. Putting things in order. Measuring the speed of a car. Making tables and graphs. Sounds like math, but it's science, too!

Active Reading As you read this page, turn the heading into a question in your mind. Then underline the parts of the text that answer the question.

Every scientist uses math. Let's say you are a marine biologist who studies whales. You *classify* whales by how much they weigh or how long they are from head to tail. You put them in *order* when you arrange them by length from smallest to largest. You *use numbers* to tell how many are alive today. You *use time and space relationships* to investigate when and where they migrate each year. You *measure* how long they are and how much food they eat. You *record and display* the results of your investigations in writing and in tables, graphs, and maps.

Beyond the Book

Do research to collect data about whale migration. Construct maps using tools to organize, examine, and evaluate your data. Construct reasonable explanations about patterns of whale migration based on the data collected as well as your map.

Classify and Order

You classify things when you put them into groups. To put things in order, you may make a list in which position matters, such as ordering bird species by how fast they fly or move.

Measure

In science and math, you measure by using tools to find length, width, height, mass, weight, volume, and elapsed time.

Use Numbers

You use numbers when you observe by counting or measuring. You also use numbers to compare and order. And, you use numbers to describe speed and force.

© Houghton Mifflin Harcourt Publishing Company

Do the Math!
Compare Numbers

Some of the world's biggest mammals live under the oceans' waves. The table gives the names of several kinds of whales and the number that scientists estimate are alive today.

Kind of Whale	Population
Beluga whale	200,000
Blue whale	14,000
Fin whale	55,000
Humpback whale	40,000
Minke whale	1,000,000
Pilot whale	1,200,000
Sei whale	54,000
Sperm whale	

1. Which two kinds of whales have the closest number alive?

_____

2. How many more Pilot whales are there than Minke whales?

_____

3. Scientists estimate there are about three hundred and sixty thousand sperm whales alive today. Write that number, using numerals, in the table.

Use Time and Space Relationships

You use timing devices, including clocks and stopwatches, to collect, record, and analyze information about time. You can predict when it will be high tide or low tide. You can also determine how the planets move in space.

Record and Display Data

You record and analyze information using tools, including notebooks and computers. You display, or show, data so that it's easy to understand by making tables, graphs, or diagrams.

© Houghton Mifflin Harcourt Publishing Company

Critical Thinking Skills

Have you ever asked yourself if the results of a scientific investigation are correct or make sense? If so, you've used critical thinking skills.

cientists in all fields use critical thinking skills to propose and examine scientific explanations and evidence related to those explanations. For example, scientists determine if an explanation is reasonable or is supported by valid data. Data collected through direct observation is called **empirical evidence**. Scientists use empirical evidence to analyze, evaluate, and critique the results of scientific investigations. To *analyze* is to think about all the pieces and parts that contribute to something. To *evaluate* is to examine something and decide if it has worth or value. To *critique* is to carefully judge something based on your knowledge, findings, and beliefs.

Logical Reasoning

When you use critical thinking, you also use logic. Logic requires you to use reason and order to figure out if something makes sense. When you use logical reasoning, you do not include your emotions or opinions. Scientists in all fields use logical reasoning to draw conclusions based on evidence.

Use Empirical Evidence

Careful observations and measurements are empirical evidence; observations that include opinions are not. For example, recording the temperature of a mixture is empirical evidence. However, saying the mixture feels warm is an opinion. When you analyze, evaluate, and critique an explanation, you see if it is based on empirical evidence.

© Houghton Mifflin Harcourt Publishing Company

Experimental Testing

Scientists perform an experiment to test a hypothesis. These experiments can be conducted in a laboratory or outdoors. Some scientific explanations are based on evidence from experiments. For example, suppose a scientist wants to find out how quickly Arctic ice freezes and thaws. He would design an experiment to test a specific hypothesis related to this question. He would then analyze the data he collected in order to help answer his question.

Observational Testing

It is not always possible to answer a question by conducting an experiment. For example, astronomers study objects in space such as planets and stars. Since these objects are very far away, the only way to study them is to observe their patterns. Scientists use observational testing to compare their patterns and draw conclusions.

Alternative Explanations

When you analyze, evaluate, and critique a scientific investigation, an important question to ask is, "Might there be another possible explanation for this data?" This would be an alternative explanation. For example, you might conclude from an investigation that bees that pollinate red flowers produce more honey than bees that pollinate yellow flowers. Other factors may also account for the difference in honey production. Always consider alternatives when you analyze, evaluate, and critique a scientific explanation.

Alternative Explanations

Milo concluded that the number of chirps crickets make each minute is based on when the sun sets at night. Suggest an alternative explanation for the number of times crickets chirp.

_____
_____
_____
_____
_____

© Houghton Mifflin Harcourt Publishing Company   (tl) ©David Boyer/National Geographic/Getty Images

When you're done, use the answer key to check and revise your work.

Fill in the missing skills in the column where they belong.

Summarize

Skills Scientists Use

Everyday Science Skills	1. _____
	2. _____
	3. _____
	4. _____

Science Investigation Skills	5. _____
	6. _____
	7. _____
	8. _____
	9. _____

Math and Science Skills	10. _____
	11. _____
	12. _____
	13. _____
	14. _____

Critical Thinking Skills	15. _____
	16. _____
	17. _____
	18. _____
	19. _____

Answer Key: 1–4, infer, communicate, compare, observe; 5–9, predict, use variables, plan and conduct investigations, draw conclusions, hypothesize; 10–14, measure, classify and order, record and display data, use time and space relationships, use numbers; 15–19, logical reasoning, use empirical evidence, observational testing, experimental testing, alternative explanations.

© Houghton Mifflin Harcourt Publishing Company ©Jose Luis Pelaez Inc./Getty Images

Name _____

Word Play

1 It's easy to get tongue-tied describing what scientists do. Look at the statements below. Switch the red words around until each statement about inquiry skills makes sense.

In order to sort his beakers and other tools, Dr. Mallory hypothesizes each object by size and shape. _____

Gabriella measures that her dog will want his favorite food for dinner, because she has observed him eat it quickly many times before. _____

Kim predicts when planning an experiment with her older brother. She keeps everything the same during their procedure, except for the one factor being tested. _____

After completing an experiment and summarizing her findings, Dr. Garcia classifies what she has learned with other scientists. _____

Dr. Jefferson studies the age of rocks and fossils. She uses variables to tell how old each specimen is. _____

Before conducting his experiment for the science fair, Derrick uses time and space relationships about which sample of fertilizer will make his tomato plant grow the fastest.

_____

To find out how long it takes Deshawn to ride his bike 100 m, Jessica communicates the time with a stopwatch. _____

© Houghton Mifflin Harcourt Publishing Company

Apply Concepts

2 Write how you would use numbers to investigate each object.

_____

_____

_____

_____

_____

3 For each picture, what kinds of observations could you record on a calendar?

_____

_____

_____

_____

_____

© Houghton Mifflin Harcourt Publishing Company

4 Shauna records the following information while conducting an investigation about plants. Circle the statements that are examples of empirical evidence. Then write to explain your choices.

- Soil temperature: 26°C
- Weight of plants: light
- Favorite plant: tulips
- Hours of sunlight: 12 hr
- Size of plants: big
- Average weekly growth: 3 cm

_____

_____

_____

5 Identify the type of testing used in each example below.

| Kate counts the number of birds that visit a feeder. | Lushen draws the different phases of the moon. | Dean records the volume of several mixtures. |

_____ _____ _____

_____ _____ _____

© Houghton Mifflin Harcourt Publishing Company

6

Trial Number	Time to Get to Cheese
2	59 seconds
4	48 seconds
6	32 seconds
8	29 seconds

The data table records the number of times a mouse ran through a maze to get to a piece of cheese.

Use logical reasoning to analyze and evaluate the data to draw a conclusion.

_____

_____

_____

_____

Enrico concludes from the data that all mice really like cheese. Is his conclusion logical? Explain.

_____

_____

_____

_____

_____

Take It Home!

There are many books in the library about scientists and how they think about the world around them. Pick a book with a family member. Find examples of the skills you've learned about and make a list.

© Houghton Mifflin Harcourt Publishing Company

TEKS **4.2B** collect and record data by observing and measuring... **4.2C** construct... bar graphs...to organize...data **4.2D** analyze data... to construct reasonable explanations... **4.2F** communicate valid...written results supported by data **4.3C** represent the natural world using models...such as stream tables... **4.4A** collect, record...information using tools...

Essential Question

How Do Scientists Collect and Use Data?

Engage Your Brain!

Find the answer to the following question in this lesson and record it here.

Are the ladybugs on this tree identical to each other? How would you investigate this question?

_____

_____

_____

_____

Active Reading

Lesson Vocabulary

List the terms. As you learn about each one, make notes in the Interactive Glossary.

_____ _____

_____ _____

_____ _____

Main Idea and Details

Details give information about a topic. The information may be examples, features, or characteristics. Active readers stay focused on the topic when they ask, What facts or information do these details add to the topic?

Inquiry Flipchart p. 5 — Rain, Rain, Come Again/Who's Wet? Who's Dry?

pp. 6–9 — Science Tools Activities

© Houghton Mifflin Harcourt Publishing Company ©Ron Sanford/Corbis

Research Is the Key

Tiny insects fly and flash on a summer night. Are you curious about them? Do you wonder how to find out what they are and how they light up? Do some research!

Active Reading As you read the next page, check the research sources you have used.

© Houghton Mifflin Harcourt Publishing Company (bkgd) ©Clearviewstock/Alamy; (cr) ©alam/Alamy; (bl) ©Getty Images/PhotoDisc;

© Houghton Mifflin Harcourt Publishing Company (bkgd) ©Clearviewstock/Alamy; (t) ©Daniella Nowitz/Corbis

Often scientists ask themselves, "What do other scientists know about this?" To find out, they do *research*. When you research, you use reference materials and talk to experts to learn what is known. So, if you want to learn what scientists know about fireflies, you can do these things:

- Use an encyclopedia.

- Read a book.

- Read science articles.

- Visit a museum.

- E-mail a scientist.

- Visit science websites.

These kinds of resources may have plenty of information about fireflies. But you will still have questions they do not answer. That's when you conduct your own investigations.

Natural history museums have insect collections as well as scientists who can answer questions about them.

Do the Research!

You just saw bees flying in and out of a hole in an old tree. You know it's not a good idea to get too close. So, how can you find out what bees do inside a tree? What research resource would you go to first? Explain why.

_____

_____

_____

_____

Science Tools

What comes to mind when you hear the word *tools*? Hammers, saws, and screwdrivers? What about computers and calculators? These are both science tools.

Active Reading As you read these two pages, circle the lesson vocabulary each time it is used.

Scientists use all kinds of tools to collect, record and analyze information. Many turn the five senses into "super-senses." Tools enable scientists to see things that are far away, to smell faint odors, to hear quiet sounds, and to feel vibrations their bodies can't.

Let's say you want to observe craters on the moon. A telescope, which makes faraway objects look closer, will turn your sense of sight into "super-vision."

Hand Lens

An ant looks larger in a magnifying box or with a hand lens.

© Houghton Mifflin Harcourt Publishing Company (bkgd) ©Clearviewstock/Alamy; (tl) ©Redmond Durrell/Alamy; (ant) ©Jack Thomas/Alamy

What if you're interested in studying tiny critters, such as leaf cutter ants? Use a hand lens to collect information about and to better analyze these ants. Hand lenses make small objects look bigger. Is the ant crawling away too fast to see it with the hand lens? Try gently placing the ant in a magnifying box. The top of the box has a lens in it, too.

Wondering what the ant's bite marks look like? Place a tiny piece of a cut leaf under a microscope. A **microscope** is a tool for looking at objects that cannot be seen with the eye alone.

▶ Predict how you could use a microscope to collect and analyze information about an ant. Make a drawing and add labels.

Microscope
Microscopes magnify objects more than hand lenses do.

© Houghton Mifflin Harcourt Publishing Company (bkgd) ©Clearviewstock/Alamy; (t) ©Redmond Durrell/Alamy; (l) ©Getty Images/PhotoDisc; (r)©Artville/Getty Images

Measurement Tools

What's the biggest bug in the world? How far can a grasshopper hop? How long can a butterfly fly? How do scientists find exact answers?

Scientists use measurement tools to collect, record, and analyze information to make their observations more exact. Think about it this way. You and your friend watch two grasshoppers hop. Your friend says, "This one jumped farther." But you think the other one jumped farther. To find out for sure, you need to measure.

There are tools to measure length or distance, mass, force, volume, and temperature. Most scientists use metric units with these tools. For example, a **pan balance** is used to measure mass with units called grams (g). A **spring scale** is used to measure force in units called newtons (N).

Pan Balance

Place the object you want to measure on one pan. Add gram masses to the other pan until the two pans balance. Add the masses together to find the total in grams (g).

Triple Beam Balance

A **triple beam balance** measures mass more exactly than a pan balance. It has one pan and three beams. To find the mass in grams, move the sliders until the beam balances.

© Houghton Mifflin Harcourt Publishing Company (bg) ©Clearviewstock/Alamy Images

Tape Measure & Meterstick

These tools are used to measure length in millimeters (mm), centimeters (cm), and meters (m).

Spring Scale

Hang an object from the hook at the end. As the spring stretches, the marker will show the size of the force in newtons (N).

Thermometer

Used to measure temperature, this tool has two sets of units: degrees Celsius (°C) and degrees Fahrenheit (°F).

Do the Math!
Make Measurements

Use the metric ruler below to collect and record information about the length of the stick insect's body. Use the correct unit.

_____

_____

Find an object in your classroom to measure with a spring scale. Write the name of the object and number of units.

_____

_____

Look at the thermometer on this page. Record the temperature in degrees Celsius (°C) and degrees Fahrenheit (°F).

_____

_____

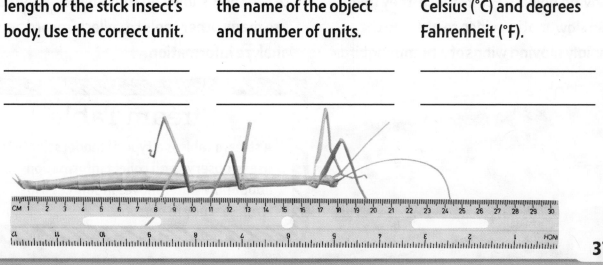

© Houghton Mifflin Harcourt Publishing Company   (tr) ©Artville/Getty Images; (b) ©Joel Sartore/Getty Images; (bg) ©Clearviewstock/Alamy Images

More Science Tools

The wings of a hummingbird beat rapidly. A river surges through a canyon. Light reflects off a mirror. Science tools help scientists observe nature in action.

Active Reading As you read these two pages, circle the names of four science tools that are described.

Many science tools help scientists make detailed observations in order to collect and record information. A camera is a tool that provides scientists with a permanent record. Scientists can use cameras to record the progress of a science experiment to analyze later. Still images help scientists study details. For example, pictures of shadows can show how they change over a day. Scientists may use video images to study animal behavior or other moving objects. For instance, they might use slow-motion video to observe the rapidly moving wings of a hummingbird.

Camera

A camera is any device that records an image. Scientists can use digital cameras, smartphones, and tablets to take pictures as a way to collect and record information.

Other tools help scientists observe events or living things that are difficult to see with the eyes alone. Geologists may use a stream table to model the movement of sediment in water. A collecting net can be used for up-close observation of living organisms. Physicists use mirrors to study and analyze how light behaves. In addition to the tools shown on these pages, scientists use many other tools to collect, record, and analyze information.

Stream Table

A stream table is a type of model scientists use to observe and collect information about how water moves in sources too large to study in person.

© Houghton Mifflin Harcourt Publishing Company   (t) ©CreativeAct-Technology series/Alamy Images; (bg) ©Clearviewstock/Alamy Images

Mirror

A mirror has a smooth, shiny surface. It can be used to collect information about how light is reflected or about optical illusions. A concave or a convex mirror can help scientists observe how light reflects. Scientists use mirrors and lasers to form 3-D pictures called holograms and to make precise measurements of distant objects.

Collecting Net

A collecting net is made up of a hoop, a handle, and netting. Scientists can use collecting nets to gather living specimens, such as insects, for close observation without causing any harm.

Lights, Camera, Action

Think of some nonliving things or events in nature. List three objects you could collect, record, and analyze information about using a still camera. List three events you could collect, record, and analyze information about using a video camera.

_____

_____

_____

_____

© Houghton Mifflin Harcourt Publishing Company (tc) ©GIPhotoStock/Photo Researchers/Getty Images; (bl) ©Clearviewstock/Alamy Images

Recording and Displaying Data

You're crawling through a tropical jungle.
A butterfly flutters by. Then another appears.
How will you keep track of how many you see?

Active Reading As you read these two pages, turn each heading into a question that will point you to the main idea. Underline the answers to your questions in the text.

A poster is one way to display data.

head

antenna

eye

pronotum

elytra

leg

wing

abdomen

© Houghton Mifflin Harcourt Publishing Company   (bkgd) ©Clearviewstock/Alamy

Recording Data

The bits of information you observe are called **data**. Some data are in the form of numbers. For example, the number of butterflies you see in an hour is a piece of data. Other data are in the form of descriptions. Examples include written notes, diagrams, audio recordings, and photographs.

Only observations are data. So when you think, "There are more butterflies here than in Canada," that's a guess, not data.

Displaying Data

The data you record as you investigate may be correct, but not easy to understand. Later, you can decide how to display the data. For example, you might use your scribbled notes from the jungle to draw a map showing where you saw each butterfly. You might compare the number of each kind of butterfly you found in a circle graph. You might use a bar graph to show the number of butterflies you saw each hour.

Data Two Ways

The table on the left lists six butterflies and the number of wing flaps each one made as it passed by an observer. The bar graph on the right can display the same data. Use the data in the table to complete the graph.

Individual Butterfly	Number of Wing Flaps in a Row
A	3
B	9
C	4
D	3
E	3
F	10

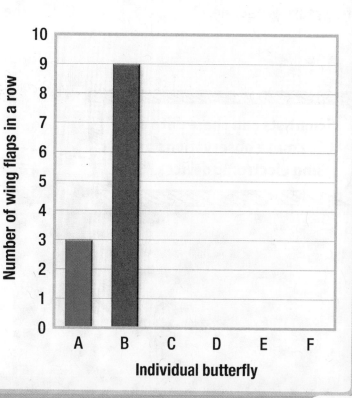

© Houghton Mifflin Harcourt Publishing Company; (bkgd) ©Clearviewstock/Alamy;

Using Data

You see on the news that the number of honeybees in the United States is decreasing. What is happening to them? How do scientists use data to solve problems and share information?

Drawing Conclusions

You've recorded your data. You've displayed it in a way that is easy to understand. Your next step is to analyze, or look for patterns in, the data. You might identify a trend, or a direction in the data over time. For example, you might conclude that the number of honeybees in your hometown has decreased by 30% in the last five years. What's next?

Communicating

Scientists communicate in many ways. They may work together to collect data. They compare their data with other scientists doing similar investigations. They report their results and conclusions by giving talks and writing reports. Conclusions often lead to new questions to investigate. Scientists are still studying why the number of honeybees is decreasing.

Scientists can share data as they make observations by using electronic devices.

4:25 PM

SEND▶

Dr. Ruiz,

Just checked the hives on Elm Street. There are many dead bees, and fewer honeycombs than last month.

Dr. Preston

© Houghton Mifflin Harcourt Publishing Company   (bkg) ©Guy Crittenden/Getty Images; (b) ©Ashley Cooper/Alamy

©Houghton Mifflin Harcourt Publishing Company (bkgd) ©Guy Crittenden/Getty Images; (t) ©George Doyle/Getty Images; (b) ©Pat Canova/Alamy

Scientists may work alone or in teams to analyze data and draw conclusions.

▶ A database is a collection of information or objects. Databases are organized so they are easy to search— like a search website. How would you search a database of insect facts to see what others have learned about the decrease in the number of honeybees?

_____

_____

_____

_____

Museums often have large collections of specimens, so scientists can compare what they have found to what's in a museum.

43

When you're done, use the answer key to check and revise your work.

The outline below is a summary of the lesson. Complete the outline.

Summarize

I. Research Is the Key

    A. Scientists do research to find out what others know.

    B. Reference sources you can use:

        1. encyclopedias

        2. _____

        3. _____

        4. _____

        5. _____

        6. _____

II. Science Tools

    A. Scientists use tools to make the senses more powerful.

    B. Tools that aid the sense of sight:

        1. telescope

        2. _____

        3. _____

        4. _____

III. _____

    A. pan balance

    B. triple beam balance

    C. spring scale

    D. tape measure/meterstick

    E. _____

IV. More Science Tools

    A. camera

    B. _____

    C. _____

    D. _____

V. Recording and Displaying Data

    A. Data are the bits of information you observe.

    B. Ways to display data:

        1. tables

        2. _____

        3. _____

Answer Key: I.B.2–6 (in any order) books, science articles, museums, contact a scientist, science websites II.B.2–4 (in any order) hand lens, magnifying box, microscope III. Measurement Tools III.E. thermometer IV.B–D (in any order) stream table, mirror, collecting net V.B.2–3 (in any order) maps, graphs

© Houghton Mifflin Harcourt Publishing Company

Name _____

Word Play

1 Put the mixed-up letters in order to spell a science term from the box.

tada ⬡⬡⬡⬡

eama supteer ⬡⬡⬡⬡ ⬡⬡⬡⬡⬡

crasheer ⬡⬡⬡⬡⬡⬡⬡⬡

priclg harce ⬡⬡⬡⬡⬡ ⬡⬡⬡⬡

croopsmice ⬡⬡⬡⬡⬡⬡⬡⬡⬡⬡

gripes clans ⬡⬡⬡⬡⬡⬡ ⬡⬡⬡⬡⬡

montumceica ⬡⬡⬡⬡⬡⬡⬡⬡⬡⬡⬡

axingbynim fog ⬡⬡⬡⬡⬡⬡⬡⬡ ⬡⬡⬡

metermother ⬡⬡⬡⬡⬡⬡⬡⬡⬡⬡⬡

lap cannaeb ⬡⬡⬡ ⬡⬡⬡⬡⬡⬡⬡

circle graph	**communicate**	**data***	**magnifying box**	**microscope***
pan balance*	**research**	**spring scale***	**tape measure**	**thermometer**

* Key Lesson Vocabulary

© Houghton Mifflin Harcourt Publishing Company ©Redmond O. Durrell/Alamy

Apply Concepts

2 Someone gives you an object. You think it's a rock, but you aren't sure. Write how you could use each resource below to do research about the object.

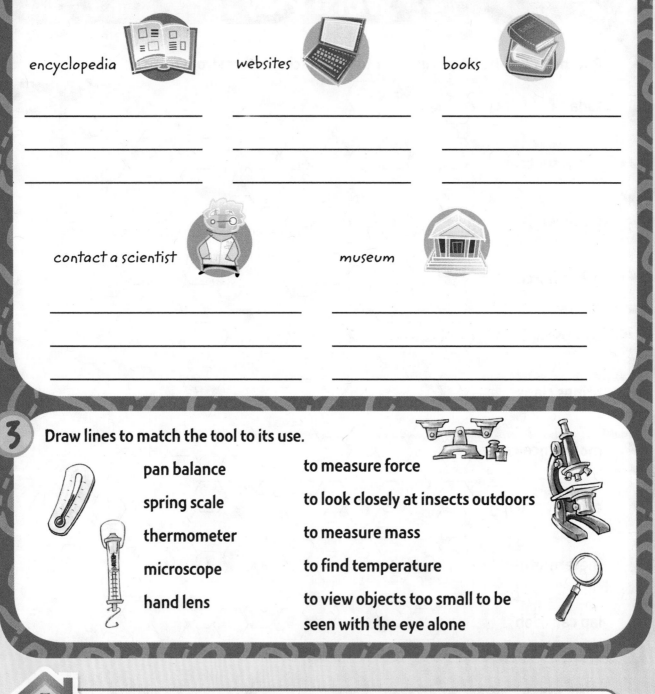

encyclopedia

_____

_____

_____

websites

_____

_____

_____

books

_____

_____

_____

contact a scientist

_____

_____

_____

museum

_____

_____

_____

3 Draw lines to match the tool to its use.

pan balance   to measure force

spring scale   to look closely at insects outdoors

thermometer   to measure mass

microscope   to find temperature

hand lens   to view objects too small to be
                     seen with the eye alone

Take It Home! Tell your family about the measurement tools scientists use. Discuss ways your family measures at home. Find and learn to use these tools. Hint: Does your kitchen have tools for measuring foods?

© Houghton Mifflin Harcourt Publishing Company

TEKS **4.2A** ...implement descriptive investigations...using appropriate equipment... **4.2B** collect...data by...measuring...and using...numerals **4.2C** construct simple tables... using tools...to organize...data **4.2F** communicate... written results... **4.4A** collect, record... information using tools, including... metric rulers...spring scales...pan balances...

Name _____

Essential Question

Why Do Scientists Compare Results?

Set a Purpose

What will you learn from this investigation?

_____

_____

_____

Think About the Procedure

Which tool will you use to measure mass?

_____

_____

_____

Which units of length will your group use? Explain your choice.

_____

_____

_____

_____

Record Your Data

In the space below, construct a simple table to collect, record, and organize your measurements.

© Houghton Mifflin Harcourt Publishing Company

Draw Conclusions

Of the three measurement tools you used, which was the easiest to use? The hardest? Explain.

_____

_____

_____

_____

_____

Analyze and Extend

1. **Why is it helpful to communicate your written results with others?**

_____

_____

_____

_____

2. **What should you do if you find out that your measurements are very different from those of other teams?**

_____

_____

_____

_____

3. **Which other characteristics of the object can you measure?**

_____

_____

_____

_____

4. **These pictures show two more measurement tools. Describe how you could use each tool to measure and collect information about an object.**

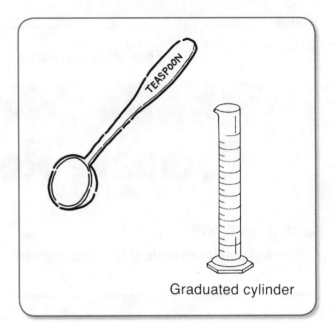
Graduated cylinder

_____

_____

_____

_____

5. **Which other questions would you like to ask about science tools?**

_____

_____

_____

_____

_____

48

© Houghton Mifflin Harcourt Publishing Company

John Diebold

Dr. John Diebold spent much of his life studying Earth's oceans. He worked in the lab and in the field. He studied volcanoes, ancient ice sheets, and faults that cause earthquakes under water. Dr. Diebold improved the design of the *air gun*, a tool used to make underwater sound waves. Then he used these sound waves to make 3-D pictures of the ocean floor.

Much of Earth's oceans are too deep to study directly. John Diebold used many tools like this air gun to help people study the ocean floor from the surface.

Meet the Inventors

These gears are many times smaller than a millimeter! Dr. Culpepper's tools can be used to assemble objects this small.

Martin Culpepper

Dr. Martin Culpepper is a mechanical engineer. He invents tools that work with machines so small you cannot see them with a regular light microscope. These machines are many times smaller than the thickness of a human hair! One day these tiny machines could be used to find cancer cells. Unlike Dr. Diebold, Dr. Culpepper does most of his research in a lab. His lab has to be dust-free—a tiny bit of dust could ruin the results of his investigations.

© Houghton Mifflin Harcourt Publishing Company (t) ©David Corcoran (t) ©Melanie Stetson Freeman/The Christian Science Monitor via Getty Images (cr) ©Sandia National Laboratories/Photo Researchers, Inc; (bg) ©Corbis; (l) ©Bolt Technology Corporation; (t) ©Getty Images Royalty Free

Field Versus Lab

In the Field Scientists often work in the field, or the world outside of labs. What did Dr. Diebold learn from his studies in the field?

_____
_____
_____
_____

Research done by Dr. Diebold and others in the field led to the development of maps like this one. The map shows rock and sediment layers beneath the ocean floor.

This tool is a tiny lifter! It moves and sets into position the incredibly small parts of tiny machines.

In the Lab Why do you think Dr. Culpepper builds machines in a lab? Why would he not build them in the field?

_____
_____
_____
_____

Think About It!

How might a scientist's work be both in the field and in a lab? Think of an example.

_____
_____
_____

© Houghton Mifflin Harcourt Publishing Company (t) ©Bad Reyt/Alamy Images; (c) ©MIT POS Lab 2001–2003; (bg) ©Corbis

TEKS **4.3C** represent the natural world using models...and identify their limitations, including accuracy and size

Essential Question

What Kinds of Models Do Scientists Use?

Engage Your Brain!

Find the answer to the following question in this lesson and record it here.

This is a scale model of the moon. What can scientists learn by studying it?

_____

_____

_____

_____

Active Reading

Lesson Vocabulary

List the terms. As you learn about each one, make notes in the Interactive Glossary.

_____

_____

_____

_____

Signal Words: Comparisons

Signal phrases show connections between ideas. Words that signal comparisons, or similarities, include *like, better than, also, alike, as close as,* and *stands for.* Active readers remember what they read because they are alert to signal phrases that identify comparisons.

© Houghton Mifflin Harcourt Publishing Company ©Dariella Nowitz/Corbis

Two-dimensional model
of the solar system

Models and Science

Native Americans had mental models for the sun, moon, and planets. Several tribes in North America tell stories of the beginning of time, when Earth did not exist. All of the animals applied mud to the shell of a turtle. Earth was born when the mud became thick and large on the turtle's back.

© Houghton Mifflin Harcourt Publishing Company

Make a Two-dimensional Model!

Good models are as close to the real thing as possible. Draw a floor plan of a room in your home. Show the doorways and windows. Show the objects that sit on the floor. Add labels. Be as accurate as you can!

A toy car. A doll's house. A person who shows off clothes on a runway. These are all models. But what is a model in science?

Active Reading As you read these two pages, draw a star next to what you think is the most important sentence. Be ready to explain why.

Scientists make models to represent the natural world. In science, a **model** represents something real that is too big, too small, too far away, or has too many parts to investigate directly. For example, our solar system is too big to see all its parts at once. So, scientists use models to investigate the motion of planets, moons, and other solar system objects. They can use the models to predict when an asteroid will pass close to Earth.

Models can take many forms. A *mental model* is a picture you make in your mind. A good thing about this kind of model is that you always have it with you! A **two-dimensional model** has length and width. It can be a drawing, a diagram, or a map.

Models do have limitations, including accuracy and size. Our solar system is so large, an accurate model would also need to be large so that it includes enough detail.

© Houghton Mifflin Harcourt Publishing Company

Other Models Scientists Use

Do the Math!
Use Fractions

You plan to make a model of the solar system. You make the tiniest ball of clay you can for Mercury. The ball is 4 mm across. If Mercury were that size, the chart shows how big all the other objects in your model would be.

Object	Diameter (mm)
Sun	1,100
Mercury	4
Venus	9
Earth	10
Mars	5
Jupiter	110
Saturn	92
Uranus	37
Neptune	36

1. Which fraction tells how the size of Mars compares to Earth?

   _____

2. Which object is about $\frac{1}{4}$ the diameter of Neptune?

   _____

3. Which object is about $\frac{1}{9}$ the diameter of Saturn?

   _____

© Houghton Mifflin Harcourt Publishing Company   ©Peter Arnold, Inc./Alamy

You see thousands of stars in the night sky. You point to a very bright star. Suddenly, you are zooming through space. As you get closer, the star gets bigger and brighter. Your trip isn't real, but it feels like it is. It's another kind of model!

Active Reading As you read these two pages, draw boxes around a clue word or phrase that signals things are being compared.

Three-Dimensional Models

The more a model is like the real thing, the better it is. If the object you want to model has length, width, and height, a **three-dimensional model** is useful. Such a model can show the positions of planets, moons, and the sun better than a two-dimensional model can.

If you want to compare sizes and distances in a model, then you make a *scale model*. The scale tells how much smaller or bigger the model is than the real thing. For example, a model railroad may have a scale of 1 to 48. This means each one inch on the model stands for 48 inches on the real train.

Computer Models

What if you want to understand how asteroids move through the solar system? You'd use a computer model. A **computer model** is a computer program that models an event or an object. Some computer models make you feel like you are moving through the solar system!

© Houghton Mifflin Harcourt Publishing Company ©Lauren Burke/Getty Images

Weather Models Save Lives

Dangerous weather can happen suddenly. Hurricanes, tornadoes, floods, and winter storms can harm people, pets, and homes. How can models save lives?

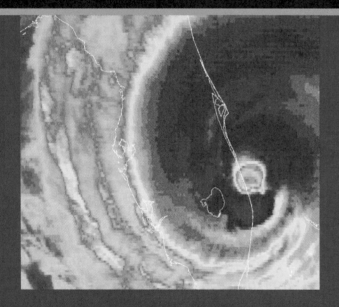

Data from Space

Satellites circle Earth 24 hours each day. Images and other weather data are beamed back to Earth. It's called *real-time* data because scientists see the pictures almost as soon as they are taken. This image shows the path of a hurricane. The colors are not real. Scientists choose them to show differences in wind speeds, heights of clouds, and other factors.

Using Models

Meteorologists use satellite data to make computer models of weather. They model hurricanes, tornadoes, and thunderstorms. The models are used to predict how and where storms will get started.

© Houghton Mifflin Harcourt Publishing Company • © Reuters/Corbis • © Getty Images

This weather model shows the height of the clouds of a storm.

Getting the Word Out

Weather reporters also use models. They make two-dimensional maps for television and Internet viewers to see. These maps can change to show how soon and where bad weather will be.

What Can We Do?

You can use models to help your family be prepared for dangerous weather. Draw a diagram of your home in your Science Notebook. Label the exits. Does your family have a safe place to meet in an emergency? Where is it?

_____

_____

_____

_____

How can your model help you in an emergency?

_____

_____

_____

_____

© Houghton Mifflin Harcourt Publishing Company (t) CI-69 Photos/Alamy (b) Image Source/Corbis

Sum It Up!

When you're done, use the answer key to check and revise your work.

Use information from the summary to complete the graphic organizer in your own words.

Summarize

For scientists, a model represents the natural world—something real that is too big, too small, too far away, or has too many parts to investigate directly. Scientists use models to investigate and understand real places and objects. Models do have limitations, including accuracy and size. Several kinds of models are used in science. Two-dimensional models, such as drawings, diagrams, and maps, have length and width. Three-dimensional models have length, width, and height. Computer models are computer programs that behave like the real thing. Some models, such as models of storms, can be used to save lives.

Main Idea: Models in science are like real things and are used to understand real things.

Detail: Two-dimensional models are flat, like a map or a diagram.

Detail:
_____
_____
_____

Detail:
_____
_____
_____
_____

© Houghton Mifflin Harcourt Publishing Company (l) ©Dorling Kindersley/Getty Images (r) ©Dorling Kindersley/Getty Images

Answer Key: 1. Three-dimensional models have length, width, and height. 2. Computer models are computer programs that act like the real thing.

Brain Check

Name _____

Word Play

1 Use the words in the box to complete the puzzle.

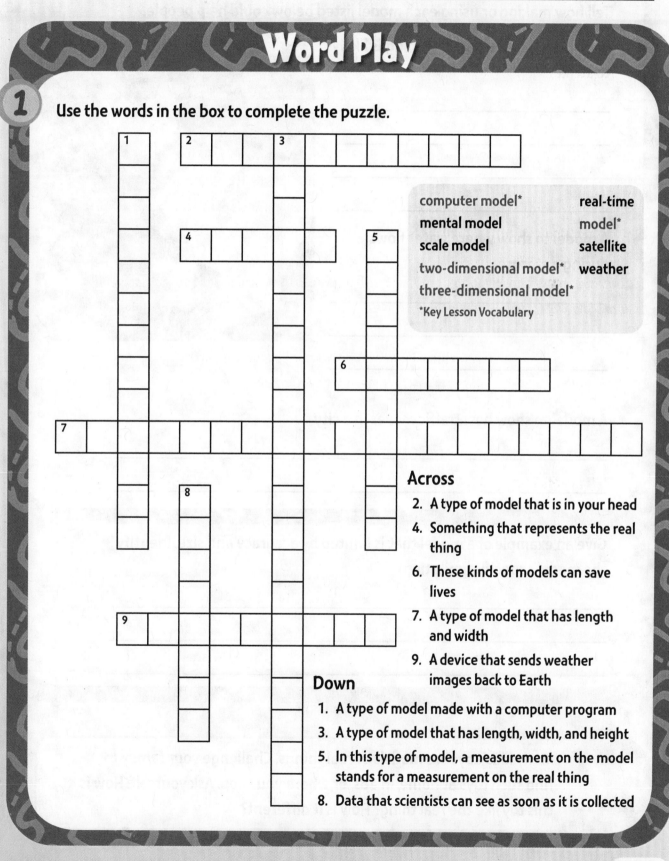

computer model*   real-time
mental model   model*
scale model   satellite
two-dimensional model* weather
three-dimensional model*

*Key Lesson Vocabulary

Across

2. A type of model that is in your head
4. Something that represents the real thing
6. These kinds of models can save lives
7. A type of model that has length and width
9. A device that sends weather images back to Earth

Down

1. A type of model made with a computer program
3. A type of model that has length, width, and height
5. In this type of model, a measurement on the model stands for a measurement on the real thing
8. Data that scientists can see as soon as it is collected

© Houghton Mifflin Harcourt Publishing Company

Apply Concepts

Tell how making or using each model listed below could help people.

2 A model to show where lightning is likely to strike

_____

_____

_____

3 A model to show where water flows during a storm

_____

_____

_____

4 A model to show how traffic moves in a city

_____

_____

5 Give an example of a model that is limited by accuracy and size. Identify the model's specific limitations.

_____

_____

_____

Take It Home!

Many kids' toys are models of real things. Challenge your family to find such toys at home, in ads, or where you shop. Ask yourself: How is this toy like the real thing? How is it different?

© Houghton Mifflin Harcourt Publishing Company ©Image Source/Corbis

TEKS **4.2A** plan and implement descriptive investigations, including... selecting and using appropriate equipment or technology... **4.3C** represent the natural world using models...and identify their limitations, including accuracy and size

Name _____

Essential Question

How Can You Model a School?

Set a Purpose
Which inquiry skills will you practice in this investigation?

_____

_____

Think About the Procedure
How will you decide which part of your school you will represent using a model?

_____

_____

_____

How will you choose the two types of models you will use?

_____

_____

_____

Record Your Observations
Identify and describe the part of your school you represented using models.

_____

_____

_____

Identify the two types of models you used and describe your models.

_____

_____

_____

_____

_____

© Houghton Mifflin Harcourt Publishing Company

Draw Conclusions

What was something you learned about your school from making the models?

_____

_____

_____

Analyze and Extend

1. Why is it helpful to compare results with others?

_____

_____

_____

_____

2. Identify your models' limitations, including its accuracy.

_____

_____

_____

_____

3. Why is it important to be accurate when making your measurements?

_____

_____

_____

4. What was the hardest part of making the models? Was size a limitation during the planning and development of your model? Explain.

_____

_____

_____

_____

_____

_____

_____

5. Why is it important for engineers to make and try out models before making a real building or bridge?

_____

_____

_____

6. What other things or places would you like to learn about by making a model? Explain why.

_____

_____

_____

7. What other questions would you like to ask about making models?

_____

_____

_____

© Houghton Mifflin Harcourt Publishing Company

Vocabulary Review

Use the terms in the box to complete the sentences.

inference
investigation
observation
pan balance
spring scale

TEKS 4.2B

1. When people collect data by using their five senses,

   they make a(n) _____.

TEKS 4.4A

2. A tool used to collect and analyze information about

   the mass of an object is a(n) _____.

TEKS 4.2A

3. When people ask questions, make observations,
   and use other methods to gather data about an event

   or object, they are doing a(n) _____.

TEKS 4.2A

4. Someone who makes a statement that explains an

   observation is making a(n) _____.

TEKS 4.4A

5. If you want to collect and analyze information about the
   pull of a force, such as the force of gravity, you would use

   a tool called a(n) _____.

Science Concepts

Fill in the letter of the choice that best answers the question.

TEKS 4.4A

6. Amira wants to compare close-up views
   of different bird feathers. Which tool
   should she use to collect and analyze
   this information?

   (A) magnet

   (B) meterstick

   (C) microscope

   (D) pan balance

TEKS 4.2B

7. Camilla is studying minerals in different
   rocks. Which would not help Camilla
   collect and record data about a rock?

   (A) measuring the volume of the rock

   (B) inferring the rock is millions of
   years old

   (C) testing the effect of dripping vinegar
   onto the rock

   (D) observing the minerals that make
   up the rock

© Houghton Mifflin Harcourt Publishing Company (border) ©NDisk/Age Fotostock

TEKS 4.3C

8. Junichi used a computer to look at this three-dimensional model of his classroom.

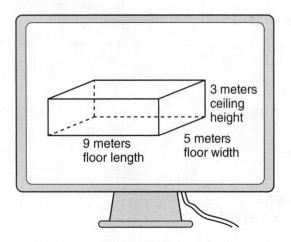

3 meters ceiling height

9 meters floor length

5 meters floor width

How can he use this model to find out if his classroom is longer than it is tall?

Ⓐ He can look at the length of the floor.

Ⓑ He can look at the height of the ceiling.

Ⓒ He can compare the length and the width.

Ⓓ He can compare the length and the ceiling height.

TEKS 4.3A

9. Julia concludes that a certain type of plant grows best in sandy soil. Rico suggests that this plant type grows best because it has the right amount of water. Which critical thinking skill is he using?

Ⓐ alternative explanation

Ⓑ experimental testing

Ⓒ logical reasoning

Ⓓ observational testing

TEKS 4.3A

10. Diego has been observing how well one plant type grows in different locations. He concludes a location with bright sunlight is the best. Which of the following is an example of empirical evidence he could use in support of his conclusion?

Ⓐ His friend told him that all plants need bright sunlight to grow.

Ⓑ Plants he kept in shade grew better than plants he kept in sunlight.

Ⓒ Plants he kept in shade did not grow as well as plants he kept in sunlight.

Ⓓ He thinks the plants he kept in sunlight would have grown better with more water.

TEKS 4.2D

11. A scientist uses steps of the scientific method to conduct an investigation. She analyzes the data she has collected and recorded through observation. What should she do next?

Ⓐ draw a conclusion

Ⓑ make a hypothesis

Ⓒ conduct an experiment

Ⓓ study the data one more time

TEKS 4.2C

12. Seiji records the number of birds he sees each day at a bird feeder. Which is the best method for Seiji to record his data?

Ⓐ bar graph   Ⓒ diagram

Ⓑ camera   Ⓓ model

© Houghton Mifflin Harcourt Publishing Company (border) ©NDisk/Age Fotostock

© Houghton Mifflin Harcourt Publishing Company   (border) ©NDisk/Age Fotostock

TEKS 4.3A

13. A scientist has spent one year conducting an experiment. He concludes that the evidence from his experiment does not support his hypothesis. What should the scientist do next?

(A) Forget this experiment and choose a new problem.

(B) Try to make up evidence that supports his hypothesis.

(C) Look at the evidence and see if he can make a new hypothesis.

(D) Look at the information and find a different way to organize his results.

TEKS 4.2D

14. Gia hypothesizes that hot water will cause a sugar cube to dissolve faster than cold water will. She investigates by filling three cups: one with hot water, one with cold water, and one with ice water. She drops a sugar cube in each cup. Which observation will help Gia decide whether her hypothesis is correct?

(A) which cup the sugar cube dissolves in first

(B) the time it takes for two sugar cubes to dissolve

(C) changes in water temperature from start to finish

(D) changes in the size of the sugar cube in cold water

TEKS 4.4A

15. The local news station asks viewers to measure the amount of rain that falls in their neighborhoods. Four measurements are shown below.

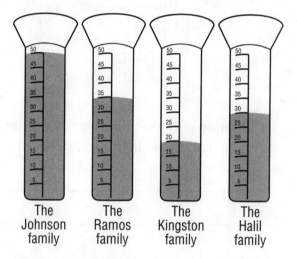

The Johnson family   The Ramos family   The Kingston family   The Halil family

Which family measures the most rain?

(A) Halil family

(B) Johnson family

(C) Kingston family

(D) Ramos family

TEKS 4.2A

16. Scientists state a hypothesis before conducting an experiment. Which step should a scientist also do before conducting an experiment?

(A) ask questions

(B) draw conclusions

(C) communicate results

(D) record and analyze results

Apply Inquiry and Review the Big Idea

Write the answers to these questions.

TEKS 4.2A

17. Luis fed his cat in the kitchen. These pictures show what Luis saw as he left the kitchen and then what he saw when he returned.

Luis figured out that the cat jumped on the table and knocked the mitt onto the floor. What inquiry skill did Luis use? Give a reason for your answer.

_____

_____

TEKS 4.2B, 4.4A

18. Write three observations about this leaf.

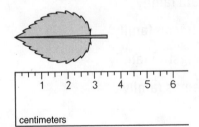

My Observations

a. _____

b. _____

c. _____

TEKS 4.2D

19. Marie collects data during an experiment. She records the mass of several soil samples, as shown in this data table.

Sample A	Sample B	Sample C
45 g	25 g	38 g

What is the average mass of these soil samples? _____.

© Houghton Mifflin Harcourt Publishing Company (border) ©NDisk/Age Fotostock

The Engineering Process

Big Idea

Engineers use scientific problem solving to design products, processes, and systems that solve human needs.

TEKS 4.2B, 4.2C, 4.2D, 4.3A, 4.3B, 4.3D, 4.4A

I Wonder Why

At different times in the past, people used stone tools such as these. Why do scientists study such tools? What can these tools tell us about how ancient people lived? *Turn the page to find out.*

© Houghton Mifflin Harcourt Publishing Company (bg) ©Steve Cole/Getty Images; (inset) ©Warren Morgan/Corbis; (border) ©NDisApp Fotostock

Here's Why Throughout history, people have designed and built tools to help meet their needs. Whether a tool is a simple stone or a high-tech electronic device, it can help solve a problem. By figuring out how an ancient tool was used, scientists can draw conclusions about the needs of the person who made it.

In this unit, you will explore the Big Idea, the Essential Questions, and the Investigations on the Inquiry Flipchart.

Levels of Inquiry Key ■ DIRECTED ■ GUIDED ■ INDEPENDENT

Big Idea Engineers use scientific problem solving to design products, processes, and systems that meet human needs.

Essential Questions

Now I Get the Big Idea!

Science Notebook

Before you begin each lesson, be sure to write your thoughts about the Essential Question.

TEKS **4.3A** in all fields of science, analyze...scientific explanations by using...observational testing...so as to encourage critical thinking by the student **4.3D** connect grade-level appropriate science concepts with...science careers...

Essential Question

What Is an Engineering Design Process?

Engage Your Brain!

Find the answer to the following question in this lesson and record it here.

Why would a car company want a wooden car?

_____

_____

_____

_____

Active Reading

Lesson Vocabulary
List the terms. As you learn about each one, make notes in the Interactive Glossary.

_____

_____

_____

Signal Words: Sequence
Signal words show connections between ideas. Words that signal sequence include *now, before, after, first,* and *next.* Active readers remember what they read because they are alert to signal words that identify sequence.

© Houghton Mifflin Harcourt Publishing Company ©DAI KUROKAWA/epa/Corbis

What Is ENGINEERING?

From the food we eat and the clothes we wear, to the cars we drive and the phones we talk on, science is at work in our lives every day.

Active Reading As you read the next page, circle the main idea of the text, and put brackets [ ] around each detail sentence.

Electrical engineers, such as Dr. Cynthia Breazeal, use their knowledge of physics to build things like Kismet the robot.

© Houghton Mifflin Harcourt Publishing Company ©Peter Menzel/Photo Researchers, Inc.

© Houghton Mifflin Harcourt Publishing Company (tl) © Construction Photography/Corbis; (cl) ©Stockbyte; (cr) ©imagebroker/Alamy

Knowledge of math and geology allows surveyors to make maps of Earth.

This biomedical engineer uses his knowledge of biology to make glass eyes.

Look around. Many of the things you see are products of engineering. **Engineering** is the use of scientific and mathematical principles to develop something practical. Some engineers use biology. Others use geology, chemistry, or physics.

Engineers use this knowledge to make something new. It might be a product, a system, or a process for doing things. Whatever it is, it's practical. People use it. Engineers develop things that people use.

▶ In the space below, draw a picture of something you can see around you that was probably designed by an engineer.

What Is the DESIGN PROCESS?

It has been said that necessity is the mother of invention. But once you find a need, how do you build your invention? That's the design process!

Active Reading As you read these two pages, draw boxes around clue words or phrases that signal a sequence or order.

What is design? **Design** means to conceive something and prepare the plans and drawings for it to be built. Engineers use the design process to develop new technology, but anyone can follow the design process.

From basic to complex, skateboards have changed over time.

© Houghton Mifflin Harcourt Publishing Company   (tr) ©Heath Korvola/Getty Images; (br) © Chet Roberts/Corbis

The design process starts with identifying a need or a problem. Next, you brainstorm and write down ideas on how to plan and build a potential solution. Once you have some options, select a solution to try. Usually, engineers test possible solutions using a prototype.

A **prototype** is an original or test model on which a real product is based. If the prototype works, then the real product is made. Usually, after testing a prototype, improvements have to be made. The prototype is then tested again. Finally, a finished product is made.

Design Process Steps

- Find a problem
- Plan and build
- Test and improve
- Redesign
- Communicate

Even something seemingly simple takes a lot of thought, planning, testing, and improvement.

How Was It Improved?

Look at the skateboards. Describe two design features that have been improved over time.

_____

_____

_____

_____

© Houghton Mifflin Harcourt Publishing Company   cl) © © George Doyle/Getty Images; (cr) ©George Doyle/Getty Images

Design
YOU CAN USE

Look at all the things you use every day. Do you have ideas about how to improve them?

Active Reading As you read these two pages, find and underline the meaning of the word *prototype*.

Who Needs It?

The first step in any design process is identifying a need or problem. Is there a chore that could be easier, a tool that could work much better, a car that could go faster or be safer? Often, the design process begins with the phrase "What if?"

Prototype!

A prototype is a test version of a design. To build a prototype, a person has to think critically to develop plans. Early sketches give a rough idea. More detailed drawings provide exact measurements for every piece. Keeping good records and drawings helps to make sure that the prototype can be replicated.

This skateboard turns fairly well. But what if it could go around curves even better?

© Houghton Mifflin Harcourt Publishing Company

Details

Draw a blueprint of a school supply, a favorite toy, or a tool. Label its parts and include exact measurements.

Sketches and detailed drawings are an important step in planning a product.

Every part of a product can become an opportunity for a design change.

wheel

trucks

deck

© Houghton Mifflin Harcourt Publishing Company   (bkgd) ©Mike McGill/Corbis

Are We DONE YET?

Now that the prototype has been built, can the final product be far behind? Yes, it can. But it might not be. It all depends.

Active Reading As you read these two pages, draw a box around the clue word or phrase that signals one thing is being contrasted with another.

Test It and Improve It!

Prototypes must be tested carefully. Observational testing helps answer questions such as, *Does it work the way it should? Is it easy to use? How does it hold up under normal conditions?*

The first prototype you build may pass all its tests. If so, the prototype can go into production. However, it is likely that testing shows that the design needs to change. Engineers use critical thinking skills to analyze the test results in order to make a new prototype. The product may need a few minor improvements, or it may need to be completely redesigned.

If a prototype works as expected, it will become a finished product.

© Houghton Mifflin Harcourt Publishing Company

Redesign and Share

Sometimes, one prototype leads to ideas for others.

When a prototype fails to meet a design goal, it may be redesigned. Redesign takes advantage of all work done before. Good design features are kept, and those that fail are discarded.

When the final working prototype is done, team members communicate the design. Sketches, blueprints, and test data and analysis are shared. Often, the product details are recorded in a legal document called a *patent*.

Spin Off!

Imagine a normal bicycle. Now think of three ways it could be modified to work better in different environments.

_____

_____

_____

_____

_____

New ideas keep the engineering design process constantly moving forward.

© Houghton Mifflin Harcourt Publishing Company   (t) ©Jeff Morgan 12/Alamy; (b) ©Darryl Leniuk/Getty Images

Sum It Up!

When you're done, use the answer key to check and revise your work.

Use information in the summary to complete the graphic organizer.

Summarize

The first step in the design process is to identify a need or a problem to be solved. The next step is to plan and build a prototype. Brainstorming ideas and drawing detailed sketches of potential solutions are important parts of this step. The third step is to test and improve a prototype. After testing, a prototype might need to be redesigned and tested again. A prototype that meets all its design goals is ready for production. The final step in the design process is to communicate to others the details of a working prototype.

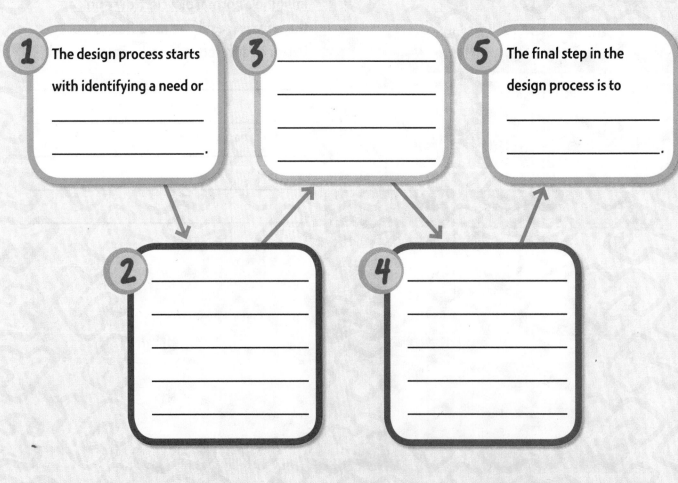

1 The design process starts with identifying a need or _____ _____ .

3 _____ _____ _____

5 The final step in the design process is to _____ _____ .

2 _____ _____ _____ _____

4 _____ _____ _____ _____

Answer Key: 1. problem to be solved. **2.** The second step in the design process is to plan and build a prototype. **3.** The third step is to test and improve the prototype. **4.** After testing, a prototype might need to be redesigned and tested again. **5.** communicate

© Houghton Mifflin Harcourt Publishing Company

Name _____

Word Play

1 Use the clues to help you write the correct word in each row. Some boxes have been filled in for you.

A. To conceive something and prepare plans to build it

B. The use of scientific and mathematical principles to develop something practical

C. A prototype may undergo many rounds of this.

D. Engineers have to be familiar with these principles.

E. The answer to a problem

F. A test version of something

G. Is identified during the first step in the design process

H. What comes after sketches, plans, and the prototype?

I. Something that people will use is described as this.

J. Engineers have to be familiar with these principles.

© Houghton Mifflin Harcourt Publishing Company   ©Daikurokawa /EPA/Corbis

Apply Concepts

2 Write numbers in the circles to put the pictures in the correct order.

3 How is a prototype different from the finished product?

_____

_____

_____

_____

_____

4 How can you use observational testing to analyze a prototype for a new type of bicycle?

_____

_____

_____

© Houghton Mifflin Harcourt Publishing Company

5 The owner of a safety apparel company asks an engineer to "design a better helmet for skateboarders." How would you improve this instruction?

_____

_____

_____

_____

_____

_____

_____

_____

6 Which job is more likely to be done by an engineer? Why?

Developing a new material that will be used to make the outer covering of vitamin capsules	Determining how vitamins are absorbed into the bloodstream

_____

_____

_____

_____

_____

_____

© Houghton Mifflin Harcourt Publishing Company

7 The engineers at an appliance company have developed a new dishwasher. It looks very different from previous models. The controls look different and work differently. The part of the machine that heats the water has been completely redesigned. Now that the plans are completed, should the company start producing thousands of these dishwashers? Why or why not?

_____

_____

_____

_____

_____

_____

_____

_____

_____

_____

_____

_____

_____

_____

Take It Home!

With your family, find a product in your home that needs improving. Suppose you work for the company that makes this product and brainstorm a new prototype to test.

© Houghton Mifflin Harcourt Publishing Company

TEKS **4.2B** ...record data by observing...and using descriptive words...such as...writing... **4.2C** construct...charts...using tools...to organize...data

Name _____

Essential Question

How Can You Design a Solution to a Problem?

Set a Purpose

What do you think you will learn from this investigation?

_____

_____

_____

_____

Think About the Procedure

How will the equipment you design be similar to safety belts and airbags in a car?

_____

_____

_____

_____

Why should you make sure the bag is tightly sealed before testing the prototype?

_____

_____

Record Your Data

Draw a chart to record the equipment and materials you used in your prototype as well as your observations from each test. Be sure to use descriptive words.

© Houghton Mifflin Harcourt Publishing Company

Draw Conclusions

Which conclusions can you draw based on your observations?

_____

_____

_____

_____

Analyze and Extend

1. Was your design successful? Why or why not?

_____

_____

_____

_____

2. Based on your results, how could you improve your design? Use descriptive words and draw how to change your prototype in the space below.

_____

_____

_____

_____

3. Were there any aspects of someone else's design you might incorporate into your design?

_____

_____

_____

_____

4. What is the difference between a successful design and a successful prototype?

_____

_____

_____

_____

_____

_____

5. Think of another design for which you would like to make a prototype. Describe your design process.

_____

_____

_____

_____

_____

_____

_____

_____

© Houghton Mifflin Harcourt Publishing Company

TEKS 4.3B draw inferences and evaluate accuracy of services and product claims found in advertisements and labels such as for toys, food, and sunscreen

Essential Question

What Is Technology?

Engage Your Brain!

Find the answer to the following question in the lesson and record it here.

This robot is riding a bicycle, just like a human, and not falling over. How is this possible?

_____

_____

_____

_____

Active Reading

Lesson Vocabulary

List the terms. As you learn about each one, make notes in the Interactive Glossary.

_____

_____

_____

Main Ideas

The main idea of a paragraph is the most important idea. The main idea may be stated in the first sentence, or it may be stated elsewhere. Active readers look for main ideas by asking themselves, What is this paragraph mostly about?

© Houghton Mifflin Harcourt Publishing Company   (r) ©Haruyoshi Yamaguchi/Corbis; (bg) ©amana images Inc./Alamy Images

Grappler

TOOLS RULE!

A bulldozer and a shovel serve the same purpose. However, because of a bulldozer's size, it can move huge amounts of material much more quickly than a shovel can.

Look in your desk. Do you see pens and pencils? Scissors? A ruler? All of these things are tools.

Active Reading As you read these two pages, put brackets [ ] around the sentences that describe a problem. Underline the sentences that describe the solution.

Planting a vegetable garden? You'll need a shovel, a rake, and a spade. All these items are tools. A **tool** is anything that helps people shape, build, or produce things to meet their needs.

Your family's toolbox probably contains a hammer and screwdrivers. Construction workers have similar tools that do the same jobs, only on a larger scale. Instead of hammering nails by hand, construction workers use tools that quickly drive nails into wood with the push of a button. Their tools are sized and powered differently to meet different needs.

© Houghton Mifflin Harcourt Publishing Company   (tl) ©David Zaitz/Alamy Images; (c) ©Brownstock Inc./Alamy Images; (bg) ©Carin Flenisch/Getty Images

Some tools are designed to do one task. You use a pen to write a note to a friend. You keep your science notes organized in a notebook. You talk to your grandmother on the phone. What if you had one tool that could do all these tasks? A smartphone is a tool that can help you send a message, organize information, *and* talk to people.

A smartphone, like all tools, is an example of technology. **Technology** is any designed system, product, or process that people use to solve problems. Technology doesn't have to be complex. The pencil you write with and the cell phone you text with are both technology. Technology changes as people's needs change.

Suppose you are building a birdhouse. How will you make each side straight? How will you cut through wire? How will you secure the nuts and bolts? Tools can help you solve these problems.

Level

Socket wrench

Problem Solved!

Fill in the chart to show problems and their solutions. In the last row, make up your own problem and identify the tool that helps solve it.

Problem	Tool that Solves It
Collect and save rainwater for later use.	
	multiplication table

© Houghton Mifflin Harcourt Publishing Company (bg) ©Rolf Hismser/Getty Images (cl) ©Edd Westmacott/Alamy Images (t) ©Brand X Pictures/Getty Images

WHAT IS TECHNOLOGY?

Vending machines, televisions, and video games are examples of technology products you know—but there are more. Technology is all around you.

Active Reading As you read this page, underline technology products. On the next page, circle the paragraph that describes examples of a technology process.

A video game is the end product of a technology process. Programming a video game involves technology you can't hold in the palm of your hand.

You've learned that technology is any designed system, product, or process. A *technology product* is anything designed to meet a need or desire. Some people think that electronics are the only type of technology product. However, most technology products do not use electricity!

This book, the desk it is on, and the backpack you use to take it home are all technology products. Your bike and the sidewalk you ride it on are technology products, too. Technology products can be very large or very small. They can be a single thing like a stone brick or made of many things put together. Some technology products, such as medicine, are made to keep us healthy. Others, such as construction tools, are made to shape the world around us. We also invent technology products just to have fun.

▶ Circle three examples of technology in this photo.

© Houghton Mifflin Harcourt Publishing Company (bg) ©Ralf Hiemisch/Getty Images; (t) ©Picture Contact BV/Alamy Images

The way a product is made is also a form of technology. A *technology process* is a series of steps used to achieve a goal or make a product. The steps in a technology process are like the steps in a scientific investigation. They are carefully designed for doing something a certain way.

Many things you do are a technology process. You follow a series of steps to make gelatin dessert, tie your shoelaces, and add music to your MP3 player. If you have ever played baseball, you are familiar with its rules. The rules of a game are a technology process.

Safety gear and clothing are types of technology that help baseball players perform. The bleachers and the backstop are types of technology that let spectators watch safely.

Play Ball

The ballpark, scoreboard, rules, and baseball equipment are all examples of technology. How can technology help deliver the game's events to people who aren't at the ballpark?

_____

_____

_____

© Houghton Mifflin Harcourt Publishing Company (bg) ©Ralf Hiemisch/Getty Images (b) ©Jules Frazier/PhotoDisc/Getty Images (c) ©PhotoDisc/Getty Images (cl) ©Ocean/Corbis (bg) ©H. Mark Weidman Photography/Alamy Images

In this factory, there are tools, robots, computers, and people. They all make up a system.

TECHNOLOGICAL SYSTEMS

The next time you ride in a car, look at how many parts it has. It took many tools and hundreds of steps to produce this technology.

Active Reading As you read this page, underline the sentence that describes what makes a designed system.

Groups of things that work together to achieve a goal make up a *system*. Tools, parts, and processes that work together form a *designed system*. Designed systems help us travel and ship goods. They help us communicate and grow our foods.

You are a part of many designed systems. Whether you ride the bus or walk to school, you are a part of a transportation system. This system is made up of the sidewalks, roads, and traffic signs. It also includes the cars, buses, planes, and trains that move people and materials from place to place.

Designed systems help us shape the world around us. When you ride around your town, you might see cars, roadways, buildings, or farm fields. All these things make up the *designed world*. The designed world is the part of your community that is designed and built by people.

Many designed systems work together in the designed world. For example, the agricultural system produces the food that we need. Ships, trains, and trucks in the transportation system carry food where it is needed.

© Houghton Mifflin Harcourt Publishing Company (t) ©Lester Lefkowitz/Getty Images; (bg) ©Ralf Hiemisch/Getty Images

A water irrigation system is a tool that helps farmers grow crops. It includes water, hoses, and pipes. It also includes the people who run the system and fix it when it breaks down.

PARTS OF A DESIGNED SYSTEM

Part	Example: Rail Transportation System
Goal—what the system aims to do	Goal—to move cargo and passengers safely from place to place
Input—what is put into the system to meet the goal	Inputs—fuel for the train, cargo, and people to ride the train
Processes—describe how the goal is to be achieved	Processes—train tracks and departure and arrival schedules
Output—the end product	Output—safe and timely delivery of people and cargo
Feedback—information that tells whether or not the output is successful	Feedback—records of whether trains left and arrived on time

A railroad system includes trains, rails, and safety signals at road crossings. The system also has parts you can't see. Radio signals keep track of where trains are. The signals raise and lower crossing arms, too.

Tech Systems

What do you think would be the goal of a farming system?

_____

_____

_____

THE GOOD AND THE BAD OF IT

A light bulb that can save you $100 a year? What's the catch?

Active Reading As you read this page, draw a box around the main idea.

Compact fluorescent lights (CFLs) and light emitting diodes (LEDs) use less energy than incandescent bulbs. However, CFLs contain mercury, which can be hazardous if the bulbs break open, and LEDs are more expensive than regular light bulbs.

Technology is constantly changing. Anyone can invent or improve a technology product or process. It takes new ideas and knowledge for technology to change. The goal of any new technology is to better meet people's needs. However, new technology can also bring new risks.

Changes in technology often involve making things safer, quicker, easier, or cheaper. For example, people once used candles and lanterns to light their homes. These things helped people see at night, but they could also cause fires. Electricity and incandescent light bulbs helped solve this problem, but this technology also has its risks.

We burn coal to generate electricity. When coal burns, harmful ash and gases are produced. The potential harm these substances can cause leads to negative feedback. Such feedback helps people think of ways to improve technology.

© Houghton Mifflin Harcourt Publishing Company (tl) ©Comstock/Getty Images; (bg) ©Ralf Hiemisch/Getty Images

Sometimes the problems with a technology are caused by the way people use technology. For instance, pesticides are helpful technology products. They are used to protect people, crops, and farm animals from harmful organisms. However, when used incorrectly, they can contaminate the soil, the water, and the air. Living things exposed to pesticides by accident can get sick and die.

Do the Math!
Interpret a Table

Use the data in the table to answer the questions below.

Light Bulb Cost Comparisons		
	25-Watt CFL	100-Watt incandescent
Cost of bulb	$3.40	$0.60
Bulb life	1,667 days (4.5 years)	167 days (about half a year)
Energy cost per year	$6.00	$25.00
Total cost over 4.5 years	$27.00	$118.50

1. How much more is the total cost of an incandescent bulb than a CFL?

_____

2. How much would your yearly energy cost be if you had 20 CFL bulbs in your home?

_____

3. Which bulb lasts longer?

_____

Airplanes can transport a lot of people at one time. However, they burn a lot of fuel and release pollution into the atmosphere. Engineers redesign airplanes to improve their performance.

© Houghton Mifflin Harcourt Publishing Company   (bg) ©Ralf Hettisch/Getty Images; (c) ©Paul Bowen/Getty Images; (b) ©Hans Neleman/Getty Images; (d) ©PhotoDisc/Getty Images

Sunscreens have labels about the SPF, or sun protection factor, within the product. An advertisement may claim that the higher the SPF, the better the sunscreen. But is that claim really true?

PRODUCT AND SERVICE CLAIMS

Commercials blare on television and on the radio. Flashing billboards line our roads and highways. Information all around you is designed to sell products and services.

Active Reading As you read these two pages, draw two lines under each main idea.

Information designed to get across a message to a viewer or listener is an **advertisement.** An advertisement tries to sell products that people might buy such as electronics, toys, clothing, food, and even sunscreen. A *product* is a good or merchandise for sale. An advertisement can also try to sell services, such as those provided for cellular phones or Internet access. Advertisements appear almost everywhere people go. They try to make a product or a service look better, more fun, or more healthful than it may actually be.

It is important to know how to evaluate advertisements in order to make informed decisions about products and services you buy. Many companies are required to place labels on products that give important information about the product. A *label* is an item used to identify the contents of something. A label may list the chemicals that make up a product. Or a label may tell the consumer at what age a child may use a toy or suggest ways to safely use it. These types of labels help protect consumers and help them evaluate products they may want to purchase.

SCREEN 15 SPF
stronger UV/AV protection
protects against sunburns
w resi

SPF 100 SUNSCREEN
Most complete protection available
Stay safe in the sun
ALL DAY LONG
ULTRA waterproof and sweatproof
4 FL OZ (118mL)

© Houghton Mifflin Harcourt Publishing Company

Advertisements try to get consumers' attention. Many advertisements make claims to generate "buzz" to attract consumers and to make them interested in purchasing the product or service. Some even make claims that cannot be proven to be true or false.

The
MOST FUN
toy helicopter
you can
buy!!

FLIES
THE HIGHEST,
THE FARTHEST,
AND THE
FASTEST!

The Best-Selling,
Handheld GPS on the Market!

Pinpoint
accuracy
guaranteed!

Flying High?

Can all claims in the helicopter advertisement be proved? Explain.

_____

_____

_____

_____

_____

_____

_____

_____

Some advertisements may sound too good to be true. Avoid judging a product or a service based on the claims made in an advertisement. You can better evaluate a product or a service by reading reviews about it from a trustworthy source.

© Houghton Mifflin Harcourt Publishing Company

OUT WITH THE OLD

Computers, cell phones, and flat-screen TVs are fun and useful. But like all technology, electronic gadgets have drawbacks.

Electronic technology seems to change at the blink of an eye. New electronic devices rapidly replace old ones. People benefit from new or improved electronic devices, but they also bring new problems.

Not long ago, most televisions and computer monitors were large, bulky things. New technology has made these large devices a thing of the past. They have been replaced by thin, lightweight flat screens.

But what do we do with old electronics? Some are taken apart and recycled; however, like the devices shown on this page, most end up in landfills. At landfills, electronics may release harmful chemicals into the environment.

Many electronic devices contain lead. Lead can be harmful to people and other organisms in the environment.

© Houghton Mifflin Harcourt Publishing Company (l) ©Michael Kerab.com/Alamy Images; (bg) ©Ralf Hiemisch/Getty Images; (tr) ©Timothy Hughes/Getty Images; (c) ©PhotoDisc/Getty Images; (tl) ©Jules Frazier/Getty Images/PhotoDisc

Electronics are helpful communication, work, and entertainment tools. They can also be a distraction. Some people spend a lot of time playing video games or on the Internet. They send text messages or listen to MP3 players while they are with other people. Some might even operate electronics while driving and cause a safety hazard for themselves and others.

People can solve these problems. They can set limits on computer and game time. They can put the phone away and pay attention to people and driving. These are ways to be responsible with technology.

▶ On the chart below, fill in the pros and cons of each electronic technology. Some examples have been provided for you.

	Pros	Cons
Television	can be educational; can provide breaking news quickly	
Smartphones		can take time away from doing other activities or being social; can cause drivers to be a hazard
Video games	fun; can be social when played with others	

© Houghton Mifflin Harcourt Publishing Company (bg) ©Ralf Hiemisch/Getty Images; (b) ©ONOKY - Photononstop/Alamy Images

When you're done, use the answer key to check and revise your work.

Complete the graphic organizer below.

1 _____ changes with new ideas and knowledge of science and engineering.

is made up of any

2 _____ is tools, parts, and processes that work together.

4 _____ is a series of steps used to achieve a goal or make a product.

3 _____ includes electronic and nonelectronic devices that meet a need or a desire.

Summarize

Fill in the missing words that help summarize ideas about technology.

A shovel is a tool that can help move dirt. A [5] _____ can do the same job in a bigger way. Tools are technology that help people shape, build, or produce things. [6] _____ changes to meet people's growing needs and desires.

A computer is an electronic product of technology. A [7] _____ is a nonelectronic product of technology. [8] _____ and [9] _____ often work in teams to develop new technology. [10] People must evaluate the accuracy of service and product claims found in _____ and on labels before making purchases. With technology, there is often risk to people and to the [11] _____.

Answer Key: 1. technology **2.** designed system **3.** product **4.** process **5.** bulldozer **6.** Technology **7.** Sample answer: wrench **8.–9.** (in any order) scientists/engineers **10.** advertisement **11.** environment

© Houghton Mifflin Harcourt Publishing Company

Name _____

Word Play

1 **Use the clues below to fill in the words of the puzzle.**

1. Any designed system, product, or process

2. Anything that helps people shape, build, or produce things to meet their needs

3. Tools, parts, and processes that work together

4. Things that are made to meet a need

5. The end product or service of a system

6. Anything that is put into a system to meet a goal

7. Information designed to get across a message to a viewer or listener

8. This is made up of all products of technology

9. A series of steps that result in a product

designed world

process   products

output   system

technology* tool*

input   advertisement*

* Key Lesson Vocabulary
_____

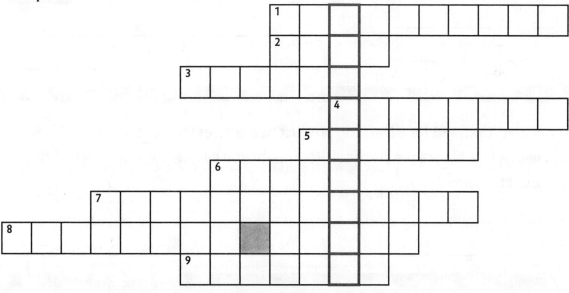

Read down the squares with red borders. The word will answer the question below. Murata Boy is a bicycling robot. He can ride forward, backward, and stop without falling over. Where does he get the ability to do it?

___ ___ ___ ___ ___ ___ ___ ___ ___

© Houghton Mifflin Harcourt Publishing Company

Apply Concepts

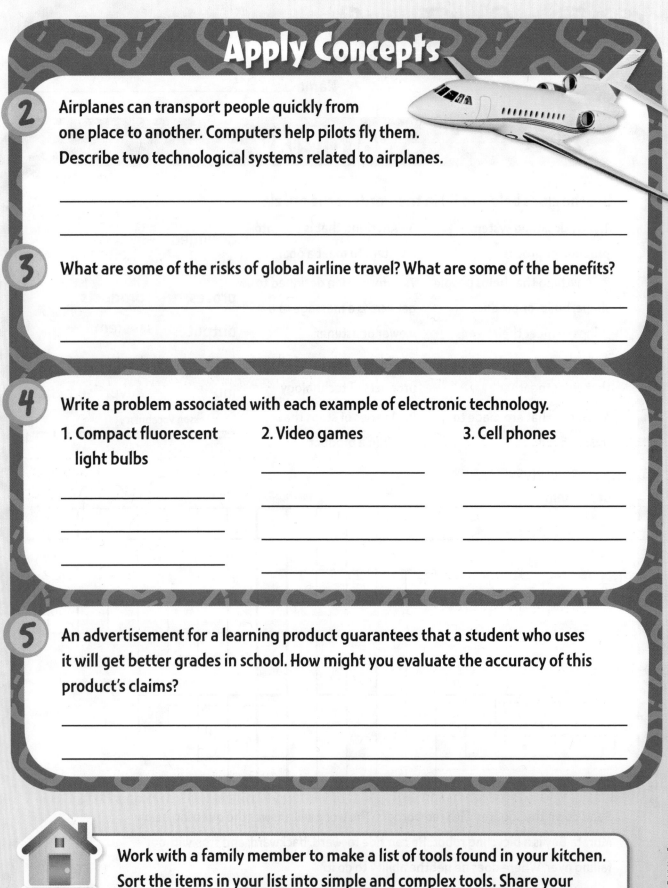

2 Airplanes can transport people quickly from one place to another. Computers help pilots fly them. Describe two technological systems related to airplanes.

_____

_____

3 What are some of the risks of global airline travel? What are some of the benefits?

_____

_____

4 Write a problem associated with each example of electronic technology.

1. Compact fluorescent light bulbs

_____

_____

_____

2. Video games

_____

_____

_____

3. Cell phones

_____

_____

_____

5 An advertisement for a learning product guarantees that a student who uses it will get better grades in school. How might you evaluate the accuracy of this product's claims?

_____

_____

Take It Home!

Work with a family member to make a list of tools found in your kitchen. Sort the items in your list into simple and complex tools. Share your work with your class. Explain how you categorized the items in your list.

© Houghton Mifflin Harcourt Publishing Company

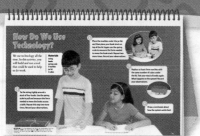

Name _____

Essential Question

How Do We Use Technology?

TEKS **4.2A** ...implement descriptive investigations, including... making inferences... **4.2B** collect... data...by measuring, using the metric system... **4.2C** construct... bar graphs...to organize...data **4.2D** analyze data...to construct reasonable explanations from data that can be...measured **4.2E** perform repeated investigations to increase the reliability of results **4.4A** collect... analyze information using tools, including...spring scales...

Set a Purpose

What do you think you will learn from this activity?

_____

_____

Think About the Procedure

What does the spring scale measure?

_____

Why is it a good idea to repeat each trial in Steps 1 and 2 three times?

_____

_____

_____

What is being modeled when some of the marbles are replaced with cubes?

_____

_____

_____

Record Your Data

Record your observations for Trials 1–3 in the space below.

Measured Force (N)			
Trial	Bare table	Marbles	Marbles and cubes
1			
2			
3			
Average			

Draw Conclusions

Calculate the average force needed to move the book stack in each setup. Show your work and record your answers in the table above.

© Houghton Mifflin Harcourt Publishing Company

Draw Conclusions (continued)

Which problem did the tool you built help solve?

_____

_____

_____

Analyze the data collected using a spring scale. Which setup required the greatest amount of force to move the books? Why?

_____

_____

_____

_____

_____

Analyze and Extend

1. Which technology products did you use to build your tool?

_____

_____

_____

2. What other objects could you have used in place of marbles?

_____

_____

_____

_____

3. In the space below, construct a bar graph to show the average force needed to move each book stack.

```
┌──────────────────────────┐
│                          │
│                          │
│                          │
│                          │
│                          │
│                          │
│                          │
│                          │
│                          │
│                          │
└──────────────────────────┘
```

4. Make an inference. What could cause the marbles to become more like cubes?

_____

_____

_____

_____

5. How could you redesign this tool to move larger things?

_____

_____

_____

_____

© Houghton Mifflin Harcourt Publishing Company

1

Dr. Ayanna Howard is a roboticist. She designs and builds robots.

2

Dr. Howard is making robots that will make decisions without the help of people.

3

To get a robot to make decisions on its own, Dr. Howard must teach the robot how to think.

4

Dr. Howard uses computer programs to teach robots. She observes the robots. Then she changes her computer programs to get better results.

8 Things
YOU SHOULD KNOW ABOUT
Ayanna Howard

5

Dr. Howard studies how robots can help explore outer space and unsafe places on Earth.

6

Dr. Howard taught a robot called SmartNav to move around things in its path. This robot could explore the surface of Mars.

7

Scientists want to understand why the ice in Antarctica is melting. Dr. Howard's SnoMote robots can safely gather data on the cracking ice sheets.

8

In 2003, Dr. Howard was named a top young inventor.

© Houghton Mifflin Harcourt Publishing Company (bkgd) ©Sharon Dupuis/Alamy; (lc) ©Corbis; (rc) ©Getty Images/PhotoDisc

Now You Be a Roboticist!

1 What is Dr. Howard investigating?

2 Why does Dr. Howard test the robots?

3 What scientific question does Dr. Howard's SnoMote help answer?

4 If you were a roboticist, what kind of robot would you make?

5 What steps would you take in making your robot?

6 Draw a picture of your robot.

1 _____
_____
_____

2 _____
_____
_____

3 _____
_____
_____

4 _____
_____
_____

5 _____
_____
_____

6

© Houghton Mifflin Harcourt Publishing Company (cables) ©Peter Dazeley/Getty Images; (electronic parts) ©Roger T. Schmidt/Getty Images

Name _____

Vocabulary Review

Use the terms in the box to complete the sentences.

advertisement
design
engineering
process
prototype
technology
technology product
tool

1. Anything that is made to meet a need or desire is

   a(n) _____.

2. To conceive of something and prepare the plans and

   drawings for it to be built is _____.

3. A designed system, product, or process that people use

   to solve problems is called _____.

4. A series of steps used to achieve a goal or make a product

   is called a(n) _____.

5. The use of scientific and mathematical principles to develop

   something practical is called _____.

6. An original or test model on which a real product is based

   is called a _____.

TEKS 4.3B

7. Information designed to get across a message to a viewer

   or listener is a(n) _____.

TEKS 4.4A

8. Anything that helps people shape, build, or produce things

   to meet their needs is called a _____.

© Houghton Mifflin Harcourt Publishing Company   (border) ©NDisk/Age Fotostock

Science Concepts

Fill in the letter of the choice that best answers the question.

TEKS 4.2D

9. A researcher is working to make winter coats warmer. The first coat is not very warm. How can she analyze her test data?

   (A) She should try again without using tools.

   (B) She should investigate a different designed system.

   (C) She should continue her work without using technology.

   (D) She should make a reasonable explanation for ways to improve the coat's design.

TEKS 4.3D

10. Sylvia works for a car company. She uses her knowledge of math and science to design dashboards that make it easier to operate cars. What is Sylvia's profession?

   (A) analyst   (C) engineer

   (B) biologist   (D) geologist

TEKS 4.4A

11. Marco is using this object to help him collect and record information for a report.

   Which statement best describes this object?

   (A) It is a tool.

   (B) It is a model.

   (C) It is a prototype.

   (D) It is a technology process.

TEKS 4.2A

12. Researchers want to build a new type of spaceship to transport astronauts to the moon. What should they do first?

   (A) They should build a model.

   (B) They should test the prototype.

   (C) They should evaluate how the prototype worked.

   (D) They should select appropriate equipment to plan a prototype.

TEKS 4.3B

13. A label on a shampoo bottle claims this shampoo will make your hair soft and shiny. How can you evaluate the accuracy of the product claim found in this label?

   (A) Try to prove that the claim is true.

   (B) Compare the label to other labels.

   (C) Judge the product based on the label.

   (D) Read reviews from a trustworthy source.

TEKS 4.2E

14. Angie tested a reflector she hopes will make bicycles safer. Her first test went well, yet she still repeated the test three more times. Which statement is true?

   (A) She skipped the step of asking "What if?"

   (B) She increased the reliability of the results.

   (C) She wasted her time by repeating the same test.

   (D) She obtained unreliable data, because there were more chances for mistakes.

© Houghton Mifflin Harcourt Publishing Company (border) ©NDisk/Age Fotostock

TEKS 4.2A

15. New solutions to problems often begin with a "What if?" question. Which "What if?" question might an engineer ask about the electrical energy station below?

- (A) What if we burned trees instead of coal?
- (B) What if we could find even more coal to burn?
- (C) What if we all threw away all of our electrical appliances?
- (D) What if we could burn coal to make electricity without polluting the air?

16. You probably use the tools shown below every day.

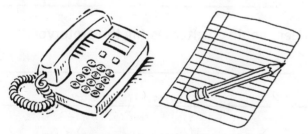

Which statement about these tools is true?

- (A) They cost about the same to produce.
- (B) They are both examples of technology.
- (C) They are examples of identical technology.
- (D) They are each designed for many different tasks.

TEKS 4.2E

17. Sometimes, a prototype tests poorly or fails completely. What should be done when that happens?

- (A) The prototype should be abandoned.
- (B) A second prototype should be built.
- (C) The prototype should be modified and repeated tests performed.
- (D) The prototype should be examined to see if it has other uses.

TEKS 4.3A

18. A fuel-efficient automobile is an example of a designed system. What is an example of feedback for such an automobile?

- (A) safe arrival at the destination
- (B) fuel for the car and the roads on which it will travel
- (C) data on how much fuel the car used to travel 100 km
- (D) to move a family of four 100 km using only 2 liters of gasoline

TEKS 4.3B

19. An advertisement claims a company's Internet service will improve your grades in school. What inferences can you make about the service claims in this advertisement?

- (A) The claim cannot be proved to be true.
- (B) The claim accurately evaluates a service.
- (C) The advertisement is there to get your attention.
- (D) The advertisement is based on a trustworthy source.

© Houghton Mifflin Harcourt Publishing Company   (border) ©NDisk/Age Fotostock

Apply Inquiry and Review the Big Idea

Write the answers to these questions.

TEKS 4.2D

20. This picture shows solar cells on the roof of a house. These cells take solar energy and convert it into electricity that appliances in the house need to function.

a. How is this an example of a designed system?

_____

_____

_____

b. Identify the goal, input, output, and feedback of this system.

_____

_____

_____

TEKS 4.2E

21. An engineer follows the design process to improve soccer shoes. First, he studies soccer shoes and learns what people like and dislike about them. Then he starts his prototype.

a. Why should the engineer build a prototype of the shoes?

_____

_____

b. Describe a part of the design process the engineer should do after testing the prototype.

_____

_____

_____

TEKS 4.2B

22. A scientist constructs a data table to record data about the SPFs of 100 sunscreens. A total of 19 sunscreens had an SPF of 8. Use numerals to record data to complete the table.

SPF	Number of Sunscreens
8	
15	23
30	
50	37

© Houghton Mifflin Harcourt Publishing Company   (border) ©NDisk/Age Fotostock

Matter

© Houghton Mifflin Harcourt Publishing Company (bg) ©Carol Dixon/Alamy Images; (inset) ©idp yellowstone collection/Alamy Images; (border) ©NDisc/Age Fotostock

Big Idea

Matter has measurable physical properties that can be used to determine how matter is classified, changed, and used.

TEKS 4.1B, 4.2A, 4.2B, 4.2C, 4.2D, 4.2E, 4.2F, 4.3D, 4.4A, 4.5A, 4.5B, 4.5C

I Wonder Why

Snow, rain, and water vapor are all forms of the same type of matter—water. Why are they so different? *Turn the page to find out.*

Here's Why Snow, rain, and water vapor are all water in different states, or forms, of matter. In each of these states, water has distinct physical properties.

In this unit, you will explore the Big Idea, the Essential Questions, and the Investigations on the Inquiry Flipchart.

Levels of Inquiry Key ■ DIRECTED ■ GUIDED ■ INDEPENDENT

Track Your Progress

Big Idea Matter has measurable physical properties that can be used to determine how matter is classified, changed, and used.

Essential Questions

Now I Get the Big Idea!

Science Notebook

Before you begin each lesson, be sure to write your thoughts about the Essential Question.

© Houghton Mifflin Harcourt Publishing Company (b) ©Carol Dixon/Alamy Images; (inset) ©dp yellowstone collection/Alamy Images; (border) ©NDisc/Age Fotostock

TEKS **4.2C** construct...bar graphs...using tools and current technology to organize...data
4.5A measure, compare, and contrast physical properties of matter, including size, mass, volume...
temperature, magnetism, and the ability to sink or float

Lesson **1**

Essential Question

What Are Physical Properties of Matter?

🧠 Engage Your Brain!

Find the answer to the following question in this lesson and record it here.

How can you compare and contrast the physical properties of the chocolate shell outside with the ice cream inside?

_____

_____

_____

_____

Active Reading

Lesson Vocabulary

List the terms. As you learn about each one, make notes in the Interactive Glossary.

_____   _____

_____   _____

_____   _____

_____   _____

Main Idea and Details

Detailed sentences give information about a topic. The information may be examples, features, characteristics, or facts. Active readers stay focused on the topic when they ask, What fact or information does this sentence add to the topic?

© Houghton Mifflin Harcourt Publishing Company

Inquiry Flipchart p. 17—Measuring Magnetism/Measuring Size

Use Your Senses

See
You can see shapes in the sandwich. What other property can you see?

_____

You can use your senses to describe a sandwich. What does it look, taste, and smell like?

Hear
When you bite into a sandwich, you might hear the crunch of the crust.

Matter
Is this sandwich made of matter? Anything that takes up space and has mass is **matter**. A characteristic of matter that you can observe or measure directly is a **physical property**.

The amount of matter in an object is its **mass**. You use a pan balance to measure mass. Less massive objects are measured in grams (g). More massive objects are measured in kilograms (kg).

Houghton Mifflin Harcourt Publishing Company (bkgd) ©G. Baden/Corbis

Taste

You can taste sweet, sour, salty, and bitter. Which would you taste in this sandwich?

_____

_____

Smell

You may smell mustard, onion, or pepper. You may even smell the fresh bread.

Feel

The bread feels soft. The dressing may feel oily. Salt and pepper feel grainy.

You start by placing the object to be measured on one side of the balance. You add known masses to the other pan until the sides balance. You add up the masses to find the mass of the object.

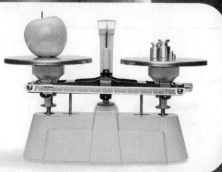

© Houghton Mifflin Harcourt Publishing Company

Describe That!

You can use these words to describe matter. Use your senses to measure and describe an object's hardness, color, taste, size, shape, odor, or texture.

Active Reading As you read these two pages, circle words or phrases that signal a detail about physical properties.

Hardness

A walnut shell is hard. The grapes are soft. Hardness describes how easily something can bend or dent.

Size

A silver dollar takes up more space than other coins. Pennies are larger than dimes.

Color

The words we use for color describe the way light bounces off an object. What colors do you see below?

_____

Taste

Crackers are salty. Candy can taste sweet or sour. Can you think of something that tastes bitter?

_____

© Houghton Mifflin Harcourt Publishing Company (fifty-cent piece) ©Q Squared Studios/Photodisc; (kiwi) ©PhotoAlto/Getty Images; (strawberry) ©Getty Images/PhotoDisc; (crackers) ©Corbis; (pepperminit candy) ©Artville/Getty Images

▶ List five properties that describe this banana.

is odor yellow

is big

Shape-banana boat

it taste like a banana

Texture

Texture describes what something feels like. The pinecone has a rough texture. The leaf feels smooth.

Odor

These shoes are stinky! Perfume has a nice smell. How can odor tell you if milk has gone bad?

_____

Shape

Objects can be long, short, flat, tall, or irregular like these keys. Shape describes an object's form. How can you describe the MP3 player?

_____

© Houghton Mifflin Harcourt Publishing Company   (iPod) ©Alamy Images Royalty Free; (keys) ©Mode Images Limited/Alamy; (perfume) ©Dirk Westphal/Getty Images

Pump Up the Volume!

You can measure mass with a pan balance. What is another property of matter that we can use tools to measure?

Active Reading As you read these two pages, underline the definition of *volume*. Circle units used to measure volume.

Volume

Volume is how much space an object takes up. The beaker on the left measures the volume of water in milliliters (mL). The beaker on the right measures the volume of an object with an irregular shape plus the volume of the water. To find the volume of just the orange, you must use subtraction:

$$\begin{cases} \text{volume of water and orange} \\ -\ \text{volume of water} \\ \hline \text{volume of orange} \end{cases}$$

© Houghton Mifflin Harcourt Publishing Company (bkgd) ©Ron Chapple Stock/Alamy

Do the Math!

Measure the Volume of Objects

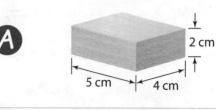

A 2 cm · 5 cm · 4 cm

B 3 cm · 3 cm · 3 cm

Find It!

The volume of a rectangular solid is found by multiplying the width by the length by the height. Find the volume for each box. The units are cubic centimeters.

Volume of Box A:

Volume of Box B:

Compare and contrast the volume of Box A with the volume of Box B. Which box has less volume?

Displacement

The dog in this tub takes up space. To make room for him, water was pushed out of the tub.

Mifflin Harcourt Publishing Company

Don't Be So Dense!

Why does the hook sink? Why doesn't it float? You must use mass and volume to find the answers.

Active Reading As you read these pages, underline the sentence that gives the main idea about density.

Density is a physical property of matter. It tells how much space (volume) a certain amount (mass) of matter takes up. In other words, **density** is the amount of matter present in a certain volume of a substance.

Density indicates how close together the particles in an object are. The density of a substance is always the same, no matter how much of the substance there is. A small piece of an eraser, for example, has the same density as a whole eraser.

This Part Floats
Objects less dense than water are able to float. This fishing float is made of plastic.

This Part Sinks
The hook and weights are metal. The density of metal is greater than that of water, which enables the metal to sink.

▶ Name three objects that are more dense than water.

_____

_____

© Houghton Mifflin Harcourt Publishing Company   (bkgd) ©PIER/Getty Images

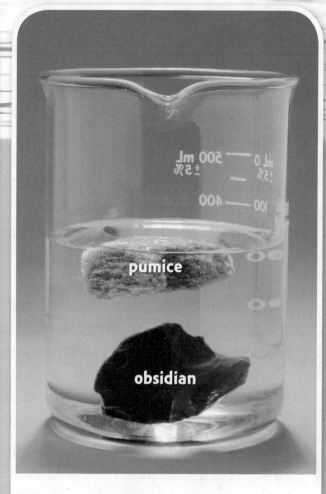

Different Densities

The density of the foam balls is different than the density of sand. Compare and contrast the ability of the foam and the sand to sink or float. Which is less dense? How do you know?

_____

_____

_____

_____

_____

More About Density

These rocks have different properties. One rock is more dense than the other. Compare and contrast the ability of each to sink or float. Which has particles that are closer together? Which has the greater density?

_____

_____

_____

_____

_____

© Houghton Mifflin Harcourt Publishing Company

You're Getting Warmer!

Going swimming? The water might be warm or cold. Temperature is a physical property of matter that can be measured.

Active Reading Compare and contrast the temperatures of the objects shown on these two pages. Mark a star next to the object with the coolest temperature. Circle the object with the warmest temperature.

Has a doctor or nurse ever measured your temperature? **Temperature** is a measure of how hot or cold something is. Everything has a temperature. A thermometer is used to measure the temperature of an object or a substance. There are two different temperature scales. Temperature is measured in degrees Celsius (°C) in the metric system and in degrees Fahrenheit (°F) in the customary system.

Cold
The air around you is made up mostly of nitrogen. Liquid nitrogen boils at a temperature of about –196 °C (–321 °F).

Warm
When a computer is on, a fan helps to keep it cool. In spite of this, chips inside the computer get warm. This chip has a temperature of 65 °C (149 °F).

© Houghton Mifflin Harcourt Publishing Company (t) ©Karl Maritila/Alamy Images; (b) ©Andrew Brookes/Corbis; (bg) ©Andre Schoenherr/Getty Images

Construct a Bar Graph to Compare Temperatures

The milk has a temperature of 2 °C. The banana has the same temperature as the air around it: 23 °C. The herbal tea has a temperature of 40 °C. Construct a bar graph to compare and contrast the three temperatures.

0

Hot
When lava bursts to Earth's surface during a volcanic eruption, it is very hot. While contact with the air cools the lava, initially it can have a temperature of 750 °C (1,382 °F).

© Houghton Mifflin Harcourt Publishing Company   (b) ©Westend61/Getty Images; (t) ©Photodisc/Getty Images; (tc) ©Nikolai Sorokin/Fotolia; (bcl) ©Photodisc/Getty Images; (bcl) ©Andre Schoenherr/Getty Images; (tr) ©Superstock

How Attractive!

Do you have drawings, photographs, or postcards stuck to your refrigerator with magnets? How do these magnets work?

Active Reading As you read these two pages, underline the definitions you find.

Magnetism is the physical property of being magnetic. The term *magnetic* can mean that something attracts certain types of metals. For example, lodestone is a magnetic rock that attracts certain metals. *Magnetic* can also mean that something can be attracted by a magnet. Iron is magnetic. An iron bar is attracted by a magnet.

Not Attracted
Like steel, aluminum is a metal. However, aluminum and steel have different physical properties. For this reason, aluminum is not attracted to magnets.

Attracted
This refrigerator is made of steel, which is attracted to magnets. Magnets are also attracted to steel. As a result, the magnets hold the pictures up on the refrigerator.

© Houghton Mifflin Harcourt Publishing Company (bg) ©Vladimir Budgar/Textures/Alamy Images

© Houghton Mifflin Harcourt Publishing Company (bg) ©Vladimir Edgar/textures/Alamy Images

Becoming Magnetic

A steel paper clip is attracted to a magnet. When a steel paper clip touches a magnet, the paper clip becomes magnetic as well. A second steel paper clip can be attracted to the first one. When the two paper clips touch, the second one becomes magnetic, too. This process is how a paper clip chain forms. The stronger the magnet is, the more paper clips it will hold.

Compare and Contrast Magnetism

Compare and contrast the magnets on this page. Which do you think is the strongest? Which is the weakest? How do you know?

_____

_____

_____

_____

Let's Sort Things Out

Shape

Study this example. Then compare and contrast the objects to sort them using other properties.

round   rectangular   other

Mass

shoes cup rock ball

Texture

banana is like hard

Paper is soft

© Houghton Mifflin Harcourt Publishing Company   (iPod) ©Alamy Images Royalty Free; (tennis ball) ©Getty Images/PhotoDisc; (crumpled paper) ©PhotoDisc/Getty Images

Imagine going into a store or a library and finding that nothing is organized. How would you find anything? How can you find your homework in a messy backpack? Organizing makes life easier. Sorting things helps us find things faster.

We can use properties to sort everything, including food, books, and clothes. The items shown are at the bottom of a closet. Sort them by each of the properties listed.

▶ Name another property you could use to sort these items.

_____

Color

the banana is yellow

Size

Hardness

© Houghton Mifflin Harcourt Publishing Company   (sneakers) ©Paul Carstairs/Alamy

Sum It Up!

When you're done, use the answer key to check and revise your work.

Use the information in the summary to complete the graphic organizer.

Summarize

All matter has physical properties. Physical properties can also be called characteristics. Some properties can be described by using your senses. You can feel hardness and see shape or color. You can feel texture and smell odor. Other properties can be measured using tools. You can measure volume with a graduated cylinder. You can measure mass with a pan balance. All matter has density. To measure an object's density, you must know its mass and volume. You can measure temperature with a thermometer. Magnetism, which is the physical property of being magnetic, can also be measured. Metals such as steel and iron are attracted by magnets, but aluminum is not.

[1] Main Idea: All matter has _____.

[2] Detail: Some properties can be _____ _____ _____.

[3] An example of one of these properties is _____ _____ _____.

[4] Other properties must be _____ _____ _____.

[5] An example of one of these properties is _____ _____ _____.

[6] Some metals are attracted to magnets, including _____ _____.

[7] Some are not, including _____ _____ _____.

© Houghton Mifflin Harcourt Publishing Company   (t) ©Paul Carstairs/Alamy; (c) ©Dirk Westphal/Getty Images

Answer Key: 1. physical properties 2. described by using your senses 3. Sample answers: hardness, color, shape, texture, and odor 4. measured 5. Sample answers: temperature, volume 6. steel and iron 7. aluminum

Brain Check

Name _____

Word Play

1. Which term best describes the physical property of each photo? Use terms only once.

mass	volume	density
hard	size	shape
texture	odor	taste

_____ _____ _____

_____ _____ _____

_____ _____ _____

© Houghton Mifflin Harcourt Publishing Company   (tl) ©Mode Images Limited/Alamy; (c) ©Artville/Getty Images

2

Use the chart below to sort the objects into two groups. Label the groups at the top of the chart.

Which properties did you use to sort the objects?

_____

_____

Can you sort the same objects into three groups?
Don't forget to label the groups at the top of your chart.

Did you use the same properties to sort the objects the second time?

_____

© Houghton Mifflin Harcourt Publishing Company   yo-yo ©PhotoDisc/Getty Images; (tr) ©Artville/Getty Images; (br) ©PhotoDisc/Getty Images

3 Compare the objects below. Identify which one has the greater mass, volume, or density.

greater mass?

greater volume?

greater density?

_____   _____   _____

4 Choose a type of matter that you had for breakfast today. List as many physical properties as you can to describe it. Trade your list with a partner, and see if you can identify the matter your partner chose based on its properties.

_____

_____

_____

_____

_____

_____

© Houghton Mifflin Harcourt Publishing Company

5 Work with a group to make a list of ten favorite books, songs, or movies. Tell how you can sort them into groups.

_____

_____

_____

_____

_____

_____

_____

6 How could you use physical properties to sort the objects in a desk drawer?

_____

_____

_____

_____

_____

_____

_____

_____

Take It Home!

Share with your family what you have learned about properties of matter. With a family member, name properties of matter you observe at mealtime or in different places in your home.

© Houghton Mifflin Harcourt Publishing Company   (tr) ©Comstock/Getty Images; (br) ©Artville/Getty Images

Inquiry Flipchart page 18

TEKS **4.2A** plan and implement descriptive investigations including… making inferences… **4.2B** collect… data by observing…using descriptive words… **4.2C** construct…charts… using tools…to organize, examine, and evaluate data **4.2D** analyze data… to construct reasonable explanations from data that can be observed and measured **4.2E** perform repeated investigations to increase the reliability of results **4.5A** measure, compare, and contrast physical properties of matter, including…the ability to sink or float

Name _____

Essential Question

Which Objects Will Sink or Float?

Set a Purpose

What will you learn from this investigation?

_____

_____

_____

_____

_____

Think About the Procedure

Why do you think scientists repeat investigations?

_____

_____

_____

_____

_____

_____

_____

Record Your Data

In the space below, construct a chart to organize and examine your data.

© Houghton Mifflin Harcourt Publishing Company

131

Draw Conclusions

Evaluate your data. Were your predictions correct?

_____

_____

_____

Analyze and Extend

1. Compare and contrast the ability of the two objects made from aluminum foil to sink or float.

_____

_____

2. Compare and contrast the ability of the two objects made from clay to sink or float.

_____

_____

_____

3. Why did you repeat the investigation and conduct multiple trials?

_____

_____

_____

4. Scientists often look at two situations in which everything is the same except for one property. Which property is the same in Steps 3 and 4? Which property was different in Steps 3 and 4? Make an inference about how that difference affected the results.

_____

_____

_____

_____

_____

_____

_____

_____

_____

_____

5. Think of other questions you would like to ask about the ability of an object to sink or float.

_____

_____

_____

_____

_____

© Houghton Mifflin Harcourt Publishing Company

Ask a Materials Scientist

Did you know that objects like these can be made from recycled plastic? Materials scientists make informed choices in the recycling of materials.

Q. What does a materials scientist do?

A. We invent new materials or improve existing materials. We might work to develop new types of paint, plastic, fabric, cardboard, or any other material you can name.

Q. What is an example of a material that materials scientists helped develop?

A. Artificial fleece is one example. We can make fleece from recycled plastic bottles that are cut apart, treated with chemicals, and then woven into fibers.

Q. How has your work changed in recent years?

A. More than ever before, scientists are working in teams. A materials scientist might work closely with experts in life science, physical science, or computer science. Everyone shares his or her knowledge and skills to reach a common goal.

Materials scientists study properties of matter. These scientists test materials to find out how strong they are and whether they stretch, bend, or resist heat.

Now It's Your Turn!

Which material would you want to invent or improve? What would the material do?

_____

_____

_____

_____

_____

_____

© Houghton Mifflin Harcourt Publishing Company (bg) ©Danita Delimont/Getty Images; (t) © Squared Studios/PhotoDisc/Getty Images; (bl) ©Getty Images

Introducing the New...

Which material described below would you use to make
a frying pan? Give reasons for using or not using each one.

Wood is strong, hard, and can last many years.
You can cut, chop, or glue it. Wood burns.

_____
_____

Plastic is strong and lightweight. It can
be flexible or keep its shape. Plastic burns.

_____
_____

Metal can be heated to a high temperature
without burning or changing shape.

_____
_____

Glass is strong and holds its shape. It can be
heated without burning or changing shape.

_____
_____

Think About It!

Hook-and-loop fastener is a type of two-layer tape often
used to fasten things, such as shoes. The hooks on one
layer stick to the loops on the other layer. How could you
make this material better?

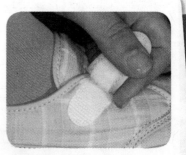

_____
_____

© Houghton Mifflin Harcourt Publishing Company (tl) ©Corbis; (tr) ©James King-Holmes/Photo Researchers, Inc.; (cl) ©F1online Digitale Bildagentur GmbH/Alamy Images; (cr) ©Paw Jones/Alamy Images; (br) ©Dr. Jeremy Burgess/Photo Researchers, Inc.

TEKS **4.5A** compare, and contrast physical properties of matter, including...states (solid, liquid, gas)... **4.5B** predict the changes caused by heating and cooling such as ice becoming liquid water and condensation forming on the outside of a glass of ice water

Essential Question

What Are the States of Water?

 Engage Your Brain!

Find the answer to the following question in this lesson and record it here.

How is the snow in this picture like an ice cube?

_____

_____

_____

_____

Active Reading

Lesson Vocabulary

List the terms. As you learn about each one, make notes in the Interactive Glossary.

_____   _____

_____   _____

_____   _____

_____

Compare and Contrast

Many ideas in this lesson are connected because they explain comparisons and contrasts—how things are alike and how they are different. Active readers stay focused on comparisons and contrasts when they ask themselves, How are these things alike? How are they different?

© Houghton Mifflin Harcourt Publishing Company   (bkgd) ©Koichi Hasegawa/Getty Images

Solids, Liquids, and Gases

Matter exists in different states. The air around us is a gas. The water we drink is a liquid. Your book is a solid.

Active Reading As you read these two pages, underline the contrasting physical properties of each state of matter.

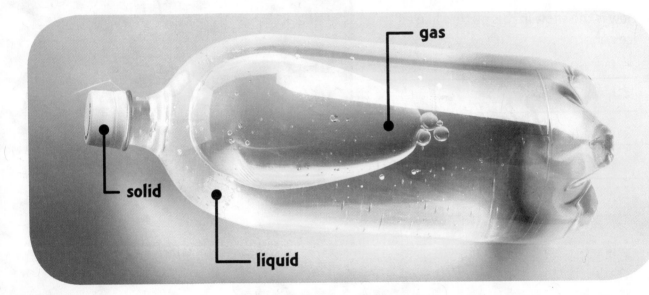

gas

solid

liquid

Solids, liquids, and gases are three **states of matter**. Most matter on Earth is classified as one of these states. Each state has a unique set of physical properties.

A **solid** has a definite volume and shape. Your desk, book, pencil, and chair are all solids. Solids stay solid unless something, such as heat, changes them.

A **liquid** has a definite volume but not a definite shape. Liquids, such as water, take the shape of whatever container holds them. A physical property of water is that it's a liquid between 0 °C and 100 °C.

A **gas** doesn't have a definite volume or shape. It expands to take up all the space in a container. If you blow up a balloon, you can see that air spreads out to fill the space. The air we breathe is a mixture of gases.

© Houghton Mifflin Harcourt Publishing Company

Gas

The air around the ice cube has water vapor in it. We can't see the water vapor, but it's there. A gas doesn't have a definite volume or shape. Particles in a gas are far apart. They are much farther apart than the particles in a liquid. They move very quickly in all directions.

▶ Complete the chart to compare and contrast the physical properties of the three states of water. Identify one way people use water in each state.

	Physical Properties	How We Use It
ice		
liquid water		
water vapor		

© Houghton Mifflin Harcourt Publishing Company

Freezing

At a certain temperature, water can freeze as heat energy is removed. Particles slow down and begin to lock into place. Water changes from a liquid to a solid. A **change of state** occurs when matter changes from one state to another.

Melting

Adding heat energy causes ice to melt. Particles speed up until they overcome the attractions that hold them in place. Water melts when it changes from a solid to a liquid.

Water Changes Form

Anything made out of snow will melt if it gains enough heat energy. Energy from the sun causes the snow to change to a liquid.

Active Reading As you read these two pages, compare changes of state. Draw a circle around changes that happen when heat is added.

© Houghton Mifflin Harcourt Publishing Company

Evaporation

When heat energy is added to water, its particles speed up. Particles that gain enough energy enter the air as water vapor. **Evaporation** is the process by which a liquid changes into a gas. Water evaporates from oceans, lakes, and rivers every day.

Condensation

When heat energy is removed from a gas, its particles slow down and clump together. **Condensation** is the process by which a gas changes into a liquid. Clouds form when water vapor condenses on particles of dust in the air.

Air contains water vapor. When the air touches the side of a cold glass, the air cools. Cool air holds less water vapor, which causes the water vapor to condense and to form liquid water on the side of the glass.

▶ Predict the changes that will take place if the condensed water continues to lose heat energy.

_____

_____

The air is warmer than the ice. When the air touches the ice, the ice gains heat energy, which causes the ice to melt and become liquid water.

▶ Predict the changes that will take place if the water continues to gain heat energy.

_____

_____

© Houghton Mifflin Harcourt Publishing Company   (l) ©Serge Krouglikoff/Digital Vision/Getty Images; (r) ©Photolibrary RF

Sum It Up!

When you're done, use the answer key to check and revise your work.

Write the vocabulary term that matches each photo and caption.

1

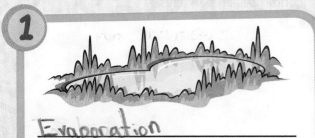

Evaporation

The sun's heat will make this water change to a gas.

2

These particles move very quickly and spread out in all directions.

Gas

3

Liquid

The water in this bottle has a definite volume and takes the shape of its container.

4

Liquid

This happens when water changes form.

Summarize

Fill in the missing words to tell about the states of matter.

Water as a solid has a definite [5] change of states and [6] Evaporation .

The particles vibrate in place. Liquid water does not have a definite [7] Condensation .

The particles [8] are condesation past each other. The air around ice

has water [9] Melting in it. Since it's a gas, its particles are very far apart.

Water's changing from a liquid to a solid is [10] Frezing .

Adding [11] change of state can make ice melt. It also can make water change from

a liquid to a gas. This is called [12] Evaporation . Water's changing from a gas to a

liquid is called [13] Melting .

© Houghton Mifflin Harcourt Publishing Company

Answer Key: 1. evaporation **2.** gas **3.** liquid **4.** change of state **5.** volume/shape **6.** volume/shape **7.** shape **8.** slide **9.** vapor **10.** freezing **11.** heat **12.** evaporation **13.** condensation

Name _____

Word Play

1 Unscramble these words. Use the highlighted letters to find the answer below.

sag
g	a	s

disol
S	o	l	i	d

qiludi
l	i	q	u	i	d

stianodocnne
c	o	d	e	n	s	a	t	i	o	n	n

rvapnotieao
e	v	a	p	o	r	a	t	i	o	n

ngecha fo ttase
c	h	a	n	g	e		o	f		s	t	a	t	e

ttases fo tmaert
t	a	s	t	e	s		o	f		m	a	t	t	e	r

tware
w	a	t	e	r

povra
v	a	p	o	r

We can find out what state water is in by finding how fast these move. What are they?

_____

Draw a star next to each word that names a state of matter.

© Houghton Mifflin Harcourt Publishing Company

Apply Concepts

2 Make a menu for a meal. The meal will have 3 solids and 3 liquids.

Solids

The tables

The rocks

The chairs

Liquids

Water

coke

Water of rain

3 Draw and label a diagram to show what happens to the particles of a substance as it changes from a solid to a liquid to a gas.

Solid

liquid

gas

4 Name an example of condensation.

_____

5 Name an example of evaporation.

_____

© Houghton Mifflin Harcourt Publishing Company   (t) ©PhotoDisc/Getty Images

Take It Home!

Make "Sunshine on a Stick"! Put an ice cube tray filled with orange juice into the freezer. When partly frozen, place a toothpick in each section. When the juice is a solid, you can eat it off the toothpicks!

TEKS **4.2B** collect and record data by…measuring, using the metric system, and using…numerals… **4.2C** construct simple tables… using tools…to organize…data **4.4A** collect…analyze information using tools, including…triple beam balances…beakers…hot plates… **4.5A** measure, compare, and contrast physical properties of matter, including…mass, volume, states (solid, liquid, gas), temperature… **4.5B** predict the changes caused by heating and cooling…

Name _____

Essential Question

How Does Water Change States?

Set a Purpose
What will you learn from this experiment?

_____

_____

Think About the Procedure
Why are you instructed to pour the ice-water mixture into the zip-top bag?

_____

_____

_____

Record your prediction from Step 3 about how the mass, volume, and temperature of the bag's contents will change when the ice melts.

_____

_____

_____

_____

Record your prediction from Step 6 about what will happen to the temperature and volume of the liquid water as it is heated.

_____

_____

_____

Record Your Data
In the space below, construct a table to organize your data and record your results.

© Houghton Mifflin Harcourt Publishing Company

Draw Conclusions

How did you use the triple beam balance to collect and analyze information about how water changes state?

_____

_____

_____

Were your predictions correct? Explain.

_____

_____

_____

_____

Analyze and Extend

1. Which properties of water changed? Which did not change?

_____

_____

_____

2. Water can exist in three states: solid, liquid, and gas. Use your data to compare and contrast these states by mass, volume, and temperature.

_____

_____

_____

_____

_____

3. Why was the mass of the zip-top bag not important?

_____

_____

_____

_____

4. What do you predict would happen to the mass of the water if you put it in a freezer rather than heating it?

_____

_____

_____

5. What do you predict would happen to the volume of the water if you put it in a freezer rather than heating it?

_____

_____

_____

6. Think of other questions you would like to ask about what happens to water during a physical change.

_____

_____

_____

_____

© Houghton Mifflin Harcourt Publishing Company

TEKS 4.3D connect grade-level appropriate science concepts with the history of science...
4.4A collect...analyze information using tools, including...computers...

S.T.E.M.
Engineering & Technology

Baby, It's Cold Inside
Refrigeration

Have you ever thought about how refrigeration has changed the way we live? We can store foods without having them rot as quickly. Spoiled foods can make people ill.

1920s

In the 1920s, electric refrigerators became available for home use. The inside of this refrigerator stayed cold without needing blocks of ice. It used an electric motor and a gas compressor to remove heat from its wooden or metal box.

1900s

By the early 1900s, many homes had iceboxes. Ice was placed in the bottom to cool the air inside the box. It became easier to cool food for longer periods of time until it could be used. These iceboxes were like coolers we use today but larger.

1800s

People put food on blocks of ice to keep it cold. The ice was cut from lakes or ponds, packed in straw, and stored in warehouses. This ice had to be replaced often.

Critical Thinking

In addition to slowing food spoilage, what is another advantage of refrigerating food?

_____

_____

_____

© Houghton Mifflin Harcourt Publishing Company (t) ©Peter Walker/Corbis; (cl) ©Corbis; (c) ©Maria Holder/Alamy Images; (cr) ©Daily Herald Archive/SSPL/Getty Images; (b) ©PhotoLink/PhotoDisc/Getty Images; (t) ©Peter Walker/Corbis; (b) ©PhotoLink/PhotoDisc/Getty Images

Make Some History

If you look closely, you will find that many of your home appliances have an *Energy Star* label. Do research to find out more about this label. Draw the Energy Star label in the space below on the timeline. Then, describe what it is and when it was first used on refrigerators.

_____

_____

_____

_____

2010s

Today's refrigerators are larger but use less energy. They have electronic controls that can be adjusted to set different parts of the refrigerator at different temperatures. Some modern refrigerators can alert people when a particular food supply is running low!

Design Your Future

Other household appliances help you save time. Think about a computer. Describe how it helps you collect and analyze information. Then, explain what you would do to improve its design.

_____

_____

_____

Build On It!

Rise to the engineering design challenge—complete **Improvise It: Build a Rubber Band Scale** on the Inquiry Flipchart.

© Houghton Mifflin Harcourt Publishing Company   (t) ©Peter Walker/Corbis; (b) ©Peter Walker/Corbis

S **4.5B** predict the changes caused by heating...such as ice becoming liquid water... compare and contrast a variety of mixtures and solutions such as rocks in sand, sand ...er, or sugar in water

Lesson **5**

ssential Question

What Are Some Physical Changes?

Engage Your Brain!

Find the answer to the following question in this lesson and record it here.

Which changes take place when melted metal is poured into a mold?

_____

_____

_____

_____

_____

Active Reading

Lesson Vocabulary

List the terms. As you learn about each one, make notes in the Interactive Glossary.

_____

_____

_____

Main Ideas

The main idea is the most important idea of a paragraph. The main idea may be stated in the first sentence, or it may be stated elsewhere. Active readers look for the main idea by asking themselves, What is this paragraph about?

Physical Changes Are All Around

Matter can be changed in many ways. In how many ways can you change a piece of paper?

Active Reading As you read, draw a line under the main idea of each paragraph.

Stacked

You can describe the physical properties of this paper, such as its size and color.

Soaked

What a mess! The paper is soggy, but it hasn't become a new substance.

Shredded

Does shredding the paper make a new substance? No, it just changes the shape of the paper into tiny pieces.

© Houghton Mifflin Harcourt Publishing Company

Think of a piece of clay. Can it be changed like paper can? If you pull bits from the clay, you change its size. If you flatten the clay, you change its shape. The size or shape may be different, but it is still clay. Changing size and shape is a physical change. A **physical change** is a change in which a new substance is not formed.

You can scratch a piece of clay until it is rough. It has a new texture, but it is still clay. You can add bits to it. It is heavier, but adding clay does not make a new substance. Changing a physical property, such as size, shape, texture, or mass, is a physical change.

▶ What are some different ways that you can make a physical change to a piece of string?

_____

_____

▶ Describe the physical change.

_____

_____

_____

Crumpled

This paper is crinkly, but it is still the original paper.

© Houghton Mifflin Harcourt Publishing Company

151

So Different, yet the Same

You get a juice pop from the freezer. As you eat the pop, it begins to drip. What causes this physical change to take place in your frozen treat?

Active Reading As you read this page, underline its main idea.

The sticky juice dripping down your arm is caused by a change in state. A change in state is a physical change that takes place when heat energy is added or removed from matter. When you take a juice pop out of the freezer, the pop begins to warm up. As a result, the solid juice begins to melt.

Melting is a change in state from a solid to a liquid. It takes place when heat energy is added to a solid.

Evaporation is a change in state from a liquid to a gas. It takes place when heat energy is added to a liquid. When the water in a melted juice pop evaporates, sugar, syrup, and food coloring are left behind.

You can make your own pops by freezing liquid juice. Freezing is a change in state from a liquid to a solid. It takes place when heat energy is removed from liquids.

Physical Changes

Making glass and candles are examples of physical changes. To make a glass pitcher, solid glass is heated. The glass melts and becomes a thick liquid. Then, the melted glass is molded or blown into shape. When the glass cools, it hardens into a solid.

152

© Houghton Mifflin Harcourt Publishing Company   (bl) ©ABED AL HAFIZ HASHLAMOUN/epa/Corbis; (br) ©PhotoStock-Israel/Alamy Images

Melt, Pour, and Mold

To make candles, people melt, pour, and mold—all these are physical changes.

1 When heat is added, the solid wax melts and becomes a liquid. You may add a color dye to the liquid wax.

2 The liquid wax takes the shape of the mold. It releases heat energy as it cools.

3 When the change in state is complete, the wax forms a solid candle.

▶ Ice is a solid. Predict which physical changes ice will undergo when it is removed from a freezer. Why do these changes take place?

_____

_____

_____

© Houghton Mifflin Harcourt Publishing Company

Mix It Up!

What do a salad, the air you breathe, and coins in a piggy bank have in common? They are all mixtures.

Active Reading As you read these two pages, underline the main idea on each page.

Sand is a tan-colored solid. Water is a liquid. If you put sand and water into a bucket, they form a mixture because their properties do not change. A **mixture** is a combination of two or more substances that keep their identities. The sand is still a tan solid, and the water is still a liquid. Neither has become a different substance.

A salad is also a mixture. When you mix lettuce, tomatoes, carrots, and other vegetables, no new substances are made. For this reason, making a mixture is a physical change.

This jar contains a mixture of rubber balls and marbles.

Mixtures

Salad dressing is a mixture. The oil and vinegar mix when shaken. If the dressing sits, the oil and vinegar will separate.

154

© Houghton Mifflin Harcourt Publishing Company

Most mixtures can be separated fairly easily. For example, you could pick all the tomatoes and carrots out of a salad. Or, you could separate the sand and water mixture by pouring it through a filter with a paper cone. The water would seep through, but the sand would not. What would happen if you poured a mixture of rocks and sand into a colander? Only the smaller sand pieces would pass through the colander's holes—not the larger rocks, which would separate this mixture.

Granola is a mixture of oats, nuts, dried fruit, and honey. The sticky honey keeps the parts of the granola mixture together.

When you mix sand with water, the sand settles to the bottom of the mixture. However, a mixture of rocks and sand stays mixed.

Compare and Contrast Mixtures

Identify two examples of mixtures. Compare and contrast these examples and describe how they are alike and different.

_____

_____

_____

_____

_____

_____

© Houghton Mifflin Harcourt Publishing Company   (c) ©nagelestock.com/Alamy Images

You Have a Solution!

A solution is a specific type of mixture. What makes up a solution?

Active Reading As you read these two pages, find and underline the definitions of important terms.

A **solution** is a mixture in which all parts are evenly mixed. Solutions can be combinations of gases, liquids, and solids. For example, what happens if you melt two solids, dissolve one in the other, then let them solidify? You have a solid solution!

Some metals are solid solutions. To make some rings, gold and another metal, such as copper, are melted together. When the liquid metals are evenly mixed, they are poured into a mold where they cool and harden to form a solid ring.

Seawater is a solution of solids that are dissolved in a liquid. Most of the solid parts of seawater are salts. Its liquid part, water, is a solvent. The *solvent* is the substance present in the largest amount and in which the other parts are dissolved.

Solutions

Seawater is a solution in which minerals and salts are dissolved in water. The necklace is a solution of gold and copper.

© Houghton Mifflin Harcourt Publishing Company   (c) ©Jupiterimages Corporation

Compare and Contrast Mixtures and Solutions

Use this chart to compare and contrast mixtures and solutions.

Mixtures	Both	Solutions

Lemonade is a solution made up of water, sugar, and lemon juice. The sugar (a solid) and the lemon juice (a liquid) are dissolved in the water, which is the solvent.

Do the Math!

Calculate Amounts

Kendra dissolved as much sugar as she could in a beaker of water. The solution had a ratio of 210 g/100 mL, or 210 grams of sugar to 100 milliliters of water.

How much sugar can be dissolved in 200 milliliters of water?

_____

_____

How much sugar can be dissolved in 700 milliliters of water?

_____

_____

© Houghton Mifflin Harcourt Publishing Company

Cleaning Up an Oily Mess

Water is a solvent in many solutions. In fact, water is called the universal solvent. Water can dissolve more things than any other known solvent.

Given enough time, rocks will dissolve in water. However, something that will *not* dissolve in water is oil. When you mix oil and water, the oil forms drops or layers that float on the water.

Oil can be messy when it gets on things. Water alone can't clean up an oily mess. People need to mix water with detergent.

Soaps, such as the types used to wash our bodies, and dishwashing and laundry detergents, have ingredients that help water break up oil and wash it away.

© Houghton Mifflin Harcourt Publishing Company

Detergent particles form bonds with water particles and reduce their ability to bond to each other. Detergent particles also form bonds with oil particles. Detergent and water work together to break up oil into smaller particles that can be washed away.

Detergents can be used to clean up the environment. In 2010, an oil rig exploded in the Gulf of Mexico spilling millions of gallons of oil. The oil affected many marine plants and animals, including water birds. The oil stuck to the birds' feathers, making it hard for them to swim, fly, and keep warm. To clean up the birds, wildlife scientists and volunteers used dishwashing detergent.

Detergent bonds with oil particles on the bird's feathers and helps water wash the particles away.

▶ Write the answer to each question in the space provided.

Why can't water alone help wash away oil?	Why is using detergent and water to clean oil a physical change?

© Houghton Mifflin Harcourt Publishing Company   (tr) ©Accent Alaska.com/Alamy Images

Sum It Up!

When you're done, use the answer key to check and revise your work.

Use the information in the summary to complete the graphic organizer.

Summarize

A physical change is a change in which no new substances are formed. A mixture is a combination of two or more substances that keep their own identities. A solution is a mixture with evenly mixed substances. In a solution, a solute is the smaller part and is the substance that is dissolved. A solvent is the substance present in the largest amount in which other parts dissolve in a solution. Because substances in a mixture retain their identities, making a mixture is a physical change.

1 Main Idea:

_____

_____

2 Detail:

_____
_____
_____
_____
_____
_____

3 Detail:

_____
_____
_____
_____
_____
_____

4 Detail:

_____
_____
_____
_____
_____
_____

Answer Key: 1. A mixture is a combination of two or more substances that keep their identities. 2.–4. (in any order) A solution is a mixture with evenly mixed substances.; Because the substances in a mixture retain their identities, making a mixture is a physical change.; In a solution, a solvent is the substance present in the largest amount in which the other parts are dissolved.

© Houghton Mifflin Harcourt Publishing Company

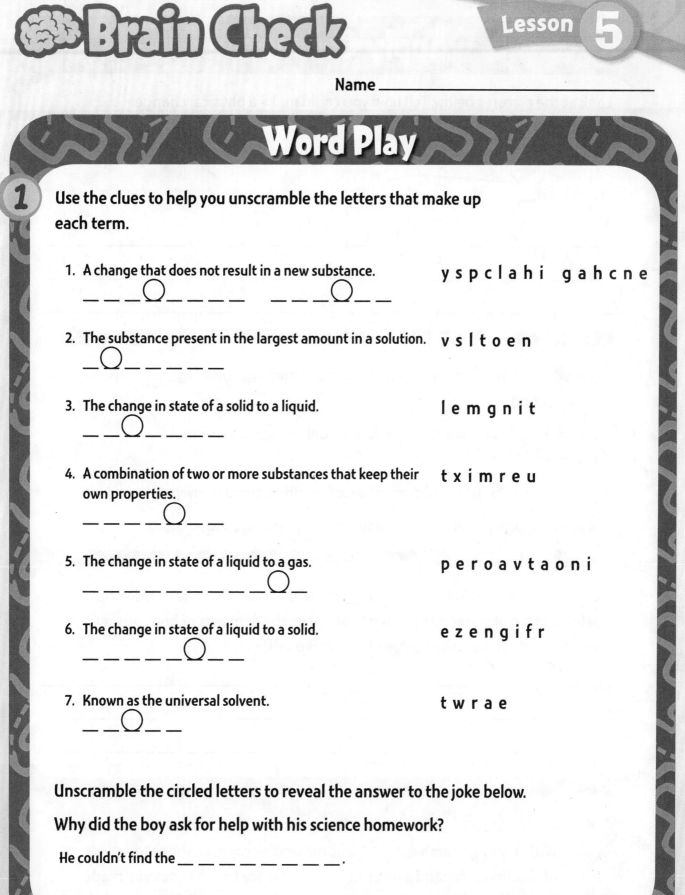

Brain Check

Name _____

Word Play

1 Use the clues to help you unscramble the letters that make up each term.

1. A change that does not result in a new substance.
_ _ _ O _ _ _ _   _ _ _ O _ _

y s p c l a h i   g a h c n e

2. The substance present in the largest amount in a solution.
_ O _ _ _ _ _

v s l t o e n

3. The change in state of a solid to a liquid.
_ _ O _ _ _ _

l e m g n i t

4. A combination of two or more substances that keep their own properties.
_ _ _ O _ _ _

t x i m r e u

5. The change in state of a liquid to a gas.
_ _ _ _ _ _ _ _ _ O _

p e r o a v t a o n i

6. The change in state of a liquid to a solid.
_ _ _ _ _ O _ _

e z e n g i f r

7. Known as the universal solvent.
_ _ O _ _

t w r a e

Unscramble the circled letters to reveal the answer to the joke below.

Why did the boy ask for help with his science homework?

He couldn't find the _ _ _ _ _ _ _ _.

© Houghton Mifflin Harcourt Publishing Company

Apply Concepts

2 Look at the pictures below. Tell how you could make a physical change to each one.

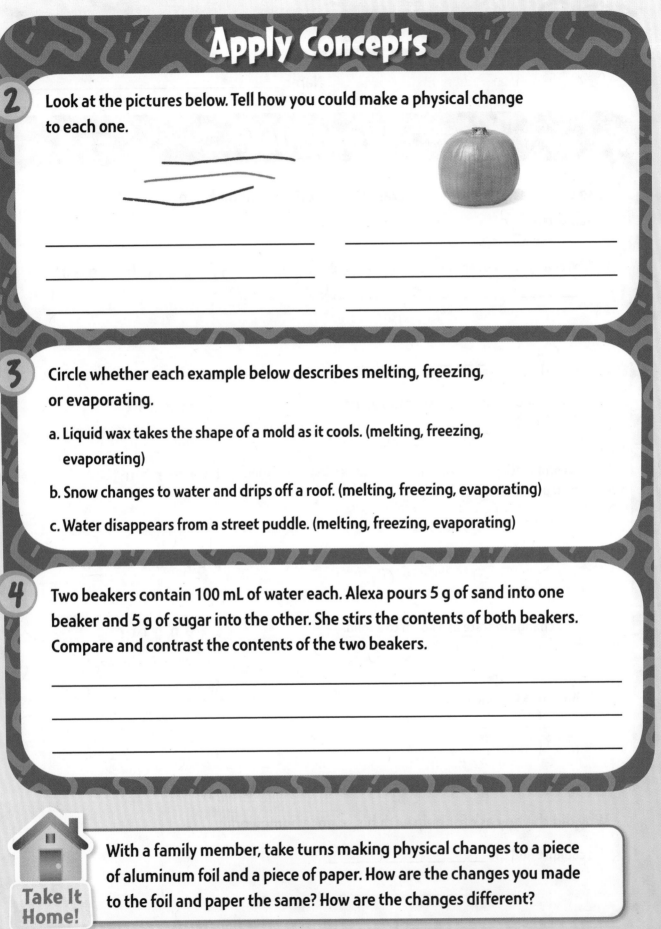

_____   _____

_____   _____

_____   _____

3 Circle whether each example below describes melting, freezing, or evaporating.

a. Liquid wax takes the shape of a mold as it cools. (melting, freezing, evaporating)

b. Snow changes to water and drips off a roof. (melting, freezing, evaporating)

c. Water disappears from a street puddle. (melting, freezing, evaporating)

4 Two beakers contain 100 mL of water each. Alexa pours 5 g of sand into one beaker and 5 g of sugar into the other. She stirs the contents of both beakers. Compare and contrast the contents of the two beakers.

_____

_____

_____

Take It Home! With a family member, take turns making physical changes to a piece of aluminum foil and a piece of paper. How are the changes you made to the foil and paper the same? How are the changes different?

© Houghton Mifflin Harcourt Publishing Company

Inquiry Flipchart page 23

TEKS **4.2A** ...implement descriptive investigations, including... using appropriate equipment... **4.2B** ...record data by observing... using descriptive words... **4.5C** compare and contrast a variety of mixtures and solutions such as... sugar in water

Name _____

Essential Question

How Can We Make a Solution?

Set a Purpose
What will you learn from this investigation?

_____

_____

_____

_____

Think About the Procedure
In this investigation, which substance is a solvent, and what does it do?

_____

_____

_____

_____

What are some variables in this investigation?

_____

_____

_____

_____

Record Your Data
Draw and describe how each cup looked after Step 2.

Before Stirring	
"Water" Cup	"Alcohol" Cup

Now draw and describe how each cup looked after Steps 3 and 4.

After Stirring	
"Water" Cup	"Alcohol" Cup

© Houghton Mifflin Harcourt Publishing Company   HMH Credits

Draw Conclusions

What did the combination of water and sugar form? Explain your answer.

_____

_____

_____

_____

What did the combination of alcohol and sugar form? Explain your answer.

_____

_____

_____

Compare and contrast the combination of water and sugar with the combination of alcohol and sugar. Describe how they are alike and different.

_____

_____

_____

_____

_____

Analyze and Extend

1. Why was it important to use the same amount of water and alcohol?

_____

_____

_____

2. Why did stirring help dissolve the sugar in the water?

_____

_____

_____

_____

3. Why is forming a mixture a physical change?

_____

_____

_____

_____

4. What other questions would you like to ask about mixtures and solutions?

_____

_____

_____

_____

_____

© Houghton Mifflin Harcourt Publishing Company   HMH Credits

Name _____

Vocabulary Review

Use the terms in the box to complete the sentences.

> condensation
> evaporation
> physical property
> solution
> states of matter

TEKS 4.5A

1. A characteristic of matter that you can observe or measure

   directly is a(n) _____.

TEKS 4.5B

2. The process by which a gas changes to a liquid

   is _____.

TEKS 4.5C

3. A mixture that has the same composition throughout because

   all the parts are mixed evenly is a(n) _____.

TEKS 4.5A

4. Solid, liquid, and gas are three _____.

TEKS 4.5B

5. The process by which a liquid changes to a gas

   is _____.

Science Concepts

Fill in the letter choice that best answers the question.

TEKS 4.5A

6. Lila is measuring the physical properties of an object. Which property is she measuring when she determines the amount of space an object takes up?

   (A) mass

   (B) density

   (C) volume

   (D) weight

TEKS 4.5A

7. Alden is measuring the physical properties of an apple. The apple has a mass of 224 g. He then slices the apple into four pieces with different sizes. What can he conclude about the mass of the pieces?

   (A) The mass of each piece is 224 g.

   (B) The total mass of the four pieces is 224 g.

   (C) Each piece has a mass that is slightly less than 56 g.

   (D) Each piece has a mass that is slightly more than 56 g.

© Houghton Mifflin Harcourt Publishing Company (border) ©NDisk/Age Fotostock

TEKS 4.5B

8. Which process names a change you could predict would happen to water due to cooling?

   Ⓐ boiling

   Ⓑ evaporating

   Ⓒ freezing

   Ⓓ melting

TEKS 4.5A

9. William is measuring, comparing, and contrasting the physical properties of matter, including temperature. Which of the following most likely has the highest temperature?

   Ⓐ hot tap water

   Ⓑ cold tap water

   Ⓒ bottled water

   Ⓓ boiling water

TEKS 4.5A

10. Which physical properties listed below describe liquids?

   Ⓐ definite shape; definite volume

   Ⓑ definite shape; no definite volume

   Ⓒ no definite shape; definite volume

   Ⓓ no definite shape; no definite volume

TEKS 4.4A, 4.5A

11. You are collecting information about an object. Which tool would you use to measure the object's mass?

   Ⓐ

   Ⓑ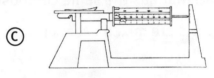

   Ⓒ

   Ⓓ

TEKS 4.5C

12. Mary Ellen is comparing and contrasting the mixtures in her kitchen. Which mixture is a solution?

   Ⓐ granola

   Ⓑ garden salad

   Ⓒ lemonade

   Ⓓ gelatin with bananas

© Houghton Mifflin Harcourt Publishing Company   (border) ©NDisk/Age Fotostock

© Houghton Mifflin Harcourt Publishing Company   (border) ©NDisk/Age Fotostock

TEKS 4.5A

13. Graciella is measuring, comparing, and contrasting the physical properties of several objects. This picture shows the setup she uses.

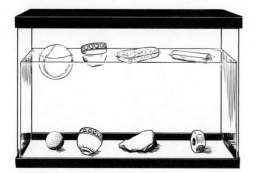

Which physical property is Graciella measuring?

(A) size

(B) mass

(C) state of matter

(D) the ability to sink or float

TEKS 4.5A

14. Ernesto is measuring, comparing, and contrasting the physical properties of objects, including magnetism. Which object do you predict Ernesto will find to be the most magnetic?

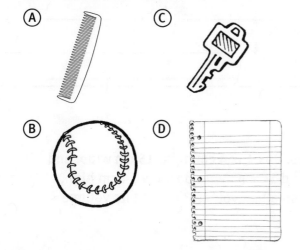

TEKS 4.5A

15. These diagrams show the particles that make up water. Which diagram shows how the particles are arranged when the water is a solid?

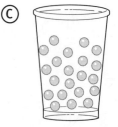
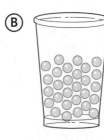
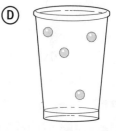

TEKS 4.5B

16. Which set of changes would you predict would take place to an ice cube that is heated?

(A) solid → gas → liquid

(B) solid → liquid → gas

(C) liquid → solid → gas

(D) liquid → gas → solid

Apply Inquiry and Review the Big Idea

Write the answers to these questions.

TEKS 4.2C

17. Linea collected these data during an investigation:

    Sample 1: 16 g; Sample 2: 4 g; Sample 3: 21 g; Sample 4: 18 g

    Construct a simple table and a bar graph to organize Linea's data.

TEKS 4.4A, 4.5A

18. Jason wants to find the volume of two irregularly shaped rocks. How could he use these tools to find the volume of these rocks?

_____

_____

_____

_____

TEKS 4.5A

19. Bhopinder compares the volumes of three boxes. Box 1 is 4 cm high, 15 cm wide, and 22 cm deep. Box 2 is 11 cm high, 10 cm wide, and 14 cm deep. Box 3 is 14 cm high, 6 cm wide, and 22 cm deep. Which box has the smallest volume? Record its volume.

_____

© Houghton Mifflin Harcourt Publishing Company (border) ©NDisk/Age Fotostock

Forms of Energy

Big Idea

Energy exists in many forms that can be transferred between objects.

TEKS 4.2B, 4.2C, 4.2D, 4.2E, 4.3A, 4.3D, 4.6A, 4.6B

I Wonder Why

This surfer lets many waves go by him before choosing one to ride. Why? *Turn the page to find out.*

© Houghton Mifflin Harcourt Publishing Company (bkgd) ©Tony Arruza/Alamy; (inset) ©Tetra Images/Alamy; (border) ©NDb/Age Fotostock

Here's Why The best waves have a lot of energy. Surfers use the energy from these waves to get a nice, long ride to shore.

In this unit, you will explore the Big Idea, the Essential Questions, and the Investigations on the Inquiry Flipchart.

Levels of Inquiry Key ■ DIRECTED ■ GUIDED ■ INDEPENDENT

Track Your Progress

Big Idea Energy exists in many forms that can be transferred between objects.

Essential Questions

Now I Get the Big Idea!

Science Notebook

Before you begin each lesson, be sure to write your thoughts about the Essential Question.

© Houghton Mifflin Harcourt Publishing Company (tr) ©Tony Arruza/Alamy Images; (inset) ©Tetra Images/Alamy Images; (border) ©NDisc/Age Fotostock

Essential Question
What Are Some Forms of Energy?

Engage Your Brain!

Find the answer to the following question in this lesson and record it here.

How does this person use energy to ride the river's rapids?

_____

_____

_____

_____

Active Reading

Lesson Vocabulary
List the terms. As you learn about each one, make notes in the Interactive Glossary.

_____   _____

_____   _____

_____   _____

_____   _____

Main Idea and Details
In this lesson, you'll read about different kinds of energy. Active readers look for main ideas before they read to give their reading a purpose. Often, the headings in a lesson state the main ideas. Preview the headings in this lesson to give your reading a purpose.

© Houghton Mifflin Harcourt Publishing Company (bkgd) ©Chris Fredriksson/Alamy

What Is Energy?

All the lights in your house need energy. So do the refrigerator and washing machine. Can you name three other things in your home or school that use energy?

Active Reading As you read these two pages, find and underline a definition of *energy*. Then circle two sources of energy.

What do you and a car have in common? You both need energy. Gasoline is the car's source of energy. This car won't go anywhere if it runs out of gas.

▶ Draw lines to match each item on the left with its source of energy.

Name something that uses electricity as a source of energy.

_____

_____

© Houghton Mifflin Harcourt Publishing Company (gas sign) ©Jason Lindsey/Alamy; (car) ©Robert Kerian/Transtock Inc./Alamy; (rocket toy) ©Daniel Hurst/Editorial/Alamy; (gas can) ©Comstock/Getty Images

Making an object move is a change. **Energy** is the ability to cause change in matter. So, everything that moves has energy.

Where does energy come from? You can see some sources of energy on these two pages. What sources of energy have you used today?

Where does this toy get its energy?

_____

_____

This man needs energy to run. Where do you think he gets it? Runners eat healthful foods such as trail mix so they will have plenty of energy.

© Houghton Mifflin Harcourt Publishing Company   (rocket toy) ©Daniel Hurst/Editorial/Alamy; (eat sign) ©Alan Copson/Getty Images; (man) ©imagebroker/Alamy

Get Moving!

Have you ever been on a roller coaster? When roller coaster cars climb a hill, they seem to stop at the top for just a moment. Then they speed down to the bottom. How does energy make this happen?

Active Reading As you read these two pages, find and underline the definition of *mechanical energy*. Then draw circles around the two parts of mechanical energy.

Something in motion, such as the girl on the pogo stick, has kinetic energy. **Kinetic energy** is the energy of motion. Something at the top of a hill, such as a roller coaster car, has potential energy. **Potential energy** is the energy something has because of its position or condition. **Mechanical energy** is the total potential energy and kinetic energy of an object.

As the roller coaster cars climb to the top of a hill, they gain potential energy. The higher the cars go, the more potential energy they have. As the cars go down a hill, their potential energy decreases because it changes to kinetic energy. The roller coaster cars have more kinetic energy when they move faster. At each point along the ride, the mechanical energy of the cars is the sum of their potential and kinetic energies.

The girl pushes the pogo stick's spring down. The spring now has potential energy. When the spring spreads out, the pogo stick goes up and has kinetic energy.

©Houghton Mifflin Harcourt Publishing Company (toy airplane) ©Dave Teel/Corbis; (sky) ©Corbis

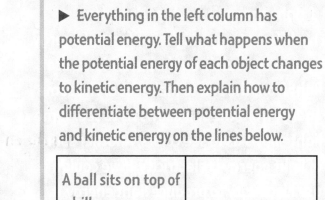

This roller coaster goes fast because of mechanical energy. That's good, because a slow roller coaster isn't much fun!

▶ Everything in the left column has potential energy. Tell what happens when the potential energy of each object changes to kinetic energy. Then explain how to differentiate between potential energy and kinetic energy on the lines below.

A ball sits on top of a hill	
A person stretches back a rubber band	
Someone gets ready to throw a paper airplane	

_____

_____

_____

_____

_____

© Houghton Mifflin Harcourt Publishing Company   (br) ©Jason Smalley/Wildscape/Alamy; (t) ©Corbis; (c) ©Jason Smalley/Wildscape/Alamy

Flash and Boom!

You see lightning flash across the sky. You hear a boom so loud it makes your heart pound. These are two forms of energy.

Light energy is made and used in different ways. Light is a form of energy that can travel through space. Plants use light from the sun to make food. The same energy from the sun allows us to see. Some light allows us to see colors. Another source of light energy is electricity. If we couldn't use electricity to produce light energy, it would be hard to work or play at night.

Another form of energy is sound. Sound is made when something moves back and forth. This back-and-forth motion is called *vibration*. Sound can move through gases, liquids, and solids. Sound cannot move through space, as light can. We cannot see sound, but we can hear it. Sound is described in different ways. *Pitch* describes how high or how low a sound is. Loud sounds have more energy than quiet sounds. Can you think of an example of a loud, high-pitched sound?

Do the Math!
Solve Real-World Problems

How far away was that lightning strike? As soon as you see a flash of lightning, count the seconds until you hear thunder. Then divide the number of seconds by 5. This number gives you the approximate distance in miles.

35 seconds _____

20 seconds _____

40 seconds _____

Lightning can be hotter than the surface of the sun. Lightning makes the air around it expand quickly. This expansion causes the boom of thunder.

Houghton Mifflin Harcourt Publishing Company   (bkgd) ©James Kay/Stock Connection/Alamy (t, tr) ©Westend61 GmbH/Alamy

▶ Describe how each member of this musical group produces sound. Write your answers in the spaces provided.

▶ How are light and sound alike? How are they different?

© Houghton Mifflin Harcourt Publishing Company (bkg) ©James Kay/Stock Connection/Alamy

Energy at Home

Do you think you could do without energy for one day? Without chemical energy, you couldn't mow the lawn. Without electrical energy, you couldn't power your MP3 player.

Active Reading As you read these two pages, draw a circle around a use of chemical energy. Draw a box around a use of electrical energy.

Electrical energy

Electrical energy

Chemical energy

©Houghton Mifflin Harcourt Publishing Company (horse) ©Tim Flach/Getty Images (car) ©Car Culture/Corbis (leaf blower) ©Hugh Threlfall/Alamy (folding chair) ©Burazin/Getty Images (porch light) ©kpzfoto/Alamy

Many things use chemical energy and electrical energy. **Chemical energy** is a form of energy than can be released by a chemical change. Chemical energy from food gives us energy. Most cars run on gasoline, a source of chemical energy. Have you ever warmed yourself by a campfire? Fire is the release of chemical energy.

Electrical energy is a form of energy that comes from electric current. Electrical energy provides the energy for most of the devices you use, such as computers and televisions. Anything plugged into a wall outlet uses electrical energy.

Where does electricity come from? In most cities, electricity is generated using the chemical energy released during the burning of fossil fuels such as coal and natural gas. The sun and wind can also be used to generate electricity.

Electrical energy

Electrical energy

Chemical energy

Chemical energy

▶ Identify the things in this scene that use chemical energy and those that use electrical energy. Write your answers in the spaces provided. Then, write to describe how chemical energy differs from electrical energy.

The difirents of Chemical and Electrical is that Electrical comes from electric current. Chemical is released by a chemical change

©Houghton Mifflin Harcourt Publishing Company (folding chain) ©Junior's Bildarchiv/Alamy; (dog) ©Junior's Bildarchiv/Alamy; (grill) ©Dorling Kindersley/Getty Images; (lawn mower) ©Stockbyte/Getty Images; (horse) ©David Robertson/Alamy; (power lines) ©Tim Flach/Getty Images;

Some Like it Hot!

Rub your hands together quickly and then press them against your face. Your hands and face feel warm. Why?

Active Reading As you read these two pages, underline the definition of *thermal energy* and circle an example of it.

Cool hands become warm when rubbed together. A toaster oven makes freshly toasted bread feel hot. An ice sculpture melts. All these changes involve the transfer of heat.

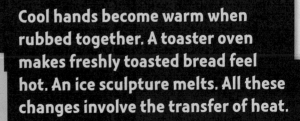

© Houghton Mifflin Harcourt Publishing Company   (cr) ©CulturalEyes/AusSoc/Alamy Images

You know that kinetic energy is the energy of motion. The particles that make up a substance are always moving. These moving particles make your rubbed hands or toast feel warm. **Thermal energy** is the total kinetic energy of the particles in a substance. The faster the particles in a substance move, the more thermal energy the substance has.

Heat is energy that moves between objects at different temperatures. It moves from warmer objects to cooler objects. Many objects around us, such as a toaster or a campfire, give off heat.

Look at the picture of the sculptor. She is using a blowtorch on a piece of metal. As she does this, the particles in the metal being touched by the torch begin to vibrate faster and faster. The metal's thermal energy is transferred, or moved, along it. As the thermal energy moves, the metal becomes heated.

Differentiate Between Heat and Thermal Energy

Write to describe how heat and thermal energy differ.

_____

_____

_____

_____

_____

_____

_____

Particles in a solid vibrate, or move back and forth, quickly. As the metal is heated, the particles move faster, which causes heat to be felt.

© Houghton Mifflin Harcourt Publishing Company (bc) ©Marwood Jenkins/Alamy Images

Energy Can Change Forms

Can you read by the light of chemical energy?
Can you use electrical energy to make something
move? You can do both of these things, and more.

Active Reading As you read these two pages, draw a line under two
examples of energy changing forms.

Chemical energy changes into
light energy in a glow stick.

© Houghton Mifflin Harcourt Publishing Company

Energy can change from one form to another. Electrical energy changes to light energy when you turn on a light switch. You may also feel the heat given off by some light bulbs. Chemical energy in gasoline changes to mechanical energy when a driver presses the gas pedal to drive.

Glow sticks have a glass tube inside them. The glass tube has chemicals inside it. When you bend the glow stick, the tube breaks. The chemicals in the tube mix with other chemicals in the glow stick. When they mix, light energy is given off.

A remote control sends radio waves to the remote-controlled car. Radio waves are another form of energy, similar to light energy. The radio waves change to electrical energy to tell the motor what to do—start, stop, or go faster. The car also has batteries inside it. The batteries change chemical energy to electrical energy to move the car.

This plant changes light energy from the sun into chemical energy in food.

Energy Changing Forms

Draw a picture to show another way energy can change form. Write a caption that describes how the two forms of energy in your picture differ.

_____

_____

© Houghton Mifflin Harcourt Publishing Company   (br) ©Mode Images Limited/Alamy; (cr) ©Inga spence/Alamy

Sum It Up!

When you're done, use the answer key to check and revise your work.

Use information in the summary to complete the graphic organizer.

Summarize

Energy is the ability to cause change in matter. Making an object move is a change. So, everything that moves has energy. Kinetic energy is the energy of motion. Potential energy is the energy something has because of its position. The mechanical energy of an object is the sum of its kinetic and potential energies. Light energy enables plants to make food and helps us see. Sound energy is caused by a vibrating object. Thermal energy is the total kinetic energy of the particles in a substance. Heat is energy that moves between objects at different temperatures. Energy can change from one form to another.

Cause → **Effect**

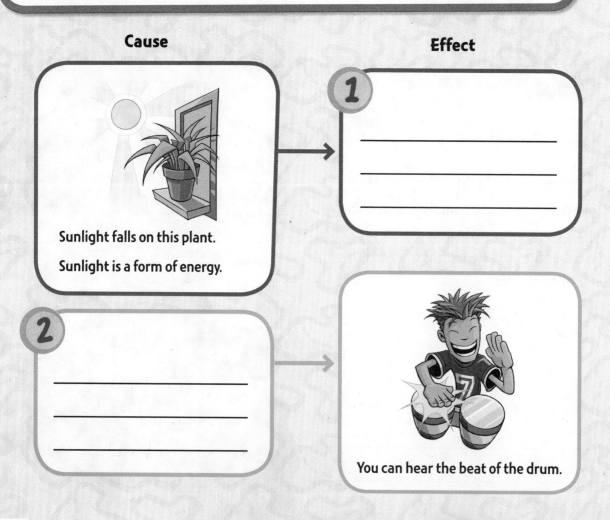

Sunlight falls on this plant.

Sunlight is a form of energy.

→ 1 ______________________

____

____

2 ______________________

____

____

→

You can hear the beat of the drum.

Answer Key: 1. The plant captures light energy from the sun and uses it to make food.
2. The drum heads vibrate to make sound.

© Houghton Mifflin Harcourt Publishing Company

4 A light bulb changes electrical energy into two other forms of energy. Identify these forms of energy and tell how they differ from one another.

_____

_____

_____

_____

5 Which of these objects has potential energy? How do you know?

_____

_____

_____

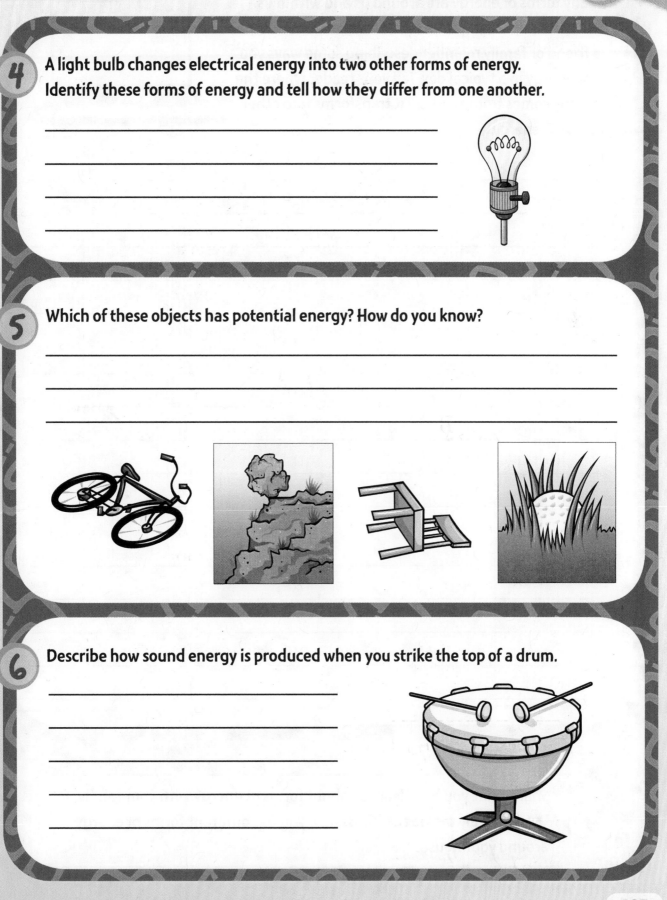

6 Describe how sound energy is produced when you strike the top of a drum.

_____

_____

_____

_____

_____

© Houghton Mifflin Harcourt Publishing Company

7 Many forms of energy are around us and within us. Write three paragraphs in the form of an e-mail to a friend or family member describing some ways you use energy in a typical day. Tell your reader where the energy comes from and how it transforms into other forms of energy.

_____

_____

_____

_____

_____

_____

_____

_____

_____

_____

_____

_____

_____

_____

Take It Home!

Share what you have learned about forms of energy with your family. With a family member, discuss how you use different forms of energy around your house.

© Houghton Mifflin Harcourt Publishing Company

TEKS **4.2B** ...record data... observing and measuring...... numerals... **4.2C** ...co....... simple tables...using tools.......ganize... data **4.2D** analy.......a...to construct reasonable ex.........ons... **4.2E** perfo.... .peated investigations to increa.......ability of results **4.3A** ....alyze scientific ex..........ons...to encourage critical ......ng... **4.6A** differentiate .....ong forms of energy, including mechanical...

Name _____

Essential Question

Where Does Energy Come From?

Set a Purpose

What will you learn from this investigation?

_____

_____

_____

_____

_____

_____

Think About th.... ....cedure

How does repeati.... ....increase the reliability of v....

_____

_____

_____

_____

Rec.... d Your Data

In .....e space below, construct a simple .....ble to record and organize your data. Be sure to use numerals.

© Houghton Mifflin Harcourt Publishing Compa....

Draw Conclusions

Analyze your data to construct a reasonable explanation. What did you observe in this investigation?

_____

_____

Analyze and Extend

1. Why do you think the ball traveled farther when it was pushed by the fully compressed spring?

_____

_____

_____

2. When you compressed the spring, it gained potential energy. What was the source of this energy?

_____

_____

_____

3. What happened to the spring's potential energy when you let go of the ball?

_____

_____

_____

4. Scientists explain that the further a spring is compressed, the more potential energy it has. Analyze why squeezing the spring halfway affects the distance the ball travels.

_____

_____

_____

_____

_____

5. Did each group in the class have the same results from the investigation? Why or why not?

_____

_____

_____

_____

_____

6. Think of other questions you would like to ask about energy and how it changes form.

_____

_____

_____

_____

_____

190

© Houghton Mifflin Harcourt Publishing Company

Essential Question

How Does Heat Move?

Engage Your Brain!

Find the answer to the following question in this lesson and record it here.

Most photographs show people and objects as we see them. What do you think this photograph shows?

_____

_____

_____

Active Reading

Lesson Vocabulary

List the terms. As you learn about each one, make notes in the Interactive Glossary.

_____

_____

_____

_____

Signal Words: Contrast

Signal words show connections between ideas. Words that signal contrasts include *unlike, different from, but,* and *on the other hand.* Active readers remember what they read because they are alert to signal words that identify contrasts.

© Houghton Mifflin Harcourt Publishing Company (bkgd) ©Ted Kinsman/Photo Researchers, Inc.

The Energy of Heat

It takes heat to shape glass or to make tea. But what is heat, exactly? Think about it for a moment. How would you define *heat*?

Active Reading As you read, circle the definitions of heat and thermal energy to differentiate between these forms of energy.

You know that *thermal energy* is the total kinetic energy of the particles of a substance. You also know that *temperature* measures how hot or cold something is. **Heat** is the energy that moves, or is transferred, between the particles of two objects or substances that differ in temperature. The difference in temperature makes the energy move.

You sense heat as a warming feeling. More precisely, you feel the change in temperature as you gain energy. Heat moves naturally from an object with a higher temperature to one with a lower temperature. In other words, heat moves from a warmer object to a cooler object.

Super Hot

You can see and feel heat moving from the flame to the glass. This melted glass is about 1,500 °C (2,732 °F)!

Incredibly Cold

This is dry ice—frozen carbon dioxide. It is really cold—about –80 °C (–112 °F).

© Houghton Mifflin Harcourt Publishing Company   (t) ©Bill Brooks/Alamy

Do the Math!
Use Temperature Scales

Temperature is measured in different scales. The two scales on this thermometer are Celsius and Fahrenheit. Write the letter of each picture at the appropriate place on the thermometer.

A

This girl's clothes trap heat near her body. Her jacket slows down energy transfer to the cold air. This girl stays warm while playing in the snow in temperatures as low as 0 °C (32 °F).

B

The water coming from this shower head is hotter than the air around it. The average temperature of shower water is 42 °C (108 °F).

D

Heat moves from the burner to the kettle, from the kettle to the water, and then from the water vapor to the air. Water boils at 100 °C (212 °F).

C

Ice cubes melt as heat transfers to them from the warm air. The puddle of water is about 20 °C (68 °F).

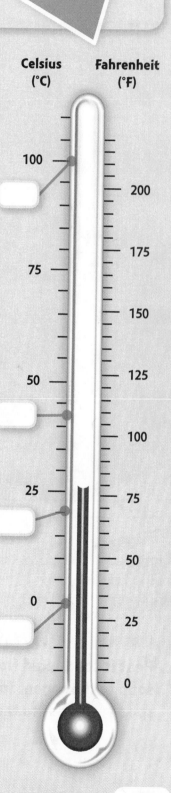

Celsius (°C)   Fahrenheit (°F)

100

200

75

175

150

50

125

100

25

75

50

0

25

0

© Houghton Mifflin Harcourt Publishing Company   (tl) ©Michael Ventura/Alamy; (tr) ©Will Stanton/Alamy; (br) ©Steve Hamblin/Alamy

Heat on the Move!

Heat can move in different ways.

Active Reading As you read these two pages, draw circles around each main idea.

Heat is conducted from your hand into the snow. The snow melts. Your hand feels cold.

Conduction

Conduction is the transfer, or movement, of heat between two objects that are touching. It can also occur *within* an object. Heat moves from inside your body to warm your skin. Your feet and hands stay warm because heat moves all around your body.

Heat is conducted from the soup to the spoon. Soon the spoon feels hot to the touch.

© Houghton Mifflin Harcourt Publishing Company (t) ©MM photo/Alamy

1. Heat is conducted from the burner to the pot to the water.

2. Heated water travels up, warming the cooler water above.

3. Cooler water sinks to the bottom, where it gets heated. The cycle repeats. This movement is called a *convection current*.

Convection

Convection is the transfer of heat within a liquid or a gas. Particles in liquids and gases move easily, and they take heat with them. Heat from a campfire warms the air around it by convection. Warmer air is always buoyed upward. In this case, the fire is the source of heat for convection.

Hot air rises above cooler air. That's what keeps a hot-air balloon in flight.

▶ Write the type of heat transfer that takes place in the following situations.

An eruption of lava on the ocean floor

_____

Winds blowing in from a warmer part of the country

_____

Feet touching a cold floor

_____

© Houghton Mifflin Harcourt Publishing Company   (t) ©Charles D. Winters/Photo Researchers, Inc.; (c) ©PhotoDisc/Getty Images; (r) ©Itani Images/Alamy

Feeling Radiant!

Heat moves by conduction between solids that are touching. Heat moves by convection through gases and liquids. But can heat travel without moving through matter? Find out.

Active Reading As you read the next page, draw boxes around the clue words or phrases that signal one thing is being contrasted with another.

Heat travels from the campfire by convection and radiation.

© Houghton Mifflin Harcourt Publishing Company   ©Getty Images/PhotoDisc

The third way heat can move is radiation. **Radiation** is the transfer of heat without matter to carry it. Heat simply leaves one object and goes directly to another. Suppose you're standing near a campfire. You can feel the heat from the fire because it warms the air. But you can also feel the heat because it warms you directly through radiation.

In some ways, radiation may be the most important way heat can move. Life on Earth needs heat from the sun. But space is a vacuum. How does heat travel through the emptiness of space? By radiation.

The room is cool and air-conditioned. On the other hand, heat radiating from this light keeps the young chickens warm.

▶ Circle the objects that are radiating heat.

Heat from the sun radiates through space and through the atmosphere before it warms this girl's face.

© Houghton Mifflin Harcourt Publishing Company (c) ©Lars Langemeier/A.B./Corbis

When you're done, use the answer key to check and revise your work.

Fill in the missing words to complete the conversation.

Summarize

Rebecca: Ow! How did my cell phone get so hot?

Abdullah: Well, there are (1) _____ ways that heat could have moved into your phone.

Rebecca: I know. If it had been sitting in sunlight, I'd know it was heated through (2) _____ . But it was in the shade.

Abdullah: Well, there's also convection.

Rebecca: Yeah, but that only happens within (3) _____ and (4) _____ . My phone's a solid.

Abdullah: Then it must have been the third way: (5) _____ .

Rebecca: But that only happens when two things are (6) _____ each other. My phone was sitting by itself.

Abdullah: Where?

Rebecca: On top of my laptop.

Abdullah: In that case, heat traveled into your phone through (7) _____ .

Rebecca: Really? How does it do that?

Abdullah: Heat moves from warm objects to (8) _____ objects. Your laptop was probably much warmer than your cell phone.

Rebecca: Maybe I'll leave it on my wooden desk from now on!

Answer Key: 1. three 2. radiation 3. liquids/gases 4. gases/liquids 5. conduction 6. touching 7. conduction 8. cool

© Houghton Mifflin Harcourt Publishing Company

Name _____

Word Play

1 Unscramble each word and write it in the boxes.

How heat moves from one end of a solid to the other

C C N O T N O I U D

☐ ☐ ☐ ☐ Ⓞ ☐ Ⓞ ☐ ☐ ☐

The topic of this lesson

T H E A

☐ Ⓞ Ⓞ ☐

What heat does during convection or conduction

S R T F N R A E S

☐ Ⓞ ☐ ☐ ☐ ☐ Ⓞ ☐ ☐

How heat moves through a liquid

T N E V C O I N C O

☐ ☐ ☐ ☐ ☐ Ⓞ ☐ ☐ ☐ ☐

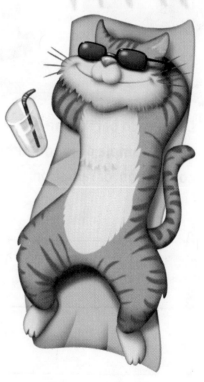

Heat moves from this source by convection and radiation

F I R M P A C E

☐ ☐ Ⓞ Ⓞ ☐ ☐ ☐

How heat travels through empty space

D O T A I R N I A

Ⓞ ☐ ☐ ☐ ☐ Ⓞ ☐ ☐ ☐

Unscramble the letters in the circles to form a word
that is related to this lesson.

_____

© Houghton Mifflin Harcourt Publishing Company

Apply Concepts

2 A transfer of heat happens between objects of different temperatures. Draw an arrow between each pair of objects to show the direction heat would travel between them.

3 Label each part of the drawing as an example of conduction, convection, or radiation.

A. _____

B. _____

C. _____

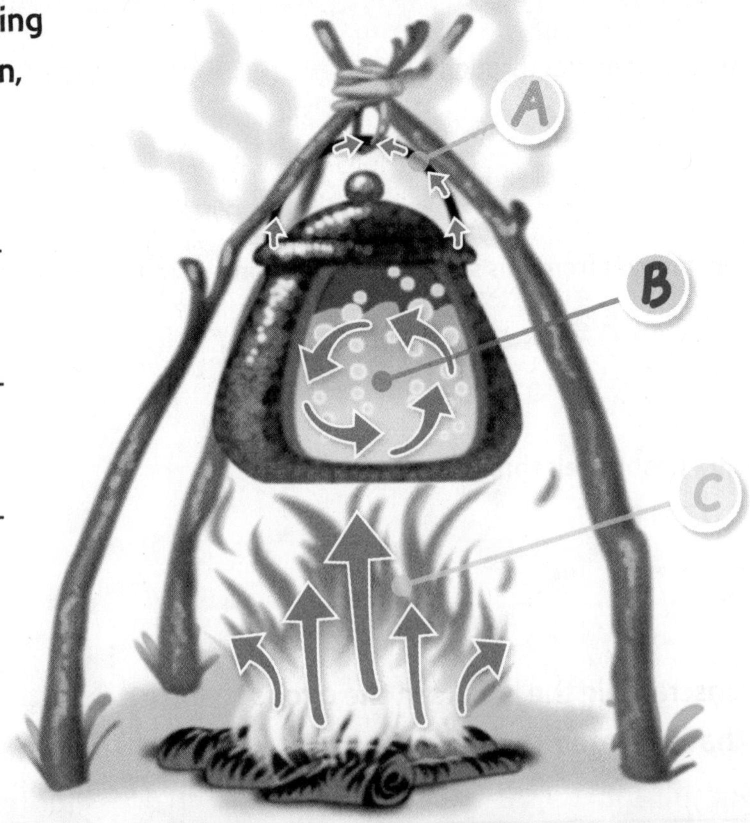

© Houghton Mifflin Harcourt Publishing Company   HMH Credits

4 Label each of the following as examples of conduction, convection, or radiation.

hot water added to bath

_____

space heater

_____

iron-on decal

_____

clothes dryer

_____

sunlight through a window

_____

sandwich press

_____

© Houghton Mifflin Harcourt Publishing Company   HMH Credits

5 In this pizza restaurant, heat is traveling in different ways. Label the examples of conduction, convection, and radiation in the spaces provided.

Take It Home! With your family, find three devices that give off heat in your home. For each device you find, discuss where the heat comes from and the way in which the heat is transferred.

© Houghton Mifflin Harcourt Publishing Company

Careers in Science

8 THINGS YOU SHOULD KNOW ABOUT Geothermal Technicians

1 *Geothermal* means heat from inside of Earth. Volcanoes, geysers, and hot springs are all sources of geothermal energy.

2 Geothermal energy is a *green energy*, which means that it is renewable, and it does not pollute the environment.

3 At geothermal energy stations, machines called *generators* convert geothermal energy into electrical energy.

4 Geothermal technicians may work inside, using computers to monitor energy production.

5 These technicians may work outside, installing and repairing equipment used to capture geothermal energy.

6 Geothermal technicians read blueprints and technical drawings as part of their work.

7 These technicans work with geothermal engineers to design and install geothermal systems.

8 To be a geothermal technician, you must complete high school as well as a special set of training courses.

© Houghton Mifflin Harcourt Publishing Company   (t) ©Martin Bond/Photo Researchers, Inc; (l) ©Bates Littlehales/National Geographic/Getty Images; (b) ©Larry Gerbrandt/Flickr/Getty Images

Show What You Know About Geothermal Technicians

Answer the five questions about geothermal technicians.

1 What type of energy do these technicians work with, and where does it come from?

_____

_____

_____

2 What do geothermal technicians do when they work outside?

_____

_____

_____

3 Why is geothermal energy green energy?

_____

_____

_____

4 What are some natural sources of geothermal energy?

_____

_____

_____

_____

5 Would you like to work as a geothermal technician? Why or why not?

_____

_____

_____

Think About It!

Would you want to heat your home using geothermal energy? Explain.

_____

_____

_____

© Houghton Mifflin Harcourt Publishing Company

Essential Question

What Are Conductors and Insulators?

Engage Your Brain!

Find the answer to the following question in this lesson and record it here.

How can these dogs stay warm in such cold weather?

_____

_____

_____

_____

_____

Active Reading

Lesson Vocabulary

List the terms. As you learn about each one, make notes in the Interactive Glossary.

_____

_____

_____

_____

Cause and Effect

Some ideas in this lesson are connected by a cause-and-effect relationship. Why something happens is a cause. What happens as a result of something else is an effect. Active readers look for effects by asking themselves, What happened? They look for causes by asking, Why did it happen?

© Houghton Mifflin Harcourt Publishing Company (bkgd) ©Hakan Hjort/Johner Images/Alamy

Inquiry Flipchart p. 27 — Sunny Side Up/Ready to Insulate!

205

Go with the Flow... of Heat

A pan in the oven gets very hot. But if you pick it up with an oven mitt, your hand stays cool. Why?

Active Reading As you read these two pages, circle lesson vocabulary each time it is used.

Heat moves through some materials very easily. In the example above, heat from the oven moved easily into the pan. But heat from the pan did not pass through the oven mitt. A material that allows heat to move through it easily is called a **conductor**. Many heat conductors also conduct electricity well.

For the most part, solids are better conductors of heat than liquids or gases are. That's because the particles that make up a solid are packed closely together. They vibrate, but don't move apart much. Heat can move quickly from one particle to another.

Glass
Glass does not conduct heat well. If you pour boiling water into a metal bowl, the outside of the bowl quickly gets hot. A glass bowl gets warm more slowly.

Stone
Marble does not conduct heat as well as metals do. But it can still conduct heat away from your body. That's why marble feels cool when you touch it.

Metal
Metals are great heat conductors. Some metals conduct heat better than others do.

© Houghton Mifflin Harcourt Publishing Company (bc) ©Ingram/Getty Images

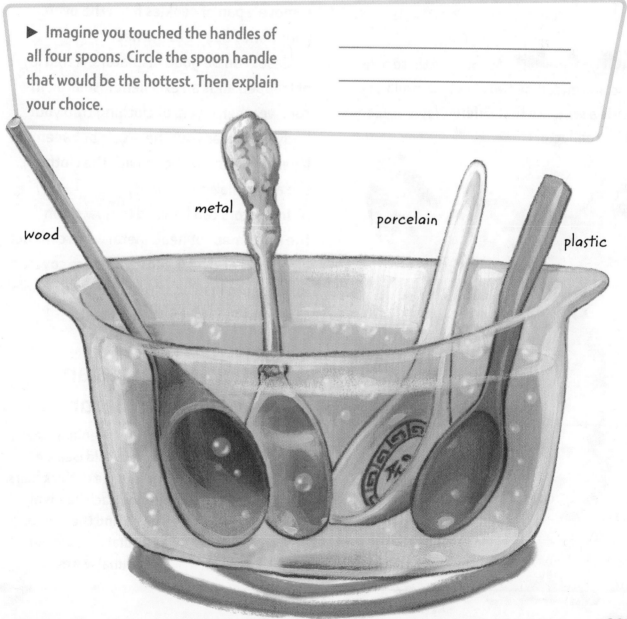

Getting Hot

This diagram shows the particles of a metal bar. The particles on this end are hot. This end was placed over a flame, but the other end wasn't.

Still Cool

The particles on this end aren't hot yet, but they will be soon. In metals, heat moves from particle to particle very easily.

▶ Imagine you touched the handles of all four spoons. Circle the spoon handle that would be the hottest. Then explain your choice.

_____

_____

_____

wood

metal

porcelain

plastic

© Houghton Mifflin Harcourt Publishing Company

Turn the Heat Around

Wearing gloves insulates your hands. The gloves trap heat near your skin.

Not all materials are conductors. Heat does not move easily—or at all—through some materials.

Active Reading As you read these pages, find and underline two effects of insulators. Circle a sentence that differentiates insulators from conductors.

Materials that do not conduct heat well are called **insulators**. Oven mitts are insulators. They are made of materials that are poor conductors of heat. When you remove a pan of cookies from the oven, your hands don't get burned.

Gases can be good insulators. A thin layer of trapped air is an excellent insulator. In cold weather, layers of clothing trap your body heat near you. There's air between the layers of clothing. Along with the clothing, the air insulates your body.

Insulators can be used to slow down the movement of heat. Metal wires conduct electricity and heat. Most wires are covered in rubber to insulate them and keep people safe from the electricity and heat.

Hair as an Insulator

Most furry animals stay warm in cold weather. Fur is made of thick hairs. Around each hair is air. The air and the fur act as insulators, keeping the animal warm.

© Houghton Mifflin Harcourt Publishing Company   (b) ©Michael Krabs/imagebroker/Alamy

Why Does a Thermos Work?

Glass lining
A layer of glass holds the tea. Glass does not conduct heat very well.

Reflection
Even in a vacuum, radiation can move energy. The facing sides of the layers are coated in silver, which act like a mirror. It reflects some heat back.

Vacuum
There is a vacuum between the inner and outer glass layers of the bottle. The vacuum keeps conduction or convection from taking place.

Still Hot
With the conduction, convection, and radiation slowed down, the tea stays hot for a long time!

▶ Although the straw house is not the sturdiest, a straw house can be well insulated. Why?

© Houghton Mifflin Harcourt Publishing Company   (tr) ©theodore liasi/Alamy

Heat Proofing a Home

All across the United States, people are trying to conserve, or save, energy. It's good for the environment, and it saves money. Heat proofing a home is one way that people can conserve energy.

When the weather is hot, you want to keep heat from coming into your home. When the weather is cold, you want to keep heat from leaving your home. It costs money to cool and heat a home! There are different ways to slow the flow of heat into or out of a house. Some things need to be done while the house is being built. Others can be done to an existing home. Insulating a home saves money. It also helps conserve energy.

© Houghton Mifflin Harcourt Publishing Company

1 Insulation

Insulation is blown inside the walls of a house. Insulation keeps heat from traveling through to the attic.

2 glass panes

2 Windows

These windows have two panes of glass to limit conduction. They also have a coating that limits heat radiation.

3 Pipes

Hot pipes radiate heat from water into the air. Wrapping them keeps the heat from escaping.

4 Soil

Soil is a great insulator. Basements are usually cool, even in the summer.

Do the Math!
Solve Real-World Problems

The Ogburn family wants to heat proof their house. They can save about $800 a year by adding insulation. Wrapping the water pipes will save an additional $5 each month. Buying new, energy-efficient windows will save them about $2,000 every year.

1. How much money will wrapping the water pipes save the Ogburns in a year?

_____

2. About how much more money will replacing the windows save each year than wrapping the water pipes?

_____

3. Write an equation to calculate how much all three things will save the Ogburns in a year.

_____

Bonus!

If new windows cost $10,500, pipe insulation costs $100, and adding insulation costs $400, in how many years will the savings pay for the cost of these home improvements?

_____

_____

_____

© Houghton Mifflin Harcourt Publishing Company

When you're done, use the answer key to check and revise your work.

Write the vocabulary term that describes each material.

1 metal cube

_____

2 a knit hat

_____

3 rubber bands

_____

Draw a box around the correct answer or answers.

[4] Heat moves easily through it.	insulator	conductor	
[5] Heat does not move easily through it.	insulator	conductor	
[6] Solids often do this to heat.	insulate	conduct	
[7] A thin layer of trapped air can do this to heat.	insulate	conduct	
[8] Which forms of heat transfer do insulated bottles prevent?	conduction	convection	radiation
[9] Wrapping hot water pipes prevents which form of heat transfer?	conduction	convection	radiation

© Houghton Mifflin Harcourt Publishing Company (tc) ©Andy Crawford/Getty Images; (tr) ©Brand X Pictures/Getty Images

Answer Key: 1. conductor **2.** insulator **3.** insulator **4.** conductor **5.** insulator **6.** conduct **7.** insulate **8.** conduction, convection, and radiation **9.** radiation

Name _____

Word Play

1 Use the clues to help you write the correct word in each row. Some boxes have been filled in for you.

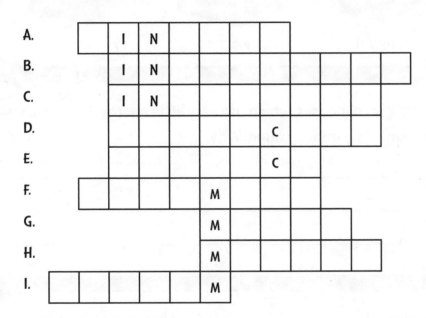

A. Some of them have two panes of glass.

B. It can be blown inside walls.

C. It slows the transfer of heat.

D. It's the opposite of answer C.

E. The silver layer of an insulated bottle does this to radiated heat.

F. Because of natural insulation, it's often the coolest part of a house.

G. It's an excellent conductor.

H. It does not conduct as well as metals do.

I. It makes conduction and convection impossible.

© Houghton Mifflin Harcourt Publishing Company

Apply Concepts

2 You are going to make a kitchen spoon. It will be used to stir hot liquids. Circle the material that will be warmest when you touch its handle.

cotton   metal   plastic   wood

3 Many people are building "green" houses, which use very little energy. Some of these houses are partially or completely underground. Why?

_____

_____

_____

4 How would you design a lunchbox that could keep hot food hot or cold food cold? Sketch a diagram of the box.

Take It Home!

Look around your kitchen with your family. Find two things that conduct heat and two things that are heat insulators.

© Houghton Mifflin Harcourt Publishing Company

TEKS **4.2B** collect...data by observing... **4.2C** construct...charts... using tools... to organize, examine, and evaluate data **4.6B** differentiate between conductors and insulators

Name _____

Essential Question

How Do Conductors and Insulators Differ?

Set a Purpose

What do you think you will learn from this experiment?

_____

_____

_____

_____

_____

State Your Hypothesis

Write your hypothesis, or testable statement.

_____

_____

_____

_____

_____

Think About the Procedure

What is the tested variable?

_____

_____

_____

_____

Which things must be the same in each setup?

_____

_____

_____

_____

_____

© Houghton Mifflin Harcourt Publishing Company

Record Your Observations

Use the space below to construct a chart to organize, examine, and evaluate the data you collected.

Draw Conclusions

Which material did heat move through more quickly?

_____

Differentiate between conductors and insulators. Which material is a conductor? Which is an insulator? How do you know?

_____

_____

_____

_____

Analyze and Extend

1. On which knife did the butter melt faster? On that knife, which pat of butter melted faster?

    _____

    _____

    _____

2. Write a hypothesis about which knife would lose heat faster. Then plan an experiment to test your hypothesis.

    _____

    _____

    _____

    _____

    _____

    _____

    _____

    _____

3. What other materials could you test this way?

    _____

    _____

    _____

4. What other questions would you like to ask about conductors and insulators?

    _____

    _____

© Houghton Mifflin Harcourt Publishing Company

TEKS 4.6A differentiate among forms of energy, including mechanical, sound, electrical, light, and heat/thermal

How It Works:
Piezoelectricity

This gas lantern has a tool that changes kinetic energy from an impact into electrical energy. Electrical energy produced this way is called *piezoelectricity*, or electricity from pressure!

Quartz is a piezoelectric material.

Gas Chamber

You don't need a match to light this lantern! It has a piezoelectric igniter. The igniter is a tool made up of a small, spring-loaded bar and a piezoelectric material.

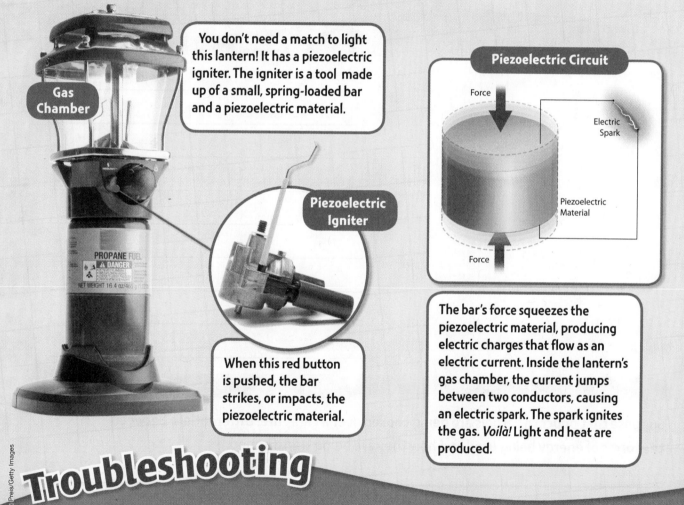

Piezoelectric Circuit

Force

Electric Spark

Piezoelectric Material

Force

Piezoelectric Igniter

PROPANE FUEL
⚠ DANGER
NET WEIGHT 16.4 oz/465 g

When this red button is pushed, the bar strikes, or impacts, the piezoelectric material.

The bar's force squeezes the piezoelectric material, producing electric charges that flow as an electric current. Inside the lantern's gas chamber, the current jumps between two conductors, causing an electric spark. The spark ignites the gas. *Voilà!* Light and heat are produced.

Troubleshooting

Why might a lantern not light up when a piezo igniter is pushed?

_____

_____

_____

© Houghton Mifflin Harcourt Publishing Company (l) ©Siede Preis/Getty Images

These solar cells transform, or change, solar energy into electrical energy. Electrical energy is changed into heat and light inside the home.

Show How It Works

The gas lantern shows some ways that energy changes take place. Kinetic energy changes into electrical energy, which ignites the natural gas. Chemical energy stored in the gas changes into heat and light. Identify different forms of energy and their sources in your classroom or home. In the space below, draw and describe how energy from one of these sources is transformed.

Suppose that popcorn kernels are being cooked over a campfire. Differentiate between the forms of energy being used and how they are being transformed.

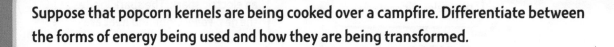

Build On It!

Rise to the engineering design challenge—complete **Design It: Solar Water Heater** on the Inquiry Flipchart.

© Houghton Mifflin Harcourt Publishing Company   (t) ©Tom Chance/Westend61 GmbH/Alamy Images

Name _____

Vocabulary Review

Use the terms in the box to complete the sentences.

conduction
conductor
convection
heat
insulator
kinetic energy
potential energy
radiation

TEKS 4.6A

1. The energy of motion is _____.

TEKS 4.6A

2. The energy something has because of its position or

   condition is _____.

TEKS 4.6A

3. The energy that moves between objects of different

   temperatures is _____.

TEKS 4.6B

4. The transfer or movement of heat between two objects

   that are touching is _____.

TEKS 4.6B

5. The transfer of heat within a liquid or a gas is

   _____.

TEKS 4.6A

6. The movement of heat without matter to carry it is

   _____.

TEKS 4.6B

7. A material that allows heat to move through it easily is

   a(n) _____.

TEKS 4.6B

8. A material that does not let heat move through it easily

   is a(n) _____.

© Houghton Mifflin Harcourt Publishing Company   (border) ©NDisk/Age Fotostock

Science Concepts

Fill in the letter of the choice that best answers the question.

TEKS 4.6A

9. When turned on, the radio display lights up and you hear sound. How does light energy differ from sound energy?

Ⓐ Light energy is measured by pitch.

Ⓑ Light energy is made from vibrations.

Ⓒ Light energy can travel through space.

Ⓓ Light energy can only be found during the day.

TEKS 4.6A

10. Niko jumps on a trampoline. The pictures below show him at different points during jumping.

At which point does Niko have the most potential energy?

Ⓐ Point 1

Ⓑ Point 2

Ⓒ Point 3

Ⓓ Point 4

TEKS 4.6A

11. Energy can change form. Which picture shows electrical energy changing into heat energy?

TEKS 4.6A

12. Ang has a pogo stick like the one shown at right. When he jumps on it, the spring squeezes toward the ground and then moves back to its starting position.

The potential and kinetic energies of the spring are forms of which type of energy?

Ⓐ chemical energy

Ⓑ electrical energy

Ⓒ magnetic energy

Ⓓ mechanical energy

TEKS 4.6A

13. Objects that vibrate make energy. Which type of energy results from vibrations that travel through the air?

Ⓐ sound

Ⓒ potential

Ⓑ chemical

Ⓓ electrical

TEKS 4.2D, 4.6B

14. Rachel tests how quickly different materials change temperature. She heats each one the same way and constructs a table to examine and evaluate her data.

Material	Starting Temperature (°C)	Temperature After Five Minutes (°C)
1	19	37
2	19	48
3	19	31
4	19	42

Which material is the best insulator?

Ⓐ Material 1

Ⓒ Material 3

Ⓑ Material 2

Ⓓ Material 4

© Houghton Mifflin Harcourt Publishing Company (border) ©NDisk/Age Fotostock

TEKS 4.6A

15. Which type of energy change takes place as a car burns fuel to race down a track?

Ⓐ electrical energy to light energy

Ⓑ kinetic energy to potential energy

Ⓒ chemical energy to kinetic energy

Ⓓ mechanical energy to kinetic energy

TEKS 4.6A

16. Rondell knows that radiation is a form of heat transfer. Which example describes a transfer of heat through radiation?

Ⓐ A cup of hot tea warms a hand.

Ⓑ A flame warms air in a hot-air balloon.

Ⓒ A puddle of water warms under the sun.

Ⓓ A pot of boiling water warms on a gas burner.

TEKS 4.6A

17. Nancy says that mechanical energy enables her clothes dryer to operate. Which form of energy listed below can Nancy use to correct her statement?

Ⓐ heat energy

Ⓑ electrical energy

Ⓒ thermal energy

Ⓓ chemical energy

TEKS 4.6A

18. A scientist measures the average kinetic energy of the particles of an object. What is he measuring?

Ⓐ heat Ⓒ insulation

Ⓑ current Ⓓ temperature

TEKS 4.6B

19. Jaden has many things on his desk at home as shown in the picture below.

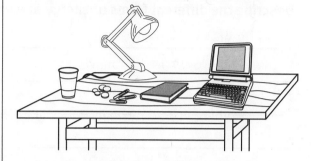

Which material was most likely used because it is a good insulator?

Ⓐ copper used for the coins

Ⓑ metal used for the computer

Ⓒ steel used for the paper clips

Ⓓ rubber used for the lamp cord

TEKS 4.6A

20. This picture shows a pot of water heating on a stovetop.

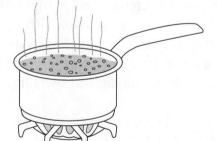

Which statement explains what happens to the water in the pot?

Ⓐ The water temperature decreases inside the pot.

Ⓑ The water will freeze when enough heat is added.

Ⓒ Heat is transferred from the water in the pot to the burner.

Ⓓ Heat is transferred from the burner to the pot and then to the water.

© Houghton Mifflin Harcourt Publishing Company   (border) ©NDisk/Age Fotostock

Apply Inquiry and Review the Big Idea

Write the answers to these questions.

TEKS 4.6A

21. Louis knows there are many forms of energy that can be observed in different systems. Study the picture to the right. Describe the different forms of energy present.

_____

_____

_____

_____

TEKS 4.6B

22. Paula is camping with her family. After their parents light a fire, Paula and her sister stand nearby to warm their hands. Her sister thinks that conduction warms their hands. Paula disagrees. Explain all methods of heat transfer taking place as they warm their hands.

_____

_____

_____

TEKS 4.6B

23. Misa puts thermometers in four boxes that are exactly alike. She covers each box with a top made of a different material. Then, Misa leaves the boxes outside on a hot, sunny day. Explain which thermometer should show the highest temperature after two hours.

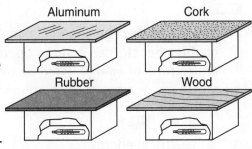

Aluminum   Cork

Rubber   Wood

_____

_____

_____

TEKS 4.6B

24. Mr. Lewis wants to put insulation around the pipes in his basement to keep heat from escaping. He measures 6 m of pipe in one area and 5 m of pipe in another area. If insulation costs $9.00 per meter, how much will Mr. Lewis spend for the cost of insulation? _____.

© Houghton Mifflin Harcourt Publishing Company   (border) ©NDisk/Age Fotostock

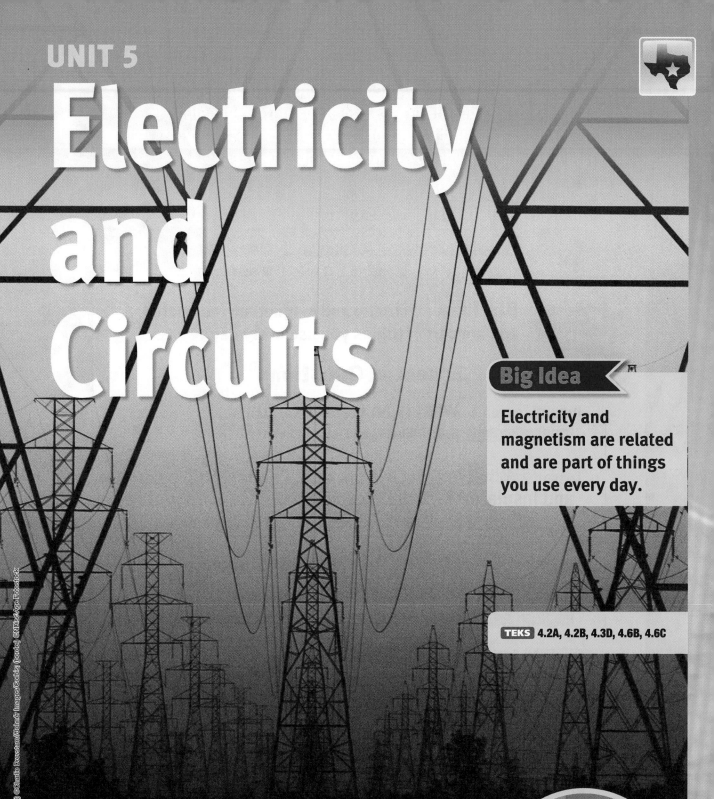

UNIT 5
Electricity and Circuits

Houghton Mifflin Harcourt Publishing Company (bg) ©Corbis; (inset) ©Charlie Drevstam/Johnér Images/Corbis; (border) ©ND/age Fotostock

Big Idea

Electricity and magnetism are related and are part of things you use every day.

TEKS 4.2A, 4.2B, 4.3D, 4.6B, 4.6C

I Wonder How

Electrical energy is important to people. How does electricity reach homes and businesses? *Turn the page to find out.*

Here's How Generating stations transform mechanical energy into electrical energy. Electrical energy travels over the electric grid. This grid is a system of transmission towers, conductors, and insulators that carries electricity from generating stations to our homes and businesses.

In this unit, you will explore the Big Idea, the Essential Questions, and the Investigations on the Inquiry Flipchart.

Levels of Inquiry Key ■ DIRECTED ■ GUIDED ■ INDEPENDENT

Track Your Progress

Big Idea Electricity and magnetism are related and are part of things you use every day.

Essential Questions

Now I Get the Big Idea!

Science Notebook
Before you begin each lesson, be sure to write your thoughts about the Essential Question.

© Houghton Mifflin Harcourt Publishing Company (bg) ©Outtlet (inset) ©Charlie Drevstam/Johnér Images/Corbis (border) ©Nibsa/Age Fotostock

Inquiry Flipchart page 30

Lesson 1
INQUIRY

TEKS 4.2A ...implement
descriptive investigations, including...
making inferences... 4.2B ...record
data...using descriptive words...
such as labeled drawings... 4.6B
differentiate between conductors and
insulators 4.6C demonstrate that
electricity travels in a closed path,
creating an electrical circuit...

Name _____

Essential Question

What Is an Electric Circuit?

Set a Purpose
What will you learn from this investigation?

_____
_____
_____
_____

Think About the Procedure
Did the order in which you arranged
the parts make a difference? Explain.

_____
_____
_____
_____

Was the procedure an experiment?
Why or why not?

_____
_____
_____
_____

Record Your Data
In the space below, draw and label a picture
of your circuit that worked. Use descriptive
words to say how the parts were connected.

Differentiate between conductors and
insulators. Place a check mark next to the
materials that enabled the bulb to light up.

Paper clip   _____

Wood craft stick   _____

Pencil lead   _____

© Houghton Mifflin Harcourt Publishing Company

Draw Conclusions

How can you build a circuit?

_____

_____

_____

_____

_____

Analyze and Extend

1. Why is it helpful to have a switch in a circuit?

_____

_____

_____

_____

_____

2. Make an inference. Why would a circuit not work when a wire is replaced with a cotton string?

_____

_____

_____

3. Look at the first part of the term *circuit*. Why do you think what you built is called a circuit?

_____

_____

_____

_____

4. Look at the picture below. Draw lines to show how three wires could be connected to make the bulbs light up.

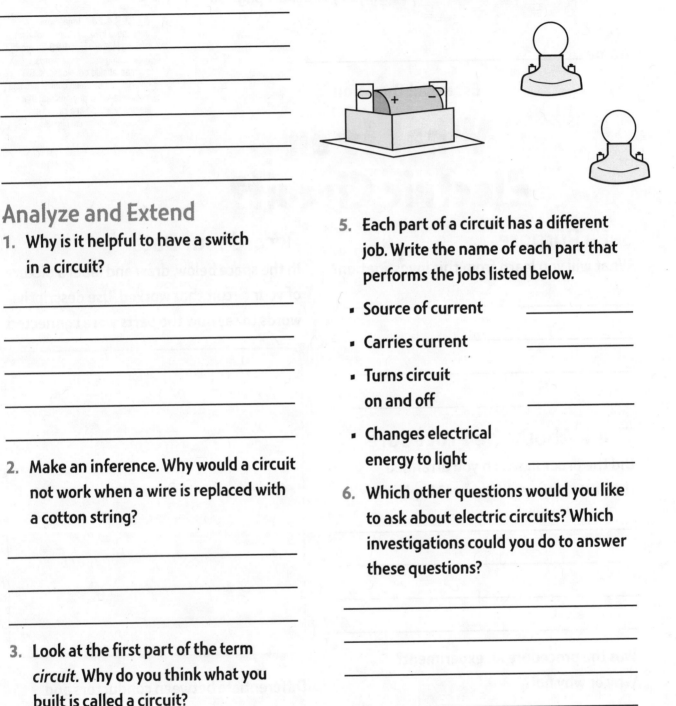

5. Each part of a circuit has a different job. Write the name of each part that performs the jobs listed below.

- Source of current   _____

- Carries current   _____

- Turns circuit
  on and off   _____

- Changes electrical
  energy to light   _____

6. Which other questions would you like to ask about electric circuits? Which investigations could you do to answer these questions?

_____

_____

_____

_____

_____

_____

_____

_____

226

© Houghton Mifflin Harcourt Publishing Company

TEKS **4.6B** differentiate between conductors and insulators **4.6C** demonstrate that electricity travels in a closed path, creating an electrical circuit...

Lesson 2

Essential Question

What Are Electric Circuits, Conductors, and Insulators?

Engage Your Brain!

Find the answer to the following question and record it here.

This picture shows the inside of a robot. What do the dark lines have to do with the robot's operation?

_____

_____

_____

Active Reading

Lesson Vocabulary

List the terms. As you learn about each one, make notes in the Interactive Glossary.

_____ _____

_____ _____

_____

Compare and Contrast

When you compare things, you look for ways in which they are alike. When you contrast things, you look for ways in which they are different. Active readers stay focused by asking themselves, How are these things alike? How are these things different?

© Houghton Mifflin Harcourt Publishing Company ©Gustoimages/Photo Researchers, Inc.

It's Shocking!

Working around electric utility lines is dangerous! How does a line worker stay safe?

Active Reading Draw a box around the sentences that differentiate between conductors and insulators.

Even on a hot day, a worker who repairs electric utility lines must be bundled up in protective clothing. The thick gloves, the bulky boots, and the hard plastic hat are heavy; however, these clothes protect the worker from an electric shock!

The rubber and plastic used in the protective clothing do not allow electric charges to flow through them. A material that resists the flow of electric charges is called an **insulator**. Electric charges flow easily through metals and some liquids. A material that readily allows electric charges to pass through it is called a **conductor**.

This worker's clothing is made up of insulators. The clothing will not allow electric charges to flow through it if the worker accidentally touches the wrong wires.

© Houghton Mifflin Harcourt Publishing Company ©Tim Wright/Corbis

The parts of a plug that you hold and the covering on the wire are insulators. The metal prongs that go into the outlet are good conductors.

Electrical appliances work when electric charges flow through them. The parts that carry electric charges are made from conductors. Insulators are wrapped around the conductors to make appliances safe to handle.

▶ Label the parts of the wire as a conductor or an insulator.

▶ Differentiate between conductors and insulators.

_____
_____
_____
_____
_____
_____
_____
_____

© Houghton Mifflin Harcourt Publishing Company   (t) ©Andy Ryan/Getty Images; (c) ©Arco Images GmbH/Alamy; (b) ©Corbis

A Path to Follow

If the wiring in a lamp does not change, why isn't the lamp on all of the time?

Active Reading Draw a box around the sentences that tell you how a closed circuit and an open circuit are different.

When you go to school and back home, your path is a loop. A **circuit** is a path along which electric charges can flow. For an electrical device to work, the circuit must form a complete loop. This type of circuit is called a *closed circuit*. There are no breaks in its path.

What happens if a loose wire gets disconnected? The path is broken, and charges cannot flow. This type of circuit is called an *open circuit*. Many circuits have a switch. A switch controls the flow of charges by opening and closing the circuit.

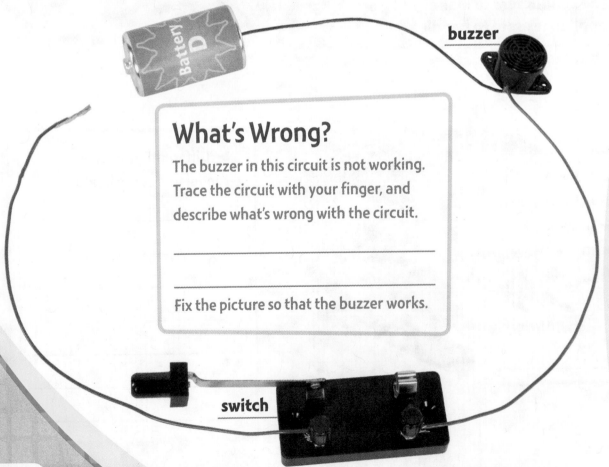

buzzer

switch

What's Wrong?

The buzzer in this circuit is not working. Trace the circuit with your finger, and describe what's wrong with the circuit.

_____

_____

Fix the picture so that the buzzer works.

© Houghton Mifflin Harcourt Publishing Company

Open Circuit

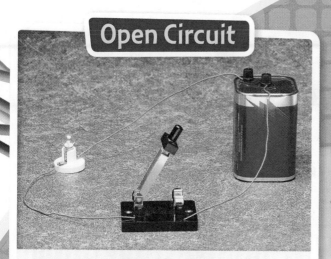

When the switch in a circuit is open, the circuit is not complete. Electric charges cannot flow, so the light stays off.

Closed Circuit

When the switch is closed, the circuit is complete. Electric charges can flow through it to light up the bulb.

▶ The filament in a light bulb is a tiny wire. It is part of the circuit. If the filament breaks, the circuit will be _____.

filament

© Houghton Mifflin Harcourt Publishing Company (inset) ©Dennis Hallinan

Who Needs a Map?

To travel from point A to point B, you usually take the shortest route. What if one of the roads on that route is blocked? Simple! You just take another road. What would happen if there were only one road between point A and point B?

Active Reading Underline the sentences that compare series circuits and parallel circuits.

Series Circuits

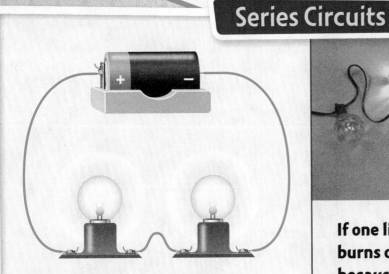

In a series circuit, electric charges must follow a single path. The charged particles move from the battery's positive terminal to its negative terminal.

▶ Draw arrows to show how charges flow in this circuit.

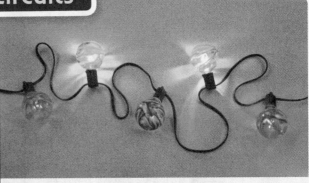

If one light bulb in a series circuit burns out, all of the lights go out, because the circuit is broken.

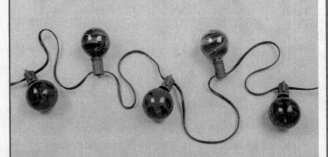

© Houghton Mifflin Harcourt Publishing Company

Suppose that the television and all the lights in a room are part of the same circuit. What would happen if one of the light bulbs burned out? It would depend on how the circuit is wired.

A **series circuit** has only one path for electric charges to follow. If any part of the path breaks, the circuit is open. Nothing works!

A circuit with several different paths for the charges to follow is called a **parallel circuit**. If one part of the circuit breaks, the charges can still flow along the other parts.

Color a Complex Circuit

1. Look at the circuit below. Color the bulb or bulbs that should be lit.
2. Draw an X on the switch that is open. Draw an arrow above the closed switch.

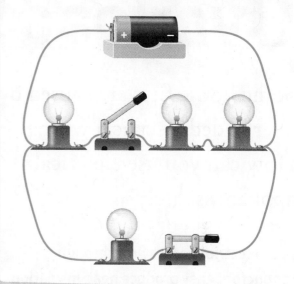

Parallel Circuits

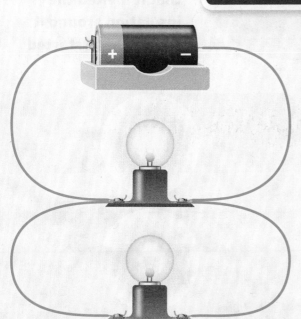

In this parallel circuit, electric charges can flow through both the top loop and the bottom loop.

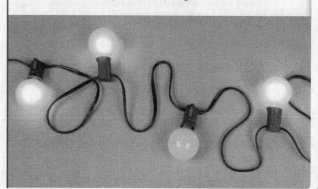

If one part of a parallel circuit breaks, only that part of the circuit stops working.

© Houghton Mifflin Harcourt Publishing Company

Circuit Overload!

Some house fires are caused by overloaded electrical wiring. How can you use electrical appliances safely?

As electric charges flow through conductors, they produce heat. Insulation protects the materials around these conductors from the heat—up to a point! If the conductor gets too hot, the insulation can melt.

To protect against fires, a fuse or a circuit breaker is added to each circuit. Fuses and circuit breakers are switches that work automatically. They open if charge flows too quickly through a circuit. The flow stops and the wires cool, which prevents a fire.

Circuit overload takes place when too many devices in one circuit are turned on. Each device needs a certain flow of charge. This flow of charge, or current, is measured in units called *amperes*, or amps.

Circuit breakers open when the number of amps is greater than a certain value. Suppose the value for a breaker is 15 amps. The breaker will open if all plugged devices draw more than 15 amps.

**television
3 amps**

**hair dryer
12.5 amps**

Wow!

This wire got so hot that it melted the insulation around it. It could have started a fire.

Never plug more appliances into a circuit than it is designed to handle!

© Houghton Mifflin Harcourt Publishing Company   (television) ©Yasuhide Fumoto/Getty Images; (hair dryer) ©PhotoDisc/Getty Images; (wire) ©FirePhoto/Alamy; (wall outlet) ©Thinkstock Images/Getty Images

With power strips like this one, it's possible to plug many devices into a single wall outlet. **That could be a big mistake!**

Should You Plug It In?

Draw a line connecting the hair dryer to one of the outlets in the power strip. Then connect the other devices you could use at the same time without overloading a 15-amp circuit breaker.

lava lamp
0.5 amp

laptop computer
1.5 amps

clothes dryer
42 amps

Do the Math!
Solve Word Problems

1. How many times as much current does a television need than a lava lamp?

_____

2. Circuit breakers are made in increments of 5 amps. What size breaker would you need for a circuit with a television, two laptops, and a lava lamp?

_____

This panel contains circuit breakers. Each breaker allows a certain number of amps of electric current to pass through one circuit.

© Houghton Mifflin Harcourt Publishing Company (power strip) ©Lawrence Manning/Corbis; (clothes dryer) ©INSADCO Photography /Alamy; (breaker box) ©David Prince/Getty Images

When you're done, use the answer key to check and revise your work.

On each numbered line, fill in the vocabulary term that matches the description.

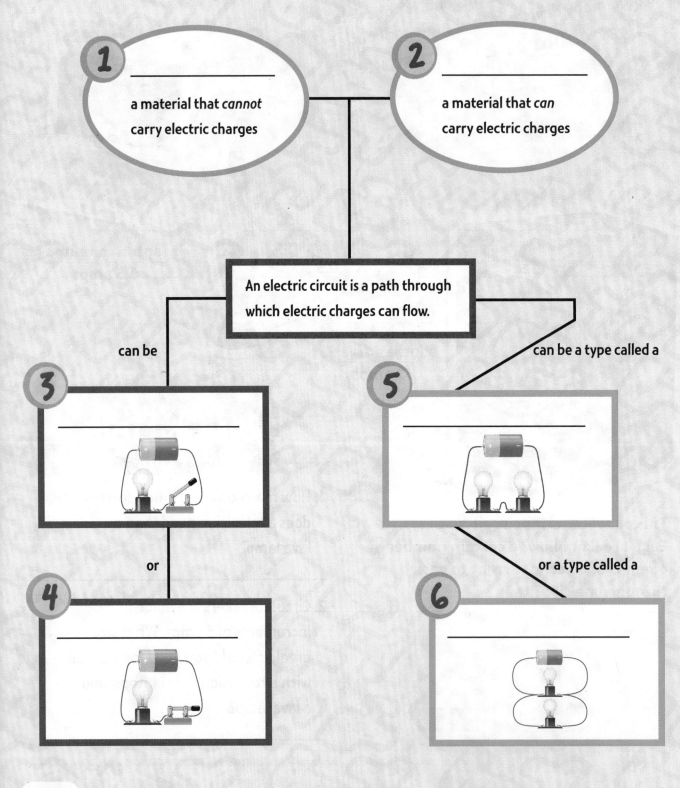

1 _____

a material that *cannot* carry electric charges

2 _____

a material that *can* carry electric charges

An electric circuit is a path through which electric charges can flow.

can be

3 _____

or

4 _____

can be a type called a

5 _____

or a type called a

6 _____

© Houghton Mifflin Harcourt Publishing Company

Answer Key: 1. insulator **2.** conductor **3.** open **4.** closed **5.** series circuit **6.** parallel circuit

Brain Check

Name _____

Word Play

1 Unscramble the scrambled word in each sentence. Write the unscrambled word after the sentence. The first one is done for you.

A. In some circuits, electrical energy is transformed into light energy by a light **lubb**.	(B) U L B 6
B. The wires in a circuit are made of a material that is a **doortuccn**.	_ _ _ _ _ _ _ (O) 10
C. A path that an electric current can follow is an electric **icurict**.	_ _ _ _ (O) (O) 4 5
D. A circuit in which electric charges can follow several different paths is called a **rallpale** circuit.	(O) _ _ _ _ _ _ 8
E. If a wire is disconnected, the circuit is an **enop** circuit.	_ _ (O) _ 9
F. The covering on electric plugs and around wires is made of an **rainulost**.	(O) _ _ _ _ _ _ (O) 2 7
G. A circuit in which all the devices are connected in a single path is a **ressie** circuit.	_ (O) _ _ _ 3
H. When a light is on, it is part of a **scolde** circuit.	(O) _ _ _ _ _ 1

Solve the riddle by writing the circled letters above in the correct spaces below.

Riddle: What is another name for
a clumsy electrician?

A _ _ _ _ C _ I _   B _ E _ K _ _ _
  1 2 3   4 5   6 7 8   9 10

© Houghton Mifflin Harcourt Publishing Company

Apply Concepts

2 Draw a closed series circuit with two light bulbs, a battery, and a switch. What would happen if one of the light bulbs blows out?

_____

_____

_____

_____

_____

3 Explain what causes an overloaded circuit. How can you prevent an overloaded circuit?

_____

_____

_____

_____

_____

4 Write the word _conductor_ or _insulator_ on each of the lines. Then differentiate between conductors and insulators. How are they different?

_____

_____

_____

_____

_____

© Houghton Mifflin Harcourt Publishing Company   (l) © Getty Images Royalty Free; (r) © Corbis

5 Suppose you are building a series circuit using a small battery and a small light bulb, and you run out of wire. What everyday objects could you use to connect the battery to the light bulb? Explain.

_____

_____

_____

6 Identify each lettered part of the circuit, and explain what each part does.

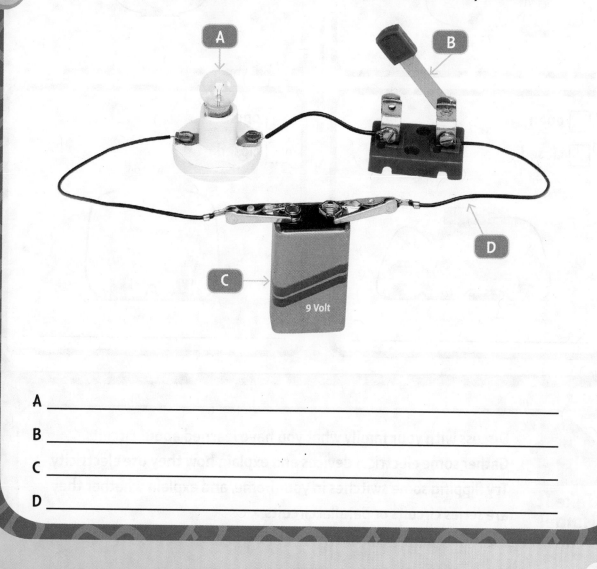

A _____

B _____

C _____

D _____

© Houghton Mifflin Harcourt Publishing Company

7 Study each of the following circuits.

- Make a check mark to show whether the circuit is open or closed.
- Draw the missing parts needed to make the open circuits work.
- Label each circuit as a series circuit or a parallel circuit.

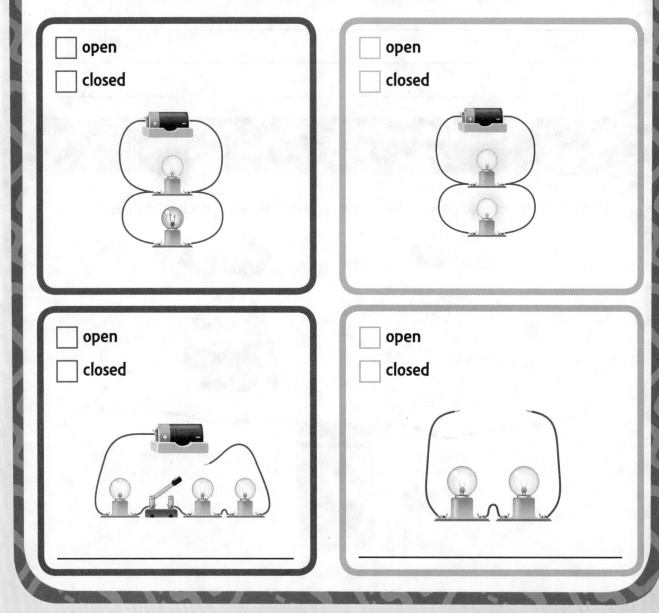

☐ open
☐ closed

☐ open
☐ closed

☐ open
☐ closed

☐ open
☐ closed

Take It Home!

Discuss with your family what you have learned about circuits. Gather some electrical devices and explain how they use electricity. Try flipping some switches in your home, and explain whether they are series circuits or parallel circuits.

© Houghton Mifflin Harcourt Publishing Company

Ask an Electrician

Q. Do electricians make electricity?

A. No. Electricity is produced in energy stations and carried to buildings through wires. Electricians work with wires to make sure the electricity moves safely.

Q. Don't electricians worry about electric shocks when they work?

A. Electricians must always turn off electricity to the wires they are working on. Electricity can be dangerous and safety is an important part of the job.

Q. What kind of training do you need to be an electrician?

A. Most electricians learn from experienced electricians while they are attending classes. During this period, they are called an apprentice.

Now It's Your Turn!

Which question would you want to ask an electrician?

_____

_____

_____

© Houghton Mifflin Harcourt Publishing Company   (bkgd) ©Jose Luis Pelaez Inc/Getty Images; (t) ©Simon Battensby/Getty Images; (br) ©Corbis

Untangle the Wires!

For each circuit, explain what would happen
when the switch at the bottom is closed.

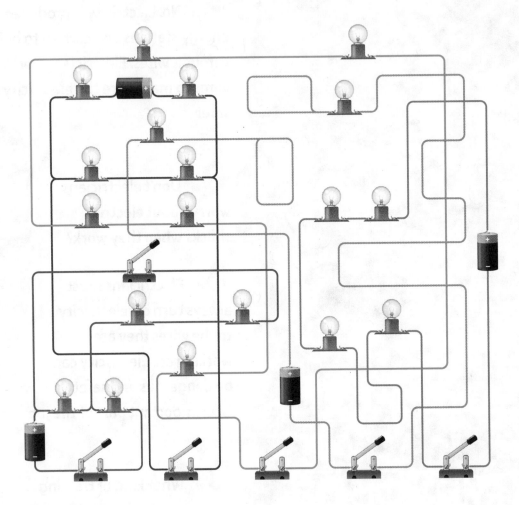

Red: _____

Purple: _____

Green: _____

Orange: _____

Blue: _____

© Houghton Mifflin Harcourt Publishing Company

TEKS **4.6C** ...explore an electromagnetic field **4.6D** design an experiment to test the effect of force on an object such as...magnetism

Lesson **3**

Essential Question

How Do We Use Electricity?

Engage Your Brain!

Find the answer to the following question in this lesson and record it here.

What types of energy is electricity being changed into in this picture?

_____

_____

_____

Active Reading

Lesson Vocabulary

List the terms. As you learn about each one, make notes in the Interactive Glossary.

_____

_____

_____

_____

Cause and Effect

Some ideas in this lesson are connected by a cause-and-effect relationship. Why something happens is a cause. What happens as a result of something else is an effect. Active readers look for effects by asking themselves, What happened? They look for causes by asking, Why did it happen?

© Houghton Mifflin Harcourt Publishing Company (bkgd) ©Tim Platt/Getty Images

Inquiry Flipchart p. 32 — Build an Electromagnet/Is There Current?

243

Electricity Has Many Uses

How did your day start? Did an alarm clock wake you? Did you turn on a light? Did you eat something out of the refrigerator? Yes? Then you used electricity!

Active Reading As you read these two pages, draw a box around the sentence that contains the main idea.

Think of all the things in your home or school that use electricity. What do they do? Devices that use electricity change electrical energy into other types of energy, such as light or heat. We use electricity to heat our homes and cook our food. We also use it to light our rooms and to keep foods cold.

A computer changes electrical energy into light, sound, and heat. When you turn on a computer, you see pictures and hear sounds. You feel heat coming off of it. A computer can be plugged into an electrical outlet. It can also run on batteries. How do the objects on these pages change electrical energy?

a ceiling fan

a television and a video game system

© Houghton Mifflin Harcourt Publishing Company   (bg) ©Corbis

Many electrical devices have electric motors. An **electric motor** is a machine that changes electrical energy into energy of motion. An electric fan uses an electric motor to move air. A refrigerator uses an electric motor to keep foods cold. What other objects in your home have electric motors? Any electric device that makes motion probably does.

an electric stove

a hair dryer and a light

Making a Better Change

A light bulb produces heat and light. Why would an engineer want to reduce the amount of heat a light bulb produces?

_____

_____

_____

© Houghton Mifflin Harcourt Publishing Company

Magnets and Magnetism

You can feel the force between two magnets. You feel magnets pull together, and you feel them push apart. How do magnets work?

Active Reading As you read these two pages, underline words or phrases that describe what causes magnets to push or pull.

Each flat surface on a ring magnet is either an *N* pole or an *S* pole.

Magnets have been used for thousands of years. A **magnet** is an object that attracts iron and a few other metals. People make magnets, but they are also found in nature. Magnets are part of many common things.

Magnetism is a physical property of matter. Magnets push and pull because of their magnetic field. A *magnetic field* is the space around the magnet where the force of the magnet acts.

Each magnet has two ends, or *poles*. A magnetic pole is the part of a magnet where its magnetic field is the strongest. One end is called the *south-seeking* pole, or *S* pole. The other is the *north-seeking* pole, or *N* pole.

Two *N* poles or two *S* poles are similar, or like, poles. If you place the *N* poles of two magnets near each other, they repel, or push away. Two *S* poles push away, too. Like poles repel each other.

An *N* pole and an *S* pole are unlike poles. If you place unlike poles of two magnets near each other, they attract, or pull toward each other.

© Houghton Mifflin Harcourt Publishing Company

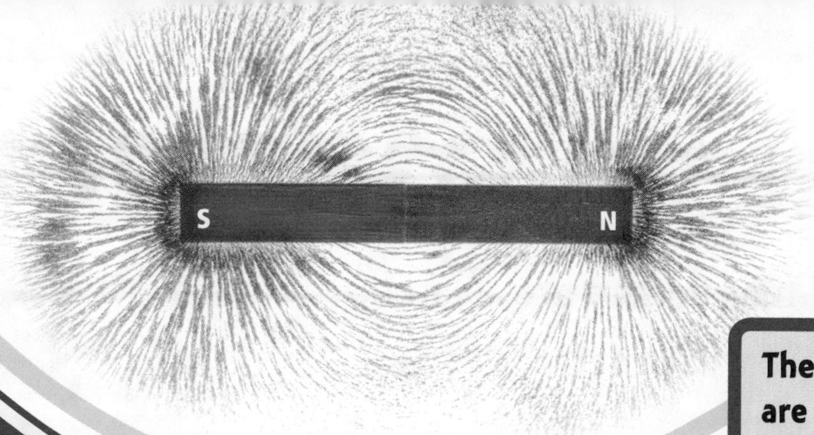

The magnetic forces are strongest around a magnet's poles.

The picture above shows a bar magnet. The iron filings around the magnet show the shape of the magnetic field. Where do you see the most iron filings? They are at the S and N poles of the magnet, which are where the magnetic field is strongest. Where do you see fewer iron filings? The middle of the magnet has fewer iron filings. The magnetic field is weakest there. The size and the type of material used to make a magnet affect its strength.

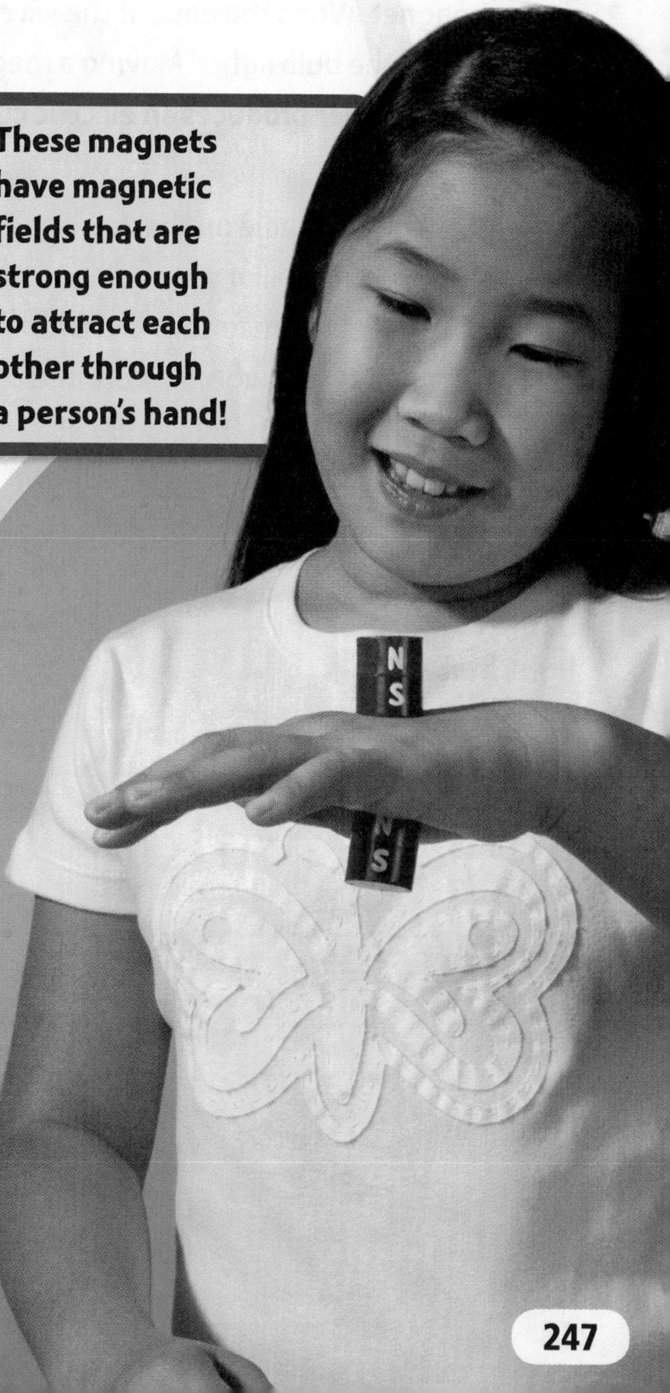

These magnets have magnetic fields that are strong enough to attract each other through a person's hand!

▶ Why are some magnets floating around the pencil in the picture on the left?

_____

_____

_____

_____

_____

© Houghton Mifflin Harcourt Publishing Company   HMH Credits

Electromagnets

Electricity and magnetism are related.
One can produce the other.

Active Reading As you read this page, circle the sentence that explains how magnetism produces an electric current.

Suppose you slide a coil of wire back and forth around a bar magnet. When the ends of the wire are attached to a light bulb, the bulb lights! Moving a magnet and a wire near each other produces an electric current.

Turning the handle on the device below turns a coil of wire inside three U-shaped magnets. Electric charges flow through the wire and the bulb lights. On the picture at right, an electric current is used to make a magnet.

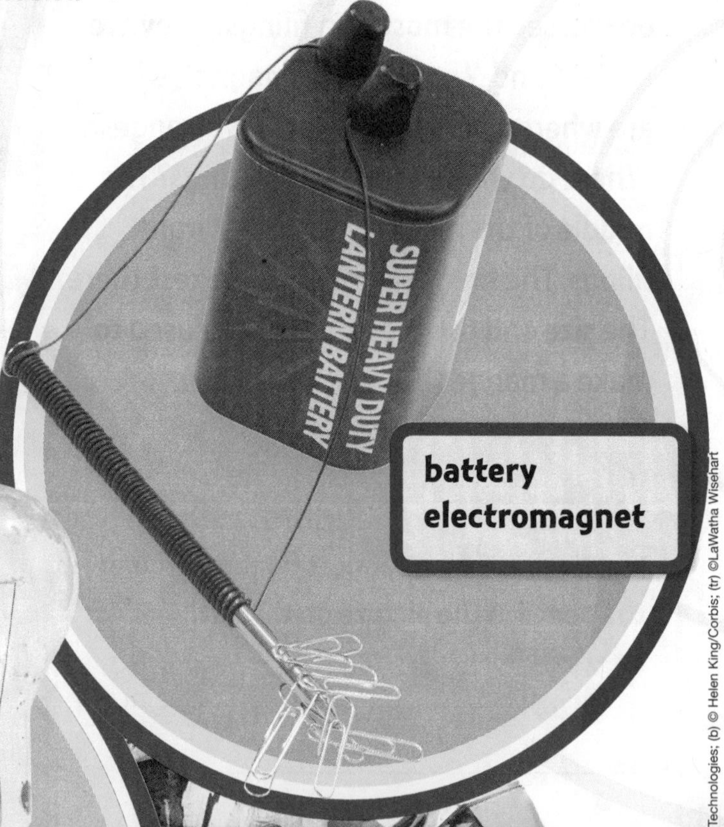

hand-cranked light bulb

battery electromagnet

SUPER HEAVY DUTY LANTERN BATTERY

Houghton Mifflin Harcourt Publishing Company (bl) ©Hemera Technologies; (b) © Helen King/Corbis; (tr) ©LaWatha Wisehart

If magnets produce electricity, can electricity make magnets? Yes! Wrapping a coil of current-carrying wire around an iron core such as a nail makes a magnet. You can use this magnet to pick up small iron objects such as paper clips. A device in which current produces magnetism is called an **electromagnet**.

Huge electromagnets are used in junkyards. They separate iron and steel objects from other objects. The operator swings the electromagnet over a pile of junk. He turns on the current. All the iron pieces are attracted by the electromagnetic field. The operator then swings the magnet over a container and turns off the current. The magnetism stops, and the iron drops into the container.

Electromagnets have become very important and useful. Today, every electric motor contains at least one electromagnet. You can also find electromagnets in telephones, doorbells, speakers, and computers. Doctors can use electromagnets to take pictures of the inside of the body.

junkyard electromagnet

What Are the Parts of an Electromagnet?

List the parts of an electromagnet. Then draw an electromagnet in the space provided.

© Houghton Mifflin Harcourt Publishing Company (b) © Helen King/Corbis; (tr) © Jeremy Walker/Photo Researchers, Inc.

Generating Electricity

We use electricity every day. How does it get
to our homes and schools?

Active Reading As you read, circle the resources used to make electricity.

hydroelectric dam

Inside a hydroelectric [hy•droh•ee•LEK•trik]
dam, the mechanical energy of falling water
is used to turn generators, which change
mechanical energy into electrical energy.

Electricity generating
stations, also known as
energy stations, may use
water, coal, or atoms to
produce the electricity
you use.

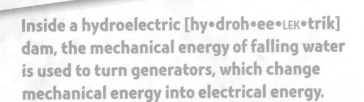

© Houghton Mifflin Harcourt Publishing Company (b) ©Mark Burnett/Photo Researchers, Inc.; (cr) ©blickwinkel/Alamy Images

windmills

Windmills have been used to grind grain or pump water. Today, wind turbines generate electricity.

Suppose you spin a magnet inside a coil of wire. A current begins to flow through the wire. You've made a **generator**, a device that converts mechanical energy to electrical energy. Huge generators in energy stations produce electricity that travels through wires to homes, schools, and businesses.

Some energy stations use falling water or wind to turn generators. Other stations convert sunlight, or solar energy, into electrical energy. These resources are called renewable resources, because they can be replaced quickly.

Most energy stations burn coal or other fuels to heat water. The water rises as steam, which turns the generators. Coal is a nonrenewable resource that will eventually run out. That's why it's important for us to conserve, or use less, electricity.

Do the Math!
Solve a Problem

Sam's electric bill was $200 for the month of June. The air conditioner accounts for $\frac{1}{2}$ of the bill, and the water heater accounts for $\frac{1}{5}$ of the bill. How much did it cost to run each appliance in June?

© Houghton Mifflin Harcourt Publishing Company   (b) ©Mark Burnett/Photo Researchers, Inc.; (tl) ©Mark Karrass/Corbis; (tr) ©Steve Hamblin/Alamy Images

When you're done, use the answer key to check and revise your work.

Use information in the summary to complete the graphic organizer.

Summarize

Electricity is used and produced in many ways. Electrical devices change electrical energy into other types of energy, such as heat, light, and sound. Many devices, including fans and refrigerators, have electric motors that change electrical energy into mechanical energy. Electricity and magnetism are related. Magnets produce a magnetic field. A magnetic field can be used to produce an electric current. An electric current can make an electromagnet. An electromagnet has a magnetic field that is turned on when there is electric current. An electromagnet can be used in a generator at an energy station. A generator changes energy of motion into electrical energy. Energy stations produce the electrical energy we use. We need to conserve electricity because some resources used by energy stations will run out.

1 Main Idea:

_____

_____

2 Detail: Electrical devices convert

_____

_____

_____

3 Detail: Magnetism and electricity are related because

_____

_____

_____

4 Detail: An electromagnet can be used in a generator at an energy station to produce

_____

_____

_____

© Houghton Mifflin Harcourt Publishing Company

Answer Key: 1. Electricity is used and produced in many ways. **2.** electrical energy into other types of energy, such as heat, sound, and light energy. **3.** Sample answer: an electric current can produce an electromagnet. **4.** electrical energy we use.

Name _____

Word Play

1 Unscramble each of the clues to form a word or a phrase from the word bank. Copy each letter in a numbered cell to the cell below with the same number.

TECGARLOETNEM

RECLICTE ROOTM

TORRAGEEN

ONECREVS

REECUSROS

GANETM

CICLETERTIY

Word Bank
conserve
electricity
electric motor
electromagnet
generator
magnet
resources

This lesson is about

Apply Concepts

2 Draw a common electrical appliance. Then explain how it changes electrical energy to other forms of energy.

_____

_____

_____

_____

© Houghton Mifflin Harcourt Publishing Company

Apply Concepts

3 Draw an *X* over each appliance that changes electrical energy to mechanical energy. You may use an appliance more than once.

Circle each appliance that is designed to change electrical energy into heat energy.

Draw a square around each appliance that changes electrical energy to sound energy.

Draw a triangle around each appliance that changes electrical energy to light energy.

4 What is the device in the picture to the right called? What would happen if you put this device near a pile of iron nails?

_____

_____

_____

5

A. What are some resources used to generate electrical energy at energy stations?

_____

_____

_____

B. Describe three ways that you can conserve electrical energy.

_____

_____

_____

Take It Home!

Discuss with your family ways that you could make informed choices to conserve electrical energy. You might talk about ways to use less energy or about things you can do by hand instead of using electrical appliances.

© Houghton Mifflin Harcourt Publishing Company

© Houghton Mifflin Harcourt Publishing Company   (l) ©Stockbyte/Alamy Images; (t) ©Image Source/Alamy Images; (c) ©Larry Lee Photography/Corbis; (r) ©PhotoLink/PhotoDisc/Getty Images; (b) ©Glen Allison/PhotoDisc/Getty Images

S.T.E.M.
Engineering & Technology

How It Works:
The Electric Grid

At home, you flip a switch and a light comes on. Electrical energy is produced at generating stations. Generating stations are part of a larger system know as the *electric grid*. Generators, high-voltage steel towers, conductors, insulators, and your household appliances are all parts of this system.

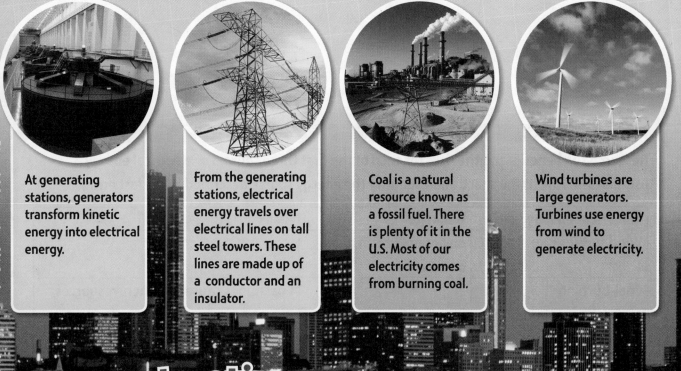

At generating stations, generators transform kinetic energy into electrical energy.

From the generating stations, electrical energy travels over electrical lines on tall steel towers. These lines are made up of a conductor and an insulator.

Coal is a natural resource known as a fossil fuel. There is plenty of it in the U.S. Most of our electricity comes from burning coal.

Wind turbines are large generators. Turbines use energy from wind to generate electricity.

Troubleshooting

During prolonged hot weather, many people use air conditioning units to remain cool. How could this affect the electric grid and the environment?

_____

_____

Show How It Works

Water falling through a turbine can generate electricity. Most hydroelectric generating stations have a dam that blocks a river. A lake forms behind the dam and provides a constant source of falling water. The dam also floods areas that were once dry land. Draw a picture that shows what you think the area behind the dam looked like before the dam was built.

A hydroelectric dam uses energy from moving water to generate electricity.

Research the benefits and the risks for each of the first three sources of electrical energy listed below. Fill out the chart. Then, identify the energy source described in the last entry.

Electrical energy source	Benefits	Risks
Wind turbines	do not pollute air, land, or water	
Coal-burning generating stations		Coal mines cause pollution; resources must be conserved and used wisely
Hydroelectric dams	use water, a renewable resource	
	do not pollute air, land, or water	These produce toxic wastes that must be stored for a very long time.

Build On It!

Rise to the engineering design challenge—complete **Build in Some Science: An Attractive Option** on the Inquiry Flipchart.

© Houghton Mifflin Harcourt Publishing Company

Name _____

Vocabulary Review

Use the terms in the box to complete the sentences.

circuit
conductor
electric motor
generator
insulator
magnet
parallel circuit

TEKS 4.6C

1. A closed path along which electric charges flow is called

   a(n) _____.

TEKS 4.5A

2. An object that attracts iron and a few other metals

   is called a(n) _____.

TEKS 4.6A

3. A device that changes electrical energy into mechanical

   energy is a(n) _____.

TEKS 4.6B

4. A material through which electricity travels easily is

   called a(n) _____.

TEKS 4.6B

5. A material that resists the movement of electricity through

   it is called a(n) _____.

TEKS 4.6A

6. A device that produces an electric current by converting
   mechanical energy to electrical energy is a(n)

   _____.

TEKS 4.6C

7. An electric circuit that has more than one path for the
   electric charges to follow is a(n)

   _____.

© Houghton Mifflin Harcourt Publishing Company   (border) ©NDisk/Age Fotostock

Science Concepts

Fill in the letter of the choice that best answers the question.

8. Clint set up equipment for an investigation, as shown in the diagram.

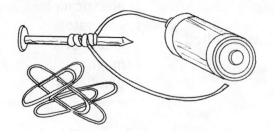

Which purpose is the most likely for Clint's investigation?

(A) to explore an electromagnetic field

(B) to test the strength of the battery

(C) to figure out what the nail is made of

(D) to see if the paper clips are magnetic

9. Electric charges can easily flow through which of the following materials?

(A) metal   (C) rubber

(B) plastic   (D) wood

10. Which materials would you use to design an experiment with an electromagnet?

(A) battery, battery holder, nail, bulb

(B) battery, battery holder, bulb, copper wire

(C) battery, battery holder, nail, copper wire

(D) battery, battery holder, switch, copper wire

11. This diagram shows an electrical plug similar to plugs used to plug in lamps.

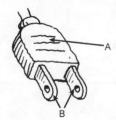

Differentiate between Part A and Part B by selecting the statement that best describes each part.

(A) A is an insulator, and B is a circuit.

(B) A is a conductor, and B is a circuit.

(C) A is an insulator, and B is a conductor.

(D) A is a conductor, and B is an insulator.

12. Jayden uses various objects to construct an electric circuit. He compares how brightly a bulb glows using each object. His results are shown below.

Object	Glow
nail	very bright
crayon	dim
eraser	very dim
pencil lead	bright

Which object is the best electrical conductor?

(A) nail   (C) crayon

(B) eraser   (D) pencil lead

© Houghton Mifflin Harcourt Publishing Company (border) ©NDisk/Age Fotostock

TEKS 4.6C

13. While planning an investigation in which she will demonstrate that electricity travels in a closed path, Harini draws four ways to connect a battery, a paper clip, a light bulb, and some wire. Which arrangement would light the bulb?

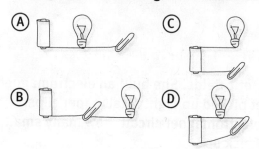

Ⓐ   Ⓒ

Ⓑ   Ⓓ

TEKS 4.6C

14. The diagram below shows a circuit.

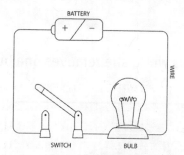

What would you need to do for the light bulb to light up and to demonstrate a complete circuit?

Ⓐ Add another battery.

Ⓑ Add another bulb.

Ⓒ Close the switch.

Ⓓ Shorten the wires.

TEKS 4.1B

15. Dams are a source of mechanical energy to generate electricity. Which natural resource provides energy for a dam?

Ⓐ coal   Ⓒ water

Ⓑ solar   Ⓓ wind

TEKS 4.6A

16. The picture below shows a large dam used to produce electricity. Water flows from the lake behind the dam to the river below it. Water passes through turbines connected to electric generators.

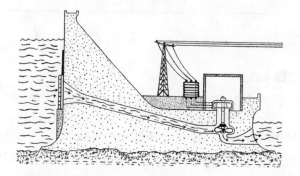

Which energy transformation takes place in the hydroelectric power plant?

Ⓐ heat energy into electrical energy

Ⓑ energy of motion into electrical energy

Ⓒ electrical energy into energy of motion

Ⓓ energy of motion and sound energy into electrical energy

TEKS 4.6C

17. When Tony left the room, he flipped the light switch. The light turned off. Which conclusion can you draw about what caused the light to go off?

Ⓐ The tiny wires inside the bulb stopped moving, so it could not make light.

Ⓑ The circuit was broken, so the electric current had no path to follow.

Ⓒ The bulb became cooler, so the light bulb stopped changing heat energy into light.

Ⓓ The electric current stopped, so light could not be changed into electrical energy.

© Houghton Mifflin Harcourt Publishing Company   (border) ©NDisk/Age Fotostock

Apply Inquiry and Review the Big Idea

Write the answers to these questions.

TEKS 4.6C

18. How could you use a magnet and some wire to explore an electromagnetic field?

_____

_____

_____

TEKS 4.2D, 4.6D

19. Kim designed an experiment to explore electromagnetic fields. She built an electromagnet using one battery. Kim found that her electromagnet picked up eight small paper clips. If Kim adds two more batteries of equal size to her electromagnet circuit, how many small paper clips do you predict the electromagnet would pick up?

_____

TEKS 4.6C

20. Eshe builds two circuits. After checking that all the bulbs work, she removes one bulb from each circuit, as shown below.

Circuit A

Circuit B

Explain why the bulb stays lit in Circuit A but goes out in Circuit B.

_____

_____

_____

_____

© Houghton Mifflin Harcourt Publishing Company   (border) ©NDisk/Age Fotostock

Forces and Motion

Big Idea

Motion can be measured and is influenced by forces such as a push, a pull, gravity, and friction.

TEKS 4.2B, 4.2E, 4.4A, 4.6D

I Wonder Why

Rides at a state fair move in many different directions and at many different speeds. Why is this so? *Turn the page to find out.*

© Houghton Mifflin Harcourt Publishing Company (bg) ©Angelo Cavalli/Getty Images (inset) ©Angelo Cavalli/Getty Images (border) ©NDisc/Age Fotostock

Here's Why Forces make objects move in straight lines, in curves, or back and forth. A force can change the speed or direction of an object.

In this unit, you will explore the Big Idea, the Essential Questions, and the Investigations on the Inquiry Flipchart.

Levels of Inquiry Key ■ DIRECTED ■ GUIDED ■ INDEPENDENT

Big Idea Motion can be measured and is influenced by forces such as a push, a pull, gravity, and friction.

Essential Questions

Now I Get the Big Idea!

Science Notebook

Before you begin each lesson, be sure to write your thoughts about the Essential Question.

© Houghton Mifflin Harcourt Publishing Company (bg) ©Angelo Cavalli/Getty Images; (inset) ©Angelo Cavalli/Getty Images; (border) ©NDisc/Age/ Fotostock

TEKS **4.6D** design an experiment to test the effect of force on an object such as a push or a pull, gravity, friction...

Essential Question

What Is Motion?

Engage Your Brain!

As you read the lesson, figure out the answer to the following question. Write the answer here.

How would you describe the motion of the hummingbird in this picture?

_____

_____

_____

_____

_____

_____

Active Reading

Lesson Vocabulary
List the terms. As you learn about each one, make notes in the Interactive Glossary.

_____   _____

_____   _____

_____   _____

Main Idea and Details
Detail sentences give information about a main idea. The details may be examples, features, characteristics, or facts. Active readers stay focused on the topic when they ask, What fact or other information does this detail add to the main idea?

© Houghton Mifflin Harcourt Publishing Company   ©Malcolm Schuyl/Alamy

Inquiry Flipchart p. 34 — Fast Walk, Slow Walk/Push or Pull

Twisting and Turning

What tells you that the person in the picture is moving? Is it possible for a person to move in more than one direction at a time? You can find out!

Active Reading

As you read the next page, find and circle details about how this girl can move.

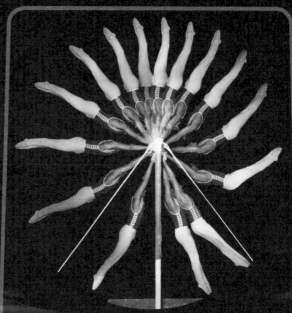

Curve

The boy's body moves in a curved path around the bar.

The blurry lines show you the directions in which the girl is moving.

Straight Line

As the girl flips down the balance beam, she moves in a straight line.

© Houghton Mifflin Harcourt Publishing Company (bkgd) ©Adastra/Getty Images; (inset) ©Gilbert Iundt; Jean-Yves Ruszniewski/TempSport/Corbis

How would you describe where your left hand is right now? Is it on top of this book, or is it touching your chin? Can you describe where it is without naming something else that is close by? No! **Position** is the location of an object in relation to a nearby object or place. The second object or place is called the *reference point*.

Now put your left hand in a different place. This change in position is **motion**. To describe your hand's motion, you'd tell in what direction it moved from its earlier position as well as how fast it moved.

The girl in the picture is in motion. Parts of her body move up and down, back and forth, in circles, and in a straight line. Her feet move in a straight line down the beam and then up and down as she flips forward.

Back and Forth

Draw a picture of something that vibrates, or moves back and forth.

▶ Name a part of the girl's body that is moving in several ways as she flips.

_____

© Houghton Mifflin Harcourt Publishing Company

Where Is It?

10

How can you tell that the penguin is moving?

Active Reading As you read the next page, underline the words that describe specific reference points.

1. The penguin has just jumped from the top of the ice.

2. The penguin is between the top of the ice and the water.

3. The penguin is entering the water.

© Houghton Mifflin Harcourt Publishing Company ©Tim Davis/Corbis

You know something is moving if its position changes against a background. The background is called the *frame of reference*.

The picture of the penguin shows three images taken as the penguin jumped off the ice. Notice that each image of the penguin has the same frame of reference. You can choose any part of that background as a reference point. The words *top of the ice* describe the reference point for Image 1. Both *top of the ice* and *the water* describe reference points for Image 2. Only *the water* describes a reference point for Image 3.

What if the images of the penguin had been in the wrong order? Could you put them in the correct order? Sure! You know that things don't fall up, so you could use the water as the reference point for each image. The image of the penguin highest above the water must be first. The image of the penguin closest to the water is last.

Look at the pictures of the horse race. In the pictures, what can you use for reference points? How can you use the reference points to put the pictures in order?

▶ Put these pictures in order by writing numbers in the circles. Then explain how you decided on the order.

_____

_____

_____

_____

© Houghton Mifflin Harcourt Publishing Company

5 meters

| 0 | 5 | 10 | 15 | 20 | 25 | 30 | 35 | 40 | 45 |

Ready! Set! Go!   `00:00` → `00:10`

The turtle, cat, and rabbit start running at the same time. How far does each of them go in 10 seconds?

Fast or Slow?

Could a turtle beat a rabbit in a race? It depends on each animal's speed.

Active Reading As you read this page, underline the definitions of *speed* and *velocity*.

One way to describe motion is to find speed, or how fast or slow something is moving. **Speed** tells you how the position of an object changes during a certain amount of time. You can measure time in hours (hr), minutes (min), or seconds (sec).

To find an object's speed, you divide how far it goes by the time it takes to get there. So if you walk 30 meters (m) in 15 seconds (sec), your speed is 2 m/sec.

$$30 \text{ m} \div 15 \text{ sec} = 2 \text{ m/sec}$$

How is velocity different from speed? **Velocity** is the speed of an object in a particular direction. Suppose you walk toward the east. If your speed is 2 m/sec, then your velocity is 2 m/sec, east.

In a race on a straight track, all the runners move in the same direction. Their velocities differ only because their speeds differ. Could a turtle win a race against a rabbit? Sure! The rabbit might run at a very slow speed—or in the wrong direction!

© Houghton Mifflin Harcourt Publishing Company   (l) ©Martin Harvey/Alamy; (r) ©Getty Images/PhotoDisc

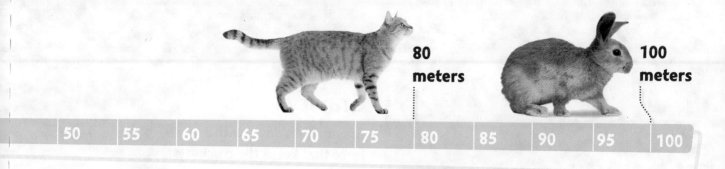

80 meters

100 meters

| 50 | 55 | 60 | 65 | 70 | 75 | 80 | 85 | 90 | 95 | 100 |

Do the Math!

Calculate Speed

1. What is the speed of the rabbit during the race?

   _____

2. What is the speed of the turtle during the race?

   _____

3. A chicken joins the race and runs at 4 m/sec. On the distance line, draw the chicken where it would be after 10 seconds.

   _____

   _____

   _____

   _____

© Houghton Mifflin Harcourt Publishing Company   (tl) ©Juniors Bildarchiv/Alamy; (tr) ©Getty Images/PhotoDisc; (cr) ©Digital Vision/Getty Images; (c) ©PhotoDisc/Getty Images; (bl) ©Getty Images/PhotoDisc; (br) ©Digital Vision/Getty Images

Pushes and Pulls

© Houghton Mifflin Harcourt Publishing Company   ©UpperCut Images/Alamy

Gravity

Gravity pulls down with a force that keeps the truck on the road.

Sand

What causes objects to start moving? What causes objects to stop moving once they are in motion?

Active Reading As you read these two pages, draw circles around two words that name types of forces.

What have you pushed or pulled today? Maybe you pushed open a door or pulled on your shoes. A push or a pull is a **force**. Suppose you want to change the way something is moving. A force can change an object's speed or direction.

Many forces act on you. *Gravity* is a force that pulls objects down to Earth. Gravity keeps you on the ground or on a chair.

Friction is a force that acts directly against the direction of motion. Friction can slow things down or make them stop.

270

Beyond the Book

Design an experiment using ramps of different heights to test the effect of the force of gravity.

Force

The force of the road on the truck pushes the truck forward.

Friction

The snow exerts a force of friction that pushes backward against the truck and slows it down.

▶ Look at the girl on the sled. Draw arrows and label *gravity*, *force*, and *friction*.

© Houghton Mifflin Harcourt Publishing Company   (b) ©Getty Images/PhotoDisc

Changing It Up

The gas pedal on a car is called an accelerator. Did you know that the brakes and steering wheel are also accelerators?

Active Reading As you read these pages, circle three phrases that tell how an object can accelerate.

You may hear people say that a car is accelerating when it speeds up. That's only partly correct. **Acceleration** is any change in velocity. Remember that velocity tells both the speed and the direction of motion. So matter accelerates if it speeds up, slows down, or changes direction.

Acceleration of any kind is caused by forces. Forces can push and pull on matter from all directions. If a force pushing against an object in one direction is greater than a force pushing in the opposite direction, the object will accelerate.

Look at the path of the fly. The fly accelerates each time it changes either its speed or its direction. Sometimes it changes both its speed and its direction at the same time!

Turn and Speed Up

In this section, the fly accelerates because it changes both its direction and its speed.

Slow Down

Here, the fly is traveling in a straight line while slowing down. This is also acceleration.

Speed Up

In this section of its path, the fly travels in a straight line. It accelerates because it is speeding up.

© Houghton Mifflin Harcourt Publishing Company (bkgd) ©Andrew Paterson/Alamy; (t) ©Anne-Marie Palmer/Alamy; (c) ©Bryan Peterson/Corbis RF/Alamy; (bl) ©CSImages/Alamy; (br) ©Stavros Markopoulos/Getty Images; (inset) ©Corbis

Stop and Start

The fly lands on the wall and stops moving. Its body doesn't accelerate. When it starts moving again, it speeds up. So it accelerates.

Change Direction

The fly's speed stays the same as it changes direction. Because its velocity changes, it accelerates.

▶ Fill in the missing parts of the table.

Item	Speed	What happens?	Acceleration?
Mouse	1 m/sec	suddenly chased by a cat	
Runner	8 m/sec	runs at the same speed around a circular track	
Train	80 km/hr	moves along a straight track	
Jet plane	300 km/hr		Yes, slows down.

© Houghton Mifflin Harcourt Publishing Company (all) ©Open Door/Alamy

Sum It Up!

When you're done, use the answer key to check and revise your work.

Read the summary statements below. Each statement is incorrect.
Change the part of the statement in blue to make it correct.

1 You know that something is
in motion when it speeds up.

_____

_____

2 Before you describe how an object
in a picture moved, you have to
choose a type of motion.

_____

3 To measure the speed of an object,
you need to know how far it traveled
and in what direction it traveled.

_____

_____

4 Gravity and friction are two types
of motion that an object can have.

_____

5 An object accelerates when it
moves left or moves right.

_____

_____

Answer Key: 1. changes its position 2. reference point 3. how long it took 4. forces that act on objects 5. speeds up, slows down, or changes direction

© Houghton Mifflin Harcourt Publishing Company (gymnast) ©Adastra/Getty Images; (penguin) ©Digital Vision/Getty Images; (rooster) ©Tim Davis/Corbis; (snowplow) ©UpperCut Images/Alamy; (fly) ©Open Door/Alamy

Word Play

Name _____

1 Important words from this lesson are scrambled in the following box. Unscramble the words. Place each word in a set of squares.

lcaoeciranet	despe	eerrfcnee	oitmon
hups	crefo	vatgiyr	ovltyiec

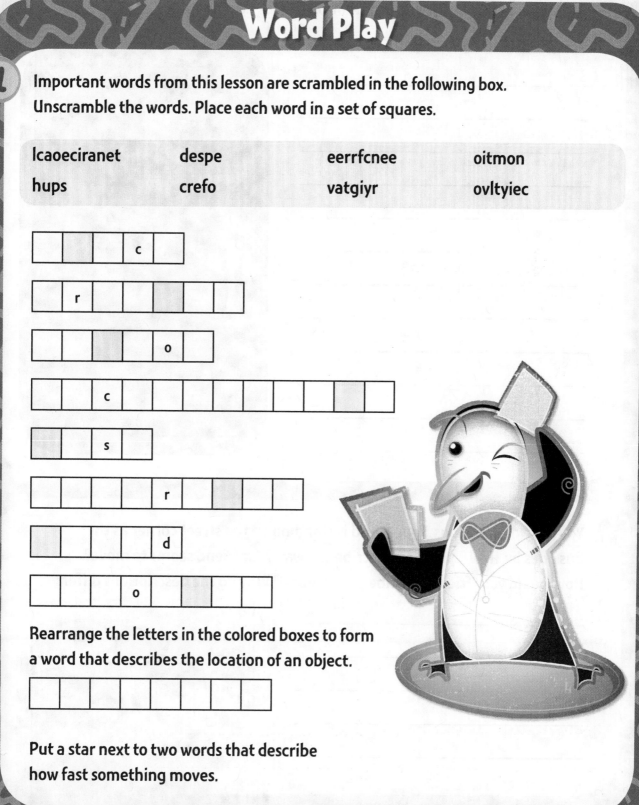

| | | | c | |

| | r | | | | | |

| | | | | o | |

| | c | | | | | | | | | | |

| | | s | | |

| | | | | | r | | | |

| | | | d | | |

| | | o | | | |

Rearrange the letters in the colored boxes to form a word that describes the location of an object.

| | | | | | | | | |

Put a star next to two words that describe how fast something moves.

© Houghton Mifflin Harcourt Publishing Company

Apply Concepts

2 Describe the motion and path of the diver. Use the words *position*, *speed*, *velocity*, and *acceleration* in your description.

_____

_____

_____

_____

_____

_____

_____

_____

_____

_____

_____

3 You are riding in a bus. Your friend is standing on the street corner as the bus goes by. How would you describe the way your friend seems to move? How would your friend describe your motion? Why do the descriptions differ?

_____

_____

_____

_____

_____

© Houghton Mifflin Harcourt Publishing Company ©Zac Macaulay/Getty Images

4

0 seconds   1 second   2 seconds   3 seconds   4 seconds   5 seconds

0 meters   2 meters   4 meters   6 meters   8 meters   10 meters

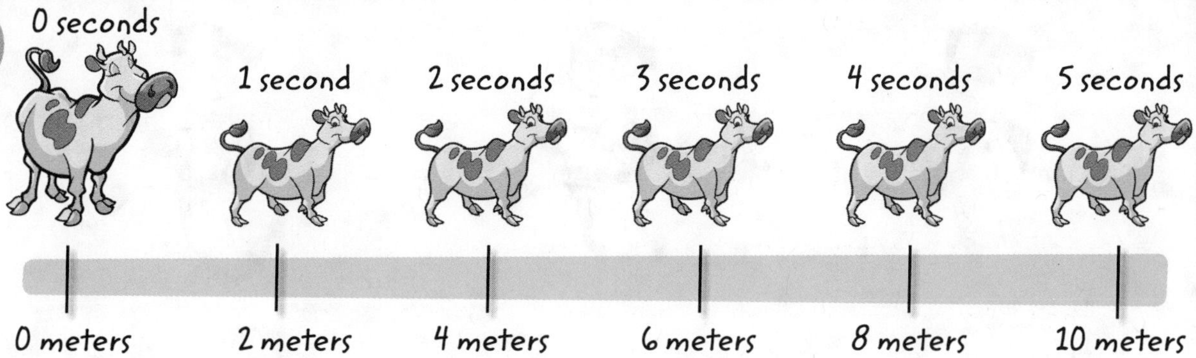

The diagram represents the motion of a cow walking in a straight line across a field. Use it to answer these questions.

a. Is the cow accelerating? Why or why not?

_____

_____

_____

_____

_____

_____

b. Calculate the speed of the cow.

_____

_____

_____

_____

c. How long will it take the cow to travel 24 meters? Describe how you found the correct answer.

_____

_____

_____

_____

d. How far will the cow travel in 35 seconds? Describe how you found the correct answer.

_____

_____

_____

_____

_____

© Houghton Mifflin Harcourt Publishing Company

5 Describe three different forces that act on you as you walk. Draw an arrow on each picture to show the direction of a force. Be sure to include gravity and friction.

_____   _____   _____

_____   _____   _____

_____   _____   _____

_____   _____   _____

_____   _____   _____

6 In each box, draw a picture that shows an object moving in the way described by the label at the top of the box.

curve

back and forth and curve

Choose three places in your community. With a family member, visit each place and look for things that move. Record what you observe in a chart. Can you identify the forces causing the motion?

Take It Home!

© Houghton Mifflin Harcourt Publishing Company

TEKS **4.2B** ...record data by observing and measuring... **4.2E** perform repeated investigations to increase the reliability of results **4.4A** collect...information using tools, including...spring scales... **4.6D** design an experiment to test the effect of force on an object such as...gravity, friction...

Name _____

Essential Question

How Do Gravity and Friction Affect Motion?

Set a Purpose

What will you learn from this investigation?

_____

_____

_____

_____

Think About the Procedure

Which forces act on the blocks when they are sitting on the table?

_____

_____

_____

_____

Why will you pull the block across several different surfaces?

_____

_____

_____

_____

Record Your Data

After you observe and measure, record your data in the table below.

Forces and Motion	
Action	**Force (N)**
Lift one block	
Lift two blocks	
Lift three blocks	
Pull block on sandpaper	
Pull block on waxed paper	
Pull block on oiled paper	

Draw Conclusions

How did you use the spring scale?

_____

_____

_____

© Houghton Mifflin Harcourt Publishing Company

Analyze and Extend

1. The block below is being pulled to the right. Draw arrows to show the forces acting on the object. Label each arrow.

2. Scientists often perform repeated investigations. Why did you repeat your force measurements three times for each surface?

_____

_____

_____

_____

3. How is an object's mass related to the upward force needed to oppose the pull of gravity in order to lift the object?

_____

_____

_____

4. Which forces acted on the block as you tried to pull it horizontally?

_____

_____

_____

_____

_____

_____

5. Why did the blocks require a different force to begin moving on the three different surfaces?

_____

_____

_____

_____

6. Which other questions would you like to ask about how gravity and friction affect motion? Which investigations could you do to answer the questions?

_____

_____

_____

_____

_____

_____

© Houghton Mifflin Harcourt Publishing Company

8 THINGS YOU SHOULD KNOW ABOUT Air Traffic Controllers

1 Air traffic controllers guide airplane traffic in the sky. They help pilots fly safely.

2 Air traffic controllers talk to pilots over the radio. Radar shows them the airplane's speed, direction, and position.

3 In the United States, most air traffic controllers work for the Federal Aviation Administration (FAA).

4 During a busy hour of travel, about 5,000 airplanes fly across the United States.

5 Some air traffic controllers work in control towers at airports. Others work far away from airports to direct airplanes as they fly.

6 Air traffic controllers must train for seven months at the FAA Academy in Oklahoma City, Oklahoma.

7 Different groups of air traffic controllers handle takeoff, in-air flight, and landing.

8 There are 200 air traffic control centers across the U. S. Each one guides the planes in its area. As a plane flies to its destination, different centers handle it.

© Houghton Mifflin Harcourt Publishing Company (tr) ©Check Six/Getty Images; (tl) ©Carol Kohen/cultura/Corbis; (cr) ©blickwinkel/Alamy Images; (cl) ©Felix Clouzot/Getty Images; (bg) ©Karen Moskowitz/Getty Images

You Be an Air Traffic Controller

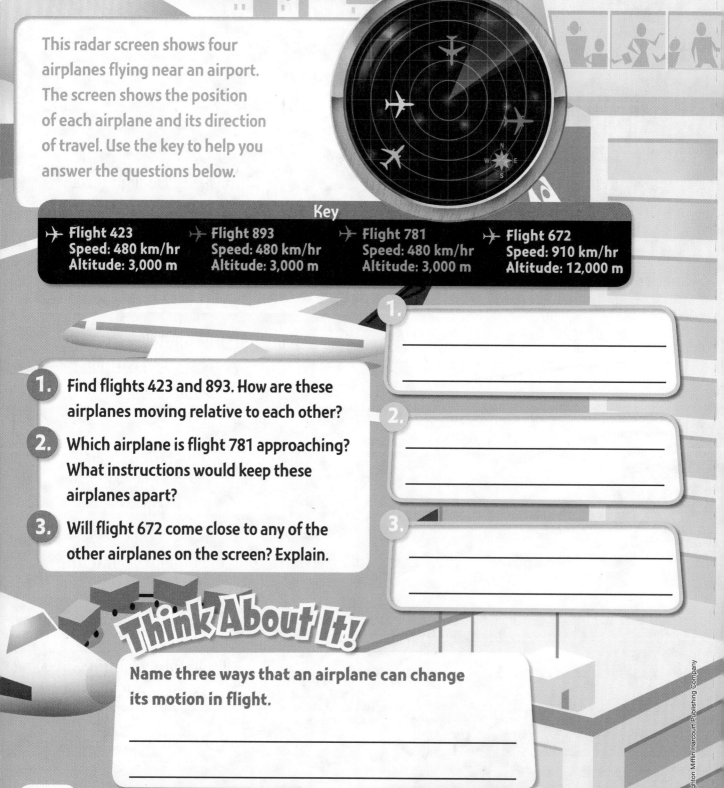

This radar screen shows four airplanes flying near an airport. The screen shows the position of each airplane and its direction of travel. Use the key to help you answer the questions below.

Key

✈ Flight 423	✈ Flight 893	✈ Flight 781	✈ Flight 672
Speed: 480 km/hr	Speed: 480 km/hr	Speed: 480 km/hr	Speed: 910 km/hr
Altitude: 3,000 m	Altitude: 3,000 m	Altitude: 3,000 m	Altitude: 12,000 m

1. Find flights 423 and 893. How are these airplanes moving relative to each other?

2. Which airplane is flight 781 approaching? What instructions would keep these airplanes apart?

3. Will flight 672 come close to any of the other airplanes on the screen? Explain.

1. _____
_____

2. _____
_____

3. _____
_____

Think About It!

Name three ways that an airplane can change its motion in flight.

_____
_____

© Houghton Mifflin Harcourt Publishing Company

TEKS 4.2B ...record data by...using descriptive words and...labeled drawings... 4.6D ...test the effect of force on an object such as...friction...

S.T.E.M.

Engineering & Technology

How It Works:

Gyroscopes

Have you ever played with a top? A top can balance on a point as it spins around its axis. The spinning motion keeps the top standing up. When the top begins to slow down, gravity makes it wobble and fall over. A gyroscope behaves like a top.

This gyroscope has a disk and axle and a central ring that swivels on an outer ring, or gimbal.

The axle is attached to the central ring. There is little friction where these parts connect, so the disk spins rapidly on the axle.

When a force acts on the gyroscope, the disk's spinning motion makes the central ring resist changing position. The rest of the gyroscope turns around the fixed central ring.

Central ring

Disk and Axle

Gimbal

Troubleshooting

Suppose that the disk of a gyroscope spins for a very short time before coming to a quick stop. What could be wrong? How would you fix it?

_____

_____

_____

© Houghton Mifflin Harcourt Publishing Company   (t) ©Ann Cutting/Getty Images;   (b) ©RYOICHI UTSUMI/Getty Images   (c) ©milos luzanin/Alamy Images;

S.T.E.M.

continued

Show How It Works

Gyroscopes are used in airplanes, boats, and spacecraft. Electronic sensors around a gyroscope tell how the vehicle has moved. Think about how data from a gyroscope might help keep a spacecraft from veering off course. In the space below, make a list of the vehicle's systems that may use data from the gyroscope.

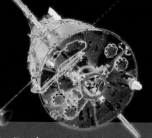

On Earth, a magnetic compass tells us which direction we are facing. A space telescope cannot use a magnetic compass. These compasses do not work in space. So, the Hubble Space Telescope uses gyroscopes to maintain direction.

_____

_____

_____

Design a toy, tool, or device with a gyroscope. Draw and label a picture of it. Use descriptive words to explain how it works.

_____

_____

How could you test the effect of friction on the gyroscope of your device?

_____

_____

_____

_____

Why does your device need a gyroscope?

_____

_____

_____

Build On It!

Rise to the engineering design challenge—complete **Improvise It: A Game of Skill and Motion** on the Inquiry Flipchart.

© Houghton Mifflin Harcourt Publishing Company (t) ©STCI/NASA 2009

Name _____

Vocabulary Review

Use the terms in the box to complete the sentences.

> acceleration
> force
> friction
> gravity
> motion
> position
> speed
> velocity

TEKS 4.6D

1. Any change in the speed or direction of an object's motion

   is _____.

TEKS 4.6D

2. A measure of an object's change in position

   during a certain amount of time is _____.

TEKS 4.6D

3. A push or a pull is a(n) _____.

TEKS 4.6D

4. The location of an object in relation to another object or

   place describes _____.

TEKS 4.6D

5. The force that acts to pull all objects down to Earth is

   _____.

TEKS 4.6D

6. An object that is changing its position is in

   _____.

TEKS 4.6D

7. A force that acts against the direction of an object's motion

   and causes it to slow or stop is _____.

TEKS 4.6D

8. The speed of an object in a particular direction is its

   _____.

© Houghton Mifflin Harcourt Publishing Company (border) ©NDisk/Age Fotostock

Science Concepts

Fill in the letter of the choice that best answers the question.

TEKS 4.6D

9. Cars, bicycles, and people are all objects that can be in motion. What is true about motion?

Ⓐ An object in motion is accelerating.

Ⓑ Motion is the change in position of an object.

Ⓒ Gravity and friction are responsible for all motion.

Ⓓ An object in motion has no speed, but it does have velocity.

TEKS 4.6D

10. The picture shows a boy as he rolls straight down a hill at a constant speed.

What is changing as the boy rolls?

Ⓐ position   Ⓒ speed

Ⓑ acceleration   Ⓓ velocity

TEKS 4.6D

11. Jared wants to test the effect of friction on an object. Which would be the best experiment for him to test this effect?

Ⓐ Use a pulley to lift several blocks.

Ⓑ Drop a ball from different heights.

Ⓒ Roll a toy car across different surfaces.

Ⓓ Use a balance to find the mass of objects.

TEKS 4.2D, 4.6D

12. The line graph records the measurement of an object's speed over time.

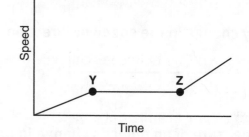

Analyze the line graph. What happens to the object between Point Y and Point Z?

Ⓐ The object is speeding up.

Ⓑ The object has no velocity.

Ⓒ The object is slowing down.

Ⓓ The object's acceleration is zero.

TEKS 4.6D

13. Renee is throwing a ball high into the air and then catching it. What is the effect of gravity on the ball?

Ⓐ It increases the mass of the ball.

Ⓑ It pulls the ball back to the ground.

Ⓒ It makes the ball's speed slow down.

Ⓓ It makes the ball's speed remain constant.

TEKS 4.6D

14. A car is stopped at a red light. The light turns green, and the car turns right around a corner. Which property of the car is changing?

Ⓐ position only   Ⓒ direction only

Ⓑ speed only   Ⓓ acceleration

© Houghton Mifflin Harcourt Publishing Company   (border) ©NDisk/Age Fotostock

TEKS 4.6D

15. Jen is walking her dog at a constant rate. They keep a constant rate as they turn a corner. Why has their velocity changed?

Ⓐ because their speed changed

Ⓑ because their direction changed

Ⓒ because their position changed

Ⓓ because their force changed

TEKS 4.2D

16. An object moves from Point A to Point B in 2 minutes at a constant rate. What is the speed of the object?

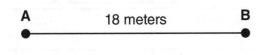

A   18 meters   B

Ⓐ 2 min/m

Ⓑ 9 m/min

Ⓒ 9 min/m

Ⓓ 18 m/min

TEKS 4.6D

17. In which example is a force causing an object to accelerate?

Ⓐ a soccer ball sitting on the ground

Ⓑ a rock sitting on a ledge at the top of a mountain

Ⓒ a train moving at constant speed around a curve in a track

Ⓓ a girl riding a bicycle at a constant speed along a straight path

TEKS 4.6D

18. A roller coaster speeds up as it travels downhill and then slows as it enters a curve. Which statement best describes the motion of the roller coaster during this trip?

Ⓐ Velocity changes, but acceleration remains constant.

Ⓑ The velocity of the roller coaster remains constant.

Ⓒ The roller coaster accelerates throughout the trip.

Ⓓ The speed of the roller coaster remains constant.

TEKS 4.6D

19. Suri designs an experiment to measure the distance each car travels when she launches it from the same starting point using the same stretched rubber band. She places a different number of magnets on each car, as shown.

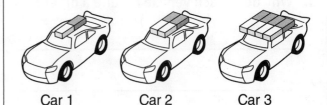

Car 1   Car 2   Car 3

How will the force of the rubber band affect the cars?

Ⓐ Car 3 will travel the longest distance.

Ⓑ Car 1 will travel the shortest distance.

Ⓒ Car 1 will be the least affected by the force acting on it.

Ⓓ Car 3 will be the least affected by the force acting on it.

© Houghton Mifflin Harcourt Publishing Company (border) ©NDisk/Age Fotostock

Apply Inquiry and Review the Big Idea

Write the answers to these questions.

TEKS 4.6D

20. Lui and Simone want to test the effects of gravity on speed. They have two equal-length tracks that start from raised platforms and then flatten out into straight, flat sections. Design an experiment Lui and Simone can conduct to test the effect of gravity.

_____

_____

_____

_____

TEKS 4.6D

21. A boy uses a rope to pull a box across the ground. What is the effect of gravity and friction on the box?

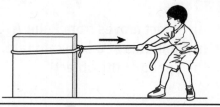

_____

_____

TEKS 4.3A

22. A truck, a car, and a bicycle are stopped at a light. The light turns green and all three begin to move. The truck uses a big engine for this acceleration while a car uses a smaller engine. The bicycle rider uses the force of his own muscles.

a. Why does each vehicle require a different amount of force to accelerate?

_____

_____

b. Suppose each vehicle is pushed forward with a force of the same size. Which

vehicle will be moving faster after one minute? Why? _____

_____

TEKS 4.6D

23. Jamal lives 2 km from his school. It takes 30 min for him to walk to school. What is Jamal's average speed during his walk—in km/hr?

_____

© Houghton Mifflin Harcourt Publishing Company (border) ©NDisk/Age Fotostock

UNIT 7
Earth's Surface

(bg) ©Gordon Cohan/National Geographic/Getty Images; ©Prisma Bildagentur AG/Alamy Images

© Houghton Mifflin Harcourt Publishing Company

Big Idea

Earth consists of useful resources, and its surface is constantly changing.

TEKS 4.3C, 4.3D, 4.7A, 4.7B, 4.7C

I Wonder How

Processes on Earth's surface shaped this mushroom rock over a long period of time. Which processes shaped this rock? *Turn the page to find out.*

Here's How Over time, water shaped the base of the rock through weathering and erosion until the rock began to look like a mushroom. Then wind weathered and eroded the rock in the final stages of its formation to polish its surface.

In this unit, you will explore the Big Idea, the Essential Questions, and the Investigations on the Inquiry Flipchart.

Levels of Inquiry Key ■ DIRECTED ■ GUIDED ■ INDEPENDENT

Track Your Progress

Big Idea Earth consists of useful resources, and its surface is constantly changing.

Essential Questions

Now I Get the Big Idea!

Science Notebook

Before you begin each lesson, be sure to write your thoughts about the Essential Question.

TEKS **4.1B** make informed choices in the use and conservation of natural resources and reusing...of materials...**4.2C** construct...maps using tools...to organize, examine, and evaluate data **4.7C** identify and classify Earth's renewable resources, including air, plants, water, and animals; and nonrenewable resources, including coal, oil, and natural gas; and the importance of conservation

Lesson **1**

Essential Question

What Are Natural Resources?

🧠 Engage Your Brain!

Find the answer to the following question in this lesson and record it here.

What types of natural resources can be found in this setting?

_____

_____

_____

_____

Active Reading

Lesson Vocabulary
List the terms. As you learn about each one, make notes in the Interactive Glossary.

_____

_____

_____

_____

Signal Words: Contrasts
Words that signal contrasts, or differences, include *unlike, but, different from,* and *on the other hand.* Active readers remember what they read because they are alert to signal words that identify contrasts.

© Houghton Mifflin Harcourt Publishing Company (bg) ©Corbis

Resources You Can Rely On

Soap, water, clothes, wood, bricks, pencils, paper. What do all these things have in common? They are all natural resources or things made from these resources.

Active Reading As you read the next page, identify and circle examples of Earth's renewable resources.

Can you identify the natural resources shown in these pictures?

© Houghton Mifflin Harcourt Publishing Company   (tl) ©Nadia Isakova/Alamy Images; (br) ©blickwinkel/Alamy Images; (t) ©PhotoDisc/Getty Images; (bc) ©Steve Hamblin/Alamy Images

▶ Look at the picture. Identify four types of renewable resources found in this setting.

_____

_____

_____

_____

Materials found in nature that are used by living things to meet their needs are called **natural resources**. Some natural resources are required to sustain life. Plants, animals, and people would die without air and water. People drink water and use it to keep clean. Some natural resources, such as water and air, are used again and again.

Natural resources that can be replaced quickly are called **renewable resources**. Trees and crops can be planted again and again. For example, if a tree is cut to make paper, a new tree can be grown in a short time to replace the old tree. Scientists also consider sunlight and wind renewable resources.

© Houghton Mifflin Harcourt Publishing Company (t) ©Dan Forer/Beateworks/Corbis

nonrenewable Resources

Not all natural resources can be replaced quickly. Some natural resources take thousands or millions of years to form.

Active Reading On these two pages, identify and circle examples of nonrenewable resources. Underline phrases that describe how they are different from renewable resources.

Natural resources that aren't replaced easily are called **nonrenewable resources**. It can take thousands or millions of years to replace a nonrenewable resource. Fossil fuels are an example of a nonrenewable resource. Coal, oil, and natural gas are types of fossil fuels. Some are used to produce electricity. Some are used to run planes, cars, and other vehicles.

Because they form so slowly, there are limited amounts of fossil fuels and other nonrenewable resources. Once nonrenewable resources are used up, they cannot be replaced in our lifetimes. If people keep using fossil fuels at the same rate they use them today, these fuels will be gone very soon.

Oil is found deep underground. It is pumped to the surface and then refined before it can be used.

© Houghton Mifflin Harcourt Publishing Company (cr) ©PhotoDisc/Getty Images; (br) PhotoDisc/Getty Images; (r) ©James Schwabel/Alamy Images

Soil takes hundreds of years to form. It is made of weathered rock and once-living plants and animals.

Limestone and aluminum are mined. Limestone is used to make cement, and aluminum is used to make cans.

Soil is a nonrenewable resource that people use to grow crops. It can be washed away if it is left uncovered or used improperly. As a result, it is important for people to conserve soil.

Minerals and rocks are other types of nonrenewable resources. A *mineral* is a nonliving solid with a crystal form. A *rock* is a solid substance made of one or more minerals. A rock that contains a valuable mineral is called an *ore*. Many minerals and rocks, such as limestone and aluminum ore, are mined. Once they have been removed from a mine, there are none left. It takes a long time for more minerals or rocks to form. It is important for people to make informed choices when using resources with a limited supply.

Do the Math!
Interpret a Graph

The graph shows the percentage of different natural resources used to produce electricity in the United States. How much comes from nonrenewable resources? _____

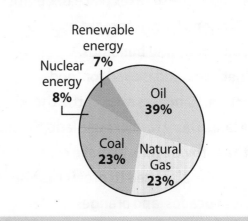

Renewable energy **7%**

Nuclear energy **8%**

Oil **39%**

Coal **23%**

Natural Gas **23%**

© Houghton Mifflin Harcourt Publishing Company   (tr) ©Jacques Jangoux/Alamy Images; (tl) ©Grant Faint/Getty Images

From Coast to Coast

You use natural resources every day. Some provide shelter. Others help you learn in school. On these pages, you will learn where some natural resources come from.

Active Reading Circle examples below of land used as a natural resource to produce food.

Every state has natural resources. Many natural resources are found in greater quantities in some parts of the United States than in others. Trees, silver, wind, coal, and fish are just a few examples of natural resources found in the United States.

People mine land to get many natural resources. Some mining is done to get valuable minerals, such as silver, iron, and copper. Mining also takes place to get fossil fuels. Other mining gets rocks used to construct roads and buildings.

Sometimes land is used for food production. Ranchers raise cattle that graze on the land. Dairy farmers use land to raise cows that provide milk to make cream and cheese. Soil is also used to grow crops, such as corn, avocados, and oranges.

Some land is used to produce *green energy*, or energy generated using renewable resources. Wind farms, solar cells, and hydroelectric dams use wind, sunlight, and water to produce electrical energy.

Forests, or areas with large numbers of trees, provide lumber. People use lumber to make paper and furniture and to build houses.

▶ Look at the Natural Resources map. Classify the resources on the map by circling the renewable resources and drawing an X on top of the nonrenewable resources.

People use land to raise livestock and grow crops.

Beyond the Book

Research resources in your state. Construct a simple map to organize, examine, and evaluate your data. Classify each resource as renewable or nonrenewable.

© Houghton Mifflin Harcourt Publishing Company (b) ©Reimar Gaertner/Alamy Images

People use trees for lumber.

People use hydroelectric dams, wind turbines, and solar panels to produce green energy.

People mine land to get minerals, rocks, and fossil fuels.

Natural Resources

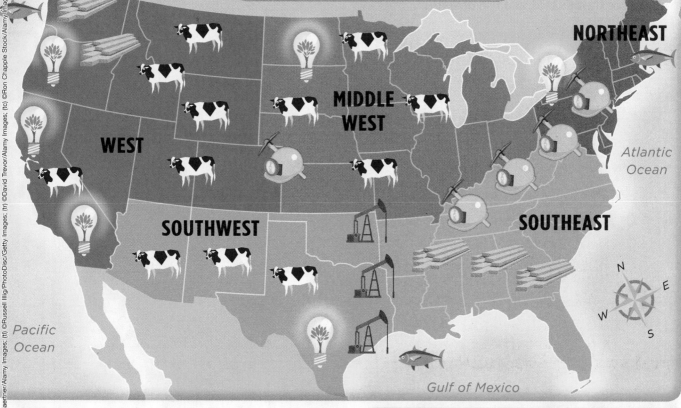

NORTHEAST

MIDDLE WEST

WEST

SOUTHWEST

SOUTHEAST

Atlantic Ocean

Pacific Ocean

Gulf of Mexico

Legend

Fisheries	Timber	Mining
Oil	Green Energy	Farming

© Houghton Mifflin Harcourt Publishing Company (b) ©Reimar Gaertner/Alamy Images; (tl) ©Russell Illig/PhotoDisc/Getty Images; (tr) ©David Trevor/Alamy Images; (tc) ©Ron Chapple Stock/Alamy Images

Flowing Down Slope

Every second, millions of gallons of water flow from the Mississippi River into the Gulf of Mexico. Where does all this water come from?

Active Reading As you read these pages, draw a star next to each sentence that describes a use of water.

The Mississippi River watershed is an important natural resource. It is home to many living things.

© Houghton Mifflin Harcourt Publishing Company

From its source as a tiny stream in northern Minnesota to where it empties into the Gulf of Mexico, the Mississippi River spans 3,782 km (2,350 mi). Along the way, it connects with hundreds of rivers and streams, including the Missouri and the Ohio Rivers.

Water from 31 states drains into the Mississippi River. All of this water makes the Mississippi River system one of the world's largest watersheds. A *watershed* is all of the land and water that drain into a river system.

A watershed is an important natural resource. States often share the water in a watershed. Virginia, for example, shares the water in the Chesapeake Bay watershed with five other states as well as the District of Columbia.

The rivers and streams in a watershed are used in many ways. For example, the Mississippi River supplies drinking water to more than 50 cities. People also use water from the Mississippi River to grow crops, for recreation, and for transportation.

A Day Without Water

How many ways do you use water each day? Make a list. Then describe what a day without water would be like.

_____

_____

_____

_____

_____

People use water for recreational activities such as fishing, canoeing, and swimming.

Farmers use water to grow food.

Cargo ships and barges use the Mississippi to move goods.

© Houghton Mifflin Harcourt Publishing Company   (c) ©Corbis; (t) ©Ariel Skelley/Blend Images/Corbis; (b) ©Rainer Schimpf/Getty Images

Let's Conserve!

What can we do to protect and conserve our natural resources?

People must recognize the importance of conservation to protect Earth's natural resources. **Conservation** is the use of less of something to make its supply last longer. It also means preserving the natural condition of the environment. People can make informed choices about how we use and conserve our natural resources to help preserve them. For example, governments have passed laws to protect the environment. As a result, millions of acres of land have been set aside to use as national and state parks and to protect the plants and animals that live in them. People, communities, and businesses can all make informed choices in order to wisely use and conserve our natural resources.

Community projects help clean up polluted streams and rivers. People volunteer to remove harmful pollutants, which makes the environment healthier for everyone. In Texas, the Blanco River Project preserves and protects the plant and animal life of the river's environment.

© Houghton Mifflin Harcourt Publishing Company   (t) ©Heike Bohnstengel/Alamy; (bc) ©Leland Bobbé/Corbis; (b) ©Stephanie Friedman/Alamy Images

Much of the trash we throw away can be recycled. Paper, glass, plastic, and metal can all be recycled based on the types of recycling programs in your area. These materials can be used to produce new products.

Many businesses have creative ways to reuse items like plastic bottles and old tires. The rubber from used sneakers can be reused by shredding them to make mulch for playgrounds.

Reusing Resources at Home

Identify an object in your home that you might reuse. Describe how you would reuse the object for another purpose.

_____

_____

© Houghton Mifflin Harcourt Publishing Company   (br) ©Mark Carper/Alamy Images;   (bl) ©Robert Ashton/Massive Pixels/Alamy Images;   (tl) ©Roger T. Schmidt/Getty Images;   (tr) ©Image Source/Getty Images

Sum It Up!

Read the summary statements below. Each one is incorrect. Change the part of the summary in blue to make it correct.

Summarize

1 Nonrenewable resources can be quickly replaced or renewed after they are used.

_____
_____
_____

2 Examples of renewable resources are rocks and coal.

_____
_____
_____

3 Oil, minerals, and soil are all renewable resources that will be gone forever once they are used up.

_____
_____
_____

4 Nonrenewable resources can take 10 or 20 years to be replaced.

_____
_____

5 You conserve natural resources so that they disappear faster.

_____
_____
_____

Answer Key: 1. Renewable resources 2. Sample answers: plants, animals, sunlight, water, air, wind 3. nonrenewable resources 4. thousands or millions of years 5. Sample answer: will be around for people in the future

302

© Houghton Mifflin Harcourt Publishing Company

Brain Check

Name _____

Word Play

1 Use the words in the box to complete each sentence.

watershed	**fossil fuels**	nonrenewable resources*	**pollution**
recycling	**natural resources***	**renewable resources***	**conservation***

*Key Lesson Vocabulary

Materials found in nature and used by living things are _____ .

All of the land and water that drain into a river system forms a _____ .

When _____ are burned, they cause pollution.

Resources that are limited and cannot be replaced quickly are called _____ .

Fish, trees, and other similar resources should be protected because if they are used too quickly, they will no longer be

_____ .

Resources such as plastic, metal, glass, and paper can be conserved by _____ them.

Harmful materials in the environment are forms of _____ .

_____ is the use of less of something to make its supply last longer.

Apply Concepts

2 Write to identify why conservation is important.

_____
_____
_____
_____

© Houghton Mifflin Harcourt Publishing Company (cr) ©Jupiterimages/Getty Images

3 Construct a two-column chart to classify the words in the box as renewable resources or nonrenewable resources.

air	coal	minerals	plants	soil	water
animals	oil	natural gas	rocks	sunlight	wind

4 Name three ways you use water. Explain how you can make informed choices in the ways you use and conserve this natural resource.

_____

_____

_____

_____

5 Make a list of five materials your family uses in one day that can be reused or recycled. Explain how you would make an informed choice in how to reuse or recycle each one.

_____

_____

Take It Home!

With your family, identify one natural resource found in your state. Research to find out where it comes from in your state. Draw a picture of the natural resource and describe how it is used.

© Houghton Mifflin Harcourt Publishing Company

TEKS 4.7B observe and identify slow changes to Earth's surface caused by weathering, erosion, and deposition from water, wind, and ice

Lesson 2

Essential Question

How Do Weathering and Erosion Shape Earth's Surface?

Engage Your Brain!

Find the answer to the following question in this lesson and record it here.

How do you think this arch formed?

_____

_____

_____

Active Reading

Lesson Vocabulary

List the terms. As you learn about each one, make notes in the Interactive Glossary.

_____

_____

_____

_____

Cause and Effect

Some ideas in this lesson are connected by a cause-and-effect relationship. Why something happens is a cause. What happens as a result of something else is an effect. Active readers look for effects by asking themselves, What happened? They look for causes by asking why it happened.

© Houghton Mifflin Harcourt Publishing Company ©Digital Vision/Getty Images

Inquiry Flipchart p. 38 — Grooving with Glaciers/Which Will Weather Faster?

305

What can Break a Boulder?

When you think of rocks, words like *hard* and *solid* may come to mind. You may think rocks can't ever break, but that's not true. Wind and water can slowly change and shape rocks.

Active Reading As you read these two pages, identify and underline all the different things that can cause a rock to weather, or break apart.

The roots of this tree broke apart the rock.

When it rains, water can get into the cracks of rocks.

When water freezes to form ice, it expands. This widens the cracks.

When water freezes again, it pushes the cracks in the rocks even wider. When this happens many times, the rock breaks apart.

© Houghton Mifflin Harcourt Publishing Company (t) ©Ola Images/Getty Images; (tbkg) ©David Edwards/Getty Images; (bbkg) ©Lee Frost/The National Trust Photolibrary/Alamy

The process of rock breaking apart is called **weathering**. Many different things can cause weathering. Flowing water can cause rocks to tumble and scrape against rocks in the riverbed. Sand blown by wind can scrape against rocks.

Living things can also cause weathering. A tree's roots can grow in a small crack in a rock. As the roots grow, it can push the rock apart until the rock breaks. Animals may dig up rocks, causing the rocks to be exposed to wind and rain.

Chemicals in water and rain that flow through and around rocks can also cause weathering. These chemicals can combine with the rock and change it so that it crumbles and wears away. Look at the statues on this page. Chemical weathering has already changed one of the statues.

WEATHERED

How Will Weathering Change What This Statue Looks Like?

Observe the statue. Describe how it may look in the future.

_____

_____

_____

_____

_____

© Houghton Mifflin Harcourt Publishing Company (l) ©Lindsey Stock/Alamy; (b) ©blickwinkel/Alamy; (tbkg) ©David Edwards/Getty Images; (bbkg) ©Lee Frost/The National Trust Photolibrary/Alamy

Rocks on the Move

Don't rocks just sit around in the sun all day?
No! Rocks can move—find out how.

Weathering is the beginning of a series of slow changes that often occur to rocks on Earth's surface. The same wind and water that can cause weathering also can carry the broken bits of rock away. The process of moving weathered rock from one place to another is called **erosion** [uh•ROH•zhuhn].

Active Reading Circle slow changes to Earth's surface due to erosion and deposition from water.

1 The erosion of rock is caused by many different natural processes. Moving water is one of the most common causes of erosion. The fast-moving water in this stream can shift or move large rocks near the top of the mountain. Together with gravity, water can cause the rocks to move downhill.

2 The water pulls the larger pieces of weathered rock along the river's bottom. As the water slows down, it has less energy. It cannot move the largest rocks and pebbles. These are left behind as the water moves on. The dropping of weathered rock by wind or moving water is known as **deposition** [dep•uh•ZISH•uhn].

© Houghton Mifflin Harcourt Publishing Company

What Happens Next?

Observe these pictures of the Yangtze River before and after a dam was built across the river. How do you think the dam affects the movement and deposition of sediment by water?

BEFORE

AFTER

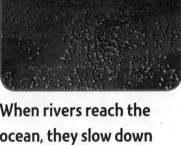

_____

_____

_____

_____

3

As the water in a river continues to slow down, more bits of weathered rock are dropped. This happens because slow-moving water has less energy than fast-moving water. So, slow-moving water can carry only very small pieces of rock, such as sand and silt. These bits of rock are called **sediment**.

4

When rivers reach the ocean, they slow down even more. As they slow down, much of the remaining sediment in the water is dropped. Over time, the sediment piles up near the mouth of the river. It forms a landform called a *delta*.

3

4

© Houghton Mifflin Harcourt Publishing Company

Blowing in the Wind

Wind is just moving air, so what can it do? A lot—wind can pick up and move sand and other sediment.

Active Reading As you read the text, identify and circle the wind's effects.

A *landform* is a natural land shape or feature. Weathering, erosion, and deposition by wind slowly form and change landforms. Wind can erode sand, moving it long distances. When the wind deposits a lot of sand in one area, *sand dunes* form. Sand dunes are often found near sandy beaches, but dunes also form far from oceans. The dunes of some deserts span thousands of kilometers.

The shape of a sand dune constantly changes. Wind sweeps up one side of a dune and lifts sand from its surface. Then, gravity pulls the sand down the other slope. An entire hill of sand gradually advances in this way.

Blowing sediment can also cause changes to other landforms. Particles carried by wind collide with exposed rock and cause weathering. Exposed rock can slowly erode, leaving interesting shapes. Mushroom rocks and arches are formed by water but shaped by the wind. Over time, they become thinner and more fragile. Eventually, gravity pulls these formations to the ground.

▶ Observe the dunes. Describe how the wind affects the direction in which the dune moves.

_____

_____

_____

_____

_____

© Houghton Mifflin Harcourt Publishing Company (bkg) ©David Nunuk/Alamy Images

Wall Arch

© Houghton Mifflin Harcourt Publishing Company (bkg) ©David Noton/Alamy Images; (t) ©National Park Service Photo; (c) ©National Park Service Photo

BEFORE

AFTER

▶ Observe the photograph of the Wall Arch. Write a sentence that explains what shaped it. Then list three processes that caused it to collapse.

_____

_____

_____

_____

_____

Utah, United States
Until its collapse in 2008, Wall Arch's opening was 22 m (72 ft) high and 10 m (33 ft) wide.

Namibia, Africa
The dunes of the Namib Desert can move up to 10 m (33 ft) each year.

Ice Carvings

Can you imagine an ice cube the size of a city?
Some chunks of ice are even larger than that!

Active Reading As you read these two pages, identify and underline
a slow change caused by deposition from ice. Then identify and circle
a slow change caused by erosion from ice.

Huge sheets of ice are called glaciers.
Glaciers are found in very cold places.
Because glaciers are made of solid ice, you
may think they do not move. But gravity
pulls glaciers downhill. The ice flows like a
very slow river. Glaciers can weather, erode,
and deposit rocks. A glacier can pick up
rocks as big as school buses!

▶ Think of two ways gravity helps
glaciers shape landforms.

_____

_____

_____

_____

Over time, erosion from ice by
glaciers formed the Great Lakes
in North America.

Russell Glacier, Canada

In this glacier, you can see
a moraine [muh • RAYNE] between
the ice flows.

CARVED BY ICE!

© Houghton Mifflin Harcourt Publishing Company (b) ©Paul A Sonders/Corbis

As a glacier moves forward, it pushes boulders against the ground beneath it, scraping and scratching rock. This can slowly change the rock by carving deep *glacial grooves* into it. The grooves can be seen when the glacier melts.

As a glacier begins to melt, the rocks and sediment it carried downhill drop out. The deposited sediment forms different land features, including hills called *moraines*.

These glacial grooves on Kelley's Island in Ohio formed when ice eroded the rock.

In the distant past, much more of Earth's surface was covered with glaciers. A huge glacier once covered most of Canada and the northern United States. The ice cut deep grooves that filled with fresh water as the glacier melted. This formed the Great Lakes. The largest, Lake Superior, is more than 400 m deep in some places!

Do the Math!
Analyze Data

As a glacier's front edge moves downhill, it is said to be advancing. A glacier that melts faster than its front edge advances is said to be retreating. Look at the data on the diagrams. Identify whether each glacier is advancing or retreating.

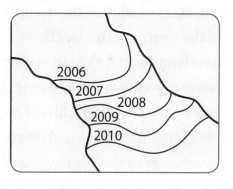

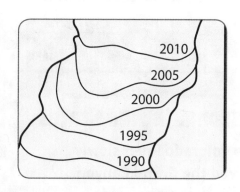

© Houghton Mifflin Harcourt Publishing Company (t) ©Mark Burnett/Photo Researchers, Inc.; (b) ©Paul A. Souders/Corbis

Can Waves Cut Caves?

Water carries rocks and sediment down a river or along a shoreline.

Active Reading As you read the text, identify and circle one effect caused by water erosion. Then identify and underline a slow change caused by deposition from water.

Moving water causes weathering and erosion. A flowing river picks up sediment along its path. The rushing sediment scrapes against the bottom and sides of the riverbed. This weathers the material along the river's path even more. River water can carve deep *canyons*. A canyon is a gorge between cliffs of rock. Deposits of sediment can build up and force river water to change directions. Curves in a river's path change over time and produce different landforms.

▶ Observe the images of the sea arch and the canyon. Identify how water caused these landforms. Then describe how these causes differ.

	→	sea arch
	→	canyon

Arizona, United States

The Colorado River slowly carved the Grand Canyon. This process occurred over millions of years.

© Houghton Mifflin Harcourt Publishing Company • (bkg) ©John Henshall/Alamy

As a river gets older, its course may change. The banks become less steep, and the distance across gets wider.

A sea arch forms when waves erode a cave all the way through a narrow cliff.

Ocean waves crash forcefully into rocks along the shore. The waves weather cliffs, erode away pieces of broken rock, and deposit the sediment in new places. Waves can cut caves into shoreline cliffs. The sediment from eroding shorelines becomes fine particles of sand. Beaches form where the sand is deposited at the water's edge.

▶ What do you think will eventually happen to this sea arch? Explain.

_____

_____

_____

WASHED AWAY BY WATER!

© Houghton Mifflin Harcourt Publishing Company   (bkg) ©John Henshall/Alamy; (t) ©blickwinkel/Alamy; (tl) ©P.A.Lawrence, LLC./Alamy

Sum It Up!

When you're done, use the answer key to check and revise your work.

Use the information in the summary to complete the cause-and-effect graphic organizers.

Summarize

Over time, wind, water, ice, gravity, plants, and animals cause rocks to break down into smaller pieces. Bits of broken-down rock, or sediment, are eroded by such agents as wind and flowing water. Eventually, the sediment is deposited. Deposited sediment forms landforms, such as deltas and sand dunes.

1

Water enters the cracks in a rock and freezes into ice. ➔ _____

2

_____ ➔ Sediment is deposited at the mouth of the river and forms a delta.

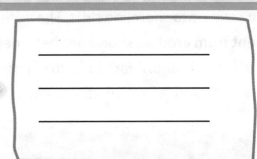

© Houghton Mifflin Harcourt Publishing Company   (tr) ©Lindsey Stock/Alamy; (br) ©NPA/Getty Images

Answer Key: 1. The ice causes the rock to crack and break apart through weathering. 2. A river erodes sediment and carries it downstream.

Brain Check

Name _____

Word Play

1 Use the words in the box to complete the puzzle.

Across

1. What process causes rocks to break down into smaller pieces?

4. What process causes eroded sediments to be dropped off in another place?

6. What is a land feature such as a sea arch or a canyon called?

7. What landform moves in the direction of the wind?

Down

2. What process carries away weathered rock?

3. What is a large sheet of flowing ice called?

5. What landform is caused by sediment deposited at the mouth of a river?

7. What are broken-down pieces of rock called?

delta	deposition*	erosion*	glacier
landform	sand dune	sediment*	weathering*

*Key Lesson Vocabulary

© Houghton Mifflin Harcourt Publishing Company   ©Susanne Masters/Alamy

Apply Concepts

2 Identify and list things that can cause slow changes to rock by weathering.

_____   _____

_____   _____

_____   _____

_____   _____

3 Explain how a plant can cause a rock to weather.

_____

_____

_____

_____

4 Identify the body of water that could erode the largest bits of sediment by circling it. Then explain how water causes slow changes to Earth's surface.

_____

_____

_____

© Houghton Mifflin Harcourt Publishing Company

5 Identify the processes—weathering, deposition, and erosion—that changed Earth's surface by causing the landforms shown below to form. Then identify whether water, ice, or wind caused each change.

_____

_____

_____

© Houghton Mifflin Harcourt Publishing Company

6 For each landform below, identify whether it was formed by erosion or by deposition. Describe how you know your answer is correct.

_____

_____

_____

_____

_____

_____

_____

_____

_____

_____

_____

_____

_____

Take It Home!

With your family, walk through your neighborhood or local park. Find objects that have been left outside for a long time. Describe how you think weathering has changed these objects.

© Houghton Mifflin Harcourt Publishing Company

S.T.E.M.
Engineering & Technology

How It Works:
Walk This Way

Measuring the distance between fossil footprints gives scientists clues about how dinosaurs walked. Studying fossilized bones tells scientists how dinosaur joints moved. Scientists use these data to make computer models to see what a walking dinosaur would have looked like.

A computer model starts with a skeleton. Then virtual muscles are added. Finally scientists are able to animate *Triceratops* in motion.

Troubleshooting

Describe some of the limitations, including accuracy and size, of modeling how a dinosaur moved.

_____

_____

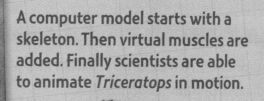

© Houghton Mifflin Harcourt Publishing Company (cl) ©The Natural History Museum, London/Alamy; (tl) ©François Gohier/Photo Researchers, Inc.; (c) HMH; (inset) ©Smithsonian Institute/Photo Researchers, Inc.; (br) ©Joe Tucciarone/Photo Researchers, Inc.

S.T.E.M.
continued

Before moving-picture cameras and computer technology, people began to study animal motion by finding ways to take rapid series of still photographs. They could look at the pictures in order to understand the animal's motion.

This famous set of images shows how a horse gallops. At one point in its stride, a horse has all four feet in the air. Write another detail that you observe about how the horse moves.

_____

_____

Research how a hummingbird flies. Draw separate images of a hummingbird in flight. How is high-speed video of hummingbirds shot?

_____

_____

Build On It!

Rise to the engineering design challenge—complete **Make a Process: Design a Fossil Exhibit Hall** in the Inquiry Flipchart.

© Houghton Mifflin Harcourt Publishing Company   (t) ©Mary Evans Picture Library/Alamy; (t) ©Francois Gohier/Photo Researchers, Inc.

TEKS **4.7A** examine properties of soils, including color and texture, capacity to retain water, and ability to support the growth of plants **4.7C** identify....Earth's...nonrenewable resources...and the importance of conservation

Lesson **3**

Essential Question

How Do Soils Form?

Engage Your Brain!

Find the answer to the following question in this lesson and record it here.

Examine the photograph of Haleakala National Park. Why is the soil red?

_____

_____

_____

_____

_____

Active Reading

Lesson Vocabulary

List the terms. As you learn about each one, make notes in the Interactive Glossary.

_____ _____

_____ _____

_____ _____

Main Ideas and Details

Detail sentences give information about a topic. The information may be examples, features, characteristics, or facts. Active readers stay focused on the topic when they ask, "What fact or information does this sentence add to the topic?"

© Houghton Mifflin Harcourt Publishing Company   (bg) © George Oze/Alamy Images

Inquiry Flipchart p. 40 — Testing Soil Absorption/Disappearing Soil

How Do SOILS Form?

Soil is the foundation for your city or town. You eat foods that are grown in soil. But what exactly is soil? Where does soil come from? How does it form?

Active Reading As you read these pages, draw a box around the word that tells how soil begins to form.

Pick up a handful of soil. You are holding something that may have begun forming a thousand years ago! It may contain billions of tiny organisms. It contains bits of rock that are millions of years old. **Soil** is a mixture of rock, organic material, water, and air in which plants can grow. Bacteria, fungi, and other tiny organisms contribute to the organic material of soil by breaking down the remains of plants and animals.

Humus, the remains of decayed plants and animals, contains nutrients that plants need to grow. Humus also helps soil retain moisture.

Earthworms loosen and mix soil as they burrow through it. The mixing increases the amount of air in soil and improves the ability of soil to drain water.

© Houghton Mifflin Harcourt Publishing Company (bg) ©John Eik III/Alamy Images (t) ©Greenshoots Communications/Alamy Images (b) ©Marin Grifsa/Alamy Images

All soils begin with weathering, the process of rock breaking apart. Many factors affect the rate of weathering. These include the type of rock and the climate of a place. After rocks have weathered, organisms need time to grow and decay, adding organic material to the broken pieces of rocks to form soil.

In a cold climate, rock weathers at a slower pace than rock in a temperate climate where freezing and melting occur regularly. In a dry climate, such as a desert, rock also weathers at a slow pace. Precipitation, especially rain, speeds weathering.

Soil Matters

What are examples of the three states of matter in soil?

Solid:

_____

_____

Liquid:

_____

_____

Gas:

_____

_____

Soil forms in stages. Rock on Earth's surface is broken down into smaller pieces. As weathering continues, layers of soil form.

exposed rock → weathered rock → developed soil

© Houghton Mifflin Harcourt Publishing Company (bg) © John Elk III/Alamy Images

Layers of SOIL

Dig deep. Soil at the surface is different from soil several inches down.

Active Reading As you read this page, circle the letter and name of each soil horizon. Put a star next to the horizon that contains the most organic material.

When soil forms, it develops layers, called **soil horizons**. Scientists use a letter to identify each soil horizon. A vertical section of soil that shows the layers is called a **soil profile**.

Horizon A is topsoil. Topsoil is a mixture of humus, minerals, and small amounts of clay and sand. The roots of most plants are here.

Horizon B is subsoil. Subsoil is clay and weathered rock. Earthworms bring subsoil to the surface. Minerals from rainwater seep down into subsoil.

Horizon C is bedrock. Bedrock is the solid rock that forms Earth's surface. It's the parent rock that breaks down as soil forms.

© Houghton Mifflin Harcourt Publishing Company

The Midwestern U.S. has just the right climate and weathering rates to form rich, fertile soils.

Sediment on slopes can be easily washed downhill. So soils on mountains and hills are often thin.

Soil varies from region to region. One reason is the makeup of the rock the soil formed from. Granite, for example, produces a different kind of soil than limestone does. Another reason is climate. In warm, moist climates, plant and animal material decays too quickly to form a thick layer of topsoil. In cold climates, few plants grow, and the rate of weathering is slow. In these areas, topsoil is usually thin.

In temperate regions, many plants lose their leaves or die in the fall and winter. These dead plants add nutrients to soil that help build up the topsoil over many years.

All the Difference

Compare the soil profiles below. Describe the ways these profiles are different.

prairie

desert

_____

_____

_____

_____

_____

_____

_____

_____

© Houghton Mifflin Harcourt Publishing Company (t) ©Gib Martinez/Alamy Images (t) ©Pat & Chuck Blackley/Alamy Images

Types of SOIL

▶ Draw boxes around the text that describes the ability of different types of soil to support plant growth. Place a star to the left of the text that describes the soil type best suited to support plant growth.

Some soil in Hawai'i is red, but the soil near you may be dark brown. Why? What's going on?

Active Reading As you read this page, circle the name of each type of soil and underline one fact about it.

Sand, silt, and clay are the main forms that the rock particles in soil take. Each can be carried by moving water and deposited as sediment. Sand and silt are often made of the same material and are distinguished by size. Silt particles are smaller than sand and bigger than clay. Clay particles are extremely fine and powdery. A lump of moist clay holds its shape when squeezed. Clay also is distinguished by the fact that it is made up of different materials from sand and silt. Each of these ingredients gives soil its texture.

The mineral content of the parent rock contributes to its color. For example, iron oxide in the soil at Haleakala National Park in Hawai'i gives it a reddish color.

Types of Soil

Scientists group soils according to the amount of sand, silt, and clay in their makeup.

sandy soil

Sandy soils are mostly sand. They feel coarse. Water passes through sandy soils quickly.

loamy soil

Loamy soils are a mix of sand, silt, and clay. Large amounts of humus make loamy soil dark in color.

clay-rich soil

Clay-rich soils are mostly clay. They have a milky color and feel smooth and wet.

© Houghton Mifflin Harcourt Publishing Company

Sandy soils do not support plant growth well because they contain little humus. Large particles of sand allow water to pass through the soil quickly. If you moisten sandy soil and squeeze it, the soil will fall through your fingers.

Most potting soil is loamy. Loamy soils are rich in humus. Loamy soils hold water better than sandy soils, so they may remain wet longer during dry periods. When you rub loamy soil between your fingers, it feels slippery and may stain your hand.

Clay-rich soils are closely packed and have very little air space. As a result, the roots of many plants are not able to break through. If you squeeze a handful of clay-rich soil, it may form a compact ball or even slip through your fingers in ribbons.

Loamy soils have a thick topsoil horizon.

Sandy soils do not have well developed horizons.

Do the Math!

Analyze Data

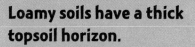

☐ Clay ☐ Sand ☐ Silt

1. Write the composition of the second sample in decimals.

   Clay: _____

   Silt: _____

   Sand: _____

2. Which sample is $\frac{1}{10}$ clay?

   _____

3. How much more clay is in the second sample than the first? Write a fraction.

   _____

4. How much less sand is in the third sample than the second? Write a decimal.

   _____

© Houghton Mifflin Harcourt Publishing Company (b) ©otog/Tetra Images/Corbis (t) ©Russ Munn/AGStockUSA/Alamy Images

SOIL Conservation

More than three-quarters of the Midwestern United States is farmland. Whether that land is used as pasture for feeding cattle or as cropland for growing corn, cotton, or wheat, the quality of the soil matters.

Soil is a *nonrenewable resource,* which means it cannot be replaced when gone. Healthy soil has organic material and contains the nutrients plants need to thrive. Farmers practice soil conservation to help keep the soil healthy and productive. *Soil conservation* is a way of managing soil that reduces erosion and maintains the nutrients plants need. Which of these images shows soil protected by soil conservation practices?

Strong winds can blow away topsoil, leaving behind soil that may not have enough nutrients to support crops.

© Houghton Mifflin Harcourt Publishing Company · (bg) ·(David Frazier/Corbis Premium RF/Alamy Images (t) ©Alan & Linda Detrick/Photo Researchers, Inc.

Growing the same crop in a field year after year can lower the nutrient level in soil. Leaving soil bare after crops have been harvested can result in wind and rain erosion. Farmers can solve both problems by rotating crops and by planting cover crops between growing seasons. For example, farmers may alternate planting crops of corn and alfalfa. Why alfalfa? Because alfalfa replaces the nitrogen that corn takes from the soil and also can be used as feed for livestock.

Windbreaks, such as the trees in this image or strips of tall plants between sections of crops, can slow or stop the erosion of topsoil by the wind.

Cause and Effect

Complete this chart. Write the cause or effect of soil conservation practices.

Cause	Effect
	Stop or slow wind erosion.
Rotate crops.	

© Houghton Mifflin Harcourt Publishing Company ∙ (t) ©David Wall/Alamy Images ∙ (t) ©Georg Gerster/Photo Researchers, Inc. ∙ (bg) ©David Frazier/Corbis Premium RF/Alamy Images

When you're done, use the answer key to check and revise your work.

1

Describe each soil horizon.

Horizon A _____

_____

_____

Horizon B _____

_____

_____

Horizon C _____

_____

_____

2

Complete the graphic organizer about soil.

Soil

Consists of | Types of

© Houghton Mifflin Harcourt Publishing Company

Answer Key: 1. Horizon A—topsoil: a dark mixture of humus, minerals, and small amounts of clay and sand Horizon B—subsoil: mostly clay and partly weathered rock Horizon C—bedrock: the solid rock that forms Earth's surface 2. Consists of—rock, water, air, organic material Types of—sandy, loamy, clay-rich

Word Play

1 Follow the directions to find the hidden term. Write the term on the line. Then draw a line from the term to its meaning.

Cross out each a, t, s, p, h, and l.
a b t e l a d h r p t o s c l a
    h k p a

_____

The remains of decayed plants and animals

Cross out each w, t, g, p, r, and f.
w r h f t u w p r m w g u r f
    w s f g

_____

A vertical section of soil that shows the layers

Cross out each b, m, c, v, w, and t.
v s t o i b m l t h m o r t i m
    z o w n

_____

The solid rock that forms Earth's surface

Cross out each d, j, p, h, z, and k.
d h p z s j z k o d k d h z i j
    p h l k p

_____

A loose mixture of rock, organic material, water, and air in which plants grow

Cross out each b, u, j, p, q, w, and z.
b q j s o p z w i b l p w z c j z
o w n p s b q e r w v j a t p i o z n

_____

A layer in a soil profile

Cross out each a, y, m, q, t, d, and x.
a s y m o i t d l p d x r o t r f z x i
    l o m e

_____

A way of managing soil that reduces erosion and maintains the nutrients plants need

bedrock*   humus*   soil*   soil conservation

soil horizon*   soil profile*

* Key Lesson Vocabulary

© Houghton Mifflin Harcourt Publishing Company

Apply Concepts

2 Identify and describe properties of clay-rich soil. Be sure to include color and texture.

_____

_____

3 The weather is hot and dry in this place. Very few plants grow here. What kind of soil would you find? Describe its properties, including its color and texture. Explain why few plants grow in it.

_____

_____

_____

_____

_____

4 Case Study: Mr. Reed is a corn farmer. Each winter, Mr. Reed lets his farmland "rest." He doesn't plant anything after he harvests the corn crop. This year, Mr. Reed's crop is small, and the plants are unhealthy.

What is the problem?	What can Mr. Reed do to solve the problem?
_____	_____
_____	_____
_____	_____

5 List the layers of soil. Circle the layer where you would find the most organic matter.

_____

Take It Home!

Put on a pair of plastic gloves. Gather a sample of soil from your neighborhood to observe. Examine the properties of your sample. How well do you think it will retain water? Can it support plant growth?

© Houghton Mifflin Harcourt Publishing Company

TEKS **4.2B** collect and record data by observing...using descriptive words...such as labeled drawings, writing... **4.2C** construct...charts... using tools...to organize, examine, and evaluate data **4.2F** communicate... oral...results supported by data **4.4A** collect...and analyze... information using tools, including... hand lenses...graduated cylinders... beakers... **4.7A** examine properties of soils, including color and texture, capacity to retain water, and ability to support the growth of plants

Name _____

Essential Question

How Can We Examine Properties of Soil?

Set a Purpose
Why is it helpful to examine properties of soil?

_____

_____

_____

Think About the Procedure
How did you use the hand lens to collect and analyze information?

_____

_____

_____

_____

Why is it important to use the same amount of water for each soil sample?

_____

_____

_____

Record Your Data
In the space below, use a tool, such as a metric ruler, to construct a chart to organize, examine, and evaluate your labeled drawings and observations.

© Houghton Mifflin Harcourt Publishing Company   HMH Credits

Draw Conclusions

What was the purpose of adding water to the soil samples? What does this property tell us?

_____

_____

_____

Which soil type did you infer is best for growing plants? Why?

_____

_____

_____

Analyze and Extend

1. Communicate your observations and conclusions orally with those of other groups. Did all groups have the same conclusions? If not, what might have made their conclusions differ?

_____

_____

_____

_____

2. What did you learn about properties of soil that surprised you?

_____

_____

_____

3. How might you directly test the ability of each type of soil to grow plants? Design and describe an experiment you could conduct. Draw a diagram of your setup.

_____

_____

_____

_____

_____

4. Think of another question you'd like to ask about the properties of soil.

_____

_____

_____

336

© Houghton Mifflin Harcourt Publishing Company   HMH Credits

People in Science

Meet the Water-Resource Scientists

Juan Enciso

Earth's supply of nonrenewable fuel resources is limited. Energy crops such as sugarcane are renewable sources of fuel, but some energy crops are grown in very dry places and must be watered using irrigation, which can be costly. Dr. Juan Enciso is an irrigation engineer who works with the Texas Agrilife Research Center to investigate and identify energy crops that will grow with little or no irrigation. Enciso hopes to find crops that will yield the most energy but require the least amount of water. His research will help people across Texas and the Southwest to produce cost-effective, alternative fuel sources that use little-to-no water.

Irrigation allows crops to be grown in very dry places.

Farouk El-Baz

Dr. Farouk El-Baz was born in Egypt. Early in his career, he worked for the Apollo space program, helping select sites for the moon landings. El-Baz began using imagery from space satellites to study Earth. He used the images to locate the courses of former rivers and to locate sources of groundwater in dry, desert regions of Earth. El-Baz's work resulted in the discovery of groundwater resources in desert areas throughout the Middle East and Africa. These discoveries provided sources of water for people in those areas.

In 1999, the Geological Society of America set up the "Farouk El-Baz Award for Desert Research" to honor excellence in dry land studies around the world.

© Houghton Mifflin Harcourt Publishing Company (t) ©Rod Santa Ana; (l) ©Paula Scully/AP Images; (bg) ©NASA

Identify Importance of Irrigation

Answer each question in the space provided.

Why is irrigation important?

_____

_____

_____

_____

How might people benefit from Dr. Enciso's work?

_____

_____

_____

_____

Why do you think Dr. El-Baz's discovery of groundwater in desert lands is important?

_____

_____

_____

_____

How did Dr. El-Baz's work with the Apollo program prepare him for his search for groundwater on Earth?

_____

_____

_____

_____

Think About It!

What are some ways people in your community might conserve water?

_____

_____

_____

© Houghton Mifflin Harcourt Publishing Company   (bg) ©Bobby Haas/Getty Images

Name _____

Vocabulary Review

Use the terms in the box to complete the sentences.

deposition
erosion
nonrenewable
  resources
renewable
  resources
sediment
soil horizon
soil profile
weathering

TEKS 4.7A

1. A vertical section of soil that shows the layers is called

   a(n) _____.

TEKS 4.7C

2. Coal, oil, and natural gas are examples of Earth's

   _____.

TEKS 4.7B

3. The process of moving weathered rock from one place

   to another is called _____.

TEKS 4.7A

4. When soil forms, it develops layers, called a(n)

   _____.

TEKS 4.7B

5. Weathering by wind, water, and ice produces

   _____.

TEKS 4.7C

6. Air, plants, water, and animals are examples of Earth's

   _____.

TEKS 4.7B

7. The process of rock breaking apart from water, wind, or ice

   is known as _____.

TEKS 4.7B

8. A river slowly erodes a steep hill, which causes sediment
   to travel downstream and to eventually drop through a

   process called _____.

© Houghton Mifflin Harcourt Publishing Company (border) ©NDisk/Age Fotostock

Science Concepts

Fill in the letter of the choice that best answers the question.

TEKS 4.7C

9. Many household items are made from renewable resources. Which object is made from a renewable resource?

Ⓐ plastic bag

Ⓒ computer keyboard

Ⓑ wooden spoon

Ⓓ motor oil

TEKS 4.7A

10. Soil is formed by the slow weathering of rock by water. Which best describes the color of loamy soil?

Ⓐ dark

Ⓑ light

Ⓒ milky

Ⓓ red

TEKS 4.7B

11. Kyle knows that slow changes to Earth's surface are caused by many things. Which would most likely be caused by deposition from ice?

Ⓐ delta

Ⓑ glacier

Ⓒ moraine

Ⓓ sand dune

TEKS 4.7B

12. Alexa observed this landform on a trip to Alaska.

What is this landform and how did it form?

Ⓐ It is a valley that was carved by a glacier.

Ⓑ It is a dune that formed as wind eroded sand.

Ⓒ It is an arch that was carved by a slow-moving river.

Ⓓ It is a delta that formed when a river deposited sediment.

TEKS 4.7A

13. Sonya is examining the properties of a soil sample. She records the following observation in her Science Notebook.

The soil feels grainy and coarse.

Which property of soil does Sonya observe?

Ⓐ color

Ⓑ texture

Ⓒ capacity to retain water

Ⓓ ability to support plant growth

© Houghton Mifflin Harcourt Publishing Company　(border) ©NDisk/Age Fotostock

TEKS 4.7B

14. An airplane pilot observed the following landform from his plane.

Delta

Which statement explains how slow changes to Earth's surface caused it to form?

(A) deposition and erosion from wind

(B) erosion and deposition from water

(C) erosion and weathering from ice

(D) weathering and deposition from wind

TEKS 4.7A

15. During science class, Lu Chen conducts an investigation to examine properties of types of soil. He constructs a chart to record his observations, as shown below.

Soil Type	Properties
1	sandy, coarse, large grains
2	fine clay-rich particles
3	milky color, smooth
4	loamy, rich in humus

Which soil type would be the least well suited to retain water?

(A) 1   (C) 3

(B) 2   (D) 4

TEKS 4.7B

16. Kaylee is doing a report on landforms caused by slow changes to Earth's surface. Which topic in her report is most likely caused by erosion and deposition from wind?

(A) glacial moraine

(B) river delta

(C) sand dune

(D) sea arch

TEKS 4.7B

17. Dewayne's family takes a trip through the desert. He observes an arch. Which statement best describes how the desert rock formed?

(A) deposition from water and ice

(B) deposition from water and wind

(C) weathering from water and ice

(D) weathering from water and wind

TEKS 4.7B

18. People use land resources to help them meet their needs. Coal is a fossil fuel that people mine from the land. They burn coal to make electricity. Which type of resource is coal?

(A) a green living resource

(B) a green energy resource

(C) a renewable energy resource

(D) a nonrenewable energy resource

© Houghton Mifflin Harcourt Publishing Company   (border) ©NDisk/Age Fotostock

Apply Inquiry and Review the Big Idea

Write the answers to these questions.

TEKS 4.3C, 4.7B

19. Anish is doing a science investigation. Her setup is shown below.

Identify two Earth processes being modeled. Describe what will happen when Anish pours the water over the sand. Predict what would happen if Anish propped up one end of the pan before she poured the water over the sand.

_____

_____

_____

_____

TEKS 4.7B

20. Slow changes to Earth's surface by water over a long period of time form many of Earth's landforms. Describe the processes that shape each of the following landforms.

a. canyon _____

_____

b. river delta _____

_____

c. sea arch _____

_____

TEKS 4.7A

21. A soil profile is 135 m deep. Horizon A is 47 m deep. Horizon C is 28 m deep. How deep is Horizon B?

_____

© Houghton Mifflin Harcourt Publishing Company (border) ©NDisk/Age Fotostock

Houghton Mifflin Harcourt Publishing Company (bg) ©Chad Ehlers/Alamy Images; (inset) ©PhotoDisc/Getty Images; (border) ©NDisc/Age Fotostock

UNIT 8

The Water Cycle and Weather

Big Idea

Water moves in a regular cycle that influences the weather.

TEKS 4.2C, 4.3D, 4.7C, 4.8A, 4.8B

I Wonder Why

As the sun rises, the sky glows red. Late morning brings sunny skies. Then puffy white clouds appear. A thunderstorm rages by late afternoon! Why? *Turn the page to find out.*

Here's Why The color of the early morning or evening sky is a clue people can use to predict changes in weather. In places where weather systems move from west to east, red skies in the morning signal an approaching storm.

In this unit, you will explore the Big Idea, the Essential Questions, and the Investigations on the Inquiry Flipchart.

Levels of Inquiry Key ■ DIRECTED ■ GUIDED ■ INDEPENDENT

Track Your Progress

Big Idea Water moves in a regular cycle that influences the weather.

Essential Questions

Now I Get the Big Idea!

Science Notebook

Before you begin each lesson, be sure to write your thoughts about the Essential Question.

© Houghton Mifflin Harcourt Publishing Company (bg) ©Chad Ehlers/Alamy Images; (inset) ©PhotoDisc/Getty Images; (border) ©NDisc/Age Fotostock

TEKS 4.7C identify...the importance of conservation 4.8B describe and illustrate the continuous movement of water above and on the surface of Earth through the water cycle and explain the role of the Sun as a major source of energy in this process

Lesson 1

Essential Question

What Is the Water Cycle?

Engage Your Brain!

Find the answer to the following question in this lesson and record it here.

Where is all this water going?

_____

_____

_____

_____

Active Reading

Lesson Vocabulary

List the terms. As you learn about each one, make notes in the Interactive Glossary.

_____   _____

_____   _____

_____   _____

_____

Sequence

In this lesson, you'll read about a process of change called the *water cycle*. As you read about the water cycle, focus on the sequence, or order, of events in the process. Active readers stay focused on a sequence when they mark the transition from one step in a process to another.

© Houghton Mifflin Harcourt Publishing Company ©Images of Africa Photobank/Alamy

Inquiry Flipchart p. 42 — Watching the Water Cycle/An Icy Observation

Water
on the Move

The water that you drink may have once been under ground or high in the sky. How does water get from Earth's surface to the air and back again?

Active Reading As you read the next page, underline sentences that explain the sun's role in the water cycle.

▶ On the diagram, draw an *X* on three places that illustrate where water evaporates from Earth's surface. Circle places that illustrate condensation of water above Earth's surface.

Earth's water is always being recycled. It evaporates from bodies of water, the soil, and even from your skin. Water exits plants' leaves through a process called transpiration. In the air, winds and clouds can help move water from one place to another.

Condensation   Transpiration

Evaporation

After it rains, this birdbath is filled with water. When the sun comes out, its energy heats the water. The birdbath becomes empty as water changes to water vapor and returns to the atmosphere.

© Houghton Mifflin Harcourt Publishing Company (bkgd) ©imagebroker/Alamy

About three-fourths of Earth's surface is covered by water. Most of the water is stored in oceans. Water moves between Earth's surface and the atmosphere through a process called the **water cycle**.

The sun provides the major source of energy for water to move through the water cycle. Sunlight heats up water near the ocean's surface. It causes water to evaporate. **Evaporation** is the change from a liquid to a gas. When water evaporates, it forms a gas called *water vapor*.

Water vapor rises into the atmosphere. The **atmosphere** is the mixture of gases that surrounds Earth. In the atmosphere, water vapor cools to form clouds. At any time, about three-fifths of Earth's surface is covered by clouds.

Precipitation

Precipitation

Glacier

Lake

Surface Runoff

River

Groundwater

© Houghton Mifflin Harcourt Publishing Company (bkgd) ©imagebroker/Alamy

What Goes Up Comes Down

What happens to water vapor after it rises into the air above Earth's surface? How does it become puffy white clouds or raindrops that fall on your head?

Active Reading As you read these pages, write numbers next to sentences and phrases to sequence and describe how water moves above Earth's surface through the water cycle.

Condensation

Think again of the ocean. Water from the ocean's surface evaporates. As water vapor rises into the atmosphere, it cools. When water vapor loses enough energy, it condenses to form liquid water. **Condensation** is the change of a gas into a liquid.

There are tiny solid particles in the atmosphere. Water vapor condenses around these particles to form water droplets. A few water droplets are almost too small to see. However, when billions of droplets are close together, they form clouds.

Clouds can be made of water droplets, ice crystals, or both. They can form high in the sky or just above the ground. *Fog* is a cloud that forms near the ground.

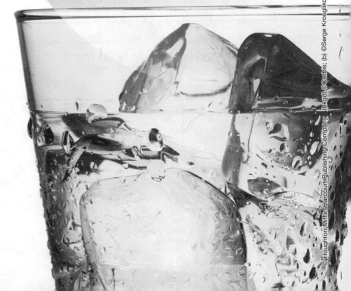

Water vapor condenses around salt and dust particles in the air to form these water droplets.

Water vapor may condense on cool surfaces, too. It's why the cool glass below seems to "sweat." *Dew* is water droplets that form on objects near the ground.

©Houghton Mifflin Harcourt Publishing Company (bkgd) ©Corbis; (b) ©Serge Krouglikoff/Digital Vision/Getty Images

Precipitation

Air currents keep water droplets in the air. But as droplets and snow crystals grow inside clouds, they become too heavy and fall to Earth as precipitation. **Precipitation** is water that falls from clouds to Earth's surface. Rain, snow, and hail are all forms of precipitation.

Precipitation that falls into the oceans may quickly evaporate back into the atmosphere. Precipitation that falls on land may be stored, it may flow across the land, or it may be used by living things. Depending on where it falls, water from precipitation may move quickly or slowly through the water cycle.

Water droplets in a cloud collide and join together. It takes many droplets to form a single raindrop.

Do the Math!
Order Fractions

A raindrop is many times bigger than a water droplet and a dust particle. The table shows the size of droplets and dust particles in relation to the size of raindrops. Order the fractions from least to greatest.

Fractions	Ordered fractions
$\frac{1}{100}$	
$\frac{1}{1}$	
$\frac{1}{5,000}$	
$\frac{1}{20}$	

Use the ordered fractions to correctly label the items on the diagram.

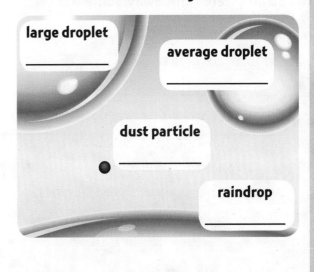

large droplet
_____

average droplet
_____

dust particle
_____

raindrop
_____

© Houghton Mifflin Harcourt Publishing Company ©Corbis

Where Does Water Go?

Most precipitation falls into oceans and evaporates back into the air. But some water takes a more roundabout path on its way through the water cycle.

Active Reading As you read these pages, identify and underline sentences and phrases that describe the movement of water on Earth's surface.

Imagine a rainstorm. Heavy rain falls on the ground. Some of this water will evaporate from shallow puddles quickly. It goes from Earth's surface directly back into the atmosphere.

Much of the rainfall will not reenter the atmosphere right away. Some will seep into the ground. Water that is stored underground is called **groundwater**. Groundwater can be found near the surface or very deep underground. Some groundwater may eventually return to the surface at places such as natural springs. Then it moves on through the water cycle.

As rainwater soaks into the ground, it fills up spaces between soil particles and cracks in rocks. Water that seeps deep underground becomes groundwater. Groundwater moves very slowly—if at all!

© Houghton Mifflin Harcourt Publishing Company ©Corbis

When glaciers melt, they quickly release stored water. Some of it may evaporate, some may seep into the ground, and some may move across the land as runoff.

Not all of the water that falls on land evaporates right away or seeps into the ground. **Runoff** is water that cannot soak into the ground and instead flows across Earth's surface. Too much precipitation may cause runoff. Runoff often flows into streams, rivers, and lakes. It may also flood low-lying areas.

Precipitation that falls in cold places may become part of a glacier. A *glacier* [GLAY•sher] is a large, slow-moving mass of ice. Water can be stored in glaciers for a very long time. Eventually, though, glaciers melt. Meltwater from glaciers can form lakes, flow into oceans, or become groundwater. Melting glaciers can increase the amount of runoff in a place.

Runaway Water

The picture shows runoff on a city street. Describe how this runoff could move through the water cycle on Earth's surface.

_____

_____

_____

_____

_____

_____

© Houghton Mifflin Harcourt Publishing Company (bkgd) ©Corbis; (tr) ©Theodore Clutter/Photo Researchers, Inc.; (br) ©Andrew Fox/Corbis

A Precious Resource

Can you name all the ways that you use water? Water is an important resource used by all living things. People often need to share and conserve their sources of fresh, clean water.

Active Reading As you read these two pages, find and underline at least three facts about aquifers.

When you turn on a faucet, water flows out. Where does it come from? People can get fresh water from rivers or lakes. They can also get fresh water from aquifers. An *aquifer* [AH•kwuh•fuhr] is a body of rock that stores groundwater. People can drill into an aquifer and pump the water to the surface.

The water in aquifers can run low if people use more than can be replaced by precipitation. Human activities can also pollute aquifers. States that share aquifers work together to find solutions to these problems. They want to make sure there is enough fresh, clean water for everyone.

The Ogallala Aquifer covers about 450,000 square kilometers and is the largest aquifer in the United States. It supplies almost one-third of all groundwater used for irrigation within the U. S.

Why Worry About Water?

Why is it important to care for our aquifers?

_____

_____

_____

© Houghton Mifflin Harcourt Publishing Company   (bkgd) ©Joseph Devenney/Getty Images

People cannot live without water. We use water for many different purposes, including recreation.

Aquifers are huge underground water reservoirs [REZ•er•vwarz]. Precipitation adds water to aquifers in places called *recharge areas*. The water in some aquifers slowly makes its way to rivers, springs, lakes, and oceans. It may take groundwater in an aquifer up to a year to travel only 25 cm.

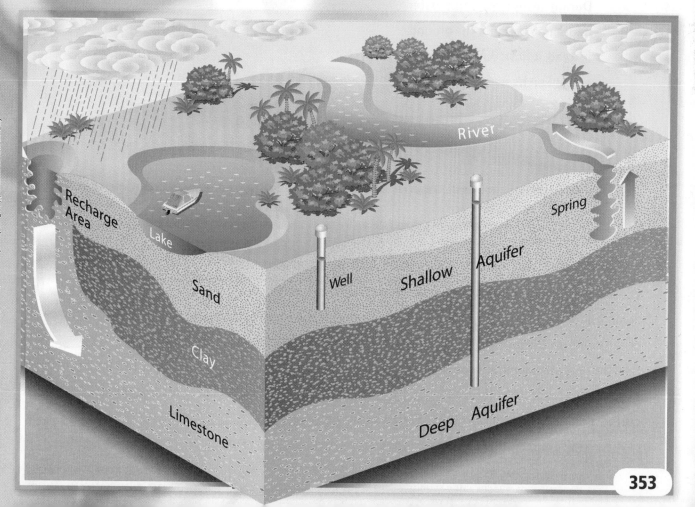

Recharge Area

Lake

Sand

Clay

Limestone

River

Well

Shallow

Spring

Aquifer

Deep Aquifer

© Houghton Mifflin Harcourt Publishing Company   (bkgd) ©Joseph Deveney/Getty Images; (tr) ©adrian brockwell/Alamy

When you're done, use the answer key to check and revise your work.

Write the term that matches each photo and caption.

1 Water can be stored for a long time in a large, slow-moving mass of ice.

_____

2 Water can also be stored underground between the spaces in soil particles or cracks in rocks.

_____

3 During heavy rains, some water might not soak into the ground. Instead, it flows down slopes and across Earth's surface.

_____

Summarize

Fill in the missing words to describe the water cycle.

The water cycle shows how water moves from Earth's surface to the 4. _____ and back again. The 5. _____ provides the energy for the water cycle. Water on the surface of the ocean heats up. During 6. _____ , it changes from a liquid to a gas. As 7. _____ rises into the atmosphere, it cools. During 8. _____ , it changes from a gas to a liquid. Billions of water droplets form a 9. _____ . When the droplets get too large for air currents to keep them up, they fall to Earth's surface as 10. _____ .

Answer Key: 1. glacier 2. groundwater 3. runoff 4. atmosphere 5. sun 6. evaporation 7. water vapor 8. condensation 9. cloud 10. precipitation

© Houghton Mifflin Harcourt Publishing Company

Name _____

Word Play

1 Use the clues to fill in the missing letters of the words.

1. g _ _ _ _ _ w _ _ ◯ _   Water stored underground
                    10

2. _ o _ d _ _ _ _ _ _ _ _ _   The changing of water from a gas to a liquid

3. _ a _ _ _   _ ◯c _ _   The movement of water from Earth's surface to the
                 7   atmosphere and back again

4. _ t _ _ _ p _ _ _ ◯ Mixture of gases that surrounds Earth
                      4

5. _ r _◯i _ _ _ _ _ t _ _ _   Water that falls from clouds to Earth's surface
        8

6. ◯u _ _ _ _ _   Water that flows across Earth's surface
   5

7. g◯_◯i _ _   A huge mass of frozen water that moves slowly
   9 6

8. _ r _ n _ _ i _ _◯_ _ _   The process in which plants return water vapor
                    3   to the atmosphere

9. ◯_ t _ _ _ _ a _ _ _   Water as a gas
   1

10. _ v _ _ o _◯t _ o _   The changing of water from a liquid to a gas
                2

Bonus: Solve the Riddle!

Use the circled letters in the clues above to solve the riddle.

What is water's favorite way to travel?

On a ___ ___ ___ ___ ___ ___ ___ ___ ___ ___
       1   2   3   4   5   6   7   8   9   10

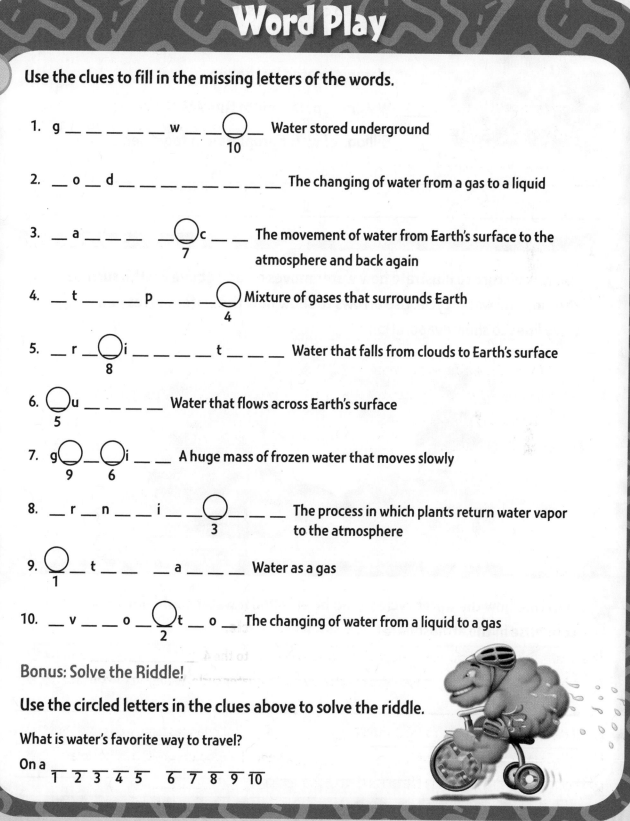

© Houghton Mifflin Harcourt Publishing Company

Apply Concepts

2 Number the sentences to place the steps of cloud formation in order. Then describe what causes water vapor to condense as it rises into the atmosphere.

_____ Water vapor condenses around tiny particles.

_____ Water is heated by the sun.

_____ Water evaporates into the air.

_____ Billions of water droplets join together.

_____

_____

3 Use this picture to illustrate how water moves on and above Earth's surface through the water cycle. Use arrows to show how the water moves and use wavy lines to show evaporation.

4 Describe how the water cycle would be affected if water could not condense in the atmosphere.

_____

_____

_____

_____

© Houghton Mifflin Harcourt Publishing Company

Name _____

5 In the spaces below, draw and label examples of water in the atmosphere as a solid, a liquid, and a gas. Hint: Wavy lines may be used to represent water vapor.

_____	_____	_____
_____	_____	_____

6 Each illustration shows a part of the water cycle. Label each as *evaporation*, *precipitation*, or *condensation*. Then describe what happens during each process.

_____	_____	_____
_____	_____	_____
_____	_____	_____

© Houghton Mifflin Harcourt Publishing Company

357

7 The picture shows stored water being used to irrigate crops. Circle and label the source of the water. How may this stored water be renewed?

_____

_____

_____

_____

8 During an ice age, water is stored in glaciers. The picture shows land area before and after an ice age. How are land area and the oceans affected during an ice age?

Land Area
■ Current Day
■ Last Ice Age

_____

_____

_____

_____

_____

9 Explain the role of the sun in the water cycle.

_____

_____

Take It Home!

Share what you have learned about water with your family. Tell them why it is important to conserve water. Set up a barrel outside to catch rainwater. Use the rainwater to wash your car or water your garden.

© Houghton Mifflin Harcourt Publishing Company

TEKS **4.2C** construct...bar graphs...using tools...to organize...data **4.8A** measure and record changes in weather...

Lesson 2

What Are Types of Weather?

Engage Your Brain!

Find the answer to the following question in this lesson and record it here.

If you are prepared, walking in the rain can be fun! What causes rain to fall?

_____

_____

_____

_____

Active Reading

Lesson Vocabulary

List the terms. As you learn about each one, make notes in the Interactive Glossary.

_____

_____

_____

Cause and Effect

What causes wind to blow or rain to fall? Many ideas in this lesson are connected by a cause-and-effect relationship. A cause explains why something happens. An effect explains what happens as a result of something else. Active readers look for causes by asking themselves, Why did it happen? They look for effects by asking, What happened?

© Houghton Mifflin Harcourt Publishing Company (bg) ©Thomas Northcut/Getty Images

Up in the Air

Quick! Describe today's weather. Is it cold and windy? Warm and dry? Many things you do depend on the weather. What *is* weather?

Active Reading As your read these pages, circle factors that help us describe weather. Then, underline a detail about each factor.

Earth's atmosphere protects living things from the sun's harmful ultraviolet rays and shields Earth from space debris. It is about 600 km (372 mi) thick, which seems very thick. However, in comparison with the rest of Earth, the atmosphere is actually quite thin.

The atmosphere is a mixture of gases. It is mostly made up of nitrogen and oxygen. The condition of the atmosphere at a given place and time is called **weather**. Weather takes place in the layer of the atmosphere closest to Earth's surface. Without the movement of gases in the atmosphere, there would be no weather.

Many factors, including air temperature, humidity, and air pressure, help us describe the weather of a place. *Air temperature* is how warm or cool the air is around us. Air temperature affects how much moisture is in the air. The air temperature also affects how we dress and what we do outside.

Do the Math!
Graph Data

Sue recorded the temperature three times in one day: 19 °C at 8:00 a.m., 31 °C at 2:00 p.m., and 26 °C at 8:00 p.m. Construct a bar graph to organize the the data.

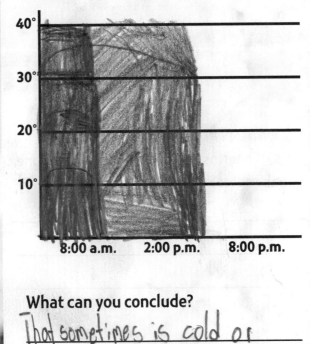

What can you conclude?

That sometimes is cold or hot

©Houghton Mifflin Harcourt Publishing Company (bg) ©OJO Images/Robert Daly/Getty Images

Humidity is the amount of water vapor in the air. When the air feels dry, we have low humidity. When the air feels damp, we have high humidity. High humidity can also affect another weather factor—precipitation. *Precipitation* is water that falls back to Earth. Depending on air temperature, precipitation falls as rain, snow, sleet, or hail.

Air pressure is the weight of the atmosphere pressing down on Earth's surface. Air temperature and humidity both affect air pressure. Changes in air pressure usually bring changes in weather.

Weather determines whether we can go for a cool dip in a pool, whether we should be careful of strong winds, or whether we can skate on a frozen lake.

What's the Weather?

Which of these pictures shows weather that is most like the day's weather where you live? Describe your current weather conditions.

I think is the strong winds why because is so cold

© Houghton Mifflin Harcourt Publishing Company (bg) ©OJO Images/Robert Daly/Getty Images; (t) ©Sandy Jones/Getty Images; (c) ©Alistair Berg/Getty Images; (b) ©UpperCut Images/Getty Images

Under Pressure

Have you heard a meteorologist talk about high and low pressure? High and low pressure describe the air around you.

Active Reading As you read these pages, circle the cause of the change in air pressure as elevation changes.

You can't feel the atmosphere pressing down on you, but it is! Air pressure is the measure of the weight of the atmosphere on Earth's surface. Changes in air pressure bring changes in weather. A *barometer* is a weather instrument used to measure changes in air pressure.

Temperature, humidity, and distance above sea level all affect air pressure. Cold air is denser than warm air, which means air pressure is higher in cold areas than in warm areas. A volume of humid air is less dense than an equal volume of dry air. As a result, humid air has lower air pressure than dry air. Most air particles are found closer to Earth's surface. Air pressure decreases as elevation, or distance above sea level, increases.

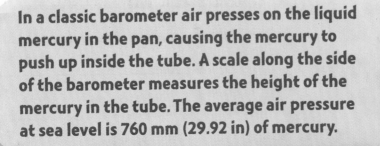

Vacuum

760 mm (29.92 in.)

Mercury

Air pressure

Air pressure

In a classic barometer air presses on the liquid mercury in the pan, causing the mercury to push up inside the tube. A scale along the side of the barometer measures the height of the mercury in the tube. The average air pressure at sea level is 760 mm (29.92 in) of mercury.

© Houghton Mifflin Harcourt Publishing Company (bg) ©PhotoDisc/Alamy Images

Dial and Pointer

Lever system

Vacuum chamber

In a modern barometer, air presses down on a vacuum chamber, a sort of airless can. As the air pressure changes, the vacuum chamber moves up or down. A lever attached to the chamber moves a pointer along a dial to measure the air pressure.

What's the Pressure?

In the picture above, record changes in weather by filling in the height of mercury inside each tube to show the air pressure at each location. In the space below, explain the air pressure you would find at each location.

in the top one will be cold because the air is so cold but the other one it would be hot because is a warm area

Air pressure is higher at the base of a mountain than at its top. The force of gravity holds most air particles close to Earth's surface. So, when you climb a mountain, the higher you go, the atmosphere thins and air pressure decreases.

© Houghton Mifflin Harcourt Publishing Company   (bg) ©PhotoDisc/Alamy Images; (t) ©Jan Tadeusz/Alamy Images

When the Wind Blows

A gentle wind can be pleasant, cooling you off when it is hot outside. However, a windstorm can cause damage. What causes wind to blow?

Active Reading As you read these pages, circle two clue words or phrases that signal a detail such as an example or an added fact.

The sun warms Earth's surface unevenly. This uneven heating causes differences in air pressure. Air moves away from areas of higher pressure to areas of lower pressure similar to how water flows downhill. This movement of air is called *wind*.

Areas near Earth's poles receive less sunlight than areas near the tropics. At the poles, the air is cold and has higher pressure. As a result, air moves along Earth's surface from the poles toward the tropics. At the tropics, air warms, rises, and moves toward the poles. These winds, called *global winds*, blow over large areas of Earth. They move large weather systems, such as hurricanes.

Local differences in temperature can also cause winds. Earth's surface heats up at different rates. For example, the side of a mountain heats up more quickly than the valley below. As a result, a valley wind forms as air moves from the valley up the side of the mountain. This is an example of a *local wind*.

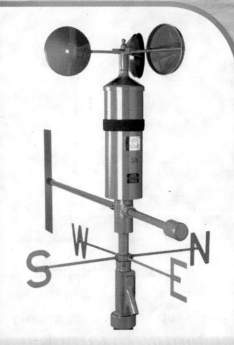

An *anemometer* measures wind speed. Wind pushes against the cups on the anemometer, causing it to spin. The rate at which the cups spin is measured and used to determine wind speed. A *wind vane* points in the direction from which the wind blows.

© Houghton Mifflin Harcourt Publishing Company. (bg) ©Tetra Images/Alamy Images; (cr) ©Paul Rapson/Photo Researchers, Inc.

Local winds move short distances and can change direction. Daily changes in temperatures can cause local winds to change direction. For example, at night, the mountainside cools quicker than the valley below. The wind at night blows from the mountainside to the valley floor. In coastal areas, daily temperature changes result in local winds known as land breezes and sea breezes.

Sea Breeze
During the day, land heats up more quickly than water. Air over the land also warms, causing the air pressure to drop. Cooler, higher-pressure air flows from over the water to the land, forming a sea breeze.

Land Breeze
At night, land loses heat more quickly than water. As the air over land cools, the air pressure rises. Cooler, higher-pressure air flows from the land toward the sea, forming a land breeze.

▶ Draw an *L* over the low pressure and a *H* over the high pressure. Then describe the direction wind is blowing and why.

Air over the land and is cooler, higher-pressure and also warms

© Houghton Mifflin Harcourt Publishing Company (bg) ©Tetra Images/Alamy Images; (b) ©LOOK Die Bildagentur der Fotografen GmbH/Alamy Images

How Clouds Form

Some clouds signal precipitation. Others signal fair weather. How can you use clouds to predict weather?

Active Reading As you read these pages, circle the three types of clouds.

Air often has some water in it. Most of the time you can't see the water because it is an invisible gas called *water vapor*. Clouds form as water vapor cools and condenses. A cloud is made up of tiny water droplets and ice crystals; these are so small that air currents can hold them up. A water droplet can be thousands of times smaller than a raindrop!

There are three main types of clouds. Cumulus clouds are white and puffy and are common on clear, sunny days. Under the right conditions, cumulus clouds can develop into massive thunderstorm clouds. Cirrus clouds look like white streaks and are high and thin. Cirrus clouds usually signal cool, fair weather. Stratus clouds are low and gray, making the day dark and gloomy. These clouds can produce or signal incoming rain or snow.

Producing a Cloud

(1) The sun warms Earth's surface, causing air to rise into the atmosphere.

(2) Water vapor in the air cools and condenses around tiny specks of dust, forming water droplets.

(3) These droplets join together, forming a cloud.

© Houghton Mifflin Harcourt Publishing Company (bg) ©Solid Photo/Alamy Images

Cirrus Clouds

Thin, cold cirrus clouds are made up of ice crystals. Fast winds blow these clouds into long streamers high up in the atmosphere.

Stratus Clouds

Stratus clouds cover the sky with a sheet of gray. Thick, wet-looking stratus clouds may produce steady, light rain or snow.

Cumulus Clouds

Cumulus clouds usually form early in the afternoon on hot, sunny days. If these clouds grow high and thick enough, they can develop into stormy cumulonimbus clouds.

Which Clouds Are in the Sky?

Draw the clouds you might see on a warm, windless, sunny afternoon. Write a statement to support your picture.

_____

_____

_____

_____

© Houghton Mifflin Harcourt Publishing Company   (bg) ©Solid Photo/Alamy Images; (t) ©Tom Mackie/Alamy Images; (c) ©David R. Frazier/Photo Researchers, Inc.; (b) ©David R. Frazier Photolibrary, Inc./Alamy Images

Some Rain, Anyone?

You might not think about rain—unless there is too much or too little of it. What causes precipitation?

Active Reading As you read this page, underline the cause of precipitation and circle kinds of precipitation.

Precipitation forms when water particles inside of clouds grow too large and fall to Earth's surface. Rain, snow, freezing rain, sleet, and hail are common kinds of precipitation.

Rain may start as ice crystals that melt as they fall to Earth's surface. Snow forms when water vapor changes directly into ice. Freezing rain occurs when falling, super-cooled raindrops do not freeze in the air but instead freeze when they strike objects near the ground.

Sleet is made of small lumps of ice. It forms when rain falls through a layer of freezing air. The raindrops turn to ice before hitting the ground.

Hail is made up of layers of ice. The layers form as air currents inside a thunderstorm cloud repeatedly lift and drop a hail particle. Each up-and-down trip adds ice to the particle. A ball of hail can be smaller than a pea or larger than a grapefruit!

Rain

Snow

Hail

A *rain gauge* measures rainfall. Rain fills the gauge, and the scale on the side shows how much rain fell.

Many factors affect the kinds of precipitation that falls in a place. For instance, snow falls in places with cold winters. It also falls in places with very high elevations. In contrast, hail might fall anywhere and at any time of year. It may even fall in places near the tropics!

People depend on precipitation to meet their water needs. Too much or too little precipitation can be a problem.

Too much precipitation can cause rivers to overflow. Floodwaters can damage crops and homes.

Too little precipitation is a *drought*. Droughts can cause the ground to dry out and plants and animals to die.

Precipitation Cause and Effect

Complete the chart. Fill in the missing cause or effect.

Cause	Effect
Snow has been melting for several weeks. Rain is predicted for the next five days.	
	The lake that supplies water to a city is very low.

© Houghton Mifflin Harcourt Publishing Company   (bg) ©imagebroker/Alamy Images (t) ©David Mark/Alamy Images; (b) ©Global Warming Images/Alamy Images

When you're done, use the answer key to check and revise your work.

Identify each weather instrument and what it measures.

1

2

3

_____

_____

Summarize

Fill in the missing words to tell about weather.

Weather is the condition of the 4. _____ at a given place and time. Factors that

affect weather include temperature and air pressure. Air moves from areas of 5. _____

air pressure to the areas of 6. _____ air pressure. This movement of air causes

7. _____ . Humidity also affects weather. Humidity is the amount of

8. _____ in the air. In the air, tiny water droplets form

9. _____ . Water falls from the sky as 10. _____ .

Answer Key: 1. anemometer/wind vane; wind speed/wind direction; 2. barometer; air pressure 3. rain gauge; amount of precipitation 4. atmosphere 5. high (or higher) 6. low (or lower) 7. wind 8. water vapor 9. clouds 10. precipitation

© Houghton Mifflin Harcourt Publishing Company (l) ©Paul Rapson/Photo Researchers, Inc.; (c) ©Jan Tadeusz/Alamy Images

Name _____

Word Play

1 Use the terms in the box to complete the crossword puzzle.

Across

3. The layer of gases that surrounds Earth
4. The weight of the atmosphere on the surface of Earth is _____ pressure.
6. Water that falls from clouds
7. A tool that points in the direction from which the wind blows
8. The amount of water vapor in the air

Down

1. The condition of the atmosphere at a given place and time
2. How warm or cool the air is around us
5. Air in motion

air pressure*   air temperature

atmosphere   humidity*

precipitation   weather*

wind   wind vane

* Key Lesson Vocabulary

© Houghton Mifflin Harcourt Publishing Company

Apply Concepts

2 Identify and describe each cloud type shown below.

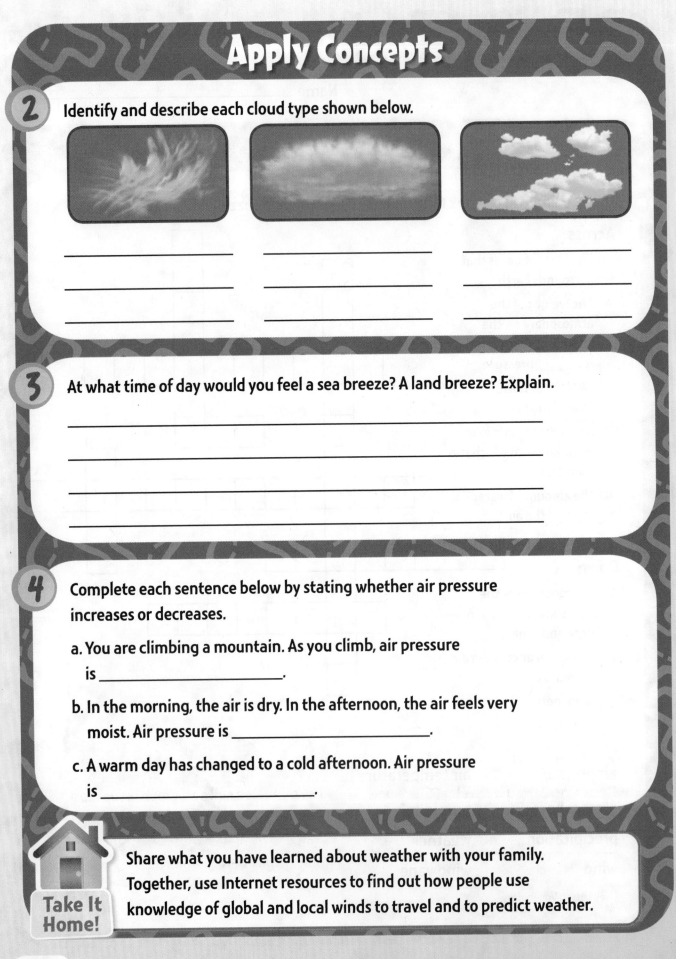

_____ _____ _____

_____ _____ _____

_____ _____ _____

3 At what time of day would you feel a sea breeze? A land breeze? Explain.

_____

_____

_____

_____

4 Complete each sentence below by stating whether air pressure increases or decreases.

a. You are climbing a mountain. As you climb, air pressure
   is _____.

b. In the morning, the air is dry. In the afternoon, the air feels very
   moist. Air pressure is _____.

c. A warm day has changed to a cold afternoon. Air pressure
   is _____.

Take It Home!

Share what you have learned about weather with your family. Together, use Internet resources to find out how people use knowledge of global and local winds to travel and to predict weather.

© Houghton Mifflin Harcourt Publishing Company

TEKS **4.8A** measure and record changes in weather and make predictions using weather maps, weather symbols, and a map key

Lesson **3**

Essential Question

How Is Weather Predicted?

Engage Your Brain!

Find the answer to the following question in this lesson and record it here.

How can a meteorologist use this picture to make predictions about the weather?

_____

_____

_____

_____

_____

Active Reading

Lesson Vocabulary

List the terms. As you learn about each one, make notes in the Interactive Glossary.

_____

_____

Main Idea and Details

The main idea of a paragraph is the most important idea. The main idea may be stated in the first sentence, or it may be stated elsewhere. Active readers look for main ideas by asking themselves, What is this paragraph mostly about?

© Houghton Mifflin Harcourt Publishing Company (bc) ©SPL/Photo Researchers, Inc.

Tracking the Weather

The weather forecasters on TV say, "Sunny and warm today, with rain tonight and tomorrow." How do they know?

Active Reading As you read this page, circle five tools used to record and collect weather data.

The forecasters have a lot of help! Meteorologists, or scientists who study weather, record and collect data from all over the world. They use automated systems at sea, on land, in the air, and in space to help track the weather.

At sea, weather buoys record and collect data on coastal weather conditions. These data help keep people in coastal cities safe. On land, weather-monitoring stations track weather conditions in remote locations. They can send advance notice about incoming weather. Scientists also use Doppler radar towers to observe how storm clouds move.

Weather balloons and weather satellites collect data from high above Earth's surface. Weather satellites can track the weather over very large areas. They also help relay data from land-based tools to meteorologists around the world.

In the United States, nearly 100 buoys like this one collect data about air temperature, air pressure, wind, and waves at sea.

© Houghton Mifflin Harcourt Publishing Company. (t) ©Orbital Imaging Corporation/Photo Researchers, Inc.; (b) ©Michael Dwyer/Alamy Images

Weather satellites orbit Earth. They record and collect weather data, such as cloud cover, and track storms, such as hurricanes. These satellites use radio signals to transmit data back to Earth.

Scientists launch weather balloons that carry tools, called *radiosondes,* into the atmosphere. A typical radiosonde measures air temperature, air pressure, and humidity.

Weather Wonder

Why do scientists use so many tools to record and collect weather data?

_____

_____

_____

_____

_____

Thousands of weather-monitoring stations record and collect data on changes in air temperature, air pressure, wind, humidity, and precipitation. Some weather stations use radar to track storms.

© Houghton Mifflin Harcourt Publishing Company   (t) ©Michael Donne/Photo Researchers, Inc. (b) ©Motoring Picture Library/Alamy Images

Air Masses and Fronts

One day, it is so cool outside. The next day, it is warm enough to wear shorts. What happened to the weather?

When cold, dry freezer air meets warm, moist room air, a mini-front is formed!

Active Reading As you read these pages, underline the definition of an air mass. Circle four characteristics that air masses may have.

Packets of air move across Earth's surface. An **air mass** is a large body of air with the same temperature and humidity throughout.

An air mass reflects the conditions of the place where it forms. Air masses that form over land are dry. Air masses that form over water are moist. Cold air masses form near the poles, and warm air masses form near the tropics.

As air masses move across an area, they can collide. The boundary between two air masses is called a **front**. Weather changes take place at fronts. For example, as a warm front passes over an area, warm air replaces cooler air and the temperature rises. The movement of air masses and fronts explains why you might be chilly one day and warm the next. At a front, stormy conditions are common.

Polar
Cold, dry

Polar
Cool, moist

Polar
Cool, moist

Tropical
Warm, moist

Tropical
Hot, dry

Tropical
Warm, moist

Air masses may form over land or water. The masses that form over land near the poles will be cold and dry. The masses that form over water near the poles will be cold and moist. Which types of air masses will form near the tropics?

© Houghton Mifflin Harcourt Publishing Company (bg) ©PhotoDisc/Getty Images

Cold Front

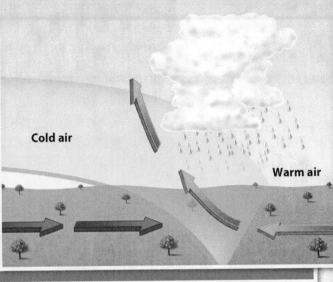

A cold front forms where a cold air mass bumps into a warmer air mass. The denser cold air pushes the warm air up. Water vapor in the air cools, and large clouds form. Thunderstorms and heavy rain often take place. Cooler temperatures follow a cold front.

Cold air

Warm air

Warm Front

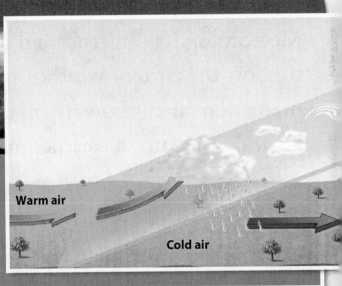

A warm front forms where a warm air mass moves over a cold air mass. A warm front forms a wider area of clouds and rain than a cold front. Steady rain or snow may fall. Warmer temperatures follow a warm front.

Warm air

Cold air

Home Front

Identify a front inside of your home. Explain where the different air masses form, the characteristics of each one, and how the two air masses meet.

_____

_____

_____

_____

© Houghton Mifflin Harcourt Publishing Company   (bg) ©PhotoDisc/Getty Images; (t) ©Michael Spence/Alamy Images; (b) ©Ray Ellis/Photo Researchers, Inc.

Mapping the Weather

Meteorologists construct and use maps to show the current weather and make predictions about how it will change. How do they make weather maps?

Active Reading As you read these two pages, put a star [*] next to the main idea of each paragraph.

Most weather forecasts are accurate within five to seven days. A *weather forecast* is a prediction about the future weather conditions of a place. Weather forecasts beyond seven days are not very accurate.

Meteorologists forecast the weather based on the local weather data and observed weather patterns. They analyze the air temperature, humidity, and air pressure data of a place. They also analyze weather patterns, such as the movement of air masses and fronts, to prepare a weather forecast. In North America, air masses and fronts generally move from west to east. Meteorologists use computers to construct maps to organize, examine, and evaluate weather data they collect. They use these maps to make predictions about the weather.

© Houghton Mifflin Harcourt Publishing Company (bg) ©PhotoDisc/Getty Images; (t) ©Chuck Eckert/Alamy Images

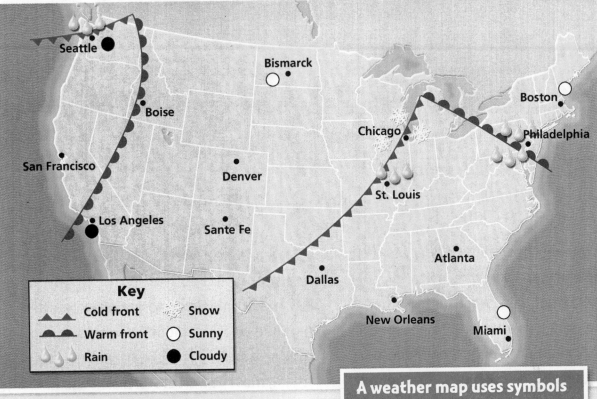

Key

Cold front		Snow	
Warm front		○ Sunny	
Rain		● Cloudy	

Recall the different tools used to monitor the weather from Earth's surface, the oceans, and the atmosphere. These tools collect lots of weather data. Computers help us store and analyze weather data and weather patterns to make *weather maps.* Meteorologists study weather maps and use them to make weather forecasts.

A weather map uses symbols to represent types of weather. The map legend tells you what each symbol means. The triangles or half circles on a front symbol point in the direction the front is moving.

Make Weather Predictions

Examine the weather map, weather symbols, and map key to make predictions about the weather and answer these questions.

- Draw a rectangle around the name of a city that has cloudy skies now but will soon have rain.

- Which type of weather will Dallas soon have, and why?

_____

_____

- Which type of weather will Philadelphia soon have, and why?

_____

_____

© Houghton Mifflin Harcourt Publishing Company (bg) ©PhotoDisc/Getty Images; (b) ©Ryan McGinnis/Alamy Images

≫ Forewarned!

Weather forecasts help us plan each day. When severe storms strike, weather forecasts can also help save lives.

Technology has changed how we measure, analyze, forecast, and share weather data. Weather tools, for example, help us accurately measure the weather conditions of a place. Modern communication technology lets scientists share weather data quickly and over long distances. These data can be used to make computer models to predict the weather.

Meteorolgists work hard at predicting the strength and path of storms. In the past, meteorologists had to rely on weather ships and weather-monitoring stations on tropical islands to track hurricanes—the largest, most powerful storms on Earth. The data from these sources were limited. As a result, predicting the strength and path of these storms was very difficult.

In September 2008, Hurricane Ike made landfall at Galveston, Texas. Satellites and airplanes recorded and collected weather data to help meteorologists make forecasts to warn people about this storm.

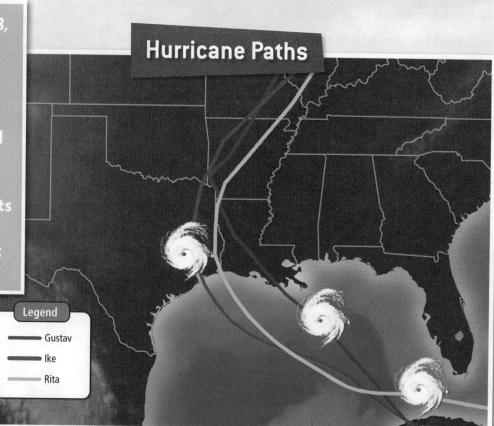

Hurricane Paths

Legend
— Gustav
— Ike
— Rita

© Houghton Mifflin Harcourt Publishing Company   (bg) ©PhotoDisc/Getty Images; (br) © CIMSS/NOAA

Starting in the 1960s, the United States launched the first of many weather-satellite systems. For the first time, scientists were able to monitor and collect data from the uninhabited parts of Earth. As a result, the accuracy of weather forecasts and hurricane tracking improved. Today, satellites along with land- and sea-based weather tools provide information to warn people about the changing weather.

Tropical Depression

Tropical Storm

Hurricane

A hurricane begins as a thunderstorm near the western coast of Africa. As its winds strengthen, the storm becomes a tropical depression. When winds reach 63 km/h (39 mph), it becomes a tropical storm. A tropical storm becomes a hurricane when there are winds of 119 km/h (74 mph) or more.

Category	Wind Speed (km/h)	Damage
1	119–153	Minimal
2	154–177	Moderate
3	178–209	Major
4	210–249	Extensive
5	> 249	Catastrophic

Do the Math!
Interpret Data

Use information from the table to answer the following questions.

1. What is the wind speed and category of hurricanes that may cause extensive damage?

_____

_____

2. How much stronger is a category 5 hurricane than a hurricane that causes only minimal damage?

_____

_____

© Houghton Mifflin Harcourt Publishing Company   (bg) ©PhotoDisc/Getty Images; (l) ©National Oceanic and Atmospheric Administration (NOAA); (c) ©NOAA/Handout/Reuters/Corbis; (r) ©HO/Reuters/Corbis

Sum It Up!

When you're done, use the answer key to check and revise your work.

Complete the details about each main idea.

1 Meteorologists collect weather data from all over the world. Some of the tools that they use include

_____
_____
_____
_____
_____

2 Air masses meet at boundaries called fronts. Weather that happens along fronts includes

_____
_____
_____
_____
_____

3 Meteorologists use weather maps to make forecasts. Symbols on weather maps indicate the weather. Symbols show

_____
_____
_____
_____
_____

4 Meteorologists use many tools to track and forecast the weather. Explain how a meteorologist might use the three tools pictured below to predict the weather.

 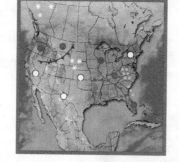 

_____
_____
_____

Answer Key: 1. weather buoys, weather balloons, weather-monitoring stations, and weather satellites. 2. thunderstorms, cloudy skies, steady rain, and windy weather. 3. precipitation, cloud cover, and fronts. 4. Sample answer: Weather satellites send data to computers on Earth. Meteorologists use computers to analyze the data and make weather maps.

© Houghton Mifflin Harcourt Publishing Company

Word Play

Name _____

1 Use the clues to unscramble the terms.

1. C A E N R I R U H _ _ _ _ _ _ _ _ ◯
   a storm with wind speeds of at least 119 km/h

2. F N O R T _ _ _ ◯ _
   the boundary between two different air masses

3. L O O S T I G R O E T M E _ _ _ _ ◯ _ _ _ _ _ _ _
   a person who studies weather and the atmosphere

4. R A I S S M A _ _ _ _ _ ◯ _
   a large body of air with the same temperature and humidity

5. R E W E A T H C A E O F T S R

   _ _ _ _ _ _ _ _ _ _ _ _ ◯ _
   a prediction of future weather conditions

6. L P O D P R E D A A R R
   ◯ _ _ _ _ _ _ _ _ _ _ _
   a tool used to see the movement of storm clouds

Solve the riddle by unscrambling the circled letters to find the missing part of the word.

What kind of radios do weather balloons carry?

RADIO_ _ _ _ _

© Houghton Mifflin Harcourt Publishing Company

Apply Concepts

2 Identify each weather instrument and describe what it does.

_____

_____

_____

_____

_____

A

B

C

3 Circle the correct answer.

Which statement best describes a hurricane?

- A swirling funnel cloud

- A short-lived, local storm

- Low sheets of thick clouds

- A large storm that forms over the ocean

4 Where does a cold, moist air mass form? What type of weather will it cause?

_____

_____

_____

_____

5 Identify the type of front shown. Use this map to predict what type of weather will take place as a result.

_____

_____

_____

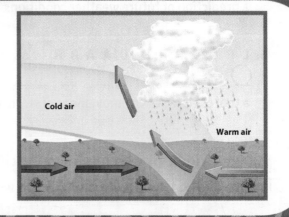

Cold air

Warm air

Work with a family member to research how severe weather affects electrical energy generation, distribution, and use. Describe what experts recommend people do to conserve energy during severe weather.

© Houghton Mifflin Harcourt Publishing Company

TEKS 4.3D connect grade-level appropriate science concepts with the history of science...
4.8A measure...changes in weather...

S.T.E.M.
Engineering & Technology

Stormy Weather:
Beaufort Wind Scale

If you were a sailor on a ship, being able to measure wind speed would be important. In the past, wind speed was estimated by observing its effect on things. Today, we use tools to measure wind speed. Read to find out how ways to measure wind speed have changed over time.

In 1805, Sir Francis Beaufort developed a scale to classify wind speed. This scale assigned levels based on sailors' observations. For example, a Force 3 wind describes a gentle breeze in which ships move steadily across the water. Force 6 describes a strong breeze that produces large waves, whitecaps, and spray. Force 11 describes a violent storm.

You can observe a flag to see how wind blows. A windsock shows the relative direction and speed of winds. The windsock droops during low wind speed. It flies straight out from the pole during high wind.

Use the text and information from reference materials to complete the Beaufort Wind Scale table.

Beaufort Wind Force	Average Wind Speed (km/h)	Description	Beaufort Wind Force	Average Wind Speed (km/h)	Description
0	0	Calm		56	Near Gale
	3	Light Air			Gale
	9	Light Breeze		82	Severe Gale
		Gentle Breeze			Storm
	24	Moderate Breeze		110	
		Fresh Breeze	12	124	Hurricane
6	44				

© Houghton Mifflin Harcourt Publishing Company (l) ©18th crd/Alamy Images; (c) ©Nanine Hartzenbusch/Getty Images; (r) ©Gregor Schuster/Getty Images

Today, wind speed is measured using anemometers.

This anemometer uses cuplike devices to measure wind speed. The faster the wind blows, the faster the cups spin. The cups are attached to sensors that measure the actual wind speed.

This digital anemometer uses spinning fans to generate magnetic pulses. Then, the instrument translates these pulses into measurements of the wind speed.

An ultrasound anemometer has pairs of sound speakers and microphones. Electronic circuits measure the time it takes for sound to travel from each speaker to its microphone. The anemometer uses the data collected to determine wind speed as well as wind direction.

Design Your Future

Use observations to design your own scale to measure changes in weather such as temperature, cloud cover, or amount or strength of rainfall. Describe how you would use the scale to measure changes in weather in your neighborhood.

_____

_____

Build On It!

Rise to the engineering design challenge—complete **Design It: Build a Wind Vane** on the Inquiry Flipchart.

© Houghton Mifflin Harcourt Publishing Company (l) ©Rafal Olkis/Alamy Images; (c) ©Aleksandr Ugorenkov/Alamy Images; (r) ©Ashley Cooper/Corbis

Inquiry Flipchart page 46

Lesson **4**
INQUIRY

TEKS 4.2C ...examine, and evaluate data **4.8A** measure and record changes in weather and make predictions using weather maps...

Name _____

Essential Question

How Can We Observe Weather Patterns?

Set a Purpose

Why is it helpful to observe, measure, and record the weather?

_____

_____

_____

Think About the Procedure

Why should the location for your weather station be sheltered from the sun?

_____

_____

_____

Why would it be useful to measure and record the weather at the same time every day?

_____

_____

_____

Record Your Data

Day	Weather Observations
	Weather Predictions

© Houghton Mifflin Harcourt Publishing Company

Draw Conclusions

How can we use tools to measure and record weather patterns?

_____

_____

_____

_____

Analyze and Extend

1. Which tools did you use to measure changes in weather? Which changes did you observe?

_____

_____

_____

_____

2. Which weather conditions were most likely to change before the weather changed?

_____

_____

_____

3. What predictions did you make using your weather map? On which weather patterns did you base your predictions?

_____

_____

_____

4. Were your predictions accurate? Explain.

_____

_____

_____

_____

5. What would have made your weather predictions more accurate?

_____

_____

_____

_____

_____

6. Find out what predictions were made by meterologists during the same period as your predictions. Evaluate how closely your data compared to their data. Which predictions were more accurate? Explain your answer.

_____

_____

_____

_____

_____

_____

© Houghton Mifflin Harcourt Publishing Company

8 THINGS YOU SHOULD KNOW ABOUT N. Christina Hsu

1 Dr. Hsu is an atmospheric scientist. She studies how Earth's atmosphere changes, and how these changes affect Earth's surface.

2 Dr. Hsu earned a Ph.D. degree in atmospheric science from the Georgia Institute of Technology.

3 Today, Dr. Hsu works for NASA—the U.S. agency that explores space and studies Earth from space.

4 Dr. Hsu studies aerosols, which are tiny particles that hang in the air. Aerosols include solids, such as smoke and soot, and liquids, such as tiny water droplets.

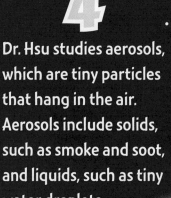

5 Dr. Hsu studies aerosols because water vapor condenses on them to form water droplets. She is interested in the source, amount, and distribution of these particles in the atmosphere.

6 Dr. Hsu uses satellites to measure and track the movement of aerosols.

7 Dr. Hsu studies the effects of aerosols blocking sunlight.

8 In 2007, Dr. Hsu received an award for exceptional achievement from NASA's Goddard Space Flight Center.

© Houghton Mifflin Harcourt Publishing Company (cr) ©PhotoDisc/Getty Images; (t) ©J.clarke/Corbis

Now You Be an Aerosol Detective!

Each clue describes a source of aerosol particles. Match each clue with the picture that illustrates it.

1. It may be quiet for years, then it releases smoke and ash with a *boom*!

2. Blustery winds launch sandy aerosols every day from dry places such as this one.

3. People are the source of this air pollution.

4. Tiny water droplets are aerosols, too. They often come from this source.

5. One little match can spark one of these.

Think About It!

How might human activities add aerosols to the atmosphere?

_____

_____

_____

© Houghton Mifflin Harcourt Publishing Company

Vocabulary Review

Use the terms in the box to complete the sentences.

> air mass
> air pressure
> condensation
> evaporation
> humidity
> precipitation
> runoff
> weather

TEKS 4.8A

1. The condition of the atmosphere at a certain place and time

   is _____.

TEKS 4.8A

2. The amount of water vapor in the air

   is _____.

TEKS 4.8A

3. The weight of the atmosphere pressing down on Earth's

   surface is _____.

TEKS 4.8A

4. A large body of air with the same temperature and humidity

   throughout is an _____.

TEKS 4.8B

5. The process by which a liquid changes to a gas

   is _____.

TEKS 4.8B

6. The process by which a gas changes into a liquid

   is _____.

TEKS 4.8B

7. Water that falls from clouds to Earth's surface

   is _____.

TEKS 4.8B

8. Water that cannot soak into the ground and instead flows

   across Earth's surface is _____.

© Houghton Mifflin Harcourt Publishing Company   (border) ©NDisk/Age Fotostock

Science Concepts

Fill in the letter of the choice that best answers the question.

TEKS 4.2D, 4.8A

9. Deanna measured the temperature and humidity every afternoon for four days. She recorded the results in this table.

Day	Temperature (°C)	Relative Humidity (%)
Monday	28 (82 °F)	90
Tuesday	27 (81 °F)	79
Wednesday	24 (75 °F)	70
Thursday	28 (82 °F)	69

By analyzing her data, which day can Deanna conclude was the hottest and most humid?

Ⓐ Monday   Ⓒ Wednesday

Ⓑ Tuesday   Ⓓ Thursday

TEKS 4.8A

10. Carl looks at a weather map and notices the following symbol. The symbol shows a warm front moving toward his town.

Based on this map key symbol, which prediction can Carl most likely make about the weather?

Ⓐ sunny, clear skies

Ⓑ cooler temperatures

Ⓒ unchanging temperatures

Ⓓ steady to heavy rain

TEKS 4.8A

11. Byron wants to measure and record changes in air pressure. Which tool should he use?

Ⓐ barometer   Ⓒ weather map

Ⓑ thermometer   Ⓓ weather vane

TEKS 4.8B

12. Which of the following sequences shows how water may move from an ocean to land and back to an ocean?

Ⓐ precipitation ➜ runoff ➜ cloud formation ➜ groundwater

Ⓑ evaporation ➜ cloud formation ➜ precipitation ➜ runoff

Ⓒ groundwater ➜ cloud formation ➜ precipitation ➜ runoff

Ⓓ cloud formation ➜ precipitation ➜ evaporation ➜ runoff

TEKS 4.8B

13. This diagram shows the water cycle.

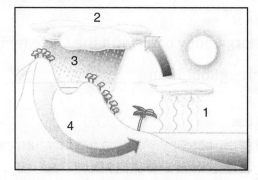

At which point in the cycle does precipitation take place?

Ⓐ 1   Ⓒ 3

Ⓑ 2   Ⓓ 4

TEKS 4.8A

14. Which of the items below will help Sarah use a weather map to predict the weather?

Ⓐ anemometer   Ⓒ map key

Ⓑ barometer   Ⓓ satellite

© Houghton Mifflin Harcourt Publishing Company (border) ©NDisk/Age Fotostock

TEKS 4.8A

15. This diagram illustrates the pattern of air movement in a coastal area.

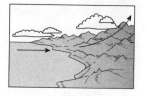

Which type of wind is illustrated in the diagram?

(A) sea breeze

(C) valley breeze

(B) land breeze

(D) coastal breeze

TEKS 4.8B

16. This picture illustrates how a puddle changes over the course of a day.

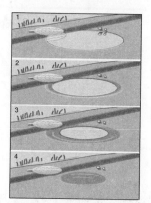

Which process is taking place?

(A) condensation

(C) precipitation

(B) evaporation

(D) runoff

TEKS 4.8B

17. Taro is studying the water cycle. He knows that energy is needed for matter to move and change state. What is a major source of energy for the water cycle process?

(A) clouds

(C) the oceans

(B) the sun

(D) chemical reactions

TEKS 4.8A

18. Jerry notices that the air pressure is rising. Based on this observation, which changes in weather might Jerry record?

(A) fair

(C) unstable

(B) stormy

(D) windy

TEKS 4.8A

19. This diagram illustrates a location where two air masses meet.

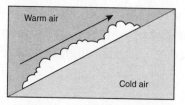

Which changes in weather might be recorded at this type of air boundary?

(A) clear and cold

(C) cloudy and rainy

(B) clear and warm

(D) windy and cold

TEKS 4.8B

20. Oceans get fresh water from precipitation and rivers. However, ocean water levels do not change very much as a result. Why are these levels not greatly affected?

(A) Water is constantly seeping into the ocean floor.

(B) Water is constantly evaporating over the ocean's surface.

(C) Water is constantly flowing back into rivers from the oceans.

(D) Water is constantly deposited back on land by ocean wave action.

© Houghton Mifflin Harcourt Publishing Company   (border) ©NDisk/Age Fotostock

Apply Inquiry and Review the Big Idea

Write the answers to these questions.

TEKS 4.8B

21. This diagram illustrates the atmosphere on a day in late winter. Precipitation is falling.

a. Which type of precipitation is likely to form in the freezing cold layer of air? Explain how you know.

_____

_____

_____

b. Draw arrows to illustrate the continuous movement of water on and above the surface of Earth through the water cycle.

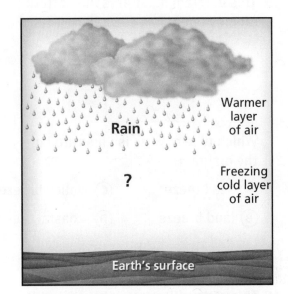

Rain

Warmer layer of air

?

Freezing cold layer of air

Earth's surface

TEKS 4.8A

22. This weather map illustrates a front moving across the Midwest. Write to describe what the symbols mean. Use the weather map and weather symbols to make a prediction about the type of weather Little Rock will have.

_____

_____

_____

_____

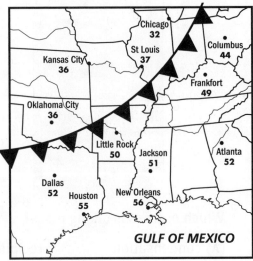

Chicago 32

St Louis 37

Columbus 44

Kansas City 36

Frankfort 49

Oklahoma City 36

Little Rock 50

Jackson 51

Atlanta 52

Dallas 52

Houston 55

New Orleans 56

GULF OF MEXICO

TEKS 4.8A

23. Ming uses a Celsius thermometer to measure and record the temperature over a three-day period. The temperature was 26°C on Monday, 20°C on Tuesday, and 17°C on Wednesday. What was the average daily temperature for the three days?

_____

© Houghton Mifflin Harcourt Publishing Company (border) ©NDisk/Age Fotostock

UNIT 9
Patterns in the Sky

MISSION CONTROL CENTER

© Houghton Mifflin Harcourt Publishing Company · (bg) ©NASA Johnson Space Center; (inset) ©Brand X Pictures/Getty Images; (border) ©NDisc/Age Fotostock

Big Idea

There are recognizable patterns among the sun, Earth, and moon system.

TEKS 4.2C, 4.2D, 4.3D, 4.4A, 4.8C

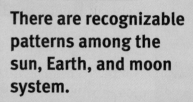

I Wonder How

People have studied space for hundreds of years. How has modern space exploration changed our lives? *Turn the page to find out.*

Here's How Space technology has led to many discoveries about our universe. In addition, technology originally invented to explore space has solved many problems here on Earth.

In this unit, you will explore the Big Idea, the Essential Questions, and the Investigations on the Inquiry Flipchart.

Levels of Inquiry Key ■ DIRECTED ■ GUIDED ■ INDEPENDENT

Track Your Progress

Big Idea There are recognizable patterns among the sun, Earth, and moon system.

Essential Questions

Now I Get the Big Idea!

Science Notebook

Before you begin each lesson, be sure to write your thoughts about the Essential Question.

TEKS **4.3D** connect grade-level appropriate science concepts with the history of science...
4.8C collect and analyze data to identify sequences and predict patterns of change in shadows, tides, seasons, and the observable appearance of the Moon over time

Essential Question

How Do the Sun, Earth, and Moon Interact?

Engage Your Brain!

Find the answer to the following question in this lesson and record it here.

Why is only part of Earth's surface visible from the moon in this picture?

_____

_____

_____

_____

Active Reading

Lesson Vocabulary
List the terms. As you learn about each one, make notes in the Interactive Glossary.

_____ _____

_____ _____

_____ _____

Cause and Effect
Some ideas in this lesson are connected by a cause-and-effect relationship. Why something happens is a cause. What happens as a result of something else is an effect. Active readers look for effects by asking themselves, What happened? They look for causes by asking, Why did it happen?

© Houghton Mifflin Harcourt Publishing Company (bg) ©iStop/Alamy Images

Night and Day

How can it be morning where you live and be nighttime in India at the same time? You cannot feel it, but Earth moves in space.

Active Reading As you read this page, draw one line under a cause of night and day. Draw two lines under an effect of night and day.

People once thought that the sun moved around Earth. After all, the sun seems to rise, to move across the sky, and to set each day. Today we know what makes it seem like the sun moves around Earth. Earth **rotates**, or turns like a top. Earth rotates around an imaginary line, called an **axis**. Earth's axis runs through it from the North Pole to the South Pole. Once every 24 hours, or once a day, Earth rotates about its axis.

Earth's rotation causes day and night. As it rotates, one side of Earth faces the sun. This part of Earth has daytime. The other side of Earth faces away from the sun and has nighttime. As Earth's rotation continues, parts of Earth cycle between day and night.

Each planet rotates at a different rate, so the length of a day is different. For example, Venus rotates so slowly that one day on Venus is equal to 225 days on Earth!

Do the Math!
Use and Represent Numbers

Find the difference between a day on Earth and a day on other planets. (1 Earth day = 24 hours)

Length of Day:

Mercury: 59 Earth days

_____

Jupiter: 9 Earth hours, 55 minutes

_____

Neptune: 16 Earth hours, 6 minutes

_____

© Houghton Mifflin Harcourt Publishing Company (t) ©Planetary Exclusives/Alamy (t) ©Corbis

Night

Day

Earth rotates on its axis from west to east. As a result, the sun appears to rise in the east and set in the west.

© Houghton Mifflin Harcourt Publishing Company (t) ©PlanetaryExclusives/Alamy

Sun-Earth-Moon System

Earth is not alone in space. You can easily spot two other bodies in the sky—the sun and the moon. How do they all move together?

Active Reading As you read these pages, underline the main idea, and circle a sentence that supports it.

The sun, Earth, and the moon form a system in space. This system is held together by gravity. *Gravity* is a force that pulls objects toward each other. Gravity pulls Earth toward the sun, holding Earth in orbit around it. An **orbit** is the path that an object takes around another object in space. Earth *revolves*, or travels around the sun. It takes Earth about 365 days to complete one revolution.

While Earth revolves around the sun, the moon revolves around Earth. Earth's gravity pulls on the moon. Like Earth, the moon also turns on its axis. It takes about a month for the moon to complete one rotation. During the same period of time, the moon makes one complete revolution around Earth. As a result, the same side of the moon always faces Earth.

Sun

The sun is so large that about 1 million Earths could fit inside it! The sun's gravity holds the Earth-moon system in place.

© Houghton Mifflin Harcourt Publishing Company

The sun, the moon, and Earth all have distinct characteristics. The sun has the largest diameter of all bodies in the solar system. An object's *diameter* is the distance from one side, through its center, to the other side.

	Makeup	Diameter	Age
Sun	hot, glowing gases; mostly helium and hydrogen	1,391,000 km (864,400 mi)	about 4.6 billion years old
Earth	rocky surface with large oceans; thick atmosphere of nitrogen and oxygen; life forms	12,756 km (7,926 mi)	about 4.5 billion years old
Moon	rocky surface; no atmosphere or water; extreme cold and heat; no known life forms	3,475 km (2,159 mi)	at least 4.5 billion years old

Moon

Earth

Earth spins quickly—more than 1,600 km/hr (1,000 mi/hr) at its equator. As Earth spins, it also speeds around the sun at more than 107,000 km/hr (67,000 mi/hr). Earth and the moon are relatively close to one another. They are about 382,000 km (237,400 mi) apart. In contrast, Earth is about 150 million km (93 million mi) from the sun.

How Do They Move?

The arrows in the picture show the two types of movements that Earth makes in space. Label each arrow with the movement it shows. Then, explain how Earth moves.

_____
_____
_____
_____
_____

Houghton Mifflin Harcourt Publishing Company (t) ©Corbis

Seasons

When it is summer in the United States, it is winter in Chile. How can two places have a different season at the same time of year?

Active Reading As you read this page, underline the cause of the seasons.

Earth rotates on its tilted axis. As Earth revolves around the sun, the direction of its tilted axis doesn't change. The tilt of Earth's axis and its orbit cause the seasons.

Earth is divided into halves called *hemispheres*. The Northern Hemisphere extends from the equator to the North Pole. The Southern Hemisphere extends from the equator to the South Pole. In June, the Northern Hemisphere is tilted toward the sun and gets more direct rays of sunlight. It has more hours of daylight and warmer weather. It is summer there.

In June, in the Southern Hemisphere, the opposite season takes place. Why? The Southern Hemisphere is tilted away from the sun and gets less direct sunlight. It has fewer hours of daylight and cooler weather. It is winter there.

In December, the Northern Hemisphere is tilted away from the sun. As a result, it is winter there. At the same time, the Southern Hemisphere is tilted toward the sun and has summer.

Home Sweet Home

Which season is it where you live? Draw a picture of the sun and Earth in the correct positions to show the season. Include the tilt of Earth's axis in your picture.

© Houghton Mifflin Harcourt Publishing Company (t) ©Getty Images/PhotoDisc

Seasons in the Northern Hemisphere

When the Northern Hemisphere is tilted away from the sun, that part of Earth has winter. When the Northern Hemisphere is tilted toward the sun, it has summer.

Winter

Fall

Spring

Summer

The Turning Tides

Have you ever spent a day at the beach? Did you notice the changing water level over the course of the day?

Active Reading As you read these two pages, draw one line under a cause. Draw two lines under an effect.

The level of the ocean rises and falls in a cycle. This rise and fall in the water level of the ocean is called a **tide**. Tides are caused by the "pull" of the sun and the moon on Earth's oceans. How does this happen?

The pull of the moon's gravity on Earth is the main cause of tides. As a result of this pull, two bulges, or swells, form in Earth's oceans. One bulge forms on the side of Earth facing the moon. The other bulge forms on the side of Earth that faces away from the moon. The higher water level in the bulges results in a *high tide*. Between the bulges, the water level is lower, resulting in a *low tide* at those places.

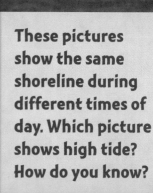

These pictures show the same shoreline during different times of day. Which picture shows high tide? How do you know?

© Houghton Mifflin Harcourt Publishing Company (bg) ©David Olsen/Alamy Images; (tr) ©Stephen Saks Photography/Alamy Images; (br) ©Edward Kinsman/Getty Images

High and Low Tides

As a result of Earth's rotation, most shorelines have two high tides and two low tides each day. The tides are usually a little more than six hours apart.

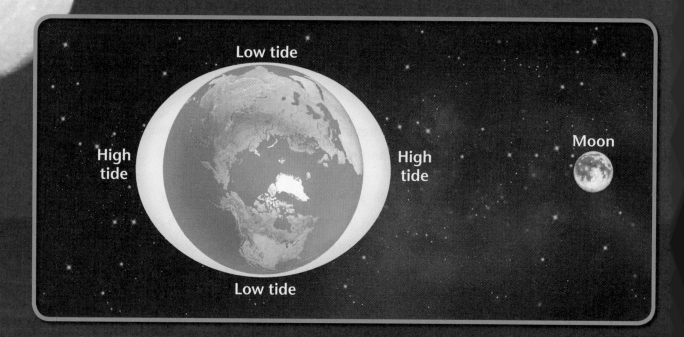

Analyze Tide Times

Day	Tides	Time
1	high	2:58 a.m.
	low	8:50 a.m.
	high	3:05 p.m.
	low	9:10 p.m.
2	high	3:46 a.m.
	low	9:45 a.m.
	high	3:58 p.m.
	low	10:00 p.m.
3	high	4:30 a.m.
	low	10:40 a.m.
	high	4:45 p.m.
	low	10:50 p.m.

Analyze the data in the tide table to identify sequences of change in tides to answer the questions.

1. How much time passes from one high tide to the next high tide on the same day?

_____

2. How much time passes from one high tide to one low tide on the same day?

_____

3. Predict when the first high tide will occur on Day 4. Explain your answer.

_____

_____

_____

Houghton Mifflin Harcourt Publishing Company   (tc) ©David Olsen/Alamy Images

Patterns in the Sky

The Big Dipper is a part of a star pattern in the night sky. To Ancient Greeks, the pattern looked like a giant bear.

Active Reading As you read these pages, draw a circle around words or phrases that provide details about constellations.

People have looked at the stars for thousands of years. A star pattern, or **constellation**, is a group of stars that seems to form a picture in the night sky. The early Greeks named constellations after animals or people from stories called *myths*. The Big Dipper is part of a constellation called *Ursa Major*, or Great Bear. Orion is a constellation named after a hunter in a Greek myth.

As Earth rotates on its axis, constellations seem to move across the night sky. Like the sun, constellations seem to rise in the east and set in the west. Stars above the North Pole, however, seem to move in a circle.

The positions of the constellations seem to change with the seasons, because we see different parts of space as Earth revolves around the sun. The stars in the constellations do change a little over time. However, it might take millions of years for a constellation to change its shape!

For thousands of years, people have seen pictures in the stars. They connect the stars to make a pattern or shape.

court Publishing Company (tc) © Bryan Allen/Corbis; (b) ©Argosy Illustration

These pictures show stars seen from the same location during summer (at left) and winter (at right). The constellations seem to change their places in the sky.

Houghton Mifflin Harcourt Publishing Company (bg) © Bryan Allen/Corbis

Connect the Stars

Connect the stars to draw a constellation. Use all or some of the stars. What is the name of your constellation?

_____

_____

Our Place in Space

At one time, people thought Earth was the center of the universe. How did we learn that this isn't true?

Long ago, astronomers believed Earth was the center of the universe. Daily observations seemed to confirm this belief. When people looked at the sky, they saw the sun, the moon, planets, and stars in motion. Naturally, they concluded that Earth was at the center of the universe. It took hundreds of years, new technology, and new observations for this idea to change.

In the 1500s, a Polish astronomer named Nicolaus Copernicus designed a new *model*, or system, of the universe. Based on new observations about the motion of the planets, he suggested that Earth and the planets revolved around the sun. Then, in the 1600s, scientists gathered more evidence to support this sun-centered model of the solar system.

Using a telescope he made, Galileo Galilei was the first to see moons orbiting Jupiter. His observation showed that all objects in space did not orbit Earth. Around this time, Johannes Kepler correctly described the shape of the planets' orbits around the sun. His calculations showed that the planets revolved around the sun in elliptical [ee▪LIP▪tih▪kuhl] orbits. All these scientists' observations changed our idea about Earth's place in space.

Earth

Beyond the Book

Suppose you are an astronomer who lived at the same time as Galileo. Write a letter to a friend explaining Galileo's discoveries, his ideas about a sun-centered universe, and the conclusions he made about them.

Houghton Mifflin Harcourt Publishing Company   (b) ©Peter Arnold, Inc./Alamy Images

When people measured time using sundials, the changing shadow cast by the sun seemed to confirm that the sun revolved around Earth. We now know that the sun doesn't revolve around Earth. Earth revolves around the sun!

What Do You Know?

Describe what you know about the sun-Earth-moon system that astronomers did not know long ago.

_____

_____

_____

_____

_____

Mars

Venus

Jupiter

Saturn

Mercury

Sun

Moon

Galileo was the first to study the night sky using a telescope. His observations helped support the sun-centered model of the solar system. The pictures here show a replica of Galileo's telescope and Jupiter and four of its moons.

Houghton Mifflin Harcourt Publishing Company (b) ©Peter Arnold, Inc./Alamy Images; (MD)Getty Images; (t) ©Gianni Tortoli/Photo Researchers, Inc.

When you're done, use the answer key to check and revise your work.

Read the summary statements below. Each one is incorrect. Change the part of the summary in blue to make the statement correct.

Summarize

1. Day and night are caused by Earth's revolution around the sun.	_____ _____
2. The discovery of moons around Jupiter proved that all objects in space revolve around Jupiter.	_____ _____ _____
3. Earth's seasons are caused by Earth's revolution and rotation in space.	_____ _____
4. During winter in the Northern Hemisphere, there are more hours of daylight and it is warmer.	_____ _____ _____
5. When it is spring in the Northern Hemisphere, the season is summer in the Southern Hemisphere.	_____ _____ _____
6. Constellations appear to move across the night sky because of Earth's tilt on its axis.	_____ _____

Answer Key: 1. Day and night are caused by Earth's rotation on its axis. 2. The discovery of moons around Jupiter proved that all objects in space do not revolve around Earth. 3. Earth's seasons are caused by Earth's revolution and the tilt of its axis. 4. During winter in the Northern Hemisphere, there are fewer hours of daylight and it is cooler. 5. When it is spring in the Northern Hemisphere, the season is fall in the Southern Hemisphere. 6. Constellations appear to move across the night sky because of Earth's rotation.

© Houghton Mifflin Harcourt Publishing Company

Name _____

Word Play

1 Unscramble letters to fill in the blanks with the words from the box below. Use the hints to help you unscramble the letters.

1. X A S I __ __ __ __
   [Hint: an imaginary line through Earth]

2. T E R A O T __ __ __ __ __ __
   [Hint: Earth's spinning in space]

3. R I B O T __ __ __ __ __
   [Hint: Earth's path in space]

4. L E O V R E V __ __ __ __ __ __ __
   [Hint: Earth does this around the sun once a year.]

5. S T E L C O N A L I O N T __ __ __ __ __ __ __ __ __ __ __ __ __
   [Hint: a pattern of stars in the night sky]

6. H M S I E E P R E H __ __ __ __ __ __ __ __ __ __
   [Hint: one half of Earth]

7. D O L E M __ __ __ __ __
   [Hint: a representation of the sun-Earth-moon system]

8. N A S S E O __ __ __ __ __ __
   [Hint: a time of year with a particular type of weather]

9. I D T E __ __ __ __
   [Hint: the rise and fall of the water level of the ocean]

model	revolve	orbit*	hemisphere	tide*
axis*	constellation*	rotate*	season	

* Key Lesson Vocabulary

© Houghton Mifflin Harcourt Publishing Company

Apply Concepts

2 Draw a picture of the sun and Earth. Draw lines to show Earth's axis and rays from the sun. Label which side of Earth has day and which side has night.

3 At sunset, the sun appears to sink down below the horizon. How would a scientist describe sunset?

_____

_____

_____

_____

© Houghton Mifflin Harcourt Publishing Company

4 The constellation Orion is seen in the night sky during winter in the Northern Hemisphere. During summer, Orion cannot be seen. Why is Orion only seen during part of the year?

_____

_____

_____

_____

_____

_____

5 Imagine you are going on a ride in a spacecraft next to Earth. Your trip takes one whole year. Describe Earth's tilt in the Northern Hemisphere during your trip. What happens as a result of the tilt?

_____

_____

_____

_____

© Houghton Mifflin Harcourt Publishing Company

6 What is a tide? What causes tides?

_____

_____

_____

7 Analyze the data in the tide table below. Use it to predict when low tide will take place on Tuesday evening. Write to explain your prediction.

Day	Tides	Time
Monday	high	3:42 a.m.
	low	9:25 a.m.
	high	4:10 p.m.
	low	9:55 p.m.
Tuesday	high	4:00 a.m.
	low	10:16 a.m.
	high	4:58 p.m.
	low	? p.m.

_____

_____

_____

Take It Home!

With an adult, observe constellations outside on a clear night. Draw a picture of a constellation you observe. What do you think the night sky will look like in three months?

© Houghton Mifflin Harcourt Publishing Company   HMH Credits

TEKS **4.3D** connect grade-level appropriate science concepts with the history of science, science careers, and contributions of scientists

People in Science

Meet the Climate Scientists

Milutin Milankovitch

During an ice age, ice sheets cover much of Earth. Why do ice ages happen? Serbian scientist Milutin Milankovitch [mih•LOO•tin mih•LAHNG•koh•vich] spent his career trying to find out. Milankovitch learned that Earth's orbit changes in cycles lasting thousands of years. He determined that these changes affect the amount of sunlight reaching Earth. As a result, during cooler periods, ice ages occur. Today, data from the ocean floor supports Milankovitch's ideas. These climate patterns are called Milankovitch cycles in his honor.

The direction of Earth's axis changes over time as part of a cycle that lasts about 23,000 years. This change affects Earth's temperature.

Dr. Maureen Raymo

Dr. Maureen Raymo is a paleoclimatologist. She studies how Earth's climate has changed over long periods of time. Like Milankovitch, Dr. Raymo studies the relationship between changes in Earth's orbit and climate. During an ice age, much of Earth's water is stored in glaciers. This affects sea level. Dr. Raymo has been able to find evidence of ancient changes in climate by studying rocks and sediment on the ocean floor. Through her research, she has been able to describe the sea level and water flow direction in ancient oceans.

© Houghton Mifflin Harcourt Publishing Company (bg) ©Sam Fried/Photo Researchers, Inc.; (br) ©Houghton Mifflin Harcourt

The Road to a New Hypothesis

Use the information below to make a timeline of the events that led Milutin Milankovitch to develop his hypothesis.

1930 Milutin Milankovitch publishes his hypothesis. He bases it on improved methods of calculating differences in Earth's orbit, axis direction, and axis tilt.

1864 James Croll explains ice ages as a result of changes in Earth's axis and the shape of its orbit around the sun.

1960s Continued research shows that Milankovitch's hypothesis explains some climate trends.

1754 Jean le Rond d'Alembert calculates how the direction in which Earth's axis is pointed changes over time.

1824 J. A. Adhemar studies d'Alembert's ideas and suggests that the change in axis direction is responsible for ice ages.

Today Dr. Raymo finds evidence in rocks and sediment on the ocean floor that supports Milankovitch's hypothesis.

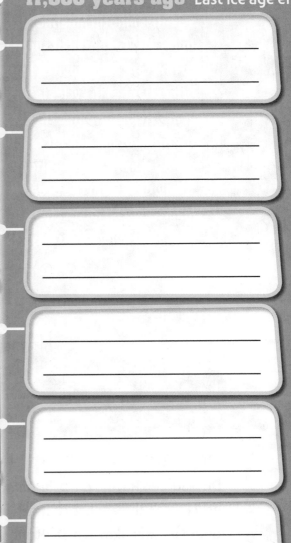

Milankovitch cycles predict ice ages as a result of Earth's motion in space.

11,500 years ago Last ice age ends.

Think About It!

Where should the following event be placed on the timeline?
Scientists find data that conflict with Milankovitch's hypothesis, which falls into disfavor.

_____

© Houghton Mifflin Harcourt Publishing Company (t) ©Radius Images/Corbis; (br) ©Houghton Mifflin Harcourt

Inquiry Flipchart page 48

TEKS 4.2B...record data by... measuring, using the metric system... and numerals... **4.2C** construct simple tables...using tools...to organize, examine, and evaluate data **4.2D** analyze data and interpret patterns to construct reasonable explanations from data that can be observed... **4.3A** in all fields of science, analyze, evaluate...scientific explanations by using...observational testing... **4.4A** collect...information using tools, including... meter sticks... **4.8C** ...analyze data to identify sequences and predict patterns of change in shadows...over time

Name _____

Essential Question

How Do Shadows Change?

Set a Purpose

Why is observational testing helpful when studying shadows?

_____

_____

_____

Think About the Procedure

Why should the location for your wooden dowel and craft paper be in a sunny place all day?

_____

_____

_____

Why is it important to measure the length of each shadow with a meterstick and record the time it was traced?

_____

_____

_____

Record Your Data

In the space below, use a metric ruler to construct a simple table to organize, examine, and evaluate your data.

© Houghton Mifflin Harcourt Publishing Company

Draw Conclusions

Compare the lengths of the shadows. Identify the pattern of change in the shadows.

_____

_____

_____

_____

How did the position of the shadows change on the craft paper?

_____

_____

_____

Analyze and Extend

1. Analyze your data. At what time was the shadow the longest? The shortest?

_____

_____

_____

2. Evaluate your data. How does the time of day affect the length of the shadow?

_____

_____

_____

_____

3. Explain how the position of the sun in the sky is related to the pattern you observed.

_____

_____

_____

_____

_____

_____

4. Were your predictions accurate? Explain.

_____

_____

_____

_____

_____

5. Suppose you are going to measure the length of a shadow from 10:00 a.m. to 12:00 p.m. Predict the pattern of change of the shadows.

_____

_____

6. How might you use the dowel and the craft paper to tell time?

_____

_____

_____

_____

© Houghton Mifflin Harcourt Publishing Company

TEKS **4.8C** collect and analyze data to identify sequences and predict patterns of change in... the observable appearance of the Moon over time.

Lesson **3**

Essential Question

What Are Moon Phases?

Engage Your Brain!

Find the answer to the following question in this lesson and record it here.

What do you observe about the moon in the night sky?

_____

_____

_____

_____

Active Reading

Lesson Vocabulary

List the terms. As you learn about each one, make notes in the Interactive Glossary.

_____

_____

_____

Sequence

Many ideas in this lesson are connected by a sequence, or order, that describes the steps in a process. Active readers stay focused on sequence when they mark the transition from one step in a process to another.

© Houghton Mifflin Harcourt Publishing Company ©Adam Jones/Danita Delimont/Alamy

Our Moon

Neil Armstrong was the first person to walk on Earth's moon. He said of the moon, "The surface is fine and powdery. I can pick it up with my toe."

The moon is Earth's satellite. A satellite is an object that moves around another larger object in space. Earth's moon is the largest and brightest object in the night sky. It looks large because it is close to Earth. But the moon is small compared to Earth. It is only about one-fourth the size of Earth. The moon has no air, wind, or liquid water. We see the moon because light from the sun reflects from it and back to Earth.

The pull of Earth's gravity keeps the moon in its orbit around Earth. We see only one side of the moon from Earth, because the moon takes the same amount of time to rotate once as it does to orbit Earth once.

We can see the moon at night (small photo) and sometimes during the day.

© Houghton Mifflin Harcourt Publishing Company (bkgd) ©Bloomimage/Corbis; (tr) ©Sigrun Eriksen/Alamy; (bc) ©Corbis

Moon and Earth

Compare the moon and Earth. How are they alike? How are they different? Complete the Venn diagram below.

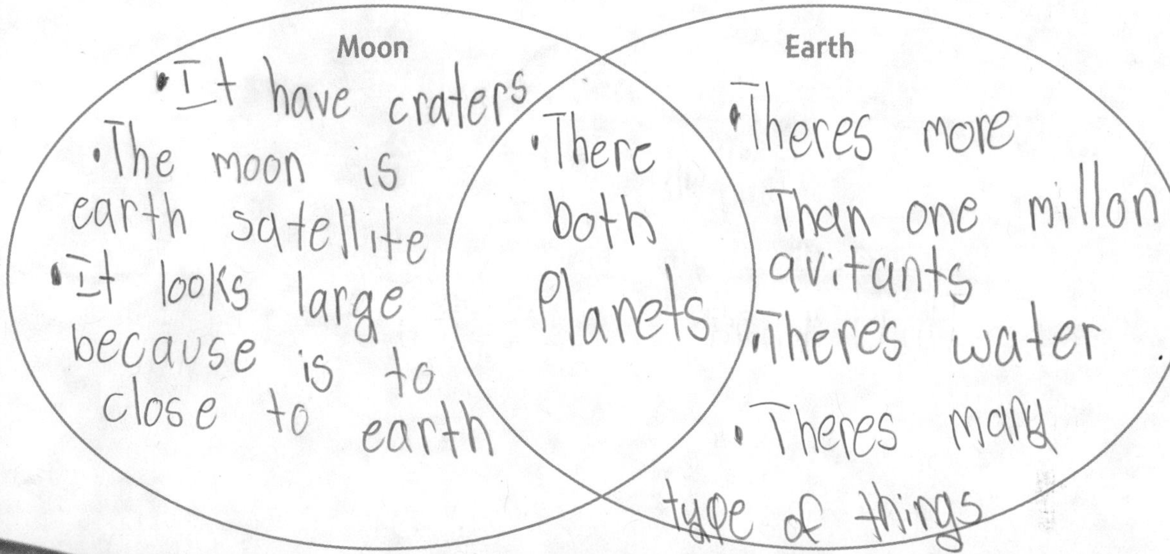

Moon | Earth

- It have craters
- The moon is earth satellite
- It looks large because is to close to earth

- There both Planets

- Theres more Than one millon avitants
- Theres water
- Theres many type of things

Rocks and chunks of debris from space slammed into the moon and formed its many craters. Craters, or pits in the ground, cover the moon's rocky surface.

There are mountains and large, flat plains. The plains on the moon's surface are called *maria* [mah•REE•uh], a Latin word meaning "seas."

© Houghton Mifflin Harcourt Publishing Company   (bkgd) ©Bloomimage/Corbis; (cr) ©Peter Arnold, Inc./Alamy

Moon Phases

One night, you might look at the moon and see a tiny sliver in the sky. A few nights later, you might see a bright, round circle. Why?

Active Reading As you read the last paragraph, write numbers next to the sentences to identify the sequence of moon phases. Then predict which phase will follow the last phase in the sequence and place a star next to it.

As Earth orbits the sun, the moon also orbits Earth. The moon reflects light from the sun. That is the light we see from Earth. As the moon travels in its orbit, different amounts of the moon's lit side can be seen from Earth.

First Quarter

New Moon

During the new moon phase, the moon is between Earth and the sun. We can't see the moon at all. During a first quarter moon, we see one-half of the moon's lit side.

© Houghton Mifflin Harcourt Publishing Company   (b) ©Dennis Hallinan/Alamy

The moon's shape does not change. The changes in the appearance of the moon's shape are known as **moon phases**.

You know that sunlight reflects from the moon to Earth. Yet the sun lights only half of the moon at any time. The motions of Earth and the moon are responsible for the phases you see. As the moon revolves around Earth, the amount of the lit part that we see from Earth changes. These different amounts of the moon's lighted side are the different phases of the moon.

Each phase of the moon has a different shape. It takes about 1 month for the moon to complete all of its phases. Then the cycle repeats.

During the new moon phase, we can't see the moon. That is because the lit part of the moon faces away from Earth. As the moon moves in its orbit around Earth, we see more of the moon's lit part. We see a full moon when all of the lit part of the moon faces Earth. Then we see less and less of the lit part again.

Do the Math!
Estimate Fractions and Percentages

Identify sequences in the observable appearance of the moon. What fraction and percent of the moon's lit side is seen during each phase? Complete the table.

	Full moon	First quarter	New moon	Third quarter
Fraction	$\frac{2}{2}$	$\frac{1}{2}$	$\frac{0}{2}$	$\frac{1}{2}$
Percent	100%	50%	0%	50%

Full Moon

Third Quarter

The lit portion grows larger until we see a full moon. This happens when Earth is between the moon and the sun. As the moon continues in its orbit, we see less of its lit portion. When it is half lit again, it is a third quarter moon.

Lunar and Solar Calendars

For thousands of years, people used the phases of the moon to make calendars and track time. These are called lunar calendars. Earth's orbit around the sun also has been used to make calendars and track time. These are called solar calendars.

The Chinese Zodiac Calendar

The Chinese zodiac calendar is based in part on the phases of the moon. Twelve animals stand for cycles of time on the calendar. Some of these animals are the tiger, rabbit, dragon, and snake. Each year is also given an animal name. For example, in 2026, it will be the "Year of the Horse." The year 2027 will be the "Year of the Sheep".

Chinese New Year comes sometime between late January and early February. It is celebrated with fancy dragon costumes.

© Houghton Mifflin Harcourt Publishing Company. (bkgd) ©Ballas and John Heaton/SCPhotos/Alamy; (br) ©Helene Rogers/Alamy

The Aztec calendar is based on Earth's orbit around the sun. Each part of the calendar has colorful animals or symbols. These symbols marked important times of the year, such as when to plant crops.

APRIL

Sunday	Monday	Tuesday	Wednesday	Thursday	Friday	Saturday
			1	2	3	4
5	6	7	8	9	10	11
12	13	14	15	16	17	18
19	20	21	22	23	24	25
26	27	28	29	30		

New Year's Day

In the United States, New Year's Day is always January 1. In China, it is on the day of the new moon. Why do you think New Year's Day always falls on a different day each year in China?

Because theres gonna be a new moon thats why

Our modern calendar is based on Earth's orbit around the sun. Each month is based roughly on the moon's phases. Once in a while, there are two full moons in one month.

© Houghton Mifflin Harcourt Publishing Company   (tl) ©Aztec/Getty Images

When you're done, use the answer key to check and revise your work.

The idea web below summarizes the lesson. Complete the web.

Summarize

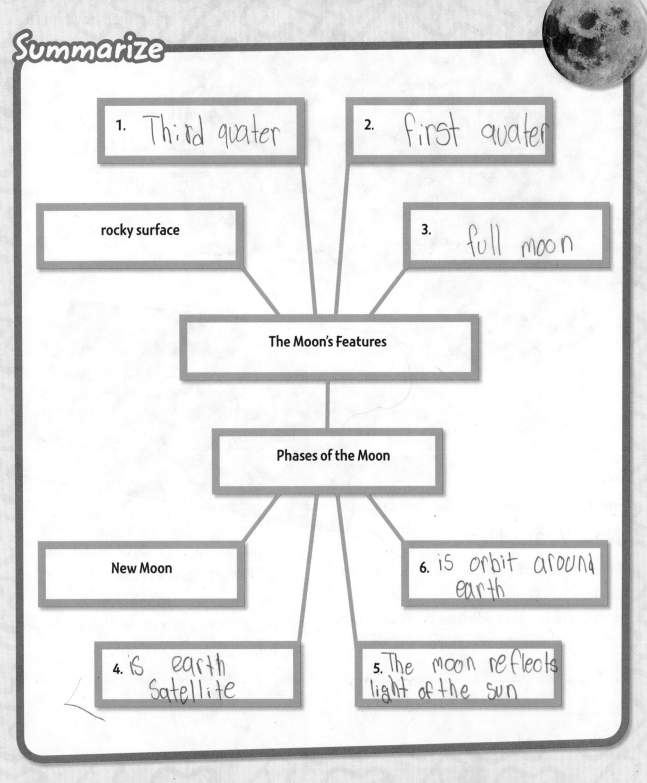

1. Third quater

2. first quater

rocky surface

3. full moon

The Moon's Features

Phases of the Moon

New Moon

6. is orbit around earth

4. is earth Satellite

5. The moon reflects light of the sun

© Houghton Mifflin Harcourt Publishing Company   (tr) ©Getty Images/PhotoDisc

Answer Key: 1.–3. Sample answers: no air or liquid water; craters, mountains and flat plains; revolves around Earth. 4. First Quarter Moon 5. Full Moon 6. Third Quarter Moon

Name _____

Word Play

1 Look at the picture and word clues. Write the answer to each clue on the blanks.

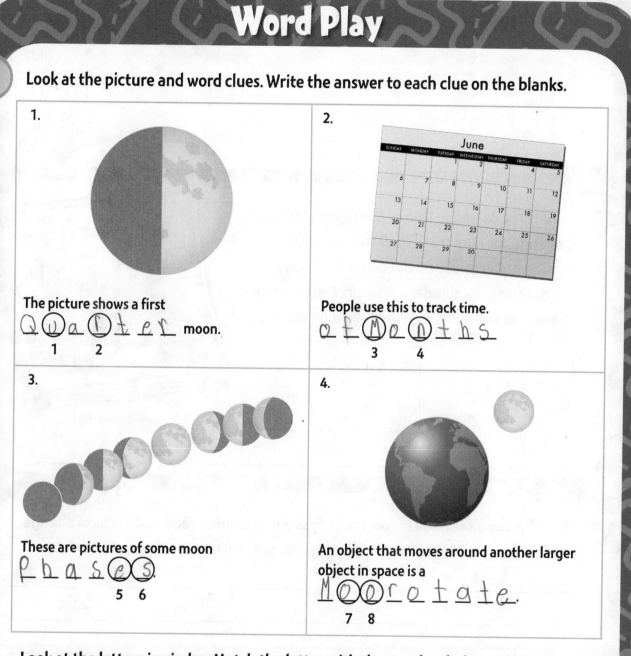

1.

The picture shows a first
Q u a **r** t e **r** moon.
   1   2

2.

People use this to track time.
a f **M** o **n** t h s
     3   4

3.

These are pictures of some moon
p h a s **e** **s**.
    5 6

4.

An object that moves around another larger object in space is a
M **o** **o** r o t a t e.
   7 8

Look at the letters in circles. Match the letter with the number below each space to solve the riddle.

What kind of cartoons does the moon watch?

M u n o r o u n e s
3 1 4 7 2   8 1 4 5 6

© Houghton Mifflin Harcourt Publishing Company

Apply Concepts

2 Draw a picture of the sun and the moon. Add lines to show light rays from the sun. Shade the part of the moon that is dark.

3 Look at the calendar. One of the moon's phases is missing for January 10th. Draw and label the missing moon phase on the calendar. Analyze the data on the calendar to predict the first moon phase that will take place the following month.

_____

_____

4 One night you see a full moon. Identify sequences and predict patterns of change in the moon over time. Predict which moon phase you will see one month later.

_____

_____

_____

Take It Home! With an adult, use a pair of binoculars to collect data on the observable appearance of the moon over time. How much detail can you see? Draw pictures of what you observe.

© Houghton Mifflin Harcourt Publishing Company

Name _____

TEKS **4.2B** ...record data by observing...using descriptive words... such as labeled drawings... **4.2F** communicate valid...results supported by data **4.8C** collect and analyze data to identify sequences and predict patterns of change in...the observable appearance of the Moon over time

Essential Question

How Does the Moon Move Around Earth?

Set a Purpose

What do you think you will learn from this activity?

_____

_____

_____

Think About the Procedure

How does the moon have to move for its marked side to always face Earth?

_____

_____

_____

The student holding the flashlight also moves. Why? How is this different from what we know about the sun?

_____

_____

_____

Record Your Data

Record data you collected below. Draw the position of the marked side of the moon with respect to Earth and the sun. Show the shaded and lit portions of the moon.

Position 1

Position 2

Position 3

Position 4

© Houghton Mifflin Harcourt Publishing Company HMH Credits

Draw Conclusions

What happens to the visible part of the moon as it moves through its orbit?

_____

_____

The moon turns as it orbits Earth. When does the moon complete a full rotation?

_____

_____

Analyze the data you recorded on the previous page. Draw to predict the position and appearance of the moon if you were to continue past Position 4. Which moon phase did you draw?

_____

Analyze and Extend

1. Predict patterns in the appearance of the moon over time. Draw and describe the moon phase that takes place when the moon is between Earth and the sun.

_____

_____

2. Use the data you collected to explain why the amount of sunlight on the moon seems to change.

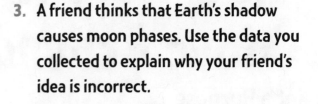

_____

_____

_____

3. A friend thinks that Earth's shadow causes moon phases. Use the data you collected to explain why your friend's idea is incorrect.

_____

_____

_____

_____

4. The same friend also thinks that the moon has a dark side where the sun never shines. How would you use the data you collected to explain why your friend's idea is incorrect?

_____

_____

_____

5. What other questions would you like to ask about moon phases?

_____

_____

_____

© Houghton Mifflin Harcourt Publishing Company   HMH Credits

TEKS 4.2D analyze data...to construct reasonable explanations from data that can be observed... 4.3D connect grade-level appropriate science concepts with...science careers....

Space Exploration

Typically, engineering design problems have many solutions. An engineer often needs to find a balance among many trade-offs to get the best solution. A *trade-off* is the giving up of one design feature to make another design feature better. The charts below show trade-off analyses for spacecraft with and without crew. The benefits and drawbacks of some major design features of each kind of mission are shown. You decide which one should blast off.

Spacecraft with Crew

Design Feature	Benefit	Drawback
living space for crew	people onboard to fix problems and run difficult science experiments	greater cost to build and to fuel; increased weight during liftoff (must store air, food, and water)
heat shield for reentry to Earth's atmosphere	safe return of crew; reusable ship	more fuel needed; less space for everything else

Spacecraft without Crew

Design Feature	Benefit	Drawback
smaller, lighter	less fuel needed; costs less to launch	less room for instruments
no living space for crew	no need to store air, food, water	no one to fix problems or watch experiments
large energy supply to last many years in space	can learn about faraway objects	spacecraft doesn't return to Earth; it cannot be reused

You Decide

Which type of spacecraft works best for space exploration? Analyze the data in the chart and use it to explain your answer.

_____

_____

© Houghton Mifflin Harcourt Publishing Company (t) ©Stockrek/Corbis; (c) ©Alain Nogues/Sygma/Corbis; (b) ©NASA

S.T.E.M.
continued

Analyze Trade-offs

Engineers think about trade-offs before designing a spacecraft. Sometimes, the trade-offs lead them to conclude that a particular solution is not worth trying.

Suppose a crew wants new space suits. Analyze the data in the chart and use the features and trade-offs of the old and new space suits to answer the questions below.

Old Space Suit		New Space Suit	
Design Feature	Trade-off	Design Feature	Trade-off
thick space suit protects astronaut against extreme temperatures and debris	hard to move around in	thinner space suit lighter and easier to move around in	may not protect as well as the old suit against extreme temperatures or debris
sturdy material and strong joints	difficult to put on quickly	has newer technologies built in	all technologies may not have been tested in space

What is the most important feature of a space suit?

_____

Do you think the benefits of the new space suit outweigh its trade-offs? Why or why not?

_____

_____

_____

Build On It!

Rise to the engineering design challenge—complete **Design It: Build a Sundial** on the Inquiry Flipchart.

© Houghton Mifflin Harcourt Publishing Company   (l) ©NASA; (r) ©NASA

Name _____

Vocabulary Review

Use the terms in the box to complete the sentences.

> axis
> constellation
> moon phase
> orbit
> rotate
> tide

TEKS 4.8C

1. A change in the appearance of the moon's shape is known

   as a(n) _____.

TEKS 4.8C

2. When things turn like a top, they _____.

TEKS 4.8C

3. Earth turns around an imaginary line called a(n)

   _____.

TEKS 4.8C

4. The path that one object takes around another object in

   space is its _____.

TEKS 4.8C

5. The rise and fall in the water level of the ocean is called a(n)

   _____.

TEKS 4.8C

6. A group of stars that seems to form a pattern in the night

   sky is a(n) _____.

Science Concepts

Fill in the letter of the choice that best answers the question.

TEKS 4.8C

7. During different seasons, you see different stars in the night sky. What causes this?

   (A) the sun's rotation

   (B) the moon's revolution

   (C) Earth's rotation

   (D) Earth's revolution

TEKS 4.8C

8. Amy notices a change in the pattern of shadows on Earth as the sun moves across the sky. What causes this change?

   (A) Earth's rotation

   (B) Earth's revolution

   (C) the moon's revolution

   (D) Earth's path as it orbits the sun

© Houghton Mifflin Harcourt Publishing Company   (border) ©NDisk/Age Fotostock

Science Concepts

Fill in the letter of the choice that best answers the question.

TEKS 4.8C

9. In the United States, an August day is usually hotter than a January day. Why is this true?

(A) The sun gives off more heat in the summer.

(B) Earth is closer to the sun in summer and farther away in winter.

(C) Earth's rotation slows down in the summer and speeds up in winter.

(D) Earth's North Pole tilts toward the sun in summer and away from it in winter.

TEKS 4.3D

10. Which scientist first described the orbits of the planets as elliptical?

(A) Isaac Newton

(B) Galileo Galilei

(C) Nicolaus Copernicus

(D) Johannes Kepler

TEKS 4.8C

11. Ashley notices changes in the moon over a one-month period. Which sequence below could Ashley have seen?

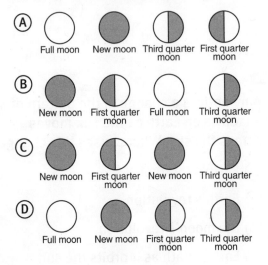

(A) Full moon, New moon, Third quarter moon, First quarter moon

(B) New moon, First quarter moon, Full moon, Third quarter moon

(C) New moon, First quarter moon, New moon, Third quarter moon

(D) Full moon, New moon, First quarter moon, Third quarter moon

TEKS 4.8C

12. The same side of the moon always faces Earth. Why is this?

(A) Half the moon faces the sun.

(B) The moon does not rotate like Earth does.

(C) The moon's revolution and rotation are about the same length.

(D) Earth blocks part of the sunlight that shines on the moon's surface.

TEKS 4.2D

13. The table below contains data showing how long it takes each planet to make one complete rotation and revolution. The numbers are in Earth days.

Planet	Time needed to make one complete rotation (Earth days)	Time needed to make one complete revolution (Earth days)
Mercury	58.6	87.96
Venus	243.0	224.7
Earth	1.0	365.26
Mars	1.02	687.0

According to the data table, which one of these statements is correct?

(A) Earth takes less time to orbit the sun than does Mars.

(B) Venus takes more time to orbit the sun than does Mars.

(C) Venus takes less time to orbit the sun than does Mercury.

(D) Mercury takes more time to orbit the sun than does Earth.

© Houghton Mifflin Harcourt Publishing Company   (border) ©NDisk/Age Fotostock

TEKS 4.2D, 4.8C

14. Adele observes the appearance of the moon over a period of time. She collects data and draws the following diagram.

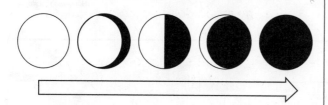

Which of the following can Adele predict will be the next moon phase?

Ⓐ full moon

Ⓑ new moon

Ⓒ first quarter moon

Ⓓ third quarter moon

TEKS 4.8C

15. The picture below is a two-dimensional model of how Earth moves in space.

How long does it take for Earth to complete one full movement as shown in this picture?

Ⓐ 1 day

Ⓑ 1 week

Ⓒ 1 month

Ⓓ 1 year

TEKS 4.8C

16. Matt and his family spend a day at the beach. Matt notices that the level of water at the dock is 2 m lower at 3:00 p.m. than it was at 9:00 a.m. What can Matt predict will happen to the level of water during the next 6 hours?

Ⓐ It will get lower.

Ⓑ It will get higher.

Ⓒ It will remain the same.

Ⓓ It will reach over the dock.

TEKS 4.8C

17. Sergei places a stick into the ground in a sunny spot at 9:00 a.m. He measures the shadow cast by the stick and records it in his Science Notebook. The length of the shadow measures 15 cm. What prediction might Sergei make about how the shadow will change during the next 3 hours?

Ⓐ It will get longer.

Ⓑ It will get shorter.

Ⓒ It will stay the same.

Ⓓ It will totally disappear.

© Houghton Mifflin Harcourt Publishing Company (border) ©NDisk/Age Fotostock

Apply Inquiry and Review the Big Idea

Write the answers to these questions.

© Houghton Mifflin Harcourt Publishing Company   (border) ©NDisk/Age Fotostock

TEKS 4.3C

18. This two-dimensional model shows the sun, Earth, and the moon. It is not drawn to scale. Use the model to explain why you can see the moon from Earth. Then identify the model's limitations.

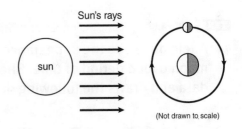

Sun's rays

sun

(Not drawn to scale)

_____

_____

TEKS 4.2D, 4.8C

19. Darnell collected data about the changes in tidal patterns at a local beach. He recorded his data in the table below.

Day	Tides	Time	Day	Tides	Time
Saturday	high	1:32 a.m.	Sunday	high	3:00 a.m.
	low	7:15 a.m.		low	9:05 a.m.
	high	2:05 p.m.		high	3:57 p.m.
	low	7:53 p.m.		low	?

a. Which pattern of change in tides can Darnell conclude from his data?

_____

_____

b. At what time might Darnell predict the next low tide will take place on Sunday? Explain.

_____

_____

TEKS 4.3D

20. Astronomers before Copernicus and Galileo knew about Earth's moon and about Mars, Jupiter, and Saturn. Do you think they knew about the moons of these planets? Explain.

_____

_____

TEKS 4.8C

21. Antoine measures the length of a stick's shadow once an hour for 4 hours beginning at 7:00 a.m. He records these measurements: 54 cm, 46 cm, 38 cm, 30 cm. Based on the shadow's pattern of change, what might he predict the length of the shadow will be after 5 hours?

_____

UNIT 10
Organisms and Their Environments

© Houghton Mifflin Harcourt Publishing Company

(bg) ©Michael Patrick O'Neill/Alamy Images; (inset) ©Aquascopic/Alamy Images; (border) ©NDisc/Age Fotostock

Big Idea

Living organisms within an ecosystem interact with one another and with their environments.

TEKS 4.2C, 4.3D, 4.9A, 4.9B

I Wonder Why

Why are these living things able to move and grow? How do they get their energy? *Turn the page to find out.*

Here's Why Living things get the energy they need to move and grow from food. Plants make their own food. Animals eat plants or other animals.

In this unit, you will explore the Big Idea, the Essential Questions, and the Investigations on the Inquiry Flipchart.

Levels of Inquiry Key ■ DIRECTED ■ GUIDED ■ INDEPENDENT

Track Your Progress

Big Idea Living organisms within an ecosystem interact with one another and with their environments.

Essential Questions

Now I Get the Big Idea!

Science Notebook
Before you begin each lesson, be sure to write your thoughts about the Essential Question.

© Houghton Mifflin Harcourt Publishing Company (bc) ©Michael Patrick O'Neill/Alamy Images; (inset) ©Aquascopic/Alamy Images; (border) ©Niko/Age Fotostock

TEKS **4.9A** investigate that most producers need sunlight, water, and carbon dioxide to make their food, while consumers are dependent on other organisms for food

Lesson **1**

Essential Question

How Do Organisms Obtain and Use Food?

Engage Your Brain!

Find the answer to the following question in this lesson and record it here.

How does this caterpillar get energy?

_____

_____

_____

_____

Active Reading

Lesson Vocabulary

List the terms. As you learn about each one, make notes in the Interactive Glossary.

_____   _____

_____   _____

_____   _____

Main Ideas

The main idea of a paragraph is the most important idea. The main idea may be stated in the first sentence, or it may be stated elsewhere. Active readers look for main ideas by asking themselves, What is this paragraph mostly about?

© Houghton Mifflin Harcourt Publishing Company ©Frans Lanting/Corbis

A Bite of Energy

Walking, jumping, playing. Where do you get the energy to move your body?

Active Reading As you read these two pages, find and underline two facts about food.

Living things need water, air, shelter, and food. Plants can make their own food. They get their nutrients from the soil. **Nutrients** are materials used by living things for growth and for other life functions.

Animals cannot make their own food. They get their nutrients from eating food. Food also gives living things energy. **Energy** is the ability to do work.

The food that you eat is broken down into smaller materials in your body. These materials are used by your cells to help you grow, move, think, and talk.

Monkeys get their energy from eating fruits and other foods.

These wheat plants produce their own food. People and other animals may in turn use these plants for food.

© Houghton Mifflin Harcourt Publishing Company (tl) ©dbimages/Alamy; (br) ©Corbis

440

Bagels are made from wheat plants. People eat bagels to get energy.

How Do You Meet Your Needs?

Like all living things, you need air, water, food, and shelter. Describe how you met your basic needs today.

_____

_____

_____

_____

Energy from food helps you run and play. It can even help your body repair cuts and broken bones.

© Houghton Mifflin Harcourt Publishing Company   (tl) ©dbimages/Alamy; (tr) ©LM Productions/Getty Images; (br) ©Getty Images/Brand X Pictures

The Food-Makers

Plants don't eat fruits and veggies.
They don't go out for hamburgers.
So how do plants get energy?

Active Reading As you read these two pages, draw a star next to the sentence you think is most important, and be ready to explain why.

sunlight

Most plants are producers. **Producers** are living things that make their own food.
Producers make their own food through a process called photosynthesis. During **photosynthesis** [foht•oh•SIHN•thuh•sis], producers use water, carbon dioxide, and the energy from sunlight to make food. This process takes place in the leaves of plants. Sunlight shines on the leaves. Water from the soil is brought up through the plant to the leaves. Carbon dioxide is taken in from the air. Cells in the leaves change these materials into sugars.

During photosynthesis, producers give off oxygen. You use this oxygen each time you breathe.
Some of the food made by producers is used for growth and other life processes. Some of the food is stored for later use.

water

© Houghton Mifflin Harcourt Publishing Company   (tulips) ©Design Pics Inc./Alamy

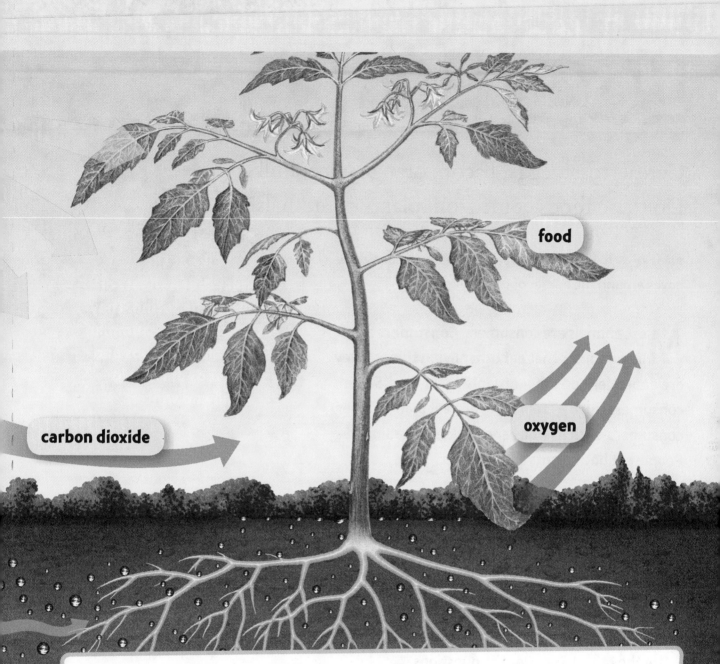

food

carbon dioxide

oxygen

The Ins and Outs of Photosynthesis

Fill in the blanks to show what happens during photosynthesis.
Some of the words are filled in for you.

Sunlight + _____ + _____ yields _____ + Oxygen

© Houghton Mifflin Harcourt Publishing Company   (tulips) ©Design Pics Inc./Alamy

The Food-Eaters

Cereal, toast, eggs, bacon, orange juice, milk.
Do these foods come from plants or animals?

Active Reading As you read these two pages, draw boxes around the names of consumers.

Most animals are consumers. **Consumers** are living things that eat other living things. They are dependent on other organisms for food. Some consumers, such as zebra and elk, eat plants. Other consumers, such as frogs and snakes, eat animals. People eat both plants and animals.

Elk eat the tender green shoots of plants in the spring. They eat grasses in the summer. Elk nibble on shrubs and the buds of trees in fall and winter.

Do the Math!
Find Fractions

The table shows how much different animals eat each day. It also shows the weigh of an average adult male animal. Use the table to answer the questions.

Animal Facts		
Animal	*How much it eats a day*	*How much it weighs*
Giant panda	20 kg	160 kg
Giraffe	25 kg	1,250 kg
Blue whale	7 metric tons	180 metric tons

1. What fraction of its body weight does the panda eat in food every day?

_____

2. What fraction of its body weight does the giraffe eat in food every day?

_____

3. What fraction of its body weight does the blue whale eat in food every day?

_____

4. Which animal eats the highest fraction of its body weight in food every day?

_____

© Houghton Mifflin Harcourt Publishing Company (t) ©Rob Crandall/Alamy; (b) ©Robert E. Barber/Alamy

A frog eats insects and other small animals. Some frogs have long tongues for catching bugs. They can catch a bug, and roll their tongues back into their mouths in about 1 second.

A heron eats mostly fish. But it will eat any animal it can swallow, including frogs and snakes.

A snake eats other animals. Some big snakes even have eaten young hippos.

© Houghton Mifflin Harcourt Publishing Company   (tl) ©Rob Crandall/Alamy;   (tl) ©Image Quest Marine/Alamy; (tr) ©Arco Images GmbH/Alamy

445

The Clean-Up Crew

The creepy, crawly things on these pages have an important role in ecosystems—they clean things up!

You may already know that vultures are scavengers. So are crabs and worms. Scavengers help clean up ecosystems by eating dead plants and animals. Any remains left by scavengers are consumed by **decomposers**, which are living things that get energy by breaking down wastes and dead plant and animal matter. They break down this matter into simpler substances. Decomposers use some of these substances, and some are returned to the air, soil, or water, where they are available to other living things. Fungi and bacteria are the two important groups of decomposers.

A blue crab is a scavenger. It eats the remains of other organisms. It is not a picky eater—it will also eat living organisms!

What Would It Look Like?

In the space below, draw what an ecosystem might look like if there were no scavengers and decomposers.

© Houghton Mifflin Harcourt Publishing Company (bkgd) ©Dennis Kunkel Microscopy, Inc./PHOTOTAKE/Alamy; (b) ©Carsten Ressinger/Alamy; (t) ©Juniors Bildarchiv/Alamy; (tr) ©Frank Greenaway/Getty Images

Mushrooms help decompose logs and other materials in forests.

Worms live in soil. They eat dead leaves and other plant parts. Their wastes help make the soil richer.

Millipedes can have more than 100 pairs of legs! They eat dead plants.

© Houghton Mifflin Harcourt Publishing Company (bkgd) ©Dennis Kunkel Microscopy, Inc./PHOTOTAKE/Alamy; (bl) ©Juniors Bildarchiv/Alamy; (t) ©Frank Greenaway/Getty Images; (tc) ©Gen Molyneux/Alamy; (cr) ©Ed Reschke/Peter Arnold, Inc./Alamy

Sum It Up!

When you're done, use the answer key to check and revise your work.

**Read the summary statements. Each one is incorrect. Change the part
of the summary in blue to make it correct.**

1 Producers eat other living things.

_____

2 Consumers make their own food.

_____

3 Crabs and earthworms are producers.

_____

4 Nutrient is the ability to do work.

_____

5 Plants use sunlight, water, and oxygen
during photosynthesis.

_____

Summarize

Fill in the Venn diagram below to compare and contrast producers and consumers.

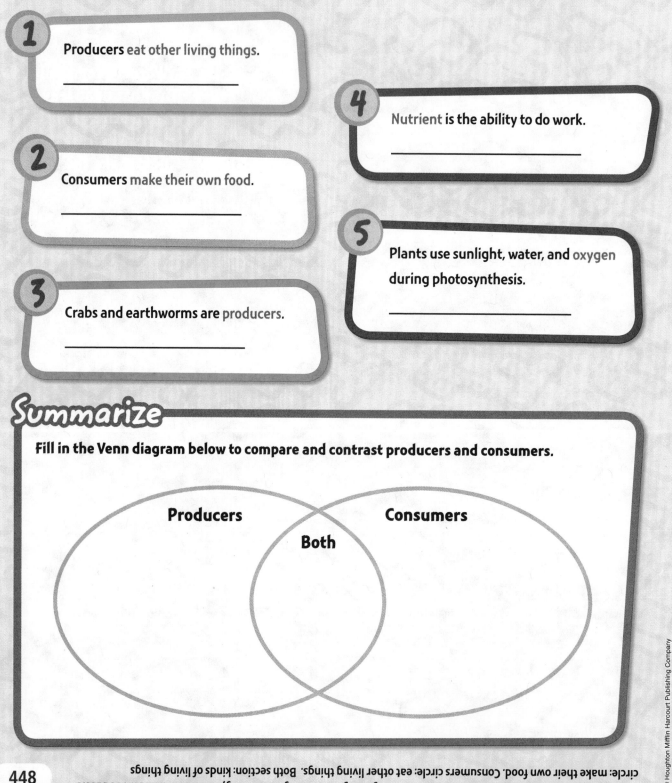

Producers   Consumers

Both

Answer Key: 1. make their own food 2. eat other living things 3. scavengers 4. Energy 5. carbon dioxide. Producers circle: make their own food. Consumers circle: eat other living things. Both section: kinds of living things

© Houghton Mifflin Harcourt Publishing Company

Name _____

Word Play

1
Use the clues to unscramble the words in the box.

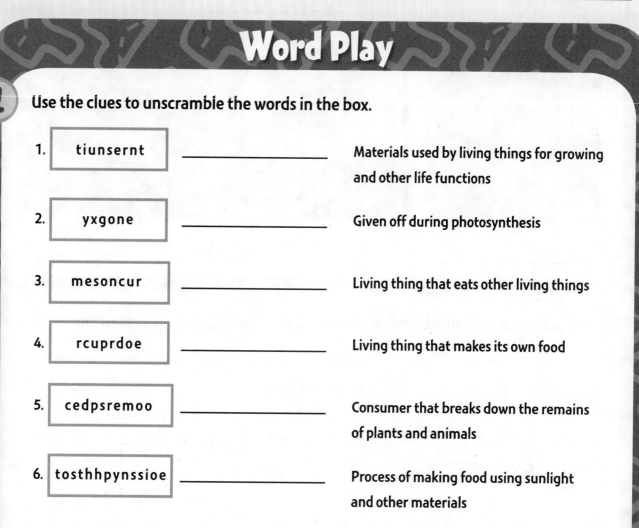

1. | tiunsernt | _____ | Materials used by living things for growing and other life functions

2. | yxgone | _____ | Given off during photosynthesis

3. | mesoncur | _____ | Living thing that eats other living things

4. | rcuprdoe | _____ | Living thing that makes its own food

5. | cedpsremoo | _____ | Consumer that breaks down the remains of plants and animals

6. | tosthhpynssioe | _____ | Process of making food using sunlight and other materials

Apply Concepts

2
What does a plant need to make its own food?

_____

_____

_____

_____

© Houghton Mifflin Harcourt Publishing Company

3 The pictures show different kinds of living things. Label each living thing as a producer, a consumer, or a decomposer.

_____   _____   _____

4 Fill in the concept map below about the roles of decomposers in ecosystems.

Decomposers Help Ecosystems

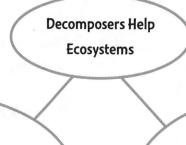

Share what you have learned about food energy with your family. Which foods keep you strong and healthy? With a family member, make a menu for a healthy meal. Help cook the meal for your family.

Take It Home!

© Houghton Mifflin Harcourt Publishing Company

TEKS **4.2B** collect and record data by observing…and using descriptive words… **4.2C** construct…charts… using…current technology to organize, examine…data **4.2D** analyze data… to construct reasonable explanations from data that can be observed… **4.2F** communicate…written results supported by data **4.9A** investigate that most producers need sunlight, water, and carbon dioxide to make their own food…

Name _____

Essential Question

What Do Plants Need to Make Food?

Set a Purpose
What will you learn from this investigation?

_____

_____

State Your Hypothesis
Write your hypothesis, or testable statement.

_____

_____

_____

Think About the Procedure
Why do you think *Elodea* is placed only in one tube?

_____

_____

_____

_____

Record Your Data
Use current technology to construct a chart to organize and evaluate your data. Plan your chart in the space below. Use descriptive words to record your data.

© Houghton Mifflin Harcourt Publishing Company

Draw Conclusions

What changes did you observe in the BTB solution during the activity?

_____

_____

_____

_____

The amount of a certain gas has increased in one of the test tubes. What can you infer about the identity of this gas and where it came from?

_____

_____

_____

_____

Analyze and Extend

1. Analyze your data. What can you conclude about what plants need to make food?

_____

_____

_____

_____

2. Why does the *Elodea* turn the water blue?

_____

_____

_____

3. Scientists use what they know to make predictions. After you blew into the water, how did your observations help you predict what would happen next?

_____

_____

_____

_____

_____

_____

4. How might you investigate the amount of sunlight producers need to make food? Design and describe an experiment you could conduct. Draw to illustrate your setup and label it using descriptive words.

_____

_____

_____

_____

_____

_____

_____

© Houghton Mifflin Harcourt Publishing Company

TEKS **4.9B** describe the flow of energy through food webs, beginning with the Sun, and predict how changes in the ecosystem affect the food web such as a fire in a forest

Essential Question

What Are Food Chains?

🧠 Engage Your Brain!

Find the answer to the following question in this lesson and record it here.

Is this frog a predator, or is it prey?

_____

_____

_____

_____

Active Reading

Lesson Vocabulary
List the terms. As you learn about each one, make notes in the Interactive Glossary.

_____   _____

_____   _____

_____

Main Ideas
The main idea is the most important idea of a paragraph or section. The main idea may be stated at the beginning, or it may be stated elsewhere. Active readers look for main ideas by asking themselves, What is this paragraph or section mostly about?

© Houghton Mifflin Harcourt Publishing Company ©Jim Zuckerman/Corbis

Food Chains

Did you know that you are fed by the sun? Find out how!

Active Reading As you read these two pages, circle common, everyday words that have a different meaning in science.

Lettuce is a plant that uses energy from the sun to make its own food. When you eat lettuce, some energy passes from the lettuce to you. You can show this relationship in a food chain. A **food chain** is the transfer of food energy in a sequence of living things. In a diagram of a food chain, arrows show how energy moves. Here is a food chain that shows how energy moves from lettuce to you.

lettuce ⟶ you

The food chain above has only two steps, or links. Food chains can have more than two links. Look at the pictures to see a food chain with five links.

Producers make up the first link. In this pond, tiny algae [AL•jee] are the producers. Mosquito larvae eat the algae. They make up the second link in this food chain.

© Houghton Mifflin Harcourt Publishing Company (c) blickwinkel/Alamy

Make a Food Chain

Choose a food that you ate for breakfast or lunch today. Make a food chain that describes the flow of energy from the sun to the food then to you.

Minnows are small fish. They eat the mosquito larvae. They make up the third link in this food chain.

Bass are bigger fish. They eat the minnows. They make up the fourth link in this food chain.

People eat the bass. People make up the last link in this food chain.

© Houghton Mifflin Harcourt Publishing Company   (cl) ©Nigel Cattlin/Alamy; (cr) ©Mark Conlin/Alamy

You Are What You Eat

A zebra and a lion are both consumers. But they eat very different foods. How can you group consumers by what they eat?

Active Reading As you read this page, underline the sentence that identifies one characteristic that is used to classify consumers.

Consumers eat other living things. They can be placed into groups according to the kind of food they eat.

- A consumer that eats only plants is a **herbivore**. A zebra is a herbivore. It eats grasses and other plants.

- A consumer that eats other animals is a **carnivore**. A lion is a carnivore. It eats zebras and other animals.

- A consumer that eats both plants and animals is an **omnivore**. People are omnivores. They eat plants such as tomatoes and animals such as fish.

- A consumer that eats dead plants and animals is a scavenger.

A crocodile is a carnivore. It eats mainly fish. But it will eat big animals, such as hippos, when it can catch them.

A rabbit is a herbivore. It eats leafy plants during spring and summer, and woody plants during fall and winter.

© Houghton Mifflin Harcourt Publishing Company • (bkgd) ©Peter Barritt/Alamy; (br) ©Corbis

Raccoons are omnivores. They eat fruit, acorns, fish, and mice. They'll eat sweet corn right from your garden!

Vultures are scavengers. They eat dead animals.

What Does It Eat?

Look at the pictures below. The top row shows different kinds of consumers. The bottom row shows the kinds of food they eat. Draw lines to match the consumers to the foods they eat. Some consumers might eat more than one kind of food.

© Houghton Mifflin Harcourt Publishing Company · (bkgd) ©Peter Barritt/Alamy; (tl) ©Rolf Nussbaumer/Alamy; (tr) ©blickwinkel/Alamy

Hunt or Be Hunted

A lion crouches in the tall grass. Nearby, a zebra nibbles on the grass. Who is the hunter? Who will be hunted?

Active Reading As you read these two pages, draw boxes around two words that are key to understanding the main idea.

Consumers are grouped by what they eat. But you can also group consumers by whether they hunt or are hunted.

A *predator* is an animal that hunts other animals. Lions are predators. They often hunt in packs. This helps them catch big animals, like hippos and rhinos. They hunt smaller animals, too.

An animal that is eaten is called *prey*. Deer, elk, and moose are all prey for wolves in the Rocky Mountains.

Some animals can be both predator and prey. A frog might eat insects in a forest. But the frog might be eaten by a snake.

A hawk can see the movement of small animals, like this mouse, from high in the sky.

© Houghton Mifflin Harcourt Publishing Company (cl) ©FLPA/Alamy; (br) ©Andrew Darrington/Alamy

Lions can run fast for short bursts. Zebras may not run as fast, but they can run for a much longer time.

Sharks feed on many kinds of prey. Fish stay in large groups to make it difficult for predators to hunt individuals.

Who's the Hunter? Who's Hunted?

Fill in the table below. Classify the animals shown on these pages as predators or prey.

Animals	
Predators	Prey

© Houghton Mifflin Harcourt Publishing Company (t) ©Steve Bloom Images/Alamy (b) ©WaterFrame/Alamy

Food Webs

A food chain shows how energy moves from one living thing to another. But living things often eat more than one kind of food. How can you show these different feeding relationships?

Active Reading As you read these two pages, draw a line under the main idea.

Lobsters eat clams. But they also eat crabs, sea stars, and mussels. Other animals, like the shark and the octopus, eat the lobster. You can use a model to show all these feeding relationships. A **food web** shows the relationships among different food chains. Food web models use arrows to show who eats what.

These green plankton are producers. They are eaten by clams, small fish, whales, and other organisms.

Desert Food Chain

Use arrows to show how energy moves from one living thing to another in this desert food chain.

© Houghton Mifflin Harcourt Publishing Company   (b) ©MarekZuk/Alamy; (cr) ©Joaquin Carrillo-Farga/Photo Researchers, Inc.

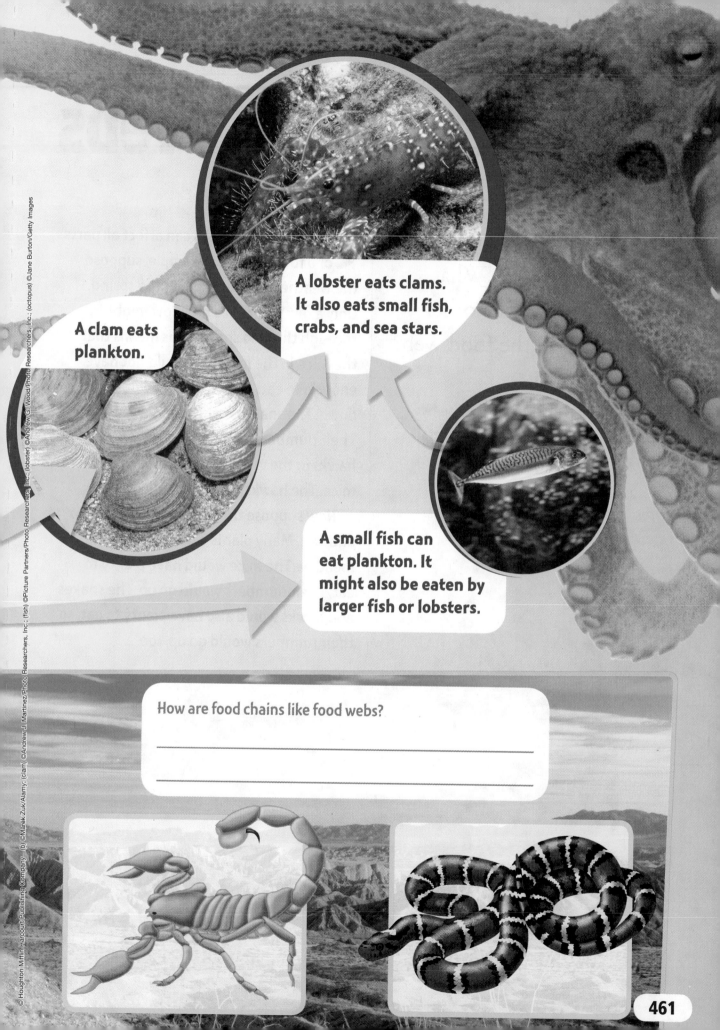

A clam eats plankton.

A lobster eats clams. It also eats small fish, crabs, and sea stars.

A small fish can eat plankton. It might also be eaten by larger fish or lobsters.

How are food chains like food webs?

_____

_____

© Houghton Mifflin Harcourt Publishing Company (b) ©Marek Zuk/Alamy; (clam) ©Andrew J. Martinez/Photo Researchers, Inc.; (fish) ©Picture Partners/Photo Researchers, Inc.; (lobster) ©Andrew G. Wood/Photo Researchers, Inc.; (octopus) ©Jane Burton/Getty Images

Changes in Food Webs

Imagine that one kind of animal disappeared. What would happen to the other living things in the food web?

Active Reading As you read these two pages, circle clue words that signal a detail such as an example or an added fact.

Changes in food webs can affect all parts of a food web. For example, suppose the weather was very cold in the spring. Only a few plants in a meadow might live through the cold spring. This means that the mice in the meadow would not have enough to eat. Their numbers would go down. The snakes in the meadow eat mice. Their numbers would also go down. The hawks in the meadow hunt snakes and mice. The hawks would be hungry, too.

Now suppose that the spring was warm and wet. Many plants would grow in the meadow. The mice would have plenty to eat. Their numbers would go up. The snakes and hawks would also have plenty to eat, so their numbers would go up, too.

© Houghton Mifflin Harcourt Publishing Company (bkgd) ©Josh Anderson/Alamy; (b) ©Kennan Ward/Corbis

Food webs can be disrupted when one member of a food web goes away. This happened in Yellowstone National Park. During the early 1900s, the gray wolf was hunted in the park. Eventually, no gray wolves were left.

The gray wolf preyed mostly on elk. The number of elk in the park increased after the wolves disappeared. In 1995, scientists returned 14 gray wolves to the park. The number of wolves has since increased. As a result, the number of elk in the park has decreased.

Other changes happened, too. Elk eat trees. Before the wolves were reintroduced, the elk overgrazed the trees in the park.

This harmed the trees. Since beavers had fewer trees to build dams with, the beaver population decreased. After the wolves were reintroduced to the park, both the trees and beavers began to thrive.

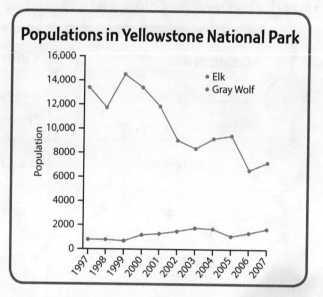

Do the Math!
Interpret Tables

The table shows the height of trees in Yellowstone National Park before and after the gray wolves returned. Study the table, and then answer the questions.

Kind of tree	Average height before 1995	Average height after 2002
Cottonwood	less than 1m	2 to 3 m
Willow	less than 1m	3 to 4 m

1. Describe the heights of the trees before the gray wolves were brought back to Yellowstone National Park.

_____

2. Describe the heights of the trees after the gray wolves were brought back to Yellowstone National Park.

_____

3. Why do you think the heights of the trees changed?

_____

_____

4. Predict how the ecosystem would have been affected if the wolves had not been returned to the park.

_____

_____

© Houghton Mifflin Harcourt Publishing Company   (bkgd) ©Josh Anderson/Alamy

Sum It Up!

When you're done, use the answer key to check and revise your work.

Match the words in Column A to their definitions in Column B.

Column A	Column B
1 _____ scavenger	a. model that shows all the feeding relationships in an ecosystem
2 _____ herbivore	b. eats other animals
3 _____ carnivore	c. eats only plants
4 _____ omnivore	d. eats dead animals and plants
5 _____ food web	e. eats both plants and animals

Summarize

The idea web below summarizes the lesson. Complete the web.

Food chains show how energy moves from one living thing to another. The first link in a food chain is always a(n) 6. _____ .

Herbivores are consumers that 7. _____ .

Omnivores are consumers that 8. _____ .

Carnivores are consumers that 9. _____ .

Scavengers are consumers that 10. _____ .

© Houghton Mifflin Harcourt Publishing Company

Answer Key: 1. d 2. c 3. b 4. e 5. a 6. producer 7. eat only plants 8. eat plants and animals 9. eat other animals 10. eat dead animals and plants

Word Play

1 Use the clues to complete the crossword puzzle.

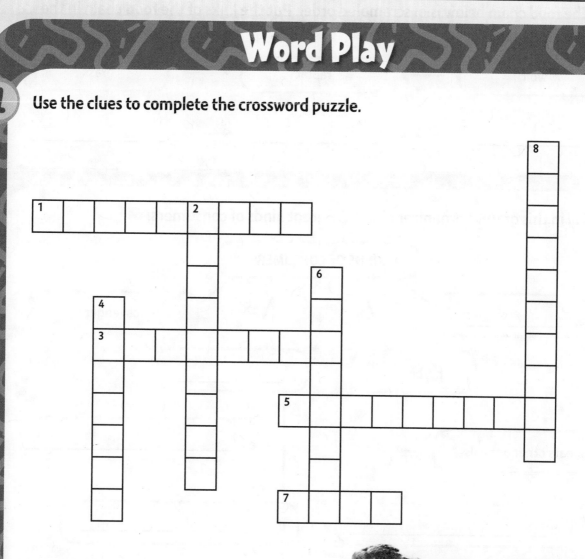

Across

1. The transfer of energy from one living thing to another
3. Consumer that eats both plants and animals
5. Consumer that eats other animals
7. Animal that is hunted

Down

2. Consumer that eats only plants
4. Shows the relationship among all the food chains in an ecosystem
6. Animal that hunts
8. Consumer that breaks down the remains of plants and animals

© Houghton Mifflin Harcourt Publishing Company ©Corbis

Apply Concepts

2 The food chain below is in scrambled order. Put the links of the food chain in the correct order.

wolf → rabbit → grass

_____ → _____ → _____

3 Fill in this graphic organizer about different kinds of consumers.

KINDS OF CONSUMERS

a. _____

herbivore

b. _____

scavenger

eats other animals

e. _____

c. _____

d. _____

4 The pictures below show a lion and a zebra. Label the animals as *predator* or *prey*.

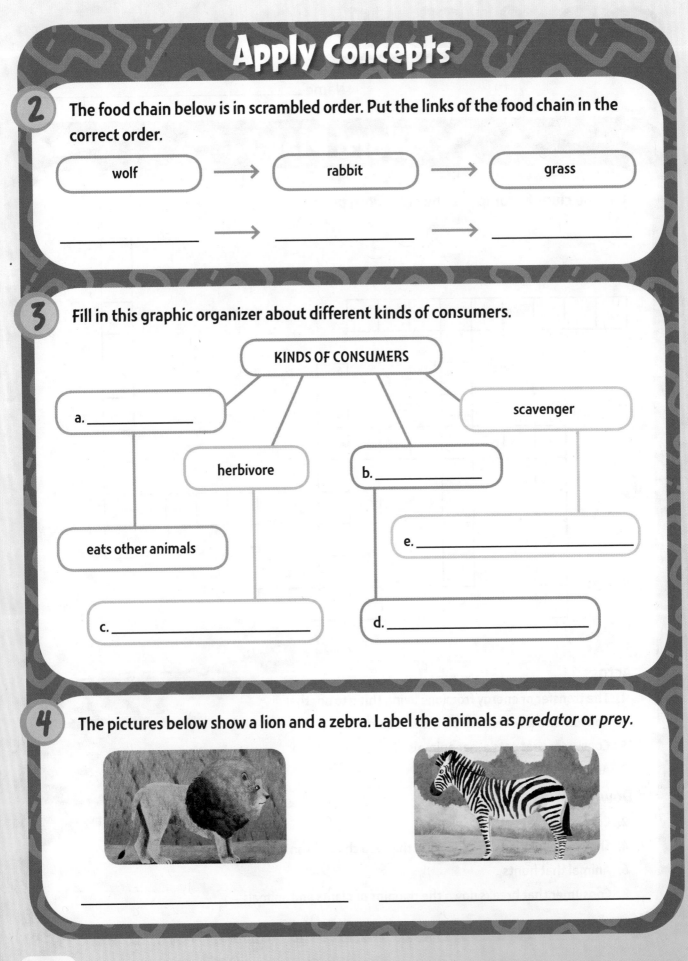

_____   _____

© Houghton Mifflin Harcourt Publishing Company

5 Use arrows to show who eats what in this pond food web. Your arrows should point from the living thing that is being eaten to the living thing that is eating. Write to describe the flow of energy through this food web, beginning with the sun.

_____

_____

_____

6 In the space below, draw a forest food web. Write to predict how this ecosystem would be affected by a change, such as a forest fire.

_____

_____

_____

_____

© Houghton Mifflin Harcourt Publishing Company

7 The pictures show different kinds of consumers. Label each consumer as a carnivore, an herbivore, an omnivore, or a scavenger.

_____

_____

_____

_____

8 The population of a predator in an area has gone up. What do you think will happen to the population of prey in the area? Explain your answer.

_____

_____

_____

_____

_____

_____

_____

Take It Home!

Share what you have learned about food chains with your family. With a family member, tell which of the foods you ate for dinner came from plants and which came from animals.

© Houghton Mifflin Harcourt Publishing Company

Inquiry Flipchart page 55

Lesson 4
INQUIRY

TEKS 4.2C construct...charts...
using tools...to organize...data
4.9B describe the flow of energy
through food webs, beginning with
the Sun, and predict how changes in
the ecosystem affect the food web...

Name _____

Essential Question

How Can We Model a Food Web?

Set a Purpose
What will you learn from this investigation?

_____
_____

Think About the Procedure
Which parts of an ecosystem will you model?

_____
_____
_____

Why is it important to have plants, animals, and decomposers in your food web?

_____
_____
_____
_____
_____
_____

Record Your Data
Construct a chart in the space below to classify the organisms in your ecosystem as producers, consumers, or decomposers. Describe how each organism gets its energy.

© Houghton Mifflin Harcourt Publishing Company

Draw Conclusions

How are ecosystems different from one another?

_____

_____

_____

What roles do plants have in a food web?

_____

_____

_____

Analyze and Extend

1. Suppose an animal with no natural predator in an ecosystem comes to live there. How would this animal affect the food web?

_____

_____

_____

2. Suppose a fungus grows on some of the plants. How might this fungus affect the food web?

_____

_____

_____

3. Predict how other changes in the ecosystem might affect the food web.

_____

_____

_____

4. In the space below, draw two food chains that overlap in your food web. Then, write a caption that describes the flow of energy through your food web, beginning with the sun.

_____

_____

_____

5. Think about other questions you would like to ask about food webs. Write your questions below.

_____

_____

_____

_____

© Houghton Mifflin Harcourt Publishing Company

People in Science

Meet the Tree-Planting Scientists

Wangari Maathai

Wangari Maathai was born in Kenya. Maathai started an organization that conserves Kenya's forests by planting trees. She recruited Kenyan women to plant native trees throughout the country. In 1977, this organization became known as the Green Belt Movement. The Green Belt Movement has planted more than 40 million trees. Maathai's work has inspired other African countries to start community tree plantings.

Seeds from nearby forests are used to grow native trees.

Willie Smits

Willie Smits works to save orangutans in Indonesia. By clearing the forests, people are destroying the orangutan's habitat. The orangutan is endangered. Smits's plan helps both orangutans and people. Smits is growing a rain forest. The new forest gives people food and rainwater for drinking, so they protect it. The sugar palm is one of the trees planted. In 2007, Smits started using sugar palms to make sugar and a biofuel called ethanol. The sugar palms provide income for the community.

Fire-resistant sugar palms help protect the forest from fires.

Smits has rescued almost 1,000 orangutan babies. However, his goal is to save them in the wild.

© Houghton Mifflin Harcourt Publishing Company • (bkgd) ©Iconotec/Alamy; (tl) ©Micheline Pelletier/Corbis; (cr) ©Wendy Stone/Corbis; (tr) ©Paula Bronstein/Liaison/Getty Images; (br) ©Redmond Durrell/Alamy

Scientist saves the Day!

Read the story about the Florida scrub jay. Draw the missing pictures to complete the story.

The Problem: Florida scrub jays are endangered. They are found only in parts of Florida with shrubs and other short plants.

Fires kill tall trees that grow in the scrub jay's habitat. But people put out the fires, so the trees survive.

Trees are now growing, so there are fewer shrubs. The scrub jays can't live there.

The Solution: Scientists and firefighters start fires that can be kept under control. These fires kill the tall trees.

Shrubs grow and the scrub jays return.

© Houghton Mifflin Harcourt Publishing Company   (bkgd) ©Jim Hargan/harganonline/Alamy; (tl) ©Papilio/Alamy.

TEKS 4.3D connect grade-level appropriate science concepts with the history of science...

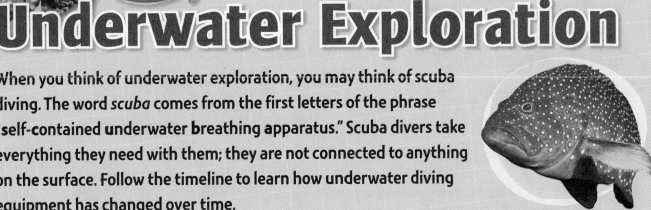

S.T.E.M.
Engineering & Technology

Underwater Exploration

When you think of underwater exploration, you may think of scuba diving. The word *scuba* comes from the first letters of the phrase "self-contained underwater breathing apparatus." Scuba divers take everything they need with them; they are not connected to anything on the surface. Follow the timeline to learn how underwater diving equipment has changed over time.

1530s
Guglielmo de Lorena—Diving Bell
Diving bells are airtight containers opened at one end. De Lorena's diving bell rested over a diver's shoulders, allowing the diver to breathe the trapped air and to walk on the ocean floor. Ropes connected the diver to the surface.

1830s
Augustus Siebe—Diving Dress
A metal diving helmet is sealed onto a watertight canvas suit. An air hose and a cable connect the diver to the surface. In this closed-circuit system, used-up air is released into the suit. The diver controls when air is released.

1940s
Jacques Cousteau and Emile Gagnan—Aqua-Lung
This breathing system passes air to a diver from a tank carried on the diver's back. This is an open-circuit system that releases used-up air into the water. Divers can swim without any cables or hoses connecting them to the surface.

Critical Thinking

How are the earliest two types of diving equipment similar?

_____

_____

_____

© Houghton Mifflin Harcourt Publishing Company (t) ©Comstock/Getty Images; (tr) ©Frank & Joyce Burek/PhotoDisc/Getty Images; (cl) ©Photos12/Alamy Images; (cr) ©Patrick Eden/Alamy Images; (bl) ©Tom Brakefield/Stockbyte/Getty Images; (br) ©Frederic Pacorel/Getty Images; (bg) ©Darryl Leniuk/Digital Vision/Getty Images

Make Some History

Research another type of diving equipment. Describe how it works and where it should be placed on the timeline.

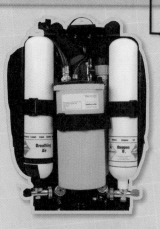

1960s
Rebreather

Rebreathers are closed-circuit systems. A diver breathes through a mouthpiece and used-up air is not released into the water. Instead, it is filtered to remove carbon dioxide and used again. This design feature extends the amount of time a diver can spend underwater.

1980s
ADS

Atmospheric Diving Suits (ADS) were developed for deep diving activities. They use rebreather technology and a hard suit that enable divers to safely dive to great depths. Modern ADS can work in water up to 610 m deep!

Design Your Future

What features do you think the next diving suit should have? What needs would those features meet?

Build On It!

Rise to the engineering design challenge—complete **Solve It: Getting Around a Dam** on the Inquiry Flipchart.

© Houghton Mifflin Harcourt Publishing Company (t) ©Alexis Rosenfeld/Photo Researchers, Inc; (c) ©Dorling Kindersley/Getty Images; (bc) ©Digital Vision/Getty Images; (b) ©Darryl Leniuk/Digital Vision/Getty Images

Vocabulary Review

Use the terms in the box to complete the sentences.

consumer
decomposer
food chain
herbivore
nutrient
photosynthesis
prey
producer

TEKS 4.9A

1. An organism that needs sunlight, water, and carbon dioxide

   to make its own food is a(n) _____.

TEKS 4.9A

2. An animal that is dependent on other organisms for food

   is a(n) _____.

TEKS 4.9A

3. A material used by living things for growth and other life

   functions is a(n) _____.

TEKS 4.9B

4. The transfer of food energy in a sequence of living things

   is a _____.

TEKS 4.9B

5. A living thing that gets energy by breaking down dead plant

   and animal matter is a(n) _____.

TEKS 4.9B

6. A consumer that eats only plants is

   a(n) _____.

TEKS 4.9B

7. An animal that is eaten by another animal is

   a(n) _____.

TEKS 4.9A

8. The process by which plants make food

   is _____.

© Houghton Mifflin Harcourt Publishing Company (border) ©NDisk/Age Fotostock

Science Concepts

Fill in the letter of the choice that best answers the question.

TEKS 4.9B

9. The picture below shows a desert food chain.

Which of the following describes how energy moves from cactus to roadrunner?

(A) from producer to producers

(B) from carnivore to carnivores

(C) from producer to herbivores

(D) from producer to consumers

TEKS 4.9B

10. Carla wants to describe the flow of energy through food chains. Which sequence is correct?

(A) Decomposer → Consumer
 → Sunlight → Producer

(B) Consumer → Sunlight
 → Producer → Decomposer

(C) Producer → Decomposer
 → Producer → Consumer

(D) Sunlight → Producer
 → Consumer → Decomposer

TEKS 4.9B

11. The picture below shows some animals you can find in grassland food chains.

Which animal is the carnivore?

(A) animal 1

(B) animal 2

(C) animal 3

(D) animal 4

TEKS 4.9A

12. Elizabeth conducts an investigation in which she adds BTB to water in a test tube. The BTB turns the water blue. When she blows through a straw into the solution, it changes color. She places an *Elodea* plant in the test tube and caps it. After several hours, the solution turns blue again. What does her investigation prove?

(A) The plant uses water.

(B) The plant uses oxygen.

(C) The plant uses nutrients.

(D) The plant uses carbon dioxide.

© Houghton Mifflin Harcourt Publishing Company (border) ©NDisk/Age Fotostock

TEKS 4.9A

13. This aquarium has many different organisms, or living things.

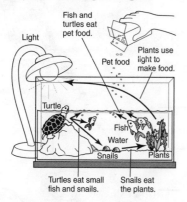

Light
Fish and turtles eat pet food.
Plants use light to make food.
Pet food
Turtle
Fish
Water
Snails
Plants
Turtles eat small fish and snails.
Snails eat the plants.

Which organism is a producer that needs sunlight to make its own food?

(A) fish   (C) snail

(B) plant   (D) turtle

TEKS 4.9B

14. Horses get energy by eating grass and oats. Florida panthers get energy from eating deer and raccoons. Raccoons get energy by eating frogs and fruit. Bobcats get energy by eating lizards and birds. Which animal is a herbivore?

(A) bobcat   (C) panther

(B) horse   (D) raccoon

TEKS 4.9A

15. For breakfast, Madison ate cereal with milk. For breakfast, a chipmunk ate seeds. How are Madison and the chipmunk alike?

(A) They are both being herbivores.

(B) They are both being carnivores.

(C) They are both getting some energy.

(D) They are both being food producers.

TEKS 4.9B

16. Emily is studying how changes in an ecosystem affect food webs. She makes these graphs to show how the number of fish and marsh birds changed in a certain area over time.

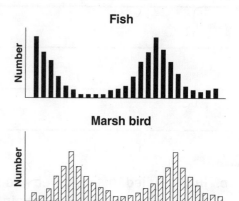

Fish
Number

Marsh bird
Number

What happened when the number of fish was highest?

(A) The bird population began to decrease.

(B) The birds moved away for lack of food.

(C) The fish population continued to increase.

(D) The bird population increased because there was more food.

TEKS 4.9A

17. Gina knows plants in her garden are producers. Which statement is true about her plants?

(A) The plants are the last link in a food chain.

(B) The plants are the last link in most food webs.

(C) The plants depend on other organisms for their food.

(D) The plants need water, sunlight, and carbon dioxide to make their own food.

© Houghton Mifflin Harcourt Publishing Company   (border) ©NDisk/Age Fotostock

Apply Inquiry and Review the Big Idea

Write the answers to these questions.

TEKS 4.9A, 4.9B

18. This illustration shows a food web.

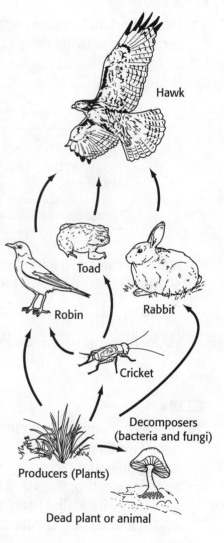

Hawk

Toad

Robin

Rabbit

Cricket

Decomposers
(bacteria and fungi)

Producers (Plants)

Dead plant or animal

a. Use an example from the food web to explain why all consumers depend on other organisms for food.

_____

_____

_____

_____

TEKS 4.9B

b. Juan studied this food web and said that hawks were the last link in every food chain shown. Vicky pointed to a different organism and said that it was the last link. Which organism did Vicky identify?Why?

_____

_____

_____

_____

TEKS 4.9B

c. Suppose the population of toads in this ecosystem suddenly decreased. Predict how this change would affect the animals in this food web.

_____

_____

_____

TEKS 4.9A

19. A deer eats about 10 kg of grasses each day. A rabbit eats about 4 kg of grasses each day. Over a one-week period, how many kilograms of grasses do these animals eat?

_____

© Houghton Mifflin Harcourt Publishing Company   (border) ©NDisk/Age Fotostock

Plants and Animals

© Houghton Mifflin Harcourt Publishing Company (bg) © Chris Mattison/Alamy Images; (inset) Chlckwinkel/Alamy Images; (border) © NitsAge Fotostock

Big Idea

Organisms have similar life processes and structures that help them survive in their environment.

TEKS 4.2B, 4.2C, 4.2D, 4.3C, 4.3D, 4.10A, 4.10B, 4.10C

I Wonder Why

This insect looks like a leaf. When it walks, it rocks back and forth. Why? *Turn the page to find out.*

Here's Why This bug is a walking leaf. It rocks back and forth when it walks, making it look like a leaf blowing in the wind. So, predators won't think this bug is food to eat!

In this unit, you will explore the Big Idea, the Essential Questions, and the Investigations on the Inquiry Flipchart.

Levels of Inquiry Key ■ DIRECTED ■ GUIDED ■ INDEPENDENT

Track Your Progress

Big Idea Organisms have similar life processes and structures that help them survive in their environment.

Essential Questions

Now I Get the Big Idea!

Science Notebook

Before you begin each lesson, be sure to write your thoughts about the Essential Question.

TEKS **4.10C** explore, illustrate, and compare life cycles in living organisms such as...radishes, or lima beans

Essential Question

How Do Plants Reproduce?

Engage Your Brain!

Find the answer to the following question in this lesson and record it here.

Bees need flowers for food. How do flowers need bees?

_____

_____

_____

_____

Active Reading

Lesson Vocabulary
List the terms. As you learn about each one, make notes in the Interactive Glossary.

_____ _____

_____ _____

_____

Signal Words
In this lesson, you will read about the sequence of stages in a plant's life cycle. Words that signal sequence include *now, before, after, first, next, start,* and *then.* Active readers look for signal words that identify sequence to help them remember what they read.

© Houghton Mifflin Harcourt Publishing Company (bg) ©Fixonnet.com/Alamy Images

How Does a
Garden Grow?

Think of some of the plants you saw on your way to school today. You might have seen trees, grasses, flowers, or even weeds. Where did all these plants come from?

Active Reading As you read the next page, circle the signal words that show the sequence in which a plant grows.

Radish Life Cycle

A seed, such as this radish seed, contains the embryo of a plant.

When a seed sprouts during a process known as **germination**, the embryo in the seed begins to grow.

When a plant grows to its full size, it reaches **maturity**. Mature plants make seeds that can grow into new plants.

As the plant continues to grow, it gets larger. It also gets more roots.

© Houghton Mifflin Harcourt Publishing Company

When a plant grows, it goes through a series of set stages. The series of stages that a living thing goes through as it develops is called a *life cycle*. It is important for people to understand plant life cycles, because most of the food we eat comes from plants.

Most plants grow from seeds. First, a seed is placed in soil, so it can sprout. Next, the plant grows until it reaches maturity. A mature plant may grow flowers or cones. Then these structures make more seeds. You will learn about flowers and cones on the next pages.

Lima Bean Life Cycle

Place the pictures in the correct sequence to illustrate the life cycle of a lima bean plant. Write a number next to each picture. Start with the seed.

Flowers and Cones

There are about 310,000 types of plants. Almost 90% of them produce seeds. How do plants produce seeds?

Active Reading As you read this page, underline the names of male plant parts and circle the names of female plant parts.

Seeds are produced in flowers and cones. Flowers and cones make reproductive cells. Male reproductive cells are called sperm. Female reproductive cells are called eggs. **Fertilization** is the process of a sperm and an egg cell joining together. A fertilized egg grows into an embryo inside a seed.

About 1,000 types of plants produce seeds in cones. In plants with cones, sperm are made in male cones and eggs are made in female cones.

Most plants produce seeds in structures called flowers. Grains of pollen, produced in parts called anthers, contain the sperm. Eggs are made in a structure called a pistil. Many flowers have both anthers and a pistil. Flowers have many other parts as well.

Petals are the outer parts of a flower.

The male organ is the stamen [STAY•muhn]. It consists of a thin stalk topped by a saclike anther, which produces pollen.

The female organ is the pistil [PIS•tuhl]. Its rounded base contains eggs.

© Houghton Mifflin Harcourt Publishing Company   (bkgd) ©Alexander Albrecht/Alamy; (inset, oranges) ©Peter Titmuss/Alamy

Most cone-bearing plants are trees. Pines, spruces, and cycads [SY•kadz] are all cone-bearing plants.

A female pine cone makes egg cells.

A male pine cone makes sperm cells.

Plant Parts

Add labels to the flower.

The Power of Pollen

In order for plant eggs to be fertilized, pollen has to move from the male parts to the female parts. How does the pollen get there?

Active Reading Underline ways plants can be pollinated.

Seed plants reproduce through pollination. **Pollination** is the process of pollen moving from a male plant part to a female plant part. There are several ways this can happen. Sometimes wind can blow the pollen from one plant to another, which is how many grasses and trees are pollinated.

Other plants are pollinated by *pollinators*. Some bees, birds, butterflies, and other animals are pollinators. For example, a butterfly goes from flower to flower drinking nectar. At each flower, the pollen on the stamens rubs off on the butterfly. When the butterfly visits the next flower, the pollen may drop off and fall on the pistil. As a result, the flower will be pollinated.

Brightly colored flower petals attract pollinators.

© Houghton Mifflin Harcourt Publishing Company (bkgd) ©Justus de Cuveland/ImageBroker/Alamy; (tr; butterfly) ©Attendo Nature/Getty Images

Some water plants are pollinated by water. Flowing water carries the pollen from plant to plant.

Pollen Cloud

Do the Math!
Work with Fractions

Animals pollinate $\frac{3}{4}$ of seed-making plants. Wind and water pollinate the other $\frac{1}{4}$ of plants. Use this information to label the parts of the circle.

Wind blows pollen from male cones. The wind may carry the pollen to a female cone.

© Houghton Mifflin Harcourt Publishing Company   (tl) ©Michele Constantini/PhotoAlto/Alamy; (tr) ©Jim Zipp/Photo Researchers, Inc.

Seeds on the Move

Unlike most animals, plants cannot move around in their environment. So how can a plant's seeds be spread from place to place?

Active Reading As you read, underline three things that help seeds move from place to place.

Animals play a big role in moving plant seeds. The base of the pistil of flowers grows into a fruit that contains the flower's seeds. Think of the seeds in an apple or in a blackberry. When an animal eats these fruits, the seeds pass through the animal's body before being deposited elsewhere.

Other animals will find and bury seeds. Think of squirrels. Squirrels bury acorns so that they will have food in the winter. The squirrels will dig up and eat most of the acorns, but they may forget a few. These acorns will grow into new oak trees.

Seeds, such as burs, can also travel on an animal's body. Other kinds of seeds are very light. They can be carried by the wind. Still other seeds, including coconuts, float in water.

Some seeds are very light. They can be blown around by the wind.

© Houghton Mifflin Harcourt Publishing Company (bkg) ©Raimund Linke/Getty Images; (cr) ©Gusto/Photo Researchers, Inc.

Some seeds are covered in little hooks. These seeds are called burs. They can easily attach to fur or even to your socks!

▶ How are each of these seeds most likely spread from place to place?

Many animals eat fruit. This helps spread the seeds contained in fruit.

_____

_____

_____

_____

© Houghton Mifflin Harcourt Publishing Company   (cl)©Stockbyte/Getty Images; (bl) ©Peter Anderson/Getty Images; (c) ©Perennou Nuridsany/Photo Researchers, Inc.; (br) ©Bill Draker/Rolfnp/Alamy; (tl) ©Gusto/Photo Researchers, Inc.

Other Ways Plants Grow

Pine trees, beans, and sunflowers all grow from seeds. Other plants do not grow from seeds. These plants grow from structures called spores.

Active Reading As you read this page, draw one line under a cause. Draw two lines under its effect.

Have you ever looked at the underside of a fern leaf? You may have seen black or brown spots, like the ones in this picture. These spots are made up of pockets filled with spores.

A **spore** is a cell that can grow into a new plant when the conditions are right. Some plants, such as mosses and ferns, grow from spores instead of seeds. Plants that grow from spores have two distinct forms in their life cycles.

Spores are released when the structures that hold them break open. Wind carries the spores to new places. If a spore lands in a good spot, it will grow into a plant.

Spores are very tiny. They can be carried long distances by the wind.

© Houghton Mifflin Harcourt Publishing Company • (b) ©Glen Allison/Getty Images; (bl) ©Getty Images

A fern leaf, or frond, is one form of the plant. Spore clusters grow on the undersides of the fronds. When the clusters burst, spores are carried by the wind.

The new plant reaches maturity when it can reproduce.

If a spore lands in a place with good light and water, it begins to grow into a tiny, flat, heart-shaped structure.

The heart-shaped structure is the other form of the plant. It produces eggs and sperm. If a sperm cell fertilizes an egg cell, a curled frond will begin to develop and push out of the ground.

► Compare and contrast the life cycles of seed plants and ferns.

Seed Plants	Both	Ferns

© Houghton Mifflin Harcourt Publishing Company (b) © Getty Images

Read the summary statements. Then match each statement with the correct image.

Summarize

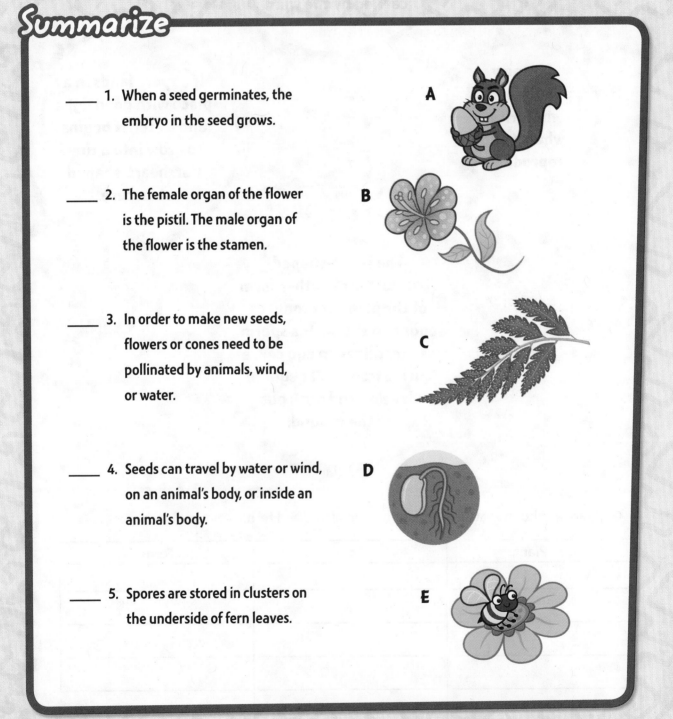

____ 1. When a seed germinates, the embryo in the seed grows.

____ 2. The female organ of the flower is the pistil. The male organ of the flower is the stamen.

____ 3. In order to make new seeds, flowers or cones need to be pollinated by animals, wind, or water.

____ 4. Seeds can travel by water or wind, on an animal's body, or inside an animal's body.

____ 5. Spores are stored in clusters on the underside of fern leaves.

A

B

C

D

E

Answer Key: 1. D 2. B 3. E 4. A 5. C

© Houghton Mifflin Harcourt Publishing Company

Word Play

Name _____

1 Use the terms in the box to complete the puzzle.

cone
cycle
fertilization*
flower
germination*
maturity*
pollen
pollination*
seed
spore*

*Key Lesson Vocabulary

Across

3. Which process happens when a sperm joins with an egg?

4. When a plant has grown enough to reproduce, it has reached which stage in its life cycle?

5. What forms when an egg within a pistil is fertilized?

6. All of the stages a plant goes through as it develops is called its life _____ .

8. Which process happens when pollen falls on a flower's pistil?

9. Which cell grows into a new plant, such as a fern or moss, if it lands in a spot with the right conditions?

Down

1. Which process happens when a small root and stem begin to grow out of a seed?

2. Which structures in seed-forming plants contain male reproductive cells?

6. Which structure do pine trees and spruce trees use to reproduce?

7. Which structure do rose bushes and apple trees use to reproduce?

© Houghton Mifflin Harcourt Publishing Company (r) ©Arco Images GmbH/Alamy Images

Apply Concepts

2 Illustrate the life cycle of a flowering plant, such as a radish or a lima bean.

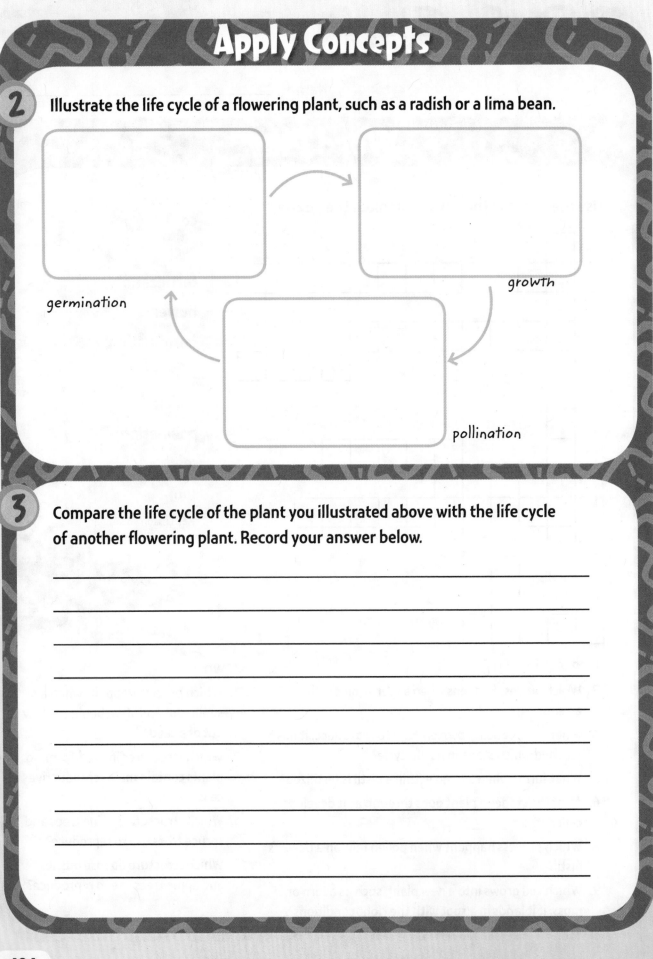

germination

growth

pollination

3 Compare the life cycle of the plant you illustrated above with the life cycle of another flowering plant. Record your answer below.

_____

_____

_____

_____

_____

_____

_____

_____

_____

© Houghton Mifflin Harcourt Publishing Company

4 List three ways a seed-forming plant can be pollinated.

1. _____
_____

2. _____
_____

3. _____
_____

5 Look at the seed shown here. How do you think this seed is spread? Explain your answer.

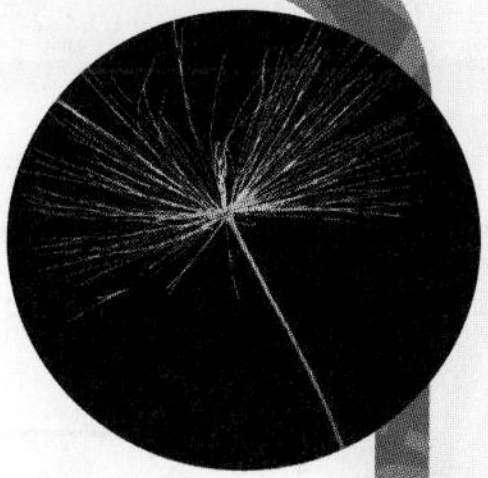

_____
_____
_____
_____

6 Draw a picture of a flower and label its parts.

© Houghton Mifflin Harcourt Publishing Company (tr) ©Steve Gschmeissner/Photo Researchers, Inc.

7 Explain how pollination is different from fertilization in flowers. (Hint: Which needs to happen first—pollination or fertilization?)

_____

_____

_____

_____

_____

8 Circle the structure(s) that plants use to reproduce.

Take It Home!

With your family, go on a walk through your neighborhood or a local park. Locate plants with flowers or cones. Explore their flowers or cones, and describe their structures and life cycles to your family members.

© Houghton Mifflin Harcourt Publishing Company

Inquiry Flipchart page 58

TEKS **4.2B** ...record data by observing... **4.2C** construct...charts... to organize...data **4.2D** analyze data to construct reasonable explanations... **4.10C** ...compare life cycles in living organisms

Name _____

Essential Question

How Can We Explore a Plant's Life Cycle?

Set a Purpose
What will you learn from this experiment?

_____

_____

Think About the Procedure
Which conditions will you control, or try to make the same, for each seed?

_____

_____

Why is it important that each seed is exposed to the same conditions?

_____

_____

_____

_____

_____

_____

_____

Record Your Data
Construct a chart in the space below to organize and record your observations and data.

© Houghton Mifflin Harcourt Publishing Company

Draw Conclusions

What would you expect to happen if you planted the germinated seeds in soil?

_____

_____

_____

Analyze and Extend

1. Compare the germination rates of the seeds. Which one germinated the fastest? The slowest?

_____

_____

_____

2. Which factors do you think determine how fast a seed germinates?

_____

_____

_____

3. Explain how you could test the effect of one of the factors you listed in Question 2 on the germination rate of seeds.

_____

_____

_____

_____

_____

4. How do you think the plant would look if it was kept in the dark? How do you think the plant would look if it was kept in low light?

_____

_____

_____

_____

_____

_____

_____

5. Compare your data with a classmate. Analyze your results and construct reasonable explanations to account for any differences in data.

_____

_____

_____

_____

_____

_____

6. What other questions do you have about how seeds germinate?

_____

_____

_____

_____

© Houghton Mifflin Harcourt Publishing Company

How It Works:
Water Irrigation System

A water irrigation system moves water to where it is needed. This water may come from rivers, lakes, or wells. Pumps and valves control water's movement into and through the system. Farmers use a control panel to determine how much and how quickly water moves through a field.

pipe and drip pipes

center pivot gear

system control panel

"A" frame

pump and check valve

wheel

Troubleshooting

Find and circle the pump on the diagram. What would happen to the irrigation system if the pump stopped working?

_____

_____

_____

© Houghton Mifflin Harcourt Publishing Company (tg) ©Peter Frank/Corbis; (br) ©Nick Koudis/Photodisc/Getty Images; (b) ©imagebroker/Alamy Images

Show How It Works

People use irrigation systems to water their vegetable gardens at home. Look at the picture of a backyard irrigation system. Label its parts. Then answer the questions.

Name some parts of the irrigation system not shown in the diagram.

_____

_____

_____

Identify some problems with this irrigation system. Then, describe how you would solve them.

_____

_____

_____

_____

Build On It!

Rise to the engineering design challenge—complete **Make a Process: Planting and Caring for a Garden** on the Inquiry Flipchart.

© Houghton Mifflin Harcourt Publishing Company (tr) ©Peter Frank/Corbis

TEKS **4.10C** explore, illustrate, and compare life cycles in living organisms such as butterflies, beetles...

Lesson **3**

Essential Question

How Do Animals Reproduce?

Engage Your Brain!

Find the answer to the following question in this lesson and record it here.

How do you think these young egrets will change as they grow up?

_____

_____

_____

_____

Active Reading

Lesson Vocabulary

List the terms. As you learn about each one, make notes in the Interactive Glossary.

_____

_____

_____

_____

Sequence

Many ideas in this lesson are in a sequence, or order, that describes the steps in a process. Active readers stay focused on sequence when they go from one stage or step in a process to another.

Inquiry Flipchart p. 60 — Breeding Brine Shrimp/Can Waxworms Stand the Heat?

501

© Houghton Mifflin Harcourt Publishing Company ©David OSborn/Alamy

Life (in) Full Circle

Like plants, animals have life cycles. Animals are born and then begin to grow up. When animals become adults, they may have young of their own. In this way, life continues to renew itself.

Active Reading As you read the next page, underline the description of each stage of an animal's life, and number the stages in the correct order.

When a bird reaches adulthood, it mates with another bird.

Over time, the bird grows. Soon it can live on its own.

After the eggs hatch, the parents feed the young birds.

After mating, a female bird lays eggs. Birds hatch from eggs.

© Houghton Mifflin Harcourt Publishing Company

Matching Game

Use the terms on the right to identify the correct life stages in each series of pictures.

Adult
Newborn
Youth

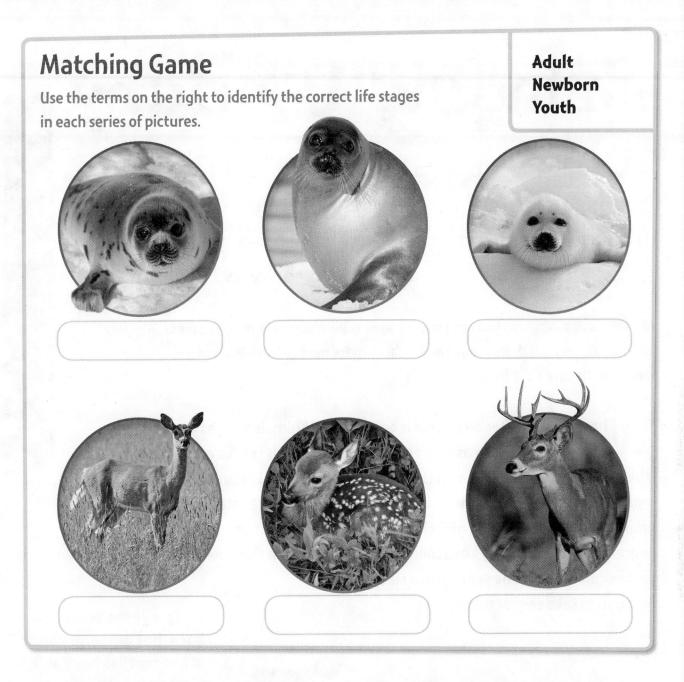

Adult animals can produce offspring. Animals such as deer and seals give birth to live young. Other animals, such as birds, lay eggs.

For example, young blue jays hatch from eggs laid by adult females. The newly hatched blue jays are then protected and cared for by their parents. After the young are born, they begin to grow and change.

Over time, newborns develop into youths. Youths continue to develop until they grow into adults. When youths grow into adults, they may produce offspring. An animal's life cycle ends when the animal dies. However, the animal's offspring will likely have offspring of their own. In this way, the life cycle repeats again and again.

© Houghton Mifflin Harcourt Publishing Company   (tl) ©Peter Arnold, Inc./Alamy; (tc) ©All Canada Photos/Alamy; (tr) ©Corbis; (cl) ©Comstock/Getty Images; (c) ©Mira/Alamy; (cr) ©Corbis

Bringing Up Baby

Like birds, many other animals hatch out of eggs. For example, most fish, reptiles, and spiders hatch from eggs. Other animals give birth to live young. Dogs, horses, and mice are all born this way.

Active Reading   As you read these pages, draw a star next to the names of animals that hatch from eggs and a check mark next to the names of animals that are born live.

What happens after an animal is born? Some animals, such as turtles, are on their own as soon as they hatch from their eggs. Their parents do not help them. Other animals, such as penguins, give their young a great deal of care. They keep their young warm and fed until the young grow strong enough to take care of themselves.

Animals such as deer, bears, and rabbits take care of their young by feeding them milk. These animals may stay with their parents for months or years until they are able to live on their own.

Birds' eggshells are hard, but alligators and other reptiles have soft, leathery shells.

©Houghton Mifflin Harcourt Publishing Company (bl) ©Mark Deeble and Victoria Stone/Getty Images; (tr) ©Juniors Bildarchiv/Alamy

► What are young kangaroos called?

_____

Cats give birth to live young.
Young cats drink their mother's milk.

Do the Math!
Solve a Problem

Raccoons usually give birth to 3 to 5 young at one time. Raccoons give birth only once a year. Suppose a female raccoon lives 10 years. She is able to give birth for 9 of those years. How many offspring will she have?

_____

_____

When kangaroos are born, they are about the size of a dime. They then develop in their mother's pouch.

© Houghton Mifflin Harcourt Publishing Company (t) ©John W Banagan/Getty Images

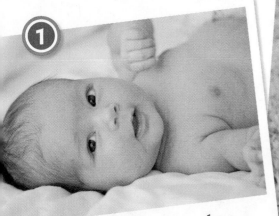

1 When babies are born, they drink their mother's milk. They have no teeth, and they are not able to walk on their own.

2 Babies grow into toddlers. Toddlers learn how to walk. They also start learning how to speak. Humans get their first set of teeth when they are toddlers.

Growing Up

Humans go through stages of development, too. It takes many years for a human baby to grow into an adult. Study these pages to see all of the growth stages humans go through.

Active Reading Put a star next to the life stage that you are currently in.

3 As a child develops, the first set of teeth is replaced by permanent teeth. The child grows and develops many physical and mental skills.

© Houghton Mifflin Harcourt Publishing Company (tl) ©Ariel Skelley/Getty Images; (c) ©Golden Pixels LLC/Alamy; (br) ©Jose Luis Pelaez Inc/Blend Images/Alamy

Growth Chart

At age 2, children are about 2 ft 10 in. tall.
By age 5, children are about 3 ft 6 in. tall.
Place these measurements into the chart.
Then, measure yourself and an adult.
Place those measurements in the chart.

How do you change as you get older?

_____

Age	Height
2	
5	
You	
Adult	

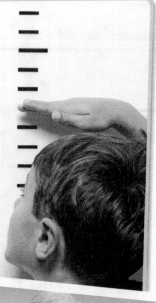

4 During the teenage years, boys and girls start looking more like adults. For example, boys start growing facial hair.

6 As an adult ages, they lose some of their physical abilities. The body changes in other ways, as well. For example, the hair turns gray.

5 During adulthood, people reach maturity. Often, adults marry and have children of their own.

© Houghton Mifflin Harcourt Publishing Company (cl) ©Jupiterimages/Getty Images; (tr) ©Dwight Eschliman/Getty Images; (cr) ©Blend Images/Alamy; (bc) ©Blend Images/Alamy

My, How You've Changed!

My

A butterfly breaking out of its chrysalis.

A young frog, or tadpole, has a long tail and no legs. As it grows, its tail becomes shorter, and it begins to grow legs. An adult frog has no tail, but has legs. The young go through a series of changes known as *metamorphosis*.

Active Reading As you read the next page, underline the sentences that contain vocabulary terms.

▶ Compare complete metamorphosis and incomplete metamorphosis. Identify two stages that occur in both life cycles.

_____

_____

_____

Complete Metamorphosis

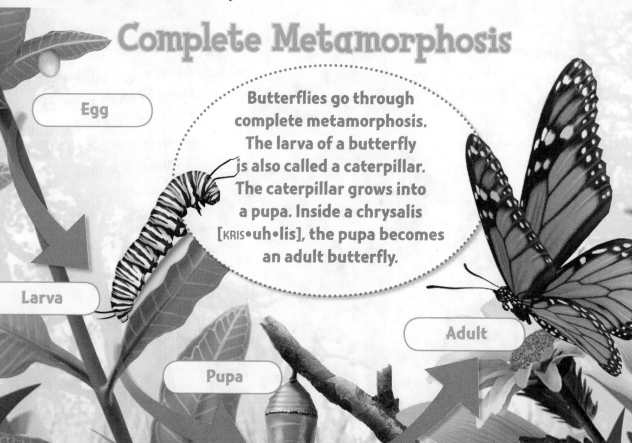

Egg

Larva

Pupa

Adult

Butterflies go through complete metamorphosis. The larva of a butterfly is also called a caterpillar. The caterpillar grows into a pupa. Inside a chrysalis [KRIS•uh•lis], the pupa becomes an adult butterfly.

© John Durak/Phototake/Alamy

© Houghton Mifflin Harcourt Publishing Company (r)

Incomplete Metamorphosis

Adult

Grasshoppers will molt five times before they reach the adult stage.

Grasshoppers go through incomplete metamorphosis. Young grasshoppers hatch as nymphs. A nymph grows and molts.

Nymph

The female grasshopper lays eggs in the soil.

Eggs

In some animals, such as ladybugs and beetles, the young look very different from the adults. In **complete metamorphosis** [met•uh•MAWR•fuh•sis], an animal goes through four different stages in its life cycle. The egg hatches into a *larva*. The larvae [LAR•vee] of many insects look like worms. A larva develops into a *pupa* [PYOO•puh] that is enclosed in a cocoon. While in the cocoon, the pupa develops into an adult moth. The adult splits its cocoon and flies out.

Some insects, such as dragonflies and termites, go through a different series of changes. In **incomplete metamorphosis**, an animal goes through three different stages in its life cycle. First, the animal hatches from the egg as a **nymph** [NIMF]. Nymphs look like tiny adults, but they don't have wings. As the nymph grows larger, it molts. Molting happens when an insect sheds its hard outer skeleton. After several moltings, the insect, which now has wings, reaches its adult stage.

© Houghton Mifflin Harcourt Publishing Company (tr) (tl) ©Tim Laman/National Geographic/Getty Images

Saving (the) Sea Turtles

Some kinds of animals are endangered. That means there are not many of them left. Scientists study the life cycles of endangered animals to try to save them and help them increase their numbers.

Sea turtles are one example of an endangered animal. Hunting, pollution, and beach erosion have caused the number of sea turtles to go down. To help sea turtles, people have learned about the sea turtle's life cycle. They have used what they learned to rear sea turtles. The turtles are then released into the wild. Over time, scientists hope this will help increase the number of sea turtles.

To rear sea turtles, eggs are collected.

© Houghton Mifflin Harcourt Publishing Company   (bl) ©Adi Weda/epa/Corbis

When the eggs hatch, the young turtles are cared for until they can be released into the wild.

▶ Examine the graph. It shows the change in the number of leatherback sea turtles in the Pacific Ocean. Why do you think it is important for humans to try to rear sea turtles?

_____

_____

_____

_____

When the turtles are ready, they are taken to a beach and released.

Leatherbacks in the Eastern Pacific Over Time

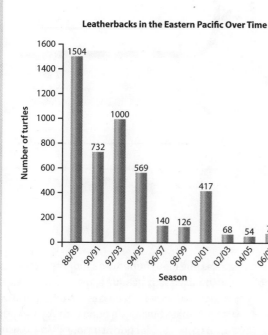

Season	Number of turtles
88/89	1504
90/91	732
92/93	1000
94/95	569
96/97	140
98/99	126
00/01	417
02/03	68
04/05	54
06/07	76

© Houghton Mifflin Harcourt Publishing Company   (t) ©Lawson Wood/Corbis; (cr) ©Reuters/Corbis; (br) ©Florian Schulz/Alamy

When you're done, use the answer key to check and revise your work.

Read the summary statements below. Each one is incorrect. Change the part of the summary in blue to make it correct.

1 Most fish and reptiles give birth to live young. →

2 Some animals, such as cows, cats, and rabbits, give birth to live young and care for the young by feeding them worms. →

3 After human babies are born, they develop into teenagers, and then they eventually grow into toddlers and then adults. →

4 Animals that have a larva stage and a pupa stage undergo incomplete metamorphosis, while animals that have a nymph stage undergo complete metamorphosis. →

5 Humans can try to help endangered animals by rearing them and releasing them into cities. →

Answer Key: 1. Most fish and reptiles hatch from eggs. **2.** Animals such as cows, cats, and rabbits give birth to live young and care for the young by feeding them milk. **3.** After human babies are born, they develop into toddlers, and then they eventually grow into teenagers and then adults. **4.** Animals that have a larva stage and a pupa stage undergo complete metamorphosis, while animals that have a nymph stage undergo incomplete metamorphosis. **5.** Humans can try to help endangered animals by rearing them and releasing them into the wild.

© Houghton Mifflin Harcourt Publishing Company

Name _____

Word Play

1 Match the words to the correct picture.

_____ 1. metamorphosis

_____ 2. incomplete metamorphosis

_____ 3. larva

_____ 4. nymph

_____ 5. molt

_____ 6. pupa

Apply Concepts

2 Circle the animals that hatch from eggs.

3 Circle the one that undergoes incomplete metamorphosis.

© Houghton Mifflin Harcourt Publishing Company

4 Illustrate and label all stages in the life cycle of a butterfly.

5 Use the Venn diagram below to compare complete metamorphosis and incomplete metamorphosis.

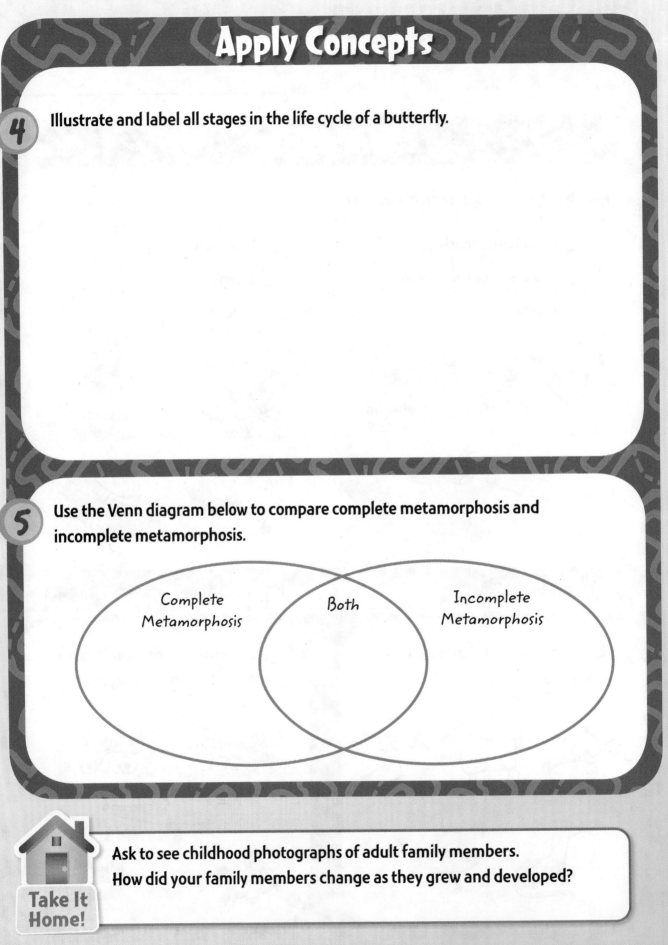

Complete
Metamorphosis

Both

Incomplete
Metamorphosis

© Houghton Mifflin Harcourt Publishing Company

Take It Home!

Ask to see childhood photographs of adult family members.

How did your family members change as they grew and developed?

Ask an Animal Behaviorist

Q. What is an animal behaviorist?

A. An animal behaviorist is a scientist. I study an animal's behavior, or how it responds to its environment. In other words, I research how animals act.

Q. Why do animals act the way they do?

A. Animals are born with some behaviors. These behaviors are called *instincts*. Birds migrate, or travel, when the seasons change. Ground squirrels hibernate during cold weather. Animals communicate using sounds or movements. These are all instincts.

Q. Do animal behaviors change as the animal grows?

A. Some animal behaviors are learned. These behaviors change with experience. In the wild, mothers teach their young to hunt. People train animals as pets, as performers, and as companions. Training animals takes time.

Now It's Your Turn!

▶ What are some ways that animals communicate?

_____

_____

_____

_____

© Houghton Mifflin Harcourt Publishing Company (bkgd) ©Kevin Schafer/Alamy; (br) ©Stocksearch/Alamy

515

Be an Animal Behaviorist

Animals do not talk in words. An animal behaviorist finds other ways to *communicate,* or share information. Find a partner and communicate without using words. Follow the steps below.

My object is a _____.

1 THINK of an object in the classroom.

2 PLAN how you will communicate the object to your partner. Write your plan.

3 Taking turns, COMMUNICATE the object to your partner.

4 DRAW what your partner communicated.

Think About It!

After seeing your partner's drawing, how can you change your plan to better communicate which object you picked?

_____

_____

© Houghton Mifflin Harcourt Publishing Company (wood texture) ©Clearviewstock/Alamy

TEKS **4.10A** explore how adaptations enable organisms to survive in their environment, such as comparing birds' beaks and leaves on plants

Essential Question

How Are Living Things Adapted to Their Environment?

Engage Your Brain!

Find the answer to the following question in this lesson and record it here.

How do the characteristics of this fox help it survive in its environment?

_____

_____

_____

_____

Active Reading

Lesson Vocabulary

List the terms. As you learn about each one, make notes in the Interactive Glossary.

_____   _____

_____   _____

_____   _____

Signal Words: Details

This lesson gives details about the types of adaptations that help plants and animals survive in different environments. Signal words, such as *for example, for instance,* and *like,* link main topics to added details. Active readers look for signal words that link a main topic to its details.

© Houghton Mifflin Harcourt Publishing Company ©Corbis

Life on the Blue Planet

Because most of Earth is covered by water, it is often called the Blue Planet. Life is found in water, on land, and everywhere in between!

Active Reading As you read this page, circle signal words that indicate details about the environment.

The **environment** consists of all the living and nonliving things in an area. Look at the picture on these pages. The environment shown here includes the animals, plants, water, soil, air, and everything else in the picture. Animals and plants depend on their environment to meet their needs. For example, the zebras in the picture get food, water, and shelter from their environment.

Earth has many types of environments. For instance, Arctic environments are very cold; tropical rainforests are very hot. Some types of environments are deep in the ocean. Others are on dry land with very little rainfall. Because there are so many types of environments on Earth, there are also many types of living things. Each living thing, or organism, is able to survive in its own environment.

All living things need food, water, air, and shelter. Organisms in the same environment share resources.

© Houghton Mifflin Harcourt Publishing Company · (bg) © Tony Camacho/Photo-Researchers, Inc.

Earth's different environments are home to many types of living things. This mountain goat's environment is different from the zebras' environment.

Do the Math!

Use Fractions

The largest environment on Earth is the ocean. Water covers about $\frac{7}{10}$ of Earth's surface. The rest is land. Use this information to determine how much of Earth's surface is land. Label the circle graph below.

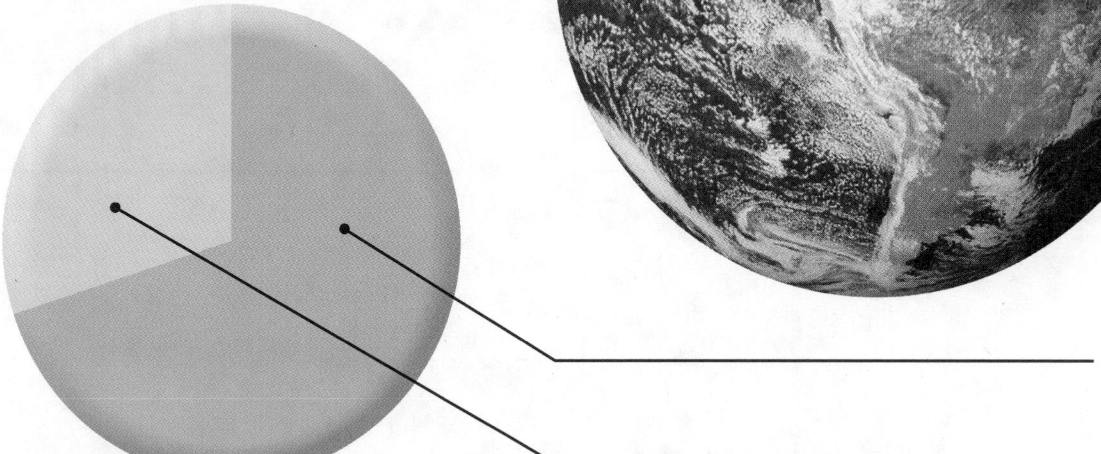

© Houghton Mifflin Harcourt Publishing Company (bl) ©Tony Camacho/Photo Researchers, Inc.; (tr) ©Photodisc/Getty Images; (tc) ©Alan and Sandy Carey/PhotoDisc/Getty Images

Who Is out on a Limb?

If you were in a forest, which bird would you expect to see up in the trees—a blue jay or an ostrich?

Active Reading As you read this page, underline the definition of *adaptation*.

Did you guess a blue jay? You are right! Blue jays are small and have feet that can grip tree branches. Ostriches are large. They have long legs and wide, strong feet. Blue jays have adaptations that help them live in trees, while ostriches do not. An **adaptation** is a characteristic that helps a living thing survive.

Ostriches live on grasslands. They have long, strong legs that enable them to run quickly in open spaces. Their brown color helps them blend in.

Prairie dogs have strong paws for digging burrows. Their brown color enables them to blend in with their environment.

© Houghton Mifflin Harcourt Publishing Company (bg) ©Digital Vision/Getty Images; (bl) ©Sam Dudgeon/HRW; (br) ©Michael Griffin/Alamy Images

A **physical adaptation** is an adaptation to a body part. Living things have different physical adaptations based on their specific environments. For example, plants and animals in open spaces have different physical adaptations than living things in forests.

In open spaces, grasses can bend in strong winds. Grassland animals have coverings to blend in with the grass. These animals may be able to run fast or have shovel-like paws for burrowing.

Living things in forests have physical adaptations to live in and around trees. Vines can climb up trees to help leaves reach sunlight they need to make food. Many forest animals can grip branches.

This blue jay's curved feet help it grip small branches. Its wings enable it to fly from branch to branch.

This sloth's long claws help it to hang from tree branches for most of its life. A sloth can even sleep without letting go of the branch.

▶ Describe the prairie dog's grassland adaptations that help it survive in its environment.

_____
_____
_____
_____
_____
_____
_____
_____
_____

© Houghton Mifflin Harcourt Publishing Company • (bg) ©Digital Vision/Getty Images; (r) ©Nigel Cattlin/Alamy Images; (tr) ©Michael Stubblefield/Alamy Images; (bl) © Corbis/Super RF/Alamy Images

Who Can Go with the Flow?

Some living things swim upstream while others go with the flow. Which adaptations do living things need in different water environments?

Active Reading As you read these two pages, circle examples of fish adaptations. Underline how these adaptations help them survive in their environment.

Imagine you live in a constantly flowing stream of water. How could you stay in the same part of the stream without being carried away? Many fish that live in streams have smooth bodies and strong tails. These characteristics help fish swim against the current. Water plants have flexible stems that allow them to bend with the flow. Many water insects are able to hold on tightly to water plants. Other insects burrow into the soil at the bottom of the stream.

This fish has a smooth, streamlined body. Its body shape allows it to swim quickly in fast-moving water.

Elodea are very flexible plants, so flowing water is less likely to break them. If a piece of elodea is pulled off, though, the piece can sprout roots and start to grow in a new part of the stream.

© Houghton Mifflin Harcourt Publishing Company (bg) ©James Schwabel/Alamy Images; (bl) ©blickwinkel/Alamy Images; (br) ©Wildlife GmbH/Alamy Images

Plants in still water, such as ponds and lakes, have different adaptations. Some plants are tall and have strong stems, so they can grow above the water. Water lilies, have wide, flat leaves that float on the water's surface to take in sunlight.

Animals that live in lakes and ponds are excellent swimmers. Many are adapted to living in deep water with little light. Catfish have whiskers that sense chemicals in the water to help them find food in the dark. Some birds wade at the shore and hunt. Their long, thin legs look like the cattails, so fish do not see them until it's too late.

Cattails grow in relatively still, shallow water, such as the water of a pond. Their stems are strong and stiff. Cattails can grow to more than 3 m tall.

Pond turtles are strong swimmers. They are also able to hold their breath for long periods of time. Their dark color allows them to stay hidden in dark, muddy water.

▶ Explain how the adaptations of the *elodea* and of the cattail enable these plants to survive in their environments.

_____

_____

_____

_____

_____

_____

© Houghton Mifflin Harcourt Publishing Company (bg) ©James Schwabel/Alamy Images; (tr) ©Corbis; (cl) ©BC photography/Alamy Images; (bg) ©Don Smetzer/Alamy Images

Who Can Take the Heat?

Deserts are places that get very little rain. Some deserts are very hot. How do plants and animals live in such hot, dry places?

Active Reading As you read these two pages, circle the words or phrases that describe the adaptations of desert plants.

Desert plants and animals have physical adaptations that help them stay cool and conserve water. The leaves and stems of many desert plants have waxy coatings to minimize water loss. Many of these plants have very long roots to reach water that is deep underground. Some desert plants have wide root systems that can absorb lots of water when it rains. Desert animals have physical adaptations to keep cool. Some have short, thin fur, or no fur at all.

Jackrabbits have large ears. Their ears release body heat and help the rabbits stay cool.

Many reptiles live in deserts. This lizard's scales help it keep water inside its body.

© Houghton Mifflin Harcourt Publishing Company (t) ©Digital Vision/Getty Images; (b) ©Design Pics Inc./Alamy Images

A **behavioral adaptation** is something an organism does to help it survive. For example, most desert animals are active at night to avoid the heat of the day. An instinct is a type of behavioral adaptation.

An **instinct** is an inherited behavior an animal knows how to do without having to learn it. For instance, jackrabbits stay crouched in one position whenever they sense danger. This instinct helps them hide from predators.

Other behaviors help organisms survive in the desert. For example, some seeds of desert plants stay dormant, or inactive, until it rains. When it rains enough, the seeds grow quickly into plants that flower and make more seeds.

Saguaro cactus flowers open and release their fragrance at night and close the next day. It is cooler at night in the desert. As a result, the flowers do not wilt as quickly as they would during the day.

▶ Describe a living thing with adaptations that help it survive in the desert. Explain how each adaptation helps.

_____

_____

_____

_____

_____

_____

_____

© Houghton Mifflin Harcourt Publishing Company (bg) ©Design Pics Inc./Alamy Images; (t) ©Mark Wallace/Alamy Images; (p) ©John Wang/Getty Images

Who Can Take the Cold?

Polar environments are very cold places. How do plants and animals survive in cold places such as Antarctica and the Arctic?

Active Reading As you read these pages, circle the words or phrases that describe polar environments.

Temperatures in Antarctica rarely get above freezing—even in summer! Plants and animals that live there have adaptations to live in extreme cold. Emperor penguins have a thick layer of fat—a physical adaptation that keeps them warm on land and in the water. To protect themselves from very cold winds, male penguins huddle together in large groups. The behavior is an instinct that helps male penguins and their newly hatched baby penguins keep warm.

The Antarctic pearlwort grows close to the ground in the warmer, wetter parts of Antarctica.

Black feathers on the backs of emperor penguins absorb heat from the sun, which helps them keep warm.

© Houghton Mifflin Harcourt Publishing Company   (bg) ©Corbis; (cr) ©Colin Harris/lightTouch Images/Alamy Images

The Arctic has extremely cold winters and very short summers. Arctic animals have thick fur and a layer of fat to keep in body heat. Some Arctic animals are often white in the winter, which helps them blend in with the snow. These characteristics are physical adaptations. Arctic animals also have behavioral adaptations. For example, many Arctic animals live in dens dug into the ground or snow during very cold months.

Most Arctic plants have short roots because the ground there is frozen the majority of the year. These plants produce seeds during the short summer when the ground isn't frozen. Most Arctic plants grow close to the ground, which helps protect them from strong, cold Arctic winds.

This prairie crocus has fuzzy hairs that cover its flowers and seeds. The hairs protect the plant from wind and trap heat from the sun.

▶ Compare the adaptations that help the desert jackrabbit and the Arctic hare survive in their environments.

_____

_____

_____

_____

_____

_____

_____

Arctic hares grow white fur in winter to blend in with the snow. They sit with their paws, tails, and ears tucked in to keep from losing body heat.

© Houghton Mifflin Harcourt Publishing Company ·bg) ©Corbis; (cr) ©Visual&Written SL/Alamy Images; (tr) ©All Canada Photos/Alamy Images

Sum It Up!

When you're done, use the answer key to check and revise your work.

The outline below is a summary of the lesson. Complete the outline.

Summarize

I. Match each description to the living thing that has that adaptation.

A. flexible stem that bends in flowing water   Arctic hare

B. grows white fur in the winter   sloth

C. long claws to hang from tree branches   saguaro

D. flowers open at night when it's cooler   prairie dog

E. long claws for digging burrows   *Elodea*

II. Identify each adaptation described below as a physical adaptation or a behavioral adaptation.

A. An ostrich has long, strong legs. _____

B. An Arctic hare sits for hours to conserve heat. _____

C. A catfish has whiskers that sense chemicals in the water. _____

D. Male penguins huddle together to stay warm. _____

E. A fish has a smooth, streamlined body. _____

Answer Key: I. A. *Elodea* B. Arctic hare C. sloth D. saguaro E. prairie dog II. A. physical B. behavioral C. physical D. behavioral E. physical

© Houghton Mifflin Harcourt Publishing Company   (b) ©Jeff Vanuga/Corbis

Name _____

Word Play

1 Complete the crossword puzzle.

Across

4. Desert animals are active at night to avoid the heat. Which type of adaptation is this?

5. Which type of behavior does an animal know how to do without having to learn it?

Down

1. What are all of the living and nonliving things in an area called?

2. A blue jay's small, curved feet help it grip branches. Which type of adaptation is this?

3. What is a body part or behavior that helps a living thing survive called?

Apply Concepts

2 Draw a circle around the plant that would most likely live in a forest.
Describe an adaptation that enables this plant to survive in its environment.

_____

© Houghton Mifflin Harcourt Publishing Company

3 Snakes and lizards are rarely found living near polar environments. Explain why.

_____

_____

_____

4

This spider monkey lives in the treetops of a tropical rainforest. Which adaptations enable it to survive in its environment?

_____

5 Why is it better for an animal to know how to hide from predators because of an instinct than to have to learn how to hide from them?

_____

_____

_____

_____

Take It Home! Take a walk with your family through your neighborhood or a local park. Look at plants and animals, and point out adaptations that enable them to survive in their environments.

© Houghton Mifflin Harcourt Publishing Company

Inquiry Flipchart page 62

Lesson 5
INQUIRY

TEKS 4.2C construct...charts...using tools...to organize...data **4.3C** represent the natural world using models... **4.10A** explore how adaptations enable organisms to survive in their environment such as comparing birds' beaks...

Name _____

Essential Question

Why Do Bird Beaks Differ?

Set a Purpose

Why do you think different birds have beaks with different shapes?

_____

_____

_____

_____

Write a statement summarizing what you plan to do in this investigation.

_____

_____

_____

_____

What will you model in this investigation?

_____

_____

_____

_____

Record Your Data

In the space below, construct a chart in which you record your observations.

Draw Conclusions

During your exploration, did some beaks work for more than one kind of food? What might this adaptation suggest about how birds are able to survive in their environments?

_____

_____

_____

_____

_____

Did one type of beak work for eating all the different foods?

_____

_____

_____

Analyze and Extend

1. Which bird's beak would be best for eating flower nectar? Which beaks would be best for picking insects out of wood and worms out of sand?

_____

_____

_____

_____

2. A toucan is a bird that eats very large, tough tropical fruit. What would you expect a toucan's beak to look like?

_____

_____

_____

3. Look at the bird beaks below. Tell which tool in the investigation was most similar to each of the beaks.

hummingbird   finch

_____   _____

macaw   shorebird

_____   _____

woodpecker   duck

_____   _____

4. Think of other questions you would like to ask about how adaptations relate to the food an animal eats.

_____

_____

_____

532

© Houghton Mifflin Harcourt Publishing Company

TEKS **4.10B** demonstrate that some likenesses between parents and offspring are inherited, passed from generation to generation...other likenesses are learned...

Lesson **6**

What Are Heredity, Instincts, and Learned Behaviors?

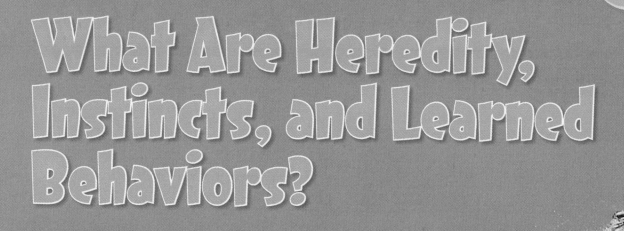

🧠 Engage Your Brain!

Find the answer to the following question in this lesson and record it here.

How did this whale learn to hunt ?

_____

_____

_____

_____

Active Reading

Lesson Vocabulary

List the terms. As you learn about each one, make notes in the Interactive Glossary.

_____

_____

_____

_____

Main Idea

The main idea of a paragraph is the most important idea. The main idea may be stated in the first sentence, or it may be stated elsewhere. Active readers look for main ideas by asking themselves, What is this paragraph mostly about?

© Houghton Mifflin Harcourt Publishing Company ©AriesStró/Alamy

Like Mother, Like Daughter

Have you ever noticed how children often look a lot like their parents? This happens because of a process known as heredity.

Active Reading As you read these two pages, circle the inherited traits.

▶ Read about this girl's traits. Then, fill in your own.

This girl's hair is brown.
Your hair color:
_____

This girl's eyes are blue.
Your eye color:
_____

This girl's ears have attached lobes.
Your ear lobes:
_____

This girl's chin has no cleft.
Your chin:
_____

© Houghton Mifflin Harcourt Publishing Company (b) ©Brad Wilson/Getty Images

Snapdragon Family Tree

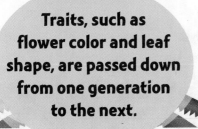

Traits, such as flower color and leaf shape, are passed down from one generation to the next.

The passing of traits from parents to offspring is **heredity**. A *trait* is a feature of an individual, such as brown eyes.

All of the features you see when you look in the mirror are traits. Most of these traits came from your parents. For example, suppose you have a friend with blue eyes. Most likely, one or both of your friend's parents also have blue eyes. Your friend inherited her eye color from her parents.

Heredity happens in other living things as well. As you can see on this page, flowers inherit their petal color from their parents. Birds inherit their beak shape. And giraffes inherit their long necks. This is why family members look similar to one other.

© Houghton Mifflin Harcourt Publishing Company

It's in the Genes

Every living thing contains chemical instructions for traits. These instructions are known as genes.

Active Reading Underline the main idea as you read each paragraph below.

Half of your genes came from your mother. The other half came from your father. Because of this, you have a mixture of traits from both of your parents.

Remember that a sperm is a male reproductive cell. It contains genes from the father. An egg is a female reproductive cell. It has genes from the mother. When the two reproductive cells join, the resulting cell has genes from both parents.

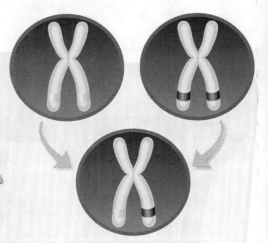

Genes [JEENZ] are instructions for traits. These instructions are carried on X-shaped chemicals. This chicken got half its genes from its mother, and half from its father.

© Houghton Mifflin Harcourt Publishing Company   (bl) ©John Mottershaw/Alamy

► What might be a benefit of making plants resistant to poison? What might be a problem with this genetic change? Record your answers in the chart below.

Benefit	Problem

The genes of these carrots have been changed so the carrots are more nutritious.

Scientists have learned a lot about how genes control traits. Today, scientists can take genes from one living thing and put them in another. This process is called genetic engineering. Scientists use genetic engineering to change a living thing's traits. For example, they can make carrots more nutritious by adding genes for different vitamins. Scientists can make plants that are not killed by poisions. Scientists can make bacteria that produce medicines. This technology is very new, so its effects are still being studied.

Mom! Why are my carrots purple?

© Houghton Mifflin Harcourt Publishing Company   (tr) ©Lew Robertson/Corbis; (br) ©Hola Images/Getty Images

Genes + Environment = You

Your genes alone do not control all of your traits. The environment you live in affects your traits, too!

Active Reading As you read this page and the next one, put a star next to a main idea, and circle a supporting detail.

Skin color can be changed by the environment. Staying in the sun can make your skin darker. Too much sun is dangerous. Be sure to always wear sunblock.

The flower color of this hydrangea [hy•DRAYN•juh] is affected by the soil. Sometimes, the flowers are pink. If the soil becomes acidic, the flowers turn blue.

© Houghton Mifflin Harcourt Publishing Company   (tr) ©Emma Innocenti/Getty Images; (bl) ©Wildscape/Alamy; (cr) ©Wildlife GmbH/Alamy

Some traits are caused when your genes and environment interact. For example, your height is controlled by genes. But it also is controlled by the kinds of foods you eat. If you did not eat nutritious food, you would not grow as tall as you could on a healthy diet.

Can you think of other traits you have that are affected by the environment?

Like you, other living things have traits caused by a mix of genes and other factors. For example, plants grow towards light.

If you leave a houseplant near a window, it will grow towards the window. No matter where you move the plant, it will start to grow towards the strongest light.

The environment can change living things in other ways, as well. For example, a tadpole is a frog larva that swims in water. If the pond tadpoles live in starts to dry up, they will undergo metamorphosis at a faster rate. They will become adult frogs faster than tadpoles left in deep ponds.

Do the Math!
Make a Number Line

The sex of alligators is affected by temperature. If an alligator egg develops at 30 °C or less, it will be a female. If it develops at 34 °C or more, it will be a male. Use this information to label the temperature line below.

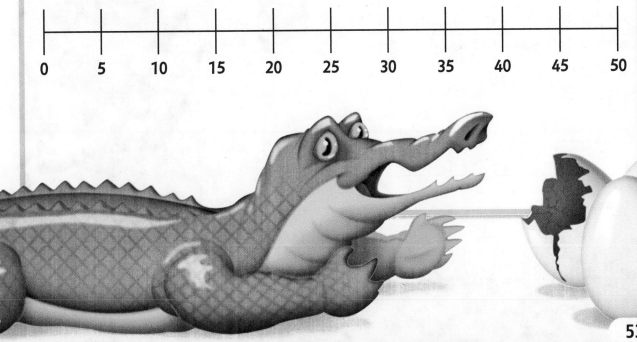

| | | | | | | | | | | |
|0|5|10|15|20|25|30|35|40|45|50|

© Houghton Mifflin Harcourt Publishing Company

Learning Your Lesson

You know a lot of things. You may know how to read a book, how to use a fork and spoon at meal time, and how to add numbers. You were not born knowing these things. Instead, you learned them.

Active Reading As you read this page and the next, underline the examples of the skills you've learned.

Think of how learning keeps you from harm. For example, you know to look both ways before crossing the street. The ability to learn helps an animal survive. A **learned behavior** is something an animal learns from experience or by watching other animals.

▶ Pets are able to learn. What are some examples of tricks you could teach a pet?

- To sit

- To stay

- _____

- _____

- _____

© Houghton Mifflin Harcourt Publishing Company   (br) ©Getty Images/PhotoDisc

This chimpanzee is using a tool to get ants to eat. It probably learned to do this by watching other chimpanzees.

Playing baseball is a learned behavior. You have to learn the rules of the game. You also have to learn how to hit the ball with the bat.

Many animals are able to learn things. Have you ever seen baby ducks following their mother? When the ducks first hatch, they recognize their mother. Everywhere the mother goes, the babies learn to follow. This helps keep the baby ducks safe.

Animals can also learn more complex behavior. Some chimpanzees learn how to make a tool for gathering termites to eat. They learn this by watching older chimpanzees make the tool from a branch. Without watching another chimpanzee do this, a young chimpanzee will not know how to make the tool.

Can you think of other examples that demonstrate a learned behavior? Working animals, such as horses and rescue dogs, are trained to help people. Dolphins and seals are taught to balance balls and jump out of the water at theme parks and aquariums.

© Houghton Mifflin Harcourt Publishing Company   (tl) ©James Balog/Getty Images; (tr) ©Erik Isakson/Tetra Images/Alamy

Insight into Instincts

Not all behaviors are learned. Animals are born knowing how to do some kinds of things.

Active Reading As you read the text below, draw a circle around all the examples of instinctive behaviors.

Behaviors that an animal is born knowing how to do are called **instincts**. Human babies have an instinct to start crying when they are hungry. Birds build nests because of instincts. Earthworms have an instinct to burrow in the ground. Like learned behaviors, instincts help an animal survive.

So how can you tell the difference between learned behaviors and instincts? Sometimes it is difficult. For example, humans have an instinct to speak a language. However, humans must learn to speak a particular language, such as English or Spanish. In this way, many behaviors are a mix of learning and instincts.

Other behaviors may be instinct alone. For example, very soon after a baby horse is born, it is able to stand up. Within a few hours, the baby horse can walk and run. The horse does not need to learn any part of this behavior. It is all instinctive.

Calves are born with an instinct to nurse by drinking milk from their mother.

© Houghton Mifflin Harcourt Publishing Company (br) ©AGStockUSA/Alamy; (tr) ©Lothar Lenz/Corbis

Spiders have an instinct to spin webs.

Geese have an instinct to migrate south in the winter.

▶ Look at the behaviors below. Which are learned and which are instincts?

	Learned	Instinct
A parrot saying, "Hello"	○	○
A fish swimming	○	○
A seal balancing a ball on its nose	○	○
A ground squirrel hibernating in the winter	○	○
A bee building a hive	○	○

© Houghton Mifflin Harcourt Publishing Company   (tr) ©Aaron Linsdau/Alamy

When you're done, use the answer key to check and revise your work.

Use the information in the summary to complete the graphic organizer.

Summarize

Living things inherit most of their traits from their parents. Inherited traits are controlled by genes. Traits can also be controlled by the environment. In animals, traits include behaviors. Instincts are behaviors that an animal is born knowing how to do. Many animals are also able to learn behaviors. They learn from experience or by watching other animals.

Main Idea: Heredity is the passing down of traits from parents to offspring.

Detail: The instinct to build a web is a trait passed from a spider to its young.

1 _____
_____
_____
_____

2 _____
_____
_____
_____
_____

© Houghton Mifflin Harcourt Publishing Company   (l) ©D. Robert & Lorri Franz/Corbis; (r) © Henrik Larsson/Shutterstock

Answer Key: 1. Sample answer: Feather color is a trait passed from a chicken to its chicks. 2. Sample answer: Hair color is a trait passed from parents to children.

Name _____

Word Play

1 Use the words in the box to complete each sentence. Then use the circled letters to answer the question below.

| gene | heredity* | instinct* |
| learned behavior* | offspring | traits |

*Key Lesson Vocabulary

The passing of characteristics from parents to their young is known as

Ⓗ_ _ _ _ Ⓔ _ .

An example of a _ _ _ _ _ _ _ ⓄⓄ_ _ _ _ Ⓞ
is a child learning to read.

A chemical instruction for a trait is known as a _ _ Ⓔ _ .

Green eyes and red hair are examples of _ _ Ⓐ_Ⓘ _ .

A bird chirping is an example of an Ⓘ_ _ _ _ _ _ _ .

A living thing's children are also known as its Ⓞ_ _ _ _ _ _Ⓝ _ .

Question:

Mice, ground squirrels, and other animals become inactive during the winter. What is the name of this instinctive behavior?

_ _ _ _ _ _ _ _ _

© Houghton Mifflin Harcourt Publishing Company ©Getty Images/PhotoDisc

Apply Concepts

2 Explain how living things inherit traits. Then describe how you would demonstrate how one trait is inherited.

_____

_____

_____

_____

_____

3 List three examples of physical traits affected by the environment.

_____

_____

_____

_____

_____

_____

_____

4 Draw and label a picture of an animal that demonstrates a learned behavior and a picture that demonstrates an inherited behavior.

Learned Behavior	**Inherited Behavior**

You perform many different learned behaviors daily. Keep a journal of some of the things you do in a week. Write down how you learned that behavior. For example, if you play tennis, record who taught you to play.

Take It Home!

© Houghton Mifflin Harcourt Publishing Company

Name _____

Vocabulary Review

Use the terms in the box to complete the sentences.

adaptation
fertilization
heredity
incomplete
 metamorphosis
instinct
nymph
pollination
spore

TEKS 4.10B

1. The passing of traits from parents to offspring

   is _____.

TEKS 4.10C

2. Animals that have three stages in their life cycles go

   through _____.

TEKS 4.10A

3. A characteristic that helps an organism survive is

   a(n) _____.

TEKS 4.10B

4. A behavior that an animal is born with is called

   a(n) _____.

TEKS 4.10C

5. The process by which a sperm cell joins with an egg cell

   is called _____.

TEKS 4.10C

6. A cell from a fern plant that can produce a new plant is

   called a _____.

TEKS 4.10C

7. An insect that hatches from an egg and looks like a tiny

   adult with no wings is a(n) _____.

TEKS 4.10C

8. The movement of sperm cells from the male part of a
   flower to the female part occurs through the process

   of _____.

© Houghton Mifflin Harcourt Publishing Company (border) ©NDisk/Age Fotostock

Science Concepts

Fill in the letter of the choice that best answers the question.

TEKS 4.10B

9. Some likenesses between parents and offspring are inherited. Other likenesses are learned. Which one is a learned behavior?

   (A) wolf hunting its prey

   (B) panda eating bamboo

   (C) beaver building a dam

   (D) rattlesnake rattling its tail

TEKS 4.10C

10. A student compares the different types of metamorphosis. Which stage below is part of incomplete metamorphosis—but not of complete metamorphosis?

    (A) adult

    (B) egg

    (C) nymph

    (D) pupa

TEKS 4.10C

11. The bristlecone pine tree produces cones that are either male or female. In contrast, the fishpoison tree has flowers that contain both male and female parts. What can you infer about these two trees?

    (A) Both trees use eggs and sperm to reproduce.

    (B) Both trees have incredibly long life cycles.

    (C) Both trees can disperse their seeds very far.

    (D) Both trees need insects to carry out pollination.

TEKS 4.10A

12. Examine the beak on the bird below.

The beak's shape enables the bird to survive in its environment because the beak is adapted to which of these actions?

(A) tearing food

(B) eating small seeds

(C) getting flower nectar

(D) digging insects from bark

TEKS 4.10C

13. Hannah is comparing the life cycles of the two plants below.

Plant A   Plant B

Which is an accurate comparison of the life cycles of these two plants?

(A) Both plants reproduce with structures called cones.

(B) Both plants reproduce with structures called flowers.

(C) Only Plant A reproduces with structures called cones.

(D) Only Plant B reproduces with structures called cones.

© Houghton Mifflin Harcourt Publishing Company   (border) ©NDisk/Age Fotostock

TEKS 4.10C

14. This picture shows a bee visiting a flower to obtain nectar.

Which process in the flower's life cycle is this bee helping carry out?

- Ⓐ pollination
- Ⓑ germination
- Ⓒ seed dispersal
- Ⓓ photosynthesis

TEKS 4.10B

15. Offspring have physical characteristics, or traits, similar to their parents. Which is an example of an inherited trait?

- Ⓐ a bird building a nest
- Ⓑ a cat nursing its kittens
- Ⓒ the hunting skills of a lion
- Ⓓ the color of a red snapdragon

TEKS 4.10A

16. Sharks can smell very small amounts of substances in ocean water. What does this physical adaptation enable the shark to do to survive in its environment?

- Ⓐ sense water temperature
- Ⓑ find a place to lay eggs
- Ⓒ find a safe place to hide
- Ⓓ find food that is far away

TEKS 4.10B

17. Monarch butterflies migrate to warm places every winter. What is their migration an example of?

- Ⓐ a trait
- Ⓒ a characteristic
- Ⓑ an instinct
- Ⓓ a learned behavior

TEKS 4.2D

18. Animals help disperse seeds in many ways. For example, a box turtle eats the fruits and seeds of many plants. The turtle digests the fruit and drops the seeds with its waste matter. This data table shows how long it takes for the turtle to digest different types of seeds.

Seed Type	Q	R	S	T
Number of Days	20	2	12	5

Which seed could the box turtle disperse the greatest distance from the parent tree?

- Ⓐ Q
- Ⓒ S
- Ⓑ R
- Ⓓ T

TEKS 4.10C

19. A mahogany tree produces seeds that look like this picture at right.

Look at the blades on the surface of this seed. What role do these blades play in the life cycle of this tree?

Fan-like blades

- Ⓐ protect the seed
- Ⓑ end the plant's life cycle
- Ⓒ store food for the seedling
- Ⓓ help disperse the tree's seeds

© Houghton Mifflin Harcourt Publishing Company   (border) ©NDisk/Age Fotostock

Apply Inquiry and Review the Big Idea

Write the answers to these questions.

20. Butterflies and grasshoppers are both insects, but their life cycles differ.

   a. Draw a diagram to illustrate the life cycle of the butterfly and of the grasshopper. Label the stages for each life cycle.

   b. Compare the life cycles of the butterfly and the grasshopper. Describe how they are alike and how they are different.

_____

_____

_____

_____

21. This picture shows organisms that live in a desert environment. Choose one of the organisms. Identify one of its physical adaptations, and describe how the adaptation helps the organism live in a desert environment.

_____

_____

_____

22. A school of tuna migrates a distance of 8,150 km. A group of monarch butterflies migrates 4,430 km. A herd of caribou migrates 1,380 km. What is the difference in migration distance between the longest and shortest migration routes?

_____

© Houghton Mifflin Harcourt Publishing Company   (border) ©NDisk/Age Fotostock

Interactive Glossary

As you learn about each term, add notes, drawings, or sentences in the extra space. This will help you remember what the terms mean. Here are some examples.

Fungi [FUHN•jeye] A kingdom of organisms that have a nucleus and get nutrients by decomposing other organisms

A mushroom is from the kingdom Fungi.

physical change [FIZ•ih•kuhl•CHAYNJ] Change in the size, shape, or state of matter with no new substance being formed

When I cut paper, the paper has a physical change.

Glossary Pronunciation Key

With every glossary term, there is also a phonetic respelling. A phonetic respelling writes the word the way it sounds, which can help you pronounce new or unfamiliar words. Use this key to help you understand the respellings.

Sound	As in	Phonetic Respelling	Sound	As in	Phonetic Respelling
a	bat	(BAT)	oh	over	(OH•ver)
ah	lock	(LAHK)	oo	pool	(POOL)
air	rare	(RAIR)	ow	out	(OWT)
ar	argue	(AR•gyoo)	oy	foil	(FOYL)
aw	law	(LAW)	s	cell	(SEL)
ay	face	(FAYS)		sit	(SIT)
ch	chapel	(CHAP•uhl)	sh	sheep	(SHEEP)
e	test	(TEST)	th	that	(THAT)
	metric	(MEH•trik)		thin	(THIN)
ee	eat	(EET)	u	pull	(PUL)
	feet	(FEET)	uh	medal	(MED•uhl)
	ski	(SKEE)		talent	(TAL•uhnt)
er	paper	(PAY•per)		pencil	(PEN•suhl)
	fern	(FERN)		onion	(UHN•yuhn)
eye	idea	(eye•DEE•uh)		playful	(PLAY•fuhl)
i	bit	(BIT)		dull	(DUHL)
ing	going	(GOH•ing)	y	yes	(YES)
k	card	(KARD)		ripe	(RYP)
	kite	(KYT)	z	bags	(BAGZ)
ngk	bank	(BANGK)	zh	treasure	(TREZH•er)

© Houghton Mifflin Harcourt Publishing Company

Interactive Glossary

A

acceleration [ak•sel•er•AY•shuhn] Any change in the speed or direction of an object's motion (p. 272)

adaptation [ad•uhp•TAY•shuhn] A trait or characteristic that helps an organism survive (p. 520)

advertisement [ad•ver•TYZ•muhnt] A public notice or announcement of information designed to communicate a message to a viewer or listener about a product or a service (p. 94)

air mass [AIR MAS] A large body of air that has the same temperature and humidity throughout (p. 376)

air pressure [AIR PRESH•er] The weight of the atmosphere pressing down on Earth (p. 361)

atmosphere [AT•muhs•feer] The mixture of gases that surrounds Earth (p. 347)

axis [AK•sis] The imaginary line around which Earth rotates (p. 398)

B

bedrock [BED•rahk] Solid rock found under soil (p. 326)

 © Houghton Mifflin Harcourt Publishing Company

behavioral adaptation
[bih•HAYV•yu•ruhl ad•uhp•TAY•shuhn]
Something an animal does that helps it
survive (p. 525)

circuit [SER•kuht] A path along which
electric charges can flow (p. 230)

C

carnivore [KAHR•nuh•vawr] A consumer
that eats only other animals (p. 456)

complete metamorphosis
[kuhm•PLEET met•uh•MAWR•fuh•sis]
A complex change that most insects undergo
that includes larva and pupa stages (p. 509)

change of state [CHAYNJ uhv STAYT]
A physical change that occurs when matter
changes from one state to another, such as
from a liquid to a gas (p. 140)

computer model [kuhm•PYOO•ter MOD•l]
A computer program that models an event
or an object (p. 55)

chemical energy
[KEM•ih•kuhl EN•er•jee] Energy that can be
released by a chemical change (p. 179)

condensation [kahn•duhn•SAY•shuhn]
The process by which a gas changes into
a liquid (pp. 141, 348)

© Houghton Mifflin Harcourt Publishing Company

Interactive Glossary

conduction [kuhn•DUK•shuhn] The transfer, or movement, of heat between two objects that are touching (p. 194)

consumer [kuhn•SOOM•er] Animals that eat plants or other animals to get energy (p. 444)

conductor [kuhn•DUK•ter] A material that allows heat or electricity to move through it easily (pp. 206, 228)

convection [kuhn•VEK•shuhn] The transfer of heat within a liquid or a gas (p. 195)

conservation [kahn•ser•VAY•shuhn] The use of less of something to make its supply last longer (p. 300)

data [DEY•tuh] Individual facts, statistics, and items of information you observe (p. 41)

constellation [kahn•stuh•LAY•shuhn] A group of stars that seems to form a picture or design in the sky (p. 406)

decomposer [dee•kuhm•POHZ•er] A living thing that gets energy by breaking down wastes and the remains of plants and animals (p. 446)

© Houghton Mifflin Harcourt Publishing Company

density [DEN•suh•tee] The amount of matter present in a certain volume of a substance (p. 118)

electrical energy [ee•LEK•trih•kuhl EN•er•jee] A form of energy that comes from electric current (p. 179)

deposition [dep•uh•ZISH•uhn] The dropping or settling of eroded materials (p. 308)

electromagnet [ee•lek•troh•MAG•nit] A temporary magnet caused by an electric current (p. 249)

design [dih•zyn] To conceive something and to prepare the plans and drawings for it to be built (p. 72)

empirical evidence [im•PIR•uh•kuhl EV•uh•duhns] Data collected through direct observation or experience (p. 24)

E

electric motor [ee•LEK•trik MOHT•er] A device that changes electrical energy into mechanical energy (p. 245)

energy [EN•er•jee] The ability to do work and to cause changes in matter (pp. 173, 440)

© Houghton Mifflin Harcourt Publishing Company

Interactive Glossary

engineering [en•juh•NIR•ing] The use of scientific and mathematical principles to develop something practical (p. 71)

evidence [EV•uh•duhns] Information collected during a scientific investigation (p. 10)

environment [en•VY•ruhn•muhnt] All the living and nonliving things that surround and affect an organism (p. 518)

F

fertilization [fur•tl•i•ZAY•shuhn] The joining together of a sperm and an egg cell (p. 484)

erosion [uh•ROH•zhuhn] The process of moving weathered rock and sediment from one place to another (p. 308)

food chain [FOOD CHAYN] The transfer of food energy in a sequence of living things (p. 454)

evaporation [ee•vap•uh•RAY•shuhn] The process by which a liquid changes into a gas (pp. 141, 347)

food web [FOOD WEB] A diagram that shows the relationships among different food chains in an ecosystem (p. 460)

© Houghton Mifflin Harcourt Publishing Company

force [FAWRS] A push or a pull (p. 270)

germination [jer•muh•NAY•shuhn] The sprouting of a seed (p. 482)

front [FRUHNT] The boundary between two air masses (p. 376)

groundwater [GROWND•waw•ter] Water located within the gaps and pores in rocks below Earth's surface (p. 350)

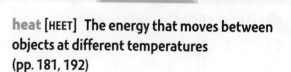

gas [GAS] The state of matter that does not have a definite volume or a definite shape (p. 136)

heat [HEET] The energy that moves between objects at different temperatures (pp. 181, 192)

generator [JEN•er•ay•ter] A device that makes an electric current by converting mechanical energy to electrical energy (p. 251)

herbivore [HER•buh•vawr] A consumer that eats only plants or other producers (p. 456)

© Houghton Mifflin Harcourt Publishing Company

Interactive Glossary

heredity [huh•RED•ih•tee] The process by which traits are passed from parents to offspring (p. 535)

humidity [hyoo•MID•uh•tee] The amount of water vapor in the air (p. 361)

humus [HYOO•muhs] The remains of decayed plants or animals in the soil (p. 324)

hypothesis [hy•PAHTH•uh•sis] A possible explanation or answer to a question; a testable statement (p. 9)

I

incomplete metamorphosis [in•kuhm•PLEET met•uh•MAWR•fuh•sis] Developmental change in some insects in which a nymph hatches from an egg and gradually develops into an adult (p. 509)

inference [IN•fer•uhns] An untested conclusion based on observations (p. 19)

instinct [IN•stinkt] A behavior an animal knows how to do without having to learn it (pp. 525, 542)

insulator [IN•suh•layt•er] A material that does not allow heat or electricity to move through it easily (pp. 208, 228)

© Houghton Mifflin Harcourt Publishing Company

investigation [in•ves•tuh•GAY•shuhn] A procedure carried out to gather data about an object or an event (p. 7)

liquid (LIK•wid) The state of matter that has a definite volume but not a definite shape (p. 136)

K

kinetic energy [kih•NET•ik EN•er•jee] The energy of motion (p. 174)

M

magnet [MAG•nit] An object that attracts iron and a few other—but not all—metals (p. 246)

L

learned behavior [LERND bee•HAYV•yer] A behavior that an animal doesn't begin life with but develops as a result of experience or by observing other animals (p. 540)

magnetism [MAG•nih•tiz•ihm] The physical property of being magnetic (p. 122)

mass [MAS] The amount of matter in an object (p. 112)

© Houghton Mifflin Harcourt Publishing Company

Interactive Glossary

matter [MAT•er] Anything that takes up space and has mass (p. 112)

mixture [MIKS•cher] A combination of two or more different substances that keep their identities (p. 154)

maturity [muh•TYOOR•ih•tee] The stage at which organisms can reproduce (p. 482)

model [MOD•l] A representation of something real that is too big, too small, too far away, or has too many parts to investigate directly (p. 53)

mechanical energy [muh•KAN•ih•kuhl EN•er•jee] The total potential and kinetic energy of an object (p. 174)

moon phase [MOON FAYZ] A change in the appearance of the moon's shape as it orbits Earth (p. 423)

microscope [MY•kruh•skohp] A tool for looking at objects that cannot be seen with the eye alone (p. 35)

motion [MOH•shuhn] A change in position of an object (p. 265)

© Houghton Mifflin Harcourt Publishing Company

N

natural resource [NACH•er•uhl REE•sawrs]
A material found in nature that people and other living things use (p. 293)

nonrenewable resource
[nahn•rih•NOO•uh•buhl REE•sawrs]
A natural resource that cannot be replaced in a reasonable amount of time (p. 294)

nutrient [NOO•tree•uhnts] A material used by living things for growth and for other life functions (p. 440)

nymph [NIMF] An immature form of an insect that undergoes incomplete metamorphosis (p. 509)

O

observation [ahb•zuhr•VAY•shuhn]
Information collected by using the five senses (p. 7)

omnivore [AHM•nih•vawr] A consumer that eats both plants and other animals (p. 456)

orbit [AWR•bit] The path of one object in space around another object (p. 400)

© Houghton Mifflin Harcourt Publishing Company

Interactive Glossary

P

pan balance [PAN BAL•uhns] A tool that measures mass with units called grams (g) (p. 36)

parallel circuit [PAIR•uh•lel SER•kit] An electric circuit that has more than one path for the electric charges to follow (p. 233)

photosynthesis [foht•oh•SIHN•thuh•sis] The process in which plants use energy from the sun to change carbon dioxide and water into sugar and oxygen (p. 442)

physical adaptation [FIZ•ih•kuhl ad•uhp•TAY•shuhn] An adaptation to a body part (p. 521)

physical change [FIZ•ih•kuhl CHAYNJ] A change in which a new substance is not formed (p. 151)

physical property [FIZ•ih•kuhl PRAHP•er•tee] A characteristic of matter that you can observe or measure directly (p. 112)

pollination [pol•uh•NEY•shuhn] The transfer of pollen from a male plant part to a female plant part of seed plants (p. 486)

position [puh•ZISH•uhn] The location of an object in relation to a nearby object or place (p. 265)

© Houghton Mifflin Harcourt Publishing Company

potential energy
[poh•TEN•shuhl EN•er•jee] Energy an object has because of its position or its condition (p. 174)

precipitation
[pree•sip•uh•TAY•shuhn] Water that falls from clouds to Earth's surface (p. 349)

producer [pruh•DOOS•er] A living thing, such as a plant, that can make its own food (p. 442)

prototype [PROH•tuh•typ] An original or test model on which something is based (p. 73)

R

radiation [ray•dee•AY•shuhn] The transfer, or movement, of heat without matter to carry it (p. 197)

renewable resource [rih•NOO•uh•buhl REE•sawrs] A natural resource that can be replaced within a reasonable amount of time (p. 293)

rotate [ROH•tayt] To turn about an axis (p. 398)

runoff [RUN•awf] Water that does not soak into the ground and instead flows across Earth's surface (p. 351)

© Houghton Mifflin Harcourt Publishing Company

Interactive Glossary

S

science [SY•uhns] The study of the natural world (p. 5)

scientist [SY•uhn•tist] A person who asks questions about the natural world (p. 5)

sediment [SED•uh•ment] Sand, bits of rock, fossils, and other matter carried and deposited by water, wind, or ice (p. 309)

series circuit [SIR•eez SER•kit] An electric circuit in which the electrical charges have only one path to follow (p. 233)

soil [SOYL] A mixture of water, air, tiny pieces of rock, and humus (p. 324)

soil horizon [SOYL huh•RIZ•uhn] A layer of soil with different physical characteristics from the layer of soil above it and the layer of soil below it (p. 326)

soil profile [SOYL PRO•fyl] A cross-section of soil that shows the various layers of soil (p. 326)

solid [SAHL•id] The state of matter that has a definite volume and a definite shape (p. 136)

© Houghton Mifflin Harcourt Publishing Company

solution [suh•LOO•shuhn] A mixture that has the same composition throughout because all the parts are mixed evenly (p. 155)

states of matter [STAYTS uhv MAT•er] The physical forms (such as solid, liquid, and gas) that matter can exist in (p. 136)

speed [SPEED] The measure of an object's change in position during a certain amount of time (p. 268)

T

technology [tek•NOL•uh•jee] Any designed system, product, or process used to solve problems (p. 87)

spore [SPAWR] A reproductive structure of some plants, such as mosses and ferns, that can form a new plant (p. 490)

temperature [TEM•per•uh•cher] The measure of the energy of motion in the particles of matter, which we feel as how hot or cold something is (p. 120)

spring scale [SPRING SKAYL] A tool used to measure forces, such as weight, in units called newtons (N) (p. 36)

thermal energy [THUR•muhl EN•er•jee] The total kinetic energy of the particles in a substance (p. 181)

© Houghton Mifflin Harcourt Publishing Company

Interactive Glossary

three-dimensional model
[THREE-di•MEN•shuh•nuhl MOD•l] A model that has the dimension of height as well as width and length (p. 55)

two-dimensional model [TOO-di•MEN•shuh•nuhl MOD•l] A model that has the dimensions of length and width only (p. 53)

tide [TYD] The rise and fall in the water level of the ocean (p. 404)

V

velocity [vuh•LAHS•uh•tee] The speed of an object in a particular direction (p. 268)

tool [TOOL] Anything used to help people shape, build, or produce things to meet their needs (p. 86)

volume [VAHL•yoom] The amount of space an object takes up (p. 116)

triple beam balance
[TRI-puhl BEEM BAL•uhns] An accurate tool to use for measuring mass (p. 36)

© Houghton Mifflin Harcourt Publishing Company

water cycle [WAWT•er SY•kuhl] The process in which water continuously moves from Earth's surface into the atmosphere and back again (p. 347)

weathering [WETH•er•ing] The breaking down of rocks on Earth's surface into smaller pieces (p. 307)

weather [WETH•er] The condition of the atmosphere at a certain place and time (p. 360)

© Houghton Mifflin Harcourt Publishing Company

Index

Note: Page numbers in **boldface** type show where terms are highlighted and defined.

© Houghton Mifflin Harcourt Publishing Company

© Houghton Mifflin Harcourt Publishing Company

Index

© Houghton Mifflin Harcourt Publishing Company

© Houghton Mifflin Harcourt Publishing Company

Index

© Houghton Mifflin Harcourt Publishing Company

© Houghton Mifflin Harcourt Publishing Company

Index

© Houghton Mifflin Harcourt Publishing Company

© Houghton Mifflin Harcourt Publishing Company

Index

© Houghton Mifflin Harcourt Publishing Company

© Houghton Mifflin Harcourt Publishing Company

Index

© Houghton Mifflin Harcourt Publishing Company

© Houghton Mifflin Harcourt Publishing Company

Index

Y

© Houghton Mifflin Harcourt Publishing Company

CoCo

1 Gold Bond Powder 6.97

~~Totls~~

1 Eqoiate ToothBruch   3.82.
        # 55332466l

2 or 3 First Aid Kil   # 566904307

5 Eq Ex Stre Chew Tums 4076205

3 Aleve # 4085984